Alexander Pope, Joseph Warton

The Works of Pope Alexander

Vol. I

Alexander Pope, Joseph Warton

The Works of Pope Alexander
Vol. I

ISBN/EAN: 9783744675192

Printed in Europe, USA, Canada, Australia, Japan

Cover: Foto ©Lupo / pixelio.de

More available books at **www.hansebooks.com**

ALEXANDER POPE ESQ.

Engraved by J. Holloway, from a Picture painted by J. Richardson,

in the possession of Benj.ⁿ Way Esq.ʳ

Published January 1st 1797 by Cadell and Davies Strand London.

THE

WORKS

OF

Alexander Pope, Esq.

IN NINE VOLUMES, COMPLETE.

WITH

NOTES AND ILLUSTRATIONS

By JOSEPH WARTON, D.D.

AND OTHERS.

VOLUME THE FIRST.

LONDON:

Printed for B. LAW, J. JOHNSON, C. DILLY, G. G. and J. ROBINSON, J. NICHOLS, R. BALDWIN, H. L. GARDNER, F. and C. RIVINGTON, J. SEWELL, T. PAYNE, J. WALKER, R. FAULDER, J. SCATCHERD, B. and J. WHITE, OGILVY and SON, T. N. LONGMAN, CADELL jun. and DAVIES, and E. POTE.

1797.

ADVERTISEMENT.

THE Public is here presented with a Complete Edition of the Works of POPE, both in Verſe and Proſe, accompanied with various Notes and Illuſtrations. The reaſon for undertaking it, was the univerſal complaint, that Dr. Warburton had disfigured and diſgraced his Edition, with many forced and far-ſought interpretations, totally unſupported by the paſſages which they were brought to elucidate. If this was only my ſingle opinion, nothing could have induced me to have delivered it with ſo much freedom; nor to have undertaken this Work after it had paſſed through the hands of Dr. Warburton. Many, however, of his Notes, that do not fall under this deſcription, are here adopted. To this Edition are now added, ſeveral Poems undoubtedly of our Author's hand; and in proſe, many Letters to different Correſpondents, which, from the circumſtances

of

of literary hiſtory which they contain, it was thought might be entertaining; together with his Thoughts on Various Subjects; his Account of the Madneſs of Dennis; the poiſoning of Edmund Curl; the Eſſay on the Origin of Sciences; the Key to the Rape of the Lock; and that piece of inimitable humour, the Fourteenth Chapter of Scriblerus, on the Double Miſtreſs; all of which were inſerted in his own Edition in quarto, 1741. And to theſe is added, alſo, one of the beſt of his critical compoſitions, his Poſtſcript to the Odyſſey.

If I have ſometimes ventured, in the following remarks, to point out any ſeeming blemiſhes and imperfections in the Works of this excellent Poet, I beg it may be imputed, not to the "dull, malignant delight," of ſeeking to find out trivial faults, but merely to guard the Reader from being miſled, by the example of a writer, in general, ſo uniformly elegant and correct.

The Notes to which the letter P. is ſubjoined, are by Mr. Pope himſelf; all which are carefully retained. Thoſe marked W. are by Dr. Warburton. For the reſt, I am anſwerable.

May 1797. JOS. WARTON.

CONTENTS

OF THE

FIRST VOLUME.

ERRATA in VOL. I.

Page xxxix. line 8, *for* Barius *read* Bavius
lxvi. — 14, *for* A. R. M. *read* H. M.
50. — ult. *for* paſtorilium *read* paſtoritium
94. — 12, *for* civitium *read* civilium
165. — 22, *for* one *read* ore
174. — 15, in note, *for* κινεν *read* κινειν
181. dele note on ver. 35.
254. line 35, in note, *for* Polyanus *read* Polyænus
271. — 9, *after* written *insert* namely
315. — 4, in note, *for* Swirten *read* Swieten.

Published June 1.1797, by Cadell & Davies. Strand.

THIS is the only Portrait that was ever drawn of Mr. POPE *at full Length.—It was done without his knowledge, as he was deeply engaged in conversation with* Mr. ALLEN *in the Gallery at* Prior Park, *by* Mr. HOARE, *who sat at the other end of the Gallery.*—POPE *would never have forgiven the Painter had he known it—He was too sensible of the Deformity of his Person to allow the whole of it to be represented.—This Drawing is therefore exceedingly valuable, as it is an Unique of this celebrated Poet.*

DIRECTIONS TO THE BINDER.

The Head of Mr. POPE to front the Title Page of the First Volume.

The Portrait of Mr. POPE to front Page ix. [A 5] of VOL. I.

THE

L I F E

OF

ALEXANDER POPE, ESQ.

THE

LIFE

OF

ALEXANDER POPE, ESQ.

ALEXANDER POPE was born, according to Mr. Spence, in Lombard-ſtreet, London, on May 22d, 1688, in the houſe of his father, who was ſo eminent a linen-draper, and traded ſo ſucceſsfully, that he gained a fortune of twenty thouſand pounds. His mother was daughter of William Turner, Eſq. of York, two of whoſe ſons died in the ſervice of Charles the Firſt, and the other became a general officer in Spain.

The feebleneſs and delicacy of his conſtitution naturally engaged the attention of his parents and relations; and he was ſtill more endeared to them by the uncommon mildneſs and ſweetneſs of temper, which he diſplayed in his childhood: And perhaps his father might ſay, as did the father of *Boileau*; "This child, if he lives, will never ſpeak ill of any "perſon." His voice, too, was ſo marvellouſly melodious, that they uſed to call him the little nightingale. He was taught to read by an aunt that was particularly fond of him, and learnt to write by copying printed books, which he did with exquiſite ſkill and dexterity. He was placed, at eight years old, under the care of *Taverner*, a Romiſh prieſt, (as his father and mother were rigid Catholics,) who taught him the rudiments of the Greek and Latin languages at the ſame time. Perhaps it may be wiſhed that, for the promotion of true taſte and literature, Greek was always taught in great ſchools before Latin, according to a hint of *Eraſmus*. Having made conſiderable improvements under *Taverner*, he was removed to a celebrated ſeminary of Catholics at *Twyford*, a pleaſant village on the banks of the Itchin near Wincheſter; a circumſtance that uſed frequently to be mentioned by the ſcholars of the neighbouring college, in their youthful compoſitions. Having written a lampoon on his maſter at Twyford, one of his firſt efforts in poetry, he was removed from thence to a ſchool kept near Hyde-park Corner. Before this removal, he had been delighted with a peruſal of *Ogilby*'s Homer, and *Sandys*'s Ovid; he frequently ſpoke, in the latter part of his life, of the exquiſite pleaſure which the peruſal of theſe two writers gave him. And having now an opportunity of ſometimes frequenting the play-houſes, our young bard was ſo delighted with theatrical performances, that he turned the chief events of the Iliad into a kind of drama, made up of a number of ſpeeches from Ogilby's tranſlation, connected with verſes of his own. He perſuaded ſome of the upper boys to act this piece, which, as an uncommon curioſity, one would have been glad to have beheld. The maſter's gardener repreſented the character of Ajax; and the actors were dreſſed after the pictures of his favourite Ogilby; which were indeed deſigned and engraved by artiſts of note. At twelve years of age, our young bard retired with his father to Binfield near Oakingham; who, unwilling to truſt the money he had gained in trade to government ſecurity, lived on the principal, which gradually was conſumed before he was aware. Another private tutor was now ſought out for his ſon; this was another prieſt, named *Dean*; from whom his pupil deriving very little advantage, he at laſt determined to ſtudy on a plan of his own; which he did with great diligence and perſeverance; devouring all books that he could procure, eſpecially poetical works. To indulge this darling paſſion, he left no calling nor profeſſion, as ſo many eminent poets and painters appear to have done: He was invariably and ſolely a poet, from the beginning of his life to the end. And it was now he firſt peruſed the writings of *Waller*, of *Spenſer*, and of *Dryden*, in the order here mentioned. Spenſer is ſaid to have made a poet of Cowley; that Ogilby ſhould give our author his firſt poetic pleaſures, is a remarkable circumſtance. But Dryden ſoon became his chief favourite, and his model. And as a desire to see eminent men is one of the first marks of a mind eager to excel, he entreated a friend to carry him to Button's coffee-house, which Dryden frequented, that he might gratify himself with the bare sight of a man whom he so much admired.

I have heard, that among works of prose, he was most fond of the second part of Sir *William Temple's* Miscellanies. How very early he began to write, cannot now be exactly ascertained; but his father frequently proposed familiar subjects to him, and after many corrections would say, "These are now good "rhymes."

Though the *Ode to Solitude*, written at twelve years of age, is said to be his earliest production, yet *Dodsley*, who was honoured with his intimacy, had seen several pieces of a still earlier date. It is remarkable that, precisely at the same age, Voltaire produced his first copy of verses on record. They were written at the request of an old invalid, to be presented, in his name, to the only son of Louis XIV. If it should be urged, that too much is said of the childish performances of these two great men, let it be remembered that it is amusing to trace the fountain of the Nile.

Cowley and Milton had written pieces of equal value at as early an age, and Tasso still earlier. Milton's Paraphrases of the 114th and 136th Psalms, made when he was only fifteen years old, are very poetical

and

and ſpirited; and Metaſtaſio was as young when he wrote Giuſtino, a tragedy.

At fourteen, he employed himſelf in tranſlating the firſt book of the Thebais of Statius, and in moderniſing the January and May of Chaucer; the Prologue of the Wife of Bath; and alſo in tranſlating the Epiſtle of Sappho to Phaon, in order to complete the careleſs verſion publiſhed under the name of Dryden, but very unequally performed. About the ſame time he gave imitations of many Engliſh poets; the beſt of which was, that of Lord Rocheſter on Silence; in which might be diſcovered the ſtrong ſenſe, and moral turn of thinking, for which he was afterwards ſo juſtly celebrated. There was no imitation of Milton *.

After ſpending a few months in London, to be inſtructed in the Italian and French languages, he returned to Binfield, and proſecuted with freſh ardour his poetical ſtudies. He wrote a Comedy; a Tragedy on the ſtory of St. Genevieve, copied by Dodſley in his Cleone; and an Epic Poem, called Alcander; all of them attempts that indicated an ardent and eager deſire of future fame. If it be ſaid, that theſe are marks of vanity and ſelf-confidence, let it be remembered that he who in youth has never graſped in his mind at more than he could perform, will never arrive at eminence and excellence in any art. At

* Mr. Harte informed me that Dryden gave Pope a ſhilling for tranſlating, when a boy, the ſtory of *Pyramus and Thiſbe.*

At ſixteen he wrote his Paſtorals; and as the firſt ſtep in the literary, as well as in the political world is of the utmoſt conſequence, theſe Paſtorals introduced him to the acquaintance, and ſoon into the friendſhip, of Sir William Trumbull, who had formerly been much in public life, Ambaſſador at Conſtantinople, and Secretary of State; and was then retired into Windſor Foreſt, near Binfield. This amiable ex-miniſter, wearied with the intrigues and buſtle of courts, was very naturally pleaſed to diſcover in his neighbourhood a youth of ſuch abilities and taſte as young Pope; and was therefore happy in his company and converſation.

It was Trumbull who circulated his Paſtorals among his friends, and firſt introduced him to Wycherley and Walſh, and the wits of that time. The Paſtorals, though written in 1704, were not publiſhed till 1709, in Tonſon's ſixth Miſcellany; which volume opened with the Paſtorals of Philips, and ended with thoſe of our Author. As examples of correct and melodious verſification, theſe Paſtorals deſerve the higheſt commendation. It has been ſaid, and indeed truly, that they want invention; and it is thought a ſufficient anſwer to obſerve, that this is to require what was never intended. But this is a confeſſion of the very fault imputed to them. There *ought* to have been invention. The diſcourſe prefixed to them is very elegantly and elaborately written; though moſt of the obſervations are taken from Rapin on Paſtoral,

publiſhed

publiſhed a few years before in Creech's Theocritus, from Walſh on Virgil's Eclogues, and from *Fontenelle;* whoſe diſſertation is as full of affected thoughts as his own Eclogues; and whom I wiſh our young poet had proſcribed for his paradoxical doctrines againſt the ancients, which he firſt broached in this diſcourſe *.

It has been my fortune, from my way of life, to have ſeen many compoſitions of youths of ſixteen years old, far beyond theſe Paſtorals in point of genius and imagination, though not perhaps of correctneſs. Their excellence, indeed, might be owing to having had ſuch a predeceſſor as Pope.

About this time old Mr. *Wycherley* courted the friendſhip, and requeſted the aſſiſtance, of our young Author, to correct his verſes, which had all the uncouth harſhneſs and aſperity of *Donne:* But Wycherley's vanity was ſoon diſguſted by the honeſt freedom and true judgment with which Pope executed the taſk he had unwillingly undertaken; a coolneſs enſued, which ended in a rupture betwixt them. "A "book has been written, ſaid a man of wit, *De morbis* "*artificum.* Among authors, jealouſy and envy are "incurable diſeaſes."

When

* But another critical treatiſe of Fontenelle deſerves to be ſpoken of in very different terms; his *Reflexions ſur la Poetique*, annexed to his life of Corneille; for this treatiſe contains ſome of the moſt true and profound remarks on dramatic poetry that can be found in any critic whatever.

When we consider the just taste, the strong sense, the knowledge of men, books, and opinions, that are so predominant in the *Essay on Criticism*, and at the same time recollect that it was written before the Author was twenty years old, we are naturally struck with astonishment; and must readily agree to place him among the first *critics*, though not, as Dr. Johnson says, "among the first *poets*," on this account alone. As a poet, he must rank much higher, for his *Eloisa*, and *Rape of the Lock*. This judgment reminds one of what the same critic has said of Dryden's *Religio Laici;* that one might have expected to have found in it, the *effulgence* of his genius; though, as he adds, on an argumentative subject; and therefore improper for a display of genius. As much as I revere and respect the memory of my old acquaintance Dr. Johnson *, and as highly as I think of his abilities, integrity, and virtue, yet must I be pardoned for saying, that I cannot possibly subscribe to many of his critical decisions; particularly to what he has said of the Lycidas, Il Penseroso, and

* The perpetual *pompousness*, and the uninterrupted *elaboration*, of the over-ornamented style of the Rambler, makes one wish that the excellent Author had recollected the opinion of Cicero; "Is enim est eloquens, qui et humilia subtiliter, et magna graviter, et mediocria *temperatè* potest dicere. Nam qui nihil potest tranquillè, nihil leniter, nihil definitè, distinctè potest dicere, is, cum non præparatis auribus inflammare rem cœpit, furere apud sanos, et quasi inter sobrios bacchari temulentus videtur."

and Latin poems of Milton; of the Sixth Book of Paradiſe Loſt; of Taſſo's Aminta; of the Rhyming Tragedies, Ode to Killigrew, and the Fables of Dryden; of Chaucer; of the Rehearſal; of Prior; of Congreve's Mourning Bride; of Blackmore; of Yalden; of Pomfret; of Dyer; of Garth; of Lyttelton; of Fielding; of Harris; of Hammond; of Beattie; of Shenſtone; of Savage; of Hughes; of Spence; of Akenſide; of Collins; of Pope's Eſſay on Man, and Imitations of Horace; and of the Odes of Gray.

The Eſſay on Criticiſm was firſt advertiſed at the end of the Spectator, No. 65. May 15, 1711, and was praiſed by Addiſon in the December following, in Number 253 of the Spectator. But Pope was not a little diſpleaſed at one ſentence in this paper, in which Addiſon ſaid, "I am ſorry to find an Author "who is very juſtly eſteemed among the beſt judges, "has admitted ſome ſtrokes of ill-nature into a very "fine poem, which was publiſhed ſome months ſince, "and is a maſter-piece of its kind." He adds, "The obſervations follow one another, like thoſe in "Horace's Art of Poetry, without that methodical "regularity which would have been requiſite in a "proſe writer." So that Addiſon did not perceive that clear order and cloſe connection, which Warburton ſtrove to diſcover, in order to give *ſome* ſhadow of propriety to a *perpetual Commentary* upon it.

The

The fierce hoſtilities of *Dennis* againſt Pope, began from ſome paſſages in this Eſſay, which this redoubted critic applied to himſelf, and never forgave; but purſued our Author, through life, in bitter invectives againſt every work he gradually publiſhed. Old Mr. Lewis, the bookſeller in Ruſſel-ſtreet, who printed the firſt edition of this Eſſay in quarto, without Pope's name, informed me, that it lay many days in his ſhop, unnoticed and unread; and that, piqued with this neglect, the Author came one day, and packed up and directed twenty copies to ſeveral great men; among whom he could recollect none but Lord Lanſdowne and the Duke of Buckingham; and that in conſequence of theſe preſents, and his name being known, the book began to be called for. This Eſſay, it is ſaid, was firſt written in proſe, according to the precept of *Vida*, in his firſt book, and the practice of *Racine*, who was accuſtomed to draw out in plain proſe, not only the ſubject of each of the five acts, but of every ſcene and every ſpeech, that he might ſee the conduct and coherence of the whole at one view, and would then ſay, "My Tragedy is "finiſhed."

The *Meſſiah* appeared firſt in the Spectator, 1712, with a warm recommendation by Steele. Nothing can be added to the juſt and univerſal approbation with which it was received and read. It raiſed the higheſt expectations of what the Author was capable of performing.

He

He was not so happy in his *Ode* on St. Cecilia's Day;* which, in respect both of subject and execution, is so manifestly inferior to that unrivalled one of his master, Dryden; but which, Dr. Johnson, by a strange perversity of judgment, pronounces to contain nothing equal to the first bombast stanza of his *Ode on Killegrew.* Pope's Ode, many years after it was written, was set to music by Dr. Greene, as were the two Chorusses to the tragedy of Brutus, by Bononcini, part of which were written by the Duke of Buckingham. Mr. Galliard set to music the Chorus of *Julius Cæsar*, entirely written by His Grace. This appears from a letter now before me, from Mr. Galliard to Mr. Duncombe.

It was at Steele's desire† that he wrote that beautiful little Ode, *The Dying Christian to his Soul*, to be set to music. But it was not quite candid and open in our Author to tell Steele, that he would see he had not only the verses of *Adrian*, but the fine fragment

* Irregular Odes, of which this is one, seem now to be universally exploded: Dr. Brown has, however, remarked, "that the return of the same measure, in the *Strophe*, Antistrophe, and Epode, of the ancient Greek Ode, was the natural consequence of its union with the *Dance*. But this union being irrecoverably lost, the unvaried measure of the Ode becomes, at best, an unmeaning thing; and indeed is an absurd one, as it deprives the Poet of that variety of measure, which often gives a great energy to the composition, by the incidental and sudden intervention of an *abrupt* or *lengthened* versification."

† In general, our Author's subjects, which is a happy circumstance for a poet, were chosen by himself.

fragment of *Sappho* in his head; and totally to ſuppreſs the name of *Flatman*, whoſe Ode he not only imitated, but copied ſome lines of it verbatim.

If we knew the hiſtory of that moſt unfortunate Lady, who is the ſubject of the ſweet and pathetic Elegy, and could relate it at large, it might give us an opportunity of enlivening theſe Memoirs, with what the Life of a retired Poet muſt unavoidably want, ſome intereſting event. No ſuch does the Life of our Author afford, who was in no public ſtation nor employment, as were Milton, Prior, and Addiſon; and who ſpent moſt of his time among his papers and books. All that can now be learnt of this Lady, is to be found in the notes on this Elegy; and is therefore not repeated in this place. A very different ſcene, and a Lady in another ſort of ſituation, appeared, in his next poem, where all was gaiety and gallantry. Lord Petre, in a frolic, carried rather beyond the bounds of delicacy and good-breeding, having cut off a favourite lock of Mrs. Arabella Fermor's hair, his rudeneſs, as it was called, was reſented, and occaſioned a ſerious rupture betwixt the two families. Mr. Caryl, a friend to both parties, deſired Mr. Pope to write a piece of raillery on this inviting ſubject, which might appeaſe their reſentment. *The Rape of the Lock*, therefore, that moſt delicious poem, in which SATIRE wears the ceſtus of VENUS, was produced in a fortnight, and appeared, 1711, in only two cantos, in a Miſcellany of Lintot. Finding it received

received with juſt and univerſal applauſe, he in the next year enlarged it into five cantos; and, by the happieſt art and judgment imaginable, enriched it with the beautiful machinery of the *Sylphs*, a ſet of inviſible beings whom he accidentally ſaw mentioned, as conſtant attendants, and as intereſted agents, in the affairs of the Ladies, not only in the Comte de Gabalis, but alſo in ſome of Madame de Sevigné's Letters. Into what a maſs of exquiſite poetry has he raiſed and expanded ſo ſlight a hint! and placed the Rape of the Lock, by this happy inſertion and addition, above all other Mock Heroic Poems whatever! Addiſon, to whom he communicated his intention of introducing this new ſpecies of machinery, did not certainly conceive the felicity and the propriety with which it would be executed; and, for that reaſon, and not from envy and jealouſy, may be candidly ſuppoſed to have diſſuaded him from the attempt. It would have been as unfortunate for him to have followed the advice of Addiſon on this occaſion, as it would have been for La Fontaine and Boileau to have liſtened to Patru, when he perſuaded the one not to attempt to write his Fables, and the other his Art of Poetry. Dennis, ſome years after, attacked this invulnerable compoſition, with equal impotence and ill-nature, endeavouring to ſhew that the intertexture of the machinery was ſuperfluous. It is remarkable that he had introduced guardian ſpirits as attendants on the favourites

vourites of Heaven, in his *Temple of Fame*, as he informs Steele in a letter on this subject; which spirits he afterwards judiciously omitted. It appears by this letter to Steele, dated November 16, 1712, that he first communicated to him at that time, *The Temple of Fame*, though he had written it two years before. Steele assures him, it contained "a thousand thou-"sand beauties;" many of which are specified in the notes of this edition, and therefore need not be here repeated. The descriptive powers of Pope are much more visible and strong in this poem, than in the next that is to be mentioned in the order of time; the *Windsor Forest* *; the first part of which was written, indeed, 1704, but the whole was not finished and published till 1713: a poem evidently written in imitation of *Cooper's Hill*, and as evidently superior to it. Denham is a writer that has been extolled far beyond his merits. Nothing can be colder and more prosaïc, for instance, than the manner in which he has spoken of the distant prospect of London and St. Paul's, and also of Edward the Third; both fine subjects for poetry. The *Claremont* of *Garth* was also another imitation of Cooper's Hill, and unworthy the Author of the *Dispensary*; it contains an unnatural mixture of wit, pleasantry, and satire, with rural description. But Thomson has carried descriptive poetry to

* I have a peculiar pleasure in mentioning another excellent descriptive piece, *The Needwood Forest of Mr. Mundy.*

to its height; and being a *true ſon of Nature*, has delineated all her moſt ſtriking objects, with a *force* and *diſtinctneſs* hitherto unparalleled.

The ſilence, the ſolitude, the gloomy ſolemnity, the pleaſing melancholy, impreſſed on our minds by the conventual ſcenes of *Eloiſa* and *Abelard*, by the ideas of long-ſounding *iſles*, and *cells*, and *lamps*, and *altars*, and *graves;* induce and allure the reader to forget the inherent indelicacy of the ſtory of theſe two unfortunate lovers. For though the "high-embowed "roof," "ſtoried windows," "ſtudious cloiſters," and "pealing organ," had been mentioned by Milton, yet this ſort of ſcenery had never before been exhibited as the *chief* and *leading* object and foundation of any poem in our language. Pope was fully ſenſible of the indelicate circumſtances above-mentioned, that attended his ſubject, and did not therefore much reliſh the manner in which Prior had ſaid, that theſe circumſtances were concealed with dexterity and ſkill, in the following elegant lines:

> He o'er the weeping nun has drawn
> Such artful folds of ſacred lawn;
> That Love with equal grief and pride
> Shall ſee the crime he ſtrives to hide;
> And ſoftly drawing back the veil,
> The God ſhall to his votaries tell,
> Each conſcious tear, each bluſhing grace
> That deck'd dear Eloiſa's face.

ALMA, p. 101.

Savage

Savage related that Pope attempted this composition in rivalship to Prior's *Nut-brown Maid.* It is not true that these very unhappy lovers "found quiet and "consolation in retirement and piety." The whole tenor of their letters contradicts this supposition. These curious letters were published in London by Dr. Rawlinson, 1718, with an extraordinary motto prefixed from Claudian, relative to Abelard's punishment, too gross to be here inserted.

After arriving at such eminence by so many capital compositions, our Author, with that just self-confidence that ought to actuate every man of real genius and ability, meditated a higher effort; something that might improve and advance his fortune as well as his fame; a translation* of Homer, which Milton is said once to have thought of executing.

This translation he proposed to print by subscription, in six volumes in quarto, for the sum of six guineas: And to the eternal honour of our country, in encouraging a work of such superlative and uncommon merit, the subscription was larger than any before known. Every man of every party, that had any, or pretended to have any taste or love of literature, sent his

* A clamour was raised at the time, that he had not sufficient learning for such an undertaking; Dr. Johnson says, that considering his irregular education, and course of life, "it is not very likely that he overflowed with Greek." Perhaps our most eminent Poets may be ranked, with respect to their learning, in the following order: Milton, Spenser, Cowley, Butler, Donne, Jonson, Akenside, Gray, Dryden, Addison.

his name; and the number of ſubſcribers were five hundred and ſeventy-five; but as ſome ſubſcribed for more than one copy, the copies delivered to ſubſcribers were ſix hundred and fifty-four. Theſe copies Lintot, who became proprietor of the work, engaged to ſupply, at his own expence, and alſo to give the Author two hundred pounds for each volume; ſo that Pope obtained, on the whole, the ſum of five thouſand three hundred and twenty pounds four ſhillings. With this money, ſo very honourably obtained, he immediately and prudently purchaſed ſeveral annuities, and particularly one of five hundred pounds a year, from the Duke of Buckingham. The work was enriched by many judicious notes by Pope himſelf, as well as by Broome, who alſo was employed to make extracts from Euſtathius, as was alſo a man of much greater learning, the celebrated Dr. Jortin, who gives the following account of the matter in his Adverſaria:

"What paſſed between Mr. Pope and me, I will "endeavour to recollect as well as I can, for it hap"pened many years ago, and I never made any me"morandum of it.

"When I was a ſoph at Cambridge, Pope was "about his Tranſlation of Homer's Ilias, and had "publiſhed part of it.

"He employed ſome perſon (I know not who he "was) to make extracts for him from Euſtathius, "which he inſerted in his notes. At that time there

" was no Latin tranſlation of that commentator.' " *Alexander Politi* (if I remember right) began that " work ſome years afterwards, but never proceeded " far in it. The perſon employed by Mr. Pope was " not at leiſure to go on with the work; and Mr. " Pope (by his bookſeller, I ſuppoſe,) ſent to Jefferies, " a bookſeller at Cambridge, to find out a ſtudent " who would undertake the taſk. Jefferies applied " to Dr. Thirlby, who was my tutor, and who " pitched upon me. I would have declined the " work, having, as I told my tutor, other ſtudies to " purſue, to fit me for taking my degree. But he— " *qui quicquid volebat valdè volebat*,—would not hear " of any excuſe. So I complied. I cannot recollect " what Mr. Pope allowed for each book of Homer; " I have a notion that it was three or four guineas. " I took as much care as I could to perform the taſk " to his ſatisfaction; but I was aſhamed to deſire my " tutor to give himſelf the trouble of overlooking my " operations; and he, who always uſed to think and " ſpeak too favourably of me, ſaid, that I did not " want his help. He never peruſed one line of it " before it was printed, nor perhaps afterwards.

" When I had gone through ſome books, (I forget " how many,) Mr. Jefferies let us know that Mr. " Pope had a friend to do the reſt, and that we " might give over.

" When I ſent my papers to Jefferies, to be con- " veyed to Mr. Pope, I inſerted, as I remember,

" ſome

" ſome remarks on a paſſage, where Mr. Pope, in " my opinion, had made a miſtake. But, as I was " not directly employed by him, but by a bookſeller, " I did not inform him who I was, or ſet my name " to my papers.

" When that part of Homer came out in which " I had been concerned, I was eager, as it may be " ſuppoſed, to ſee how things ſtood; and much " pleaſed to find that he had not only uſed almoſt " all my notes, but had hardly made any alteration " in the expreſſions. I obſerved alſo, that, in a " ſubſequent edition, he corrected the place to " which I had made objections.

" I was in ſome hopes, in thoſe days, (for I was " young,) that Mr. Pope would make inquiry about " his *co-adjutor*, and take ſome civil notice of him. " But he did not; and I had no notion of obtruding " myſelf upon him.—I never ſaw his face."

The firſt four books * were publiſhed 1715, and the largeneſs of the ſubſcription enabled him alſo to purchaſe the houſe at Twickenham, beſides the annuities above-mentioned; to which he removed, having perſuaded his father to ſell his little property at Binfield.

But

* Dr. Johnſon ſays, the firſt conſiderable work publiſhed by ſubſcription was Dryden's Virgil; but the folio edition of Paradiſe Loſt was ſo publiſhed ſome years before.

But now the pleaſure he took in the ſucceſs of his great undertaking, was diminiſhed and interrupted by an unforeſeen accident. At the very time when the Firſt Volume of Pope's Iliad was publiſhed, a Tranſlation of the Firſt Book appeared under the name of *Tickell*; and though Addiſon lived in terms of friendſhip with Pope, and had warmly encouraged him to undertake this work, yet Pope had reaſon to think that this Firſt Book was the work of Addiſon himſelf, and not of Tickell. The reaſons of this ſuſpicion, and of a conduct ſo unaccountable in a man of Addiſon's character, are given by Pope himſelf in the following words, faithfully tranſcribed by me from *Spence*'s Anecdotes.

" There had been a coldneſs between Mr. Addiſon " and me for ſome time; and we had not been in " company together, for a good while, any where " but at Button's coffee-houſe, where I uſed to ſee " him almoſt every day. On his meeting me there " one day in particular, he took me aſide, and ſaid " he ſhould be glad to dine with me at ſuch a " tavern, if I ſtaid till thoſe people were gone " (Budget and Philips). We went accordingly; " and after dinner Mr. Addiſon ſaid, " That he had " wanted for ſome time to talk with me; that his friend " Tickell had formerly, whilſt at Oxford, tranſlated " the Firſt Book of the Iliad; that he deſigned to " print it, and had deſired him to look it over; that he

" muſt

" muſt therefore beg that I would not deſire him " to look over my Firſt Book, becauſe, if he did, it " would have the air of double-dealing." I aſſured " him that I did not at all take it ill of Mr. Tickell " that he was going to publiſh his Tranſlation; that " he certainly had as much right to tranſlate any " Author as myſelf; and that publiſhing both was " entering on a fair ſtage. I then added, that I " would not deſire him to look over my Firſt Book " of the Iliad, becauſe he had looked over Mr. " Tickell's; but could wiſh to have the benefit of " his obſervations on my Second, which I had then " finiſhed, and which Mr. Tickell had not touched " upon. Accordingly I ſent him the Second Book " the next morning; and Mr. Addiſon a few days " after returned it with very high commendations. " Soon after it was generally known that Mr. " Tickell was publiſhing the Firſt Book of the Iliad, " I met Dr. Young in the ſtreet; and, upon our " falling into that ſubject, the Doctor expreſſed a " great deal of ſurpriſe at Tickell's having had ſuch " a Tranſlation ſo long by him. He ſaid, that it was " inconceivable to him, and that there muſt be ſome " miſtake in the matter; that each uſed to commu- " nicate to the other whatever verſes they wrote, " even to the leaſt things; that Tickell could not " have been buſied in ſo long a work there, without " his knowing ſomething of the matter; and that he " had never heard a ſingle word of it till on this

 " occaſion.

"occaſion. This ſurpriſe of Dr. Young, together "with what Steele has ſaid againſt Tickell in rela- "tion to this affair, makes it highly probable that "there was ſome underhand dealing in that buſineſs; "and indeed Tickell himſelf, who is a very fair "worthy man, has ſince, in a manner, as good as "owned it to me."

Great and juſt was Pope's indignation on this occaſion, eſpecially when Addiſon declared at Button's, that both verſions were good; but that Tickell had more of Homer. "I appeal, ſaid Pope, to the people as "my rightful judges, and while they are not inclined "to condemn me, ſhall not fear the high-fliers at "Button's."

At one time he intended to print together all the four verſions that had been given of this Firſt Book, by *Dryden*, *Maynwaring*, *himſelf*, and *Tickell* *; at another, to make a cloſe, and minute, and rigorous criticiſm on every paſſage of the laſt that ſeemed defective. In the collection of his Letters, in this edition, many particulars of this unhappy quarrel, and the ſentiments of his friends, may be found, which are not therefore here detailed. Every candid reader muſt wiſh that the charge againſt ſo amiable a man as was Addiſon, could be totally refuted. It moſt certainly

* Mr. Watts the printer, a man of integrity, aſſured a friend of Mr. Nichols, that the Tranſlation of the Firſt Book of the Iliad was in Tickell's hand-writing, but much corrected and interlined by Addiſon.

certainly is not, though it was expected it would have been done effectually in what has been lately said on the subject by the learned Author of *Warburton's Life*, who is of opinion, that Tickell might have begun and finished his First Book of Homer four years before Lord Halifax's death, though known to Lord Halifax only four months before his death, and might intended to have dedicated the work to this Lord. Well convinced of the rashness and uncertainty of judging merely by different *styles*, I hardly venture to say, that the *style* of this version is apparently very unlike *Tickell*'s way of writing. With his usual frankness and good-nature, Steele once endeavoured to reconcile these two great angry rivals; but, in the interview he procured, they so bitterly upbraided each other with envy, arrogance, and ingratitude, that they parted with increased aversion and ill-will. Pope was chiefly irritated at the calm and contemptuous unconcern with which Addison affected to address him in this conversation.

With respect to Pope's Translation, in general, it is certainly very spirited and splendid throughout; an unwearied fire, ἄκαμαλον πῦρ, pervades the whole work; but it must be allowed to be too full of antithesis, hyperbole, and exaggeration; every part and every object is equally ornamented; "the naked "nature," "is covered with gold and jewels." No two things can be so unlike, as the Iliad of Homer, and the Iliad of Pope; "to colour the images;" "to

" point the ſentences;" " to laviſh Ovidian graces," on the ſimple Grecian, is to put a bag-wig on Mr. TOWNLEY's fine buſto of the venerable old bard.

Pope had now leiſure and ability to gratify his favourite paſſion of laying out grounds, which he diſplayed with taſte and judgment, at his pleaſant villa, cloſe to the banks of the Thames; where, by a happy contrivance to join two pieces of ground together, he built a beauty on neceſſity, and turned a ſubterraneous paſſage into a romantic grotto, which he adorned with valuable ores, ſpars, and minerals; many of which were preſented to him by Dr. *Borlaſe*, the celebrated antiquary and hiſtorian of *Cornwall*. The ſpot was viſited and admired by the firſt men of this country, and frequently by *Frederic* Prince of Wales, who was happy to contribute to its beauty and ornament, as will be ſeen by the Letter here annexed *.

His father did not live long to behold and to enjoy the proſperity and reputation of his ſon, but died at Twickenham, 1717, ſuddenly, " and without a " groan," in his ſeventy-fifth year; and was celebrated

* " Dear Sir,

" Since my laſt, I have received His Royal Highneſs's commands, to let you know, that he has a mind to preſent you with ſome urns, or vaſes, for your garden; and deſires you would write me word, what number, and ſize, will ſuit you beſt. You may have ſix ſmall ones for your laurel circus, or two large ones to terminate points, as you like beſt. He wants to have your anſwer ſoon.—Adieu."

brated with equal elegance, tenderneſs, and gratitude, in the Epiſtle to Arbuthnot. In this year alſo he collected all his Poems, and publiſhed them, with a very judicious Preface, in a beautiful edition, in folio, and in quarto.

In the year 1720, when the publication of the Iliad was completed, which he began 1712, he became one of the infatuated adventurers in the famous and fatal South-Sea ſcheme, and luckily withdrew the ſum of money he had hazarded, without being a great loſer.

As the æras of a mere author's life can be marked only by the ſeries of his publications, which however ſhew the progreſs of his genius and labours, I proceed to obſerve, that, in 1721, he publiſhed the exquiſite Poems of his friend Parnell, to which he prefixed the fine Epiſtle to Lord Oxford; and in the ſame year engaged with Tonſon to give an edition of Shakeſpeare, in ſix quarto volumes; for which he received the ſum of two hundred and ſeventeen pounds twelve ſhillings. For this edition he was juſtly attacked by Theobald, firſt in *Shakeſpeare Reſtored*, and afterwards in a formal edition, to which Warburton contributed many remarks; and by Theobald many deficiencies, errors, and miſtakes were pointed out. Pope was ſo mortified by this failure, that from this time, it is ſaid, he became an enemy to collators, commentators, and verbal critics, hinting that he miſcarried in this undertaking, for which he was not qualified,

by

by having a mind too great for ſuch minute employment *.

Soon afterwards he gave out Propoſals for a Tranſlation of the *Odyſſey*; and took for his co-adjutors, Fenton and Broome; the former of whom, both from his genius and learning, was eminently qualified for the taſk. He, himſelf, tranſlated only twelve books; and at the end of the notes, which were compiled by Broome †, a falſe ſtatement was given of their reſpective ſhares; but it is now aſcertained by Spence's papers, that Fenton tranſlated the firſt, fourth, nineteenth, and twentieth Books; and Broome the ſecond, ſixth, eighth, eleventh, twelfth, ſixteenth, eighteenth, and twenty-third Books. Lintot agreed to pay Pope one hundred pounds for each volume; the number of ſubſcribers was five hundred and ſeventy-four; and of copies eight hundred and nineteen. He is ſaid to have given to Fenton for his aſſiſtance,

* On this occaſion Mallet addreſſed to him an Epiſtle on *Verbal Criticiſm*; full of affected contempt for a ſort of learning with which Mallet, as well as Pope, was unacquainted. This Epiſtle procured him the friendſhip of Pope, who commends it in his Letters, though Mallet was afterwards the perſon that Bolingbroke employed to revile the memory of Pope, for publiſhing the Idea of a Patriot King: The moſt unmeaning of all Bolingbroke's Treatiſes, and which, as ſaid Count Powniatowſki, the late unhappy King of Poland, proves nothing at all.

† But the poſtſcript to the notes was written by Pope himſelf, and is ſo fine a piece of criticiſm, that it is inſerted in this edition, among his proſe pieces.

aſſiſtance, three hundred pounds; and to Broome five hundred.

About this time he was full of grief and anxiety, on account of the impeachment of his friend Biſhop Atterbury, for whom he ſeems to have felt the greateſt affection and regard. And being ſummoned before the Lords at the trial, to give ſome account of Atterbury's domeſtic life and employments, not being uſed to ſpeak in a large aſſembly, he made ſeveral blunders in the few words he had to utter.

In 1726, Mr. Joſeph Spence, Fellow of New College in Oxford, but not yet Profeſſor of Poetry, as Dr. Johnſon imagined him to be, (my father holding that office at the time,) publiſhed an *Eſſay on the Odyſſey*, in a dialogue betwixt *Philypſus* and *Antiphaus*, after the manner of Bouhours and Dryden on the Drama, in which its beauties and blemiſhes were minutely conſidered. The candour, the politeneſs, the true taſte, and judgment, with which this criticiſm was conducted, were ſo very acceptable and pleaſing to Pope, that he immediately courted the acquaintance of the ingenious Author, who, notwithſtanding Dr. Johnſon's invidious aſſertion, was an excellent ſcholar, and earneſtly invited him to ſpend ſome time with him at Twickenham; and I have now before me a Letter which Spence wrote from thence, to his intimate friend Mr. Pitt, the tranſlator of *Vida* and *Virgil*, deſcribing to him the uncommonly kind and

and friendly manner in which he was received and treated. By the favour of Dr. Lowth, the late excellent Bishop of London *, I have seen a copy of this *Essay on the Odyssey*, with marginal observations written in Pope's own hand, and generally acknowledging the justness of Spence's observations; and in a few instances pleading, humorously enough, that some favourite lines might be spared. I speak from experience, when I say, that I know no critical treatise better calculated to form the taste of young men of genius, than this *Essay on the Odyssey*. And lest it should be thought that this opinion arises from my partiality to a friend with whom I lived so many years in the happiest intimacy; I will add, that this also was the opinion of three persons, from whose judgment there can be no appeal, Dr. Akenside, Bishop Lowth, and Mr. James Harris. The two valuable preferments which Spence obtained, the Prebend of Durham, and the Professorship of Modern History in Oxford, were owing to the interest which Pope, among some of his powerful friends, exerted in his favour. And it was upon Pope's recommendation that he travelled with Lord Middlesex, which was the foundation of his future good fortune.

To this learned and amiable man, on whose friendship I set the greatest value, am I indebted for most of the

* Who transmitted an account of his friend Spence's life to Dr. Kippis, to be inserted in the Biographia Britannica, which I have read with great pleasure, and which I presume is among the papers left by that learned and candid compiler.

the anecdotes relating to Pope mentioned in this edition, which he communicated to me when I was making him a viſit, 1754, at Byfleet in Surrey; a pleaſant villa which had been preſented to him by Lord Lincoln.

The only bad accident Pope, in the courſe of his life, ever met with, was at the cloſe of this year, when he was overturned in a deep water, and was with difficulty ſnatched out of his coach by the poſtilion, with a force that broke the glaſs, and cut two of his fingers ſo deſperately, that, though he was attended by St. André, a ſkilful and eminent ſurgeon, he loſt the uſe of them. On which occaſion Voltaire wrote to him a letter, which, as a ſpecimen of his Engliſh, is here inſerted in a note*.

Swift,

* "Sir,

"I hear this moment of your ſad adventure. That water you fell in, was not Hippocrene's water, otherwiſe it would have reſpected you. Indeed, I am concerned beyond expreſſion for the danger you have been in, and more for your wounds. Is it poſſible that thoſe fingers which have written the Rape of the Lock, and the Criticiſm, which have dreſſed Homer ſo becomingly in an Engliſh coat, ſhould have been ſo barbarouſly treated? Let the hand of Dennis, or of your poetaſters, be cut off, yours is ſacred. I hope, Sir, you are now perfectly recovered; really your accident concerns me as much as all the diſaſters of a maſter ought to affect his ſcholar. I am ſincerely, Sir, with the admiration which you deſerve,

"Your moſt humble ſervant,

"In my Lord Bolingbroke's houſe, "Voltaire.
Friday at noon, Nov. 16, 1726."

N. B. If Voltaire is frequently quoted in the following ſheets, it is becauſe he was a man of wit and penetration, though an unbeliever;

Swift, coming to England, 1727, joined with Pope in publiſhing, in four volumes octavo, their Miſcellaneous Pieces, in proſe and verſe; to which Pope wrote a Preface, complaining, among other inſtances, of the ill uſage he had received from bookſellers, and of the liberty Curll had taken in publiſhing his juvenile Letters, purchaſed from a Mrs. Thomas, a miſtreſs of Mr. Cromwell. The two moſt remarkable paſſages in this Preface are, where they ſay, "That in ſeveral "parts of our lives, we have written ſome things "which we may wiſh never to have thought on:" And when they alſo ſay, "In regard to two perſons "only, we wiſh our raillery, though ever ſo tender, "or reſentment ever ſo juſt, had not been indulged. "We ſpeak of Sir T. Vanbrugh, who was a man of "wit and of honour; and of Mr. Addiſon, whoſe "name

believer; which, however, never appears in his tragedies; becauſe he was the moſt celebrated of all our Author's contemporary poets; becauſe he was an admirer and acquaintance of Pope; becauſe they wrote on ſimilar ſubjects; becauſe he had made particular remarks on many of our Author's pieces; and becauſe both of them were patronized by Bolingbroke. I have been always as ready to cenſure his inconſiſtencies as to praiſe his talents. At this time he was ſupported and careſſed by the Britiſh court and nobility, and particularly by Queen Caroline, to whom he dedicated the quarto edition of his Henriade, publiſhed by ſubſcription in London. The Marquis d' Argenſon, his intimate friend, ſays of him, 1736: "Plaiſe au ciel que la magie de ſon ſtyle n'accrédite pas des fauſſes opinions & des idées dangereuſes, qu'il ne deſhonore pas ce ſtyle charmant en proſe & en vers, en le faiſant ſervir à des ouvrages dont les ſujets ſoient indignes & du peintre & du coloris; & qu'il ne devienne pas le chef d'une ſecte à qui il arrivera, comme à bien d'autres, que les ſectateurs ſe tromperont ſur les intentions de leur Patriarche!"

"name deserves all respect from every lover of "learning."

And now, in the year 1728, too much exasperated by the rude attacks of impotent scribblers, and forgetting what he had said in the before-mentioned Preface, "that it is to be lamented that Virgil let "pass a line which told posterity he had two enemies "called Bavius and Mævius," he determined to crush his adversaries in a mass, by one strong and decisive blow, and wrote his *Dunciad:* The history of which, is so very minutely related by Pope himself, in a Dedication which he wrote to Lord Middlesex, under the name of *Savage*, who, by the way, assisted Pope in finding out many particulars of these Scribblers' lives, that it ought it be inserted in this place.

"I will relate the war of the *Dunces*, (for so it has "been commonly called,) which began in the year "1727, and ended in 1730.

"When Dr. Swift and Mr. Pope thought it pro-"per, for reasons specified in the Preface to their "Miscellanies, to publish such little Pieces of theirs, "as had casually got abroad, there was added to "them the *Treatise of the Bathos*, or the *Art of Sink-"ing in Poetry.* It happened, that in one Chapter "of this Piece the several species of bad Poets were "ranged in classes, to which were prefixed almost "all the Letters of the Alphabet (the greatest "part of them at random); but such was the num-"ber of poets eminent in that art, that some one or

" other took every letter to himſelf: All fell into " ſo violent a fury, that, for half a year or more, the " common newſpapers (in moſt of which they had " ſome property, as being hired writers) were filled " with the moſt abuſive falſehoods and ſcurrilities " they could poſſibly deviſe. A liberty no way to " be wondered at in thoſe people, and in thoſe " papers, that for ſo many years, during the uncon- " trouled licence of the preſs, had aſperſed almoſt " all the great characters of the age; and this with " impunity, their own perſons and names being ut- " terly ſecret and obſcure.

" This gave Mr. Pope the thought, that he had " now ſome opportunity of doing good, by detect- " ing, and bringing into light, theſe common ene- " mies of mankind; ſince, to invalidate this univer- " ſal ſlander, it ſufficed to ſhew what contemptible " men were the authors of it. He was not without " hopes, that, by manifeſting the dulneſs of thoſe, " who had only malice to recommend them, either " the bookſellers would not find their account in " employing them, or the men themſelves, when diſ- " covered, want courage to proceed in ſo unlawful " an occupation. This it was that gave birth to the " *Dunciad;* and he thought it an happineſs, that, " by the late flood of ſlander on himſelf, he had ac- " quired ſuch a peculiar right over their names as " was neceſſary to this deſign.

" On

" On the 12th of May 1729, at St. James's, that " poem was presented to the King and Queen (who " had before been pleased to read it) by the Right " Honourable Sir Robert Walpole: and some days " after the whole impression was taken and dispersed " by several noblemen and persons of the first dis- " tinction.

" It is certainly a true observation, that no people " are so impatient of censure as those who are the " greatest slanderers, which was wonderfully exem- " plified on this occasion. On the day the book " was first vended, a crowd of authors besieged the " shop; intreaties, advices, threats of law and bat- " tery, nay, cries of treason, were all employed to " hinder the coming out of the *Dunciad*: on the " other side, the booksellers and hawkers made as " great an effort to procure it. What could a few " poor authors do against so great a majority as the " public? There was no stopping a torrent with a " finger, so out it came.

" Many ludicrous circumstances attended it. The " *Dunces* (for by this name they were called) held " weekly clubs, to consult of hostilities against the " author: one wrote a Letter to a great Minister, " assuring him, Mr. Pope was the greatest enemy the " government had: and another bought his image " in clay, to execute him in effigy; with which sort " of satisfaction the gentlemen were a little com- " forted.

"Some falſe editions of the book having an owl "in their frontiſpiece, the true one, to diſtinguiſh it, "fixed in its ſtead an aſs laden with authors. Then "another ſurreptitious one being printed with the "ſame aſs, the new edition in octavo returned for "diſtinction to the owl again. Hence aroſe a great "conteſt of bookſellers againſt bookſellers, and ad-"vertiſements againſt advertiſements; ſome recom-"mended the edition of the owl, and others the edi-"tion of the aſs; by which names they came to be "diſtinguiſhed, to the great honour alſo of the gen-"tlemen of the *Dunciad.*"

The complete edition of the Dunciad was elegantly printed in quarto, by Dodd, 1729, with large Notes, and an Appendix, under the name of *Cleland*, but written by Pope himſelf. As to the conduct of this poem, the awkward additions made to it, and the many unhappy alterations it underwent, we muſt refer to the remarks in the Fifth Volume of this Edition.

After enjoying for two years a complete triumph over *Horneck*, and *Rome*, and *Gildon*, and *Concanen*, and *Oldmixon*, and the nameleſs fabricators of the *Popiad*, and *Martiniad*, he printed, in folio, 1731, (for this was the original title,) "An Epiſtle to "Richard Earl of Burlington, occaſioned by his "publiſhing Palladio's Deſigns of the Baths, Arches, "Theatres, &c. of Ancient Rome."

The gang of ſcribblers immediately roſe up together, and accuſed him of malevolence and ingratitude, in in having ridiculed the houſe, gardens, chapel, and dinners, of the Duke of Chandos at *Canons*, (who had lately, as they affirmed, been his benefactor,) under the name of *Timon*. He peremptorily and poſitively denied the charge, and wrote an exculpatory letter to the Duke, with the aſſeverations of which letter, as the laſt Duke of Chandos told me, his anceſtor was not perfectly ſatisfied.

It ought to be added, that the many reſpectable authors, who have, ſince this Epiſtle, treated of the art of laying out grounds and gardens, have acknowledged the juſtneſs and propriety of the rules and precepts delivered by Pope, in this highly-finiſhed piece. What relates to architecture is ſhorter, and perhaps not equal to the reſt.

Adhering to the chronological order in which the *Ethic Epiſtles* were publiſhed, I am next to obſerve, that there appeared, in 1732 *, "Of the Uſe of "Riches, an Epiſtle to the Right Hon. Allen Lord "Bathurſt," folio; which he has treated in ſo maſterly a way, as to have almoſt exhauſted the ſubject. I never ſaw this very amiable old nobleman, whoſe wit, vivacity, ſenſe, and integrity are well known; but he repeatedly expreſſed his diſguſt, and his ſurpriſe, at finding, in later editions, this *Epiſtle* awkwardly

* In the Epiſtles to Lord Burlington and Lord Bathurſt, ſays Johnſon, Warburton has endeavoured to find a train of thought which was never in the writer's head.

awkwardly converted into a *Dialogue*, in which he has but little to ſay. And I remember he once remarked, "that this line,

"P. But you are tir'd. I'll tell a tale. B. Agreed;—

"was inſupportably inſipid and flat." Pope almoſt annually viſited, and frequently praiſed, his fine improvements, and many plantations, at Cirenceſter.

It was in this year alſo, 1732 *, that, determined to wait in ſecret the opinion of the public, he publiſhed, what he had for eight years at leaſt been revolving in his mind, the Firſt Epiſtle of his *Eſſay on Man;* the Second followed in the ſame year; the Third in 1733; and the Fourth in 1734.

He enjoyed in private the various ſuſpicious † ſurmiſes of thoſe who pretended to point out the right author, and once puniſhed the vanity and petulance of *Mallet*, who, being aſked by him what new publication there was, anſwered, "Only an inſignificant "thing, called, An Eſſay on Man;" on which Pope ſtruck him dumb, and filled him with confuſion, by ſaying, "I wrote it." The nature, the merits, the tendency of this work, are ſo much enlarged upon in

* About this time died *Gay*, for whom he appears to have felt the trueſt tenderneſs and affection. And Swift was ſo affected at the news of Gay's death, that he delayed to open a letter, which he thought contained the affecting intelligence, for many days.

† In the edition in 12mo, 1735, by Dodſley, they were called, Ethic Epiſtles, the Firſt Book; and not Eſſay on Man; and the four Epiſtles to Lord Burlington, &c. were called, Ethic Epiſtles, the Second Book.

in the Notes to this Edition *, that to them the reader must be referred: observing only, that up and down were scattered so many splendid and striking sentiments of religion and virtue, that for many years it was not, till Crousaz † attacked it, suspected to contain tenets hostile to the Christian revelation, though not to natural religion. That Pope himself, some years afterwards, wished it might be otherwise interpreted, may appear,

* After the noble panegyric our Poet has bestowed on his guide Bolingbroke at the end of this *Essay*, his conduct in clandestinely printing the Patriot King may seem indefensible. On considering coolly and impartially the circumstances that attended this improper Publication, I am inclined to think, that he did not print 1500 copies of that Treatise from avarice or treachery; but from too eager a desire to spread, as he thought, the reputation of his friend, whom he idolized.

† *Warburton*, who, in the early part of his life, was a censurer of Pope, and had said, in a letter to *Concanen*, with whom he was intimate, that Pope borrowed by necessity, and who had assisted Theobald in his Notes on Shakspeare, now stept forth with a vigorous defence of the Doctrines of the Essay on Man, against the objections of *Crousaz*; which defence was first published in a Monthly Literary Journal, but was afterwards collected into a volume, and dedicated to Mr. Allen of Bath; with remarks on Fate and Free Will, of which poor *Allen* could understand little. With this vindication Pope was so delighted that he eagerly sought the acquaintance of Warburton, and told him, he understood his opinions better than he did himself; which acquaintance made the fortune of Warburton, and ultimately got him a wife and a bishopric. Bolingbroke reproached Pope with this new connexion, and said, "You have at your elbow a foul-mouth'd and dogmatical critic." It is asserted, that, some years before, Warburton, in a literary club held at Newark, produced and read a Dissertation *against* the Doctrines of the Essay on Man.

appear, from a curious Letter to Racine the Son, who had accused him of infidelity, here inserted.

LETTRE
DE M. POPE A M. RACINE.

" J'AUROIS eu l'honneur, Monsieur, de répon-
" dre plutôt à votre lettre, si je n'avois pas toujours
" attendu le beau présent dont vous m'avez honoré.
" J'ai reçu enfin votre Poëme sur la Religion. Le
" plaisir que me causa cette lecture eût été sans mé-
" lange, si je n'avois eu le chagrin de voir que vous
" m'imputiez des principes que j'abhorre. Je ne m'en
" suis consolé qu'en lisant l'endroit de votre avertisse-
" ment ou vous déclarez que n'entendant pas l'origi-
" nal Anglois vous ne pouvez pas juger de l'*Essai
" sur l'Homme* par vous même; & que vous n'attaque
" pas mes principes, mais les fausses conséquences qu'on
" en a tirées, & les dangereuses maximes que quelques
" personnes ont cru y trouver. Cet aveu est une
" preuve éclatante de votre candeur, de votre pru-
" dence, & de votre charité.

" Je puis vous assurer, Monsieur, que votre entière
" ignorance de notre Langue, m'a été beaucoup moins
" fatale que la connoissance imparfaite qu'en avoient
" mes traducteurs, qui les a empêché de penétrer mes
" véritables sentimens. Toutes les beautés de la ver-
" sification de M. D. R . . . ont été moins honora-
" bles à mon Poëme, que ses méprises continuelles
" sur

" ſur mes raiſonnemens & ſur ma doctrine ne lui ont " été préjudiciables. Vous verrez ces mépriſes re- " levées & réfutées dans l'ouvrage Anglois que j'ai " l'honneur de vous envoyer. Cet ouvrage eſt un " commentaire critique & philoſophique par le ſça- " vant Auteur *de la Divine Légation de Moiſe.*

" Je me flatte que le Chevalier de Ramſay, rempli " comme l'eſt d'un zele ardent pour la vérité, vou- " dra bien vous en expliquer le contenu. Alors je " m'en rapporterai à votre juſtice, & je me flatte que " tous vos ſoupçons ſeront diſſipés.

" En attendant ces éclairciſſemens, je ne ſçaurois " me refuſer le plaiſir de répondre nettement à ce " que vous deſirez ſçavoir de moi.

" Je déclare donc hautement & très-ſincèrement, " que mes ſentimens ſont diamétralement oppoſés à " ceux de Spinoza & même à ceux de Leibnitz, puiſ- " qu'ils ſont parfaitement conformés à ceux de M. " Paſcal & de M. l'Archevêque de Fenelon, & que " je ſerois gloire d'imiter la docilité du dernier, en " ſoumettant toujours toutes mes opinions particu- " lières aux déciſions de l'Egliſe.

" Je ſuis, avec, &c.

" A Londres,
" le 1 Septembre 1742."

Voltaire has affirmed, " that Pope, to his know- " ledge, had not ſkill enough in the French language " to have been able to have written this Letter to Ra-

"cine; and that if he really wrote it, he muſt ſud-"denly have been bleſt with a gift of tongues, as a "reward for writing ſo admirable a work as the "*Eſſay on Man.*"

"If you would read," ſays Metaſtaſio, "this poem "without ſcruple, I recommend to you the excellent "tranſlation in *terza rima*, lately publiſhed, 1770, by "Count Giuſ. Ferrero di Lauriano. In the judicious, "chriſtian, and learned notes with which he has illuſ-"trated the work, you will ſee the innocence of the "original evidently proved. You will find in Pope "a great poet and a deep philoſopher; but not ſuch "axioms as are neceſſary to ſupport his own ſyſtem."

Few pieces can be found that, for depth of thought, and penetration into the human mind and heart, excel the Epiſtle to Lord Cobham, firſt publiſhed 1733. This nobleman appears to have been much courted by the wits and writers of his time. Congreve addreſſed two Epiſtles in a pleaſing and flowing ſtyle to him, and in a manner very Horatian. The moſt laboured of the two ends with a thought much cenſured by Swift; "that men have been always the "ſame:"

"That virtue now is neither more nor leſs,
"And vice is only varied in the dreſs;
"Believe it, men have always been the ſame,
"And Ovid's Golden Age is but a dream."

Among

Among the many inſcriptions at *Stow*, that to the memory * of *Congreve* is expreſſed with a particular warmth of affection. *Cobham* being diſmiſſed from the command of his regiment, by a pretty violent act of the Miniſter, againſt whoſe meaſures he had voted, particularly on the Exciſe Bill, became a popular character among the patriots. To him *Glover* inſcribed his *Leonidas*, a poem much read and celebrated at its firſt publication; as to a perſon highly diſtinguiſhed by his diſintereſted zeal, and unſhaken fidelity to his country, not leſs in civil life than in the field; and Dr. King introduced him, in his *Templum Libertatis*, as a principal figure, under the name of *Varius;* a long and languid work, that certainly leant more to Republicaniſm than to Jacobitiſm, though *King* was commonly, and as I think, from my knowledge of him at that period of his life, falſely reckoned a Jacobite; for he was for ever ridiculing, as I well remember, the doctrine of paſſive obedience and non-reſiſtance. But it was the cant of that time, and the art of the Miniſter and his adherents, to ſtigmatize every man that dared to oppoſe his meaſures with that odious and contemptible name.

Cobham, in his retirement from the court and buſineſs, employed himſelf in making and beautifying the

* Dr. Young once expreſſed himſelf to me in very harſh terms, of what he termed the vanity of Congreve, in bequeathing by his will ten thouſand pounds to the Ducheſs of Marlborough, and nothing to Mrs. Bracegirdle, who had been long his favourite, and to whom he had many obligations.

the celebrated gardens at Stow, of which Lord Peterborough ſays to Pope, on his viſiting them, "I went "thither to ſee what I had ſeen, and was ſure to like. I "had the idea of thoſe gardens ſo fixed in my imagi-"nation by many deſcriptions, that nothing ſurpriſed "me; immenſity and Vanbrugh appear in the "whole, and in every part. I confeſs the ſtately "*Sacchariſſa* at Stow; but am content with my "little *Amoret*:" meaning *Bevis Mount*, near Southampton.

Lord Cobham wrote two Letters to Pope on occaſion of this Epiſtle, which are ſo full of good ſenſe, that they ought to be brought forward, and inſerted in this place, as they are not found in the collection of our Author's Letters.

"Stowe, Nov. 1, 1733.

"THOUGH I have not modeſty enough not to be "pleaſed with your extraordinary compliment, I have "wit enough to know how little I deſerve it. You "know all mankind are putting themſelves upon the "world for more than they are worth, and their "friends are daily helping the deceit. But I am "afraid I ſhall not paſs for an abſolute patriot; how-"ever, I have the honour of having received a pub-"lic teſtimony of your eſteem and friendſhip, and "am as proud of it as I could be of any advantage "which could happen to me. As I remember, when "I ſaw the Brouillion of this Epiſtle, it was per-

"plexed;

" plexed; you have now made it the contrary, and, " I think, it is the cleareſt and the cleaneſt of all " you have wrote. Don't you think you have be- " ſtowed too many lines on the old Letcher? The " inſtance itſelf is but ordinary, and I think ſhould " be ſhortened or changed. Thank you; and be- " lieve me to be moſt ſincerely yours,

" COBHAM."

" Stowe, Nov. 8, 1733.

" I LIKE your Letcher better now 'tis ſhorter; and " the Glutton is a very good Epigram. But they " are both appetites, that from nature we indulge, " as well for her ends as our pleaſure. A Cardinal, " in his way of pleaſure, would have been a better " inſtance. What do you think of an old Lady " dreſſing her ſilver locks with pink, and ordering " her coffin to be lined with white quilted ſattin, with " gold fringes? Or Counſellor Vernon, retiring to " enjoy himſelf with five thouſand a year which he " had got, and returning back to Chancery to get " a little more, when he could not ſpeak ſo loud as " to be heard? or a Judge turned out coming again " to the bar?—I mean that a paſſion or habit, that " has not a natural foundation, falls in better with " your ſubject, than any of our natural wants; which " in ſome degree we cannot avoid purſuing to the " laſt; and if a man has ſpirits or appetite enough " to take a bit of either kind at parting, you may " condemn

" condemn him, but you would be proud to imitate " him.

" I congratulate you upon the fine weather. 'Tis " a ſtrange thing that people of condition, and men " of parts, muſt enjoy it in common with the reſt of " the world. But now I think on't, their purſuits " are generally after points of ſo great importance, " that they do not enjoy it at all. I won't trouble " you any longer, but with the aſſurance of what I " hope you are perfectly convinced of, that I am " moſt ſincerely yours,

" COBHAM."

The firſt ſpecimen of our Author's happy and judicious Imitations of Horace, was given, 1733, folio, with this title, " The Firſt Satire of the Second " Book of Horace, imitated in a Dialogue between " Alexander Pope of Twickenham, in Comm. " Midd. Eſq. on the one part, and his learned " Council on the other." A minute detail of the beauties and blemiſhes of this Imitation is given in the ſucceeding Notes of this Edition. And I will here only obſerve, that, perhaps, it may deſerve conſideration, whether the beſt manner of imitating the Satires and Epiſtles of Horace, which approach ſo near to comedy and to common converſation, would not be to adopt the *familiar* blank verſe, which my lamented friend, Mr. Colman, has ſo very ſucceſsfully employed in his *Terence*; a ſort of verſe no more

more resembling that of Milton, than the Hexameters of *Homer* resemble those of *Theocritus*. I cannot forbear adding, that Mr. Christopher Pitt has imitated the Seventh Satire of Horace, Book II. the Nineteenth Epistle of Book II. the Fourth Epistle, Book I. and the Tenth and Eighteenth of Book I. with a *freedom* and a facility of versification truly Horatian.

A death of such consequence as that of a fond mother to so affectionate a son as was our Author, must not be omitted to be here mentioned; which happened this year. Nothing can be more interesting and affecting than the request he made to his friend Mr. Richardson, the painter, to come to Twickenham, and take a sketch of his mother just after she was dead, June 20, 1733: "It would afford (says "he) the finest image of a Saint expired, that ever "painting drew."

It was in the year 1734, that the fine Epistle to Dr. Arbuthnot was, according to the first edition in folio, first printed. Afterwards it underwent two material alterations; it was intitled, improperly and fantastically enough, *A Prologue to the Satires*; and its form was changed into that of a *Dialogue*, in which a man possessed of so much wit, humour, literature, science, and taste, as was Arbuthnot, makes a very indifferent figure, and says little indeed. Pope in this *Epistle*, for so I shall continue to call it, has succeeded in what Cowley calls a nice and difficult task, to speak of himself with dignity and grace.

It is evident he had Boileau in his eye, who has given an interesting picture of his father, family, and fortunes, and even of his own person and manners.

> Libre dans ses discours, mais pourtant toujours sage,
> Assez foible de corps, assez doux de visage;
> Ni petit, ni trop grand, tres-peu voluptueux,
> Ami de la vertu plutôt que vertueux.
>
> EPITRE x. 89.

But no passage in Boileau equals the pathetic tenderness with which our Author speaks of his attention to his aged mother.

This was succeeded, 1735, by the Epistle on the *Characters of Women*, in an Advertisement to which, he asserted, but in truth was not believed, that no *one character* was drawn from the life. Here again he may claim a manifest superiority over the Tenth Satire of Boileau, on the same subject: a subject that had been handled by Young, eight years before, and though not indeed in a style so close, correct, and nervous as that of our Author, but with many playful and truly Horatian strokes of a delicate raillery and ridicule, gently touching the foibles of the sex, with a more cautious and tender hand. As general and vague criticism is useless, I shall venture to hint, that the portraits in Young, of *Zantippe;* of *Delia*, the chariot-driver; of *Daphne*, the critic; of *Lemira*, the sick lady; of the *Female Philosopher;* of the *Theologist;* of the *Languid Lady;* of *Thalestris*, the swearer; of *Lyce*, the old beauty; of *Alicia*, the

sloven;

floven; of the *Female Atheist*; and the *Female Gamester*; are all of them drawn with truth and fpirit, and will not fuffer by being compared with the portraits exhibited by Pope. And the Introductions to thefe Satires, particularly the Addrefs to the Incomparable Lady *Betty Germain*, are, perhaps, as elegant and well-turned as any thing in our language. After reading thefe Pieces, fo full of a knowledge of the world, and difcriminations of characters, one is totally at a lofs to know what Pope could mean by faying, that though Young was a man of genius, yet that he wanted common fenfe.

There was always a friendfhip betwixt our Author and Young; though Harte affured me, that Pope took amifs the preffing Letter Young confcientioufly wrote to him; which Letter Harte had feen, urging Pope to write fomething on the fide of Revelation, in order to take off the impreffions of thofe doctrines which the Effay on Man feemed to convey. To this Young alludes in the conclufion of his Firft *Night Thoughts*, a work in which, fays Johnfon, "he has "exhibited a very wide difplay of original poetry, "variegated with deep reflections and ftriking al- "lufions, a wildernefs of thought, in which the "fertility of fancy fcatters flowers of every hue and "every odour. In the whole, there is a magnificence, "like that afcribed to Chinefe Plantations; the mag- "nificence of vaft extent, and endlefs diverfity." This eloquent eulogium makes amends for the unfriendly

friendly and uncandid Life prefixed to it. Johnſon adds, " He had forgotten to mention the *Revenge*, " till a friend *reminded him of it*." So little did he value dramatic poetry.

Though he did not put his name to the looſe Imitation of the Second Satire of Horace, intitled, " Sober Advice from Horace to the Young Gentle-" men about Town," printed 1736, yet was he indiſputably the Author of it; and ſuffered his friend Dodſley to publiſh it as ſuch, in one edition in 12mo; and is in plain terms charged with it by Bolingbroke, in one of his Letters.

No leſs than four of his Imitations of Horace appeared 1737, which, by the artful accommodations of modern ſentiments to ancient, by judicious applications of ſimilar characters, and happy parallels, are become ſome of the moſt pleaſing and popular of all his Works, eſpecially to readers of years and experience. Theſe are, the Sixth Epiſtle of the Firſt Book of Horace to Mr. Murray (to whom he alſo addreſſed an Imitation of the Ode to Venus); the Second Satire of the Second Book to Mr. Bethel; the Firſt Epiſtle of the Firſt Book of Epiſtles to Lord Bolingbroke; the Firſt Epiſtle of the Second Book to the King; the Second Epiſtle of this Book to Colonel Dormer. Of theſe Imitations, that to the King, Lord Bolingbroke, and Mr. Murray afterwards Lord Mansfield, are the beſt; and that to Mr. Bethel the feebleſt. The Epiſtle to Auguſtus, at firſt read and underſtood,

by

by ſome ſuperficial courtiers, as a compliment to George II. as ſoon as the bitter and ſarcaſtic irony in it was diſcovered, gave great offence.

Mr. Allen of Bath, having long deſired our Author to publiſh a Collection of his Letters, from which, he ſaid, a perfect ſyſtem of morals might be extracted, offered to be at the coſt of a publication of them. Pope refuſed this offer; but in the year 1737, publiſhed an edition of them in quarto, by a large ſubſcription; and a ſecond volume, with the Memoirs of Scriblerus, 1741. I think it proper to give an account of the manner in which this correſpondence was procured, in the words of Dr. Johnſon.

" One of the paſſages of Pope's Life, which ſeems to deſerve ſome inquiry, was a publication of Letters between him and his friends, which falling into the hands of Curll, a rapacious bookſeller of no good fame, were by him printed and ſold. This volume containing ſome Letters from Noblemen, Pope incited a proſecution againſt him in the Houſe of Lords for breach of privilege, and attended himſelf to ſtimulate the reſentment of his friends. Curll appeared at the bar, and, knowing himſelf in no great danger, ſpoke of Pope with very little reverence. *He has*, ſaid Curll, *a knack of verſifying, but in proſe I think myſelf a match for him.* When the orders of the Houſe were examined, none of them appeared to have been infringed;

Curll went away triumphant, and Pope was left to ſeek ſome other remedy.

" Curll's account was, that one evening a man in a clergyman's gown, but with a lawyer's band, brought and offered to ſale a number of printed volumes, which he found to be Pope's Epiſtolary Correſpondence; that he aſked no name, and was told none; but gave the price demanded, and thought himſelf authoriſed to uſe this purchaſe to his own advantage.

" That Curll gave a true account of the tranſaction, it is reaſonable to believe, becauſe no falſehood was ever detected; and when ſome years afterwards I mentioned it to Lintot, the ſon of Bernard, he declared his opinion to be, that Pope knew better than any body elſe how Curll obtained the copies, becauſe another parcel was at the ſame time ſent to himſelf, for which no price had ever been demanded, as he made known his reſolution not to pay a porter, and conſequently not to deal with a nameleſs agent.

" Such care had been taken to make them public, that they were ſent at once to two bookſellers; to Curll, who was likely to ſeize them as a prey; and to Lintot, who might be expected to give Pope information of the ſeeming injury. Lintot, I believe, did nothing, and Curll did what was expected. That to make them public was the only purpoſe, may

be

be reaſonably ſuppoſed, becauſe the numbers offered to ſale by the private meſſengers, ſhewed that hope of gain could not have been the motive of the impreſſion.

" It ſeems that Pope, being deſirous of printing his Letters, and not knowing how to do, without imputation of vanity, what has in this country been done very rarely, contrived an appearance of compulſion; that when he could complain his Letters were ſurreptitiouſly publiſhed, he might decently and defenſively publiſh them himſelf.

" Pope's private correſpondence, thus promulgated, filled the nation with praiſe of his candour, tenderneſs, and benevolence, the purity of his purpoſe, and the fidelity of his friendſhip. There were ſome Letters which a very good, or a very wiſe man would wiſh ſuppreſſed; but, as they had been already expoſed, it was impoſſible now to retract them."

In the various ſorts of compoſition in which the Engliſh have excelled, we have perhaps the leaſt claim to excellence in the article of Letters of our celebrated countrymen. The beſt in this Collection, are of Swift and Arbuthnot, of Peterborough and Trumbull, as written from the heart, and in an eaſy, familiar ſtyle. Thoſe of Bolingbroke are in the form of diſſertations; and thoſe of Pope himſelf, like the elegant and ſtudied Epiſtles of Pliny and Balſac. All of them are over-crowded with profeſſions of integrity and disinterestedness, with trite reflections on contentment and retirement; a disdain of greatness and courts; a contempt of fame; and an affected strain of commonplace morality. They seem to be chiefly valuable for some literary particulars incidentally mentioned.

Being now, in the year 1738, closely connected with the most able opposers of the Ministry and the Court, he wrote the Two Dialogues that took their title from the year in which they were composed, and which are, perhaps, all things considered, some of the strongest Satires ever written in any age or any country. Every species of sarcasm and mode of style are here alternately employed; ridicule, reasoning, irony, mirth, seriousness, lamentation, laughter, familiar imagery, and high poetical painting. Many persons in power were highly provoked, but the name of Pope prevented a prosecution, for what Paxton wished to have called a libel. But about the same time, Paul Whitehead, a very inferior poet, publishing *Manners*, gave an opportunity for repressing what was thought too great a liberty of the press. He left in his poem a very unguarded line,

"And Sherlock's shop and Henley's are the same."

For this line, the Bishop of Salisbury summoned Whitehead to appear before the House of Lords. As he could not be found, his printer, Dodsley, was taken and conveyed, as he himself informed me, to a spunging-house in the Butcher-row, under the custody of of a meſſenger, which coſt him ſeventy pounds. The next morning the neighbouring ſtreet was crowded with the carriages of ſome of the firſt noblemen and gentlemen, who came to offer him their ſervices, and to be his bail. Among the reſt, he told me, were Lord Cheſterfield, Lord Marchmont, Lord Granville, Lord Bathurſt, Lord Eſſex, Mr. Lyttelton, Mr. Pulteney, &c. &c. His proſecution was intended as a hint to Pope, and he underſtood it as ſuch; and did not publiſh a *Third* Dialogue, which he certainly had deſigned to do; part of it now firſt appears in this edition *.

Ceaſing from politics, Pope amuſed himſelf, in 1740, in republiſhing *Selecta Carmina Italorum;* but he took no notice of the edition from which he borrowed his collection, called, *Anthologia,* printed in London in 12mo. 1684, with a moſt judicious preface, and one of the beſt pieces of modern latinity, falſely aſcribed to Atterbury; which he omitted, I think,

* About this time he was honoured with the favour and friendſhip of Frederic Prince of Wales, who was then in oppoſition to the Court. And Mr. Glover told me, that being with Mr. Pope at Twickenham, ſoon after he had publiſhed Leonidas, the Prince, attended by Mr. Lyttelton, one evening paid them a viſit; the latter privately deſired Pope and Glover, that they would join with him in diſſuading the Prince to ride a vicious horſe he was fond of; and among other things urged on the ſubject, Pope ſaid with earneſtneſs to the Prince, " I hope, Sir, the people of " England will not be made miſerable by a *ſecond* horſe!" alluding to the accident that befel King William. " I think," (added Pope, whiſpering afterwards to Mr. Glover,) " this ſpeech was " pretty well for me!"

think, very improperly. What he added was a very indifferent Poem of *Aonius Palearius*, *De Immortalitate Animi* *, in Three Books; when he might have enriched his Collection by many more Pieces of *Vida*, *Ant. Flaminius*, *Cotta*, *Sannazarius*, *Politianus*, *Molza*, and the *Strozzi*, and a number of more exquiſite morſels than thoſe which he has inſerted, if he had conſulted the ten volumes of the *Carmina Illuſtrium Poetarum*, printed at Florence 1720, and *Carmina Quinque Poetarum*, Flor. 1720.

In the year 1742, he was unfortunately perſuaded, by Dr. Warburton, to write the Fourth Book of the Dunciad †; which I cannot forbear conſidering as an injudicious and incongruous addition to that Poem, for reaſons aſſigned in the notes to it; as I alſo do the degrading *Tibbald*, 1743, from being the Hero of that Poem, and ſubſtituting *Cibber* in his place, for reaſons alſo there aſſigned. What provocations he might have received from Cibber, is a thing entirely out of the queſtion; the matter to be conſidered is, whether Cibber was a Hero *proper*, or not, for the Dunciad. It is to be lamented, that, in this inſtance, our Author's *indignation* got the better of what he poſſeſſed in an eminent degree, his judgment; and that the laſt effort of

* Very inferior to Mr. Hawkins Brown's Latin Poem on this ſubject. A. Palearius was burnt as a heretic.

† The Fourth Book of the Dunciad, ſaid Shenſtone, is doubtleſs Mr. Pope's dotage, τȣ̃ Διὸς ἐνύπνια; flat in the whole, and including, with ſeveral tolerable lines, a number of weak, obſcure, and even punning ones. Letter 13.

of his genius, which might have been employed on subjects so much higher, and more important, should be wasted in expressing this resentment. After all, the chief fault of the Dunciad, in its last state, is the violence and the vehemence of its satire, and the excessive height to which it is carried; and which may, therefore, be justly compared to that marvellous column of boiling water near *Mount Hecla*, thrown upwards, above ninety feet, by the force of a subterraneous fire.

Pope is said to have planned, at different times, *three* Works that he did not finish. *One* was, a Translation of Passages of Greek Poets of different *Ages*, as Specimens of their different *Manners*. *Another*, was the History of the Rise and Progress of Poetry in England, which he divided into six different Schools: 1. The School of Provence; 2. of Chaucer; 3. of Petrarch; 4. of Dante; 5. of Spencer, and Translators from Italian; 6. of Donne. The *other* and third Work, was no less than an *Epic* Poem, the subject of which was *Brutus*, grandson of *Æneas*; who, after many adventures and obstacles, establishes a form of government of the best kind imaginable, in Great Britain. Brutus was to be assisted by Guardian Angels in his attempt, and opposed by a set of Evil Beings. The Plan which he had drawn up for this work, will be given at length in a subsequent Volume. He intended to have written it in Blank Verse; a circumstance worth the consideration of the defenders of

 rhyme.

rhyme. It is remarkable, that the very firſt Poem, any thing like an Epic Poem, that appeared in France, was on this identical ſubject of Brutus arriving in England. It was written by Euſtache, or rather Wace, in the reign of Louis the Seventh, who aſcended the throne 1137, the huſband of Eleanora, married, after a divorce, to our Henry the Second. The Author called it, *Le Roman de Brut.* Every piece of poetry was, at that time, denominated a Romance. The Latin language ceaſed to be commonly ſpoken in France about the ninth century; and was ſucceeded by what was called the Romance-tongue, a mixture of the language of the Francs and of bad Latin.

And now, about the year 1744, his health and ſtrength began viſibly to decline. Beſides his conſtant head-achs, and ſevere rheumatic pains, he had been afflicted, for five years, with an aſthma, which was ſuſpected to be occaſioned by a dropſy on the breaſt, and which, not the ſkill of the many able phyſicians who were always ready and eager to attend him, could relieve. In the month of May 1744, he evidently grew worſe and more infirm. He had frequent deliriums; and as Dodſley told me, with tears in his eyes, Pope aſked him one day, as he ſat by his bed-ſide, "What great arm is that I ſee coming out of the "wall?" Recovering another day from one of theſe deliriums, he ſaid to Spence, "I am ſo certain "of the Soul's being immortal, that I ſeem to feel it "within

"within me, as it were by intuition." Mrs. Martha Blount * unfeelingly neglected him in his laſt illneſs, and coming one day to his houſe, enquired of the amiable Lord Marchmont, who had conſtantly attended him with friendſhip and affection, "What, is "he not dead yet?" Very different was the behaviour of Bolingbroke, who, as Spence related to me, ſtanding, in one of his laſt interviews with Pope, behind his chair, and looking earneſtly down upon him, repeated ſeveral times, interrupted with ſobs, "O great "God, what is man! I never knew a perſon that "had ſo tender a heart for his particular friends, or "a warmer benevolence for all mankind!" It was Mr. Hooke, a bigoted papiſt, a quietiſt, a friend † of Ramſay, and diſciple of Fenelon, who perſuaded Pope to be attended by a prieſt, that he might die like his father and mother; an argument that had much weight with ſo dutiful a ſon. And ſuch was the fervour of his devotion, that, as Chiſelden, the ſurgeon,

* Mr. Swinburne, the traveller, who was her relation, informs me, that ſhe died in 1762, at her houſe in Berkley Square, Piccadilly, where he frequently viſited her, and much gratified him by promiſing to leave him all the MSS. ſhe had in her poſſeſſion, but ſhe died without a will, and the MSS. were never recovered. He tells me, ſhe was a little, neat, fair, prim, old woman, eaſy and gay in her manner and converſation, but ſeemed not to poſſeſs any extraordinary talents. Her eldeſt ſiſter Tereſa had uncommon wit and abilities.

† When Mr. Hooke aſked him, Whether he would not die as his father and mother had done, and whether he ſhould not ſend for a prieſt? he anſwered, "I do not ſuppoſe it to be eſſential, "but it will look right, and I thank you for putting me in mind of "it."

ſurgeon, who was preſent, related to Dr. Hoadly, he exerted all his ſtrength to throw himſelf out of his bed, that he might receive the laſt ſacraments kneeling on the floor. A few hours after the prieſt retired, Bolingbroke came over from Batterſea, and expreſſed great indignation at this tranſaction. It was in the evening of the thirtieth day of May 1744, that he had the happineſs of dying with the greateſt tranquillity, aged fifty-ſix years.

He was interred at Twickenham, near his father and mother; and the Biſhop of Glouceſter erected a monument to his memory, with the following inſcription:

" ALEXANDRO POPE, A. R. M.
GUL. *Epiſcopus Gloceſtrienſis,*
Amicitiæ Cauſâ,
Fac. cur. 1761.
Poeta loquitur.

" For one, who would not be buried in Weſtminſter Abbey:

" Heroes and Kings, your diſtance keep,
In peace let one poor Poet ſleep;
Who never flattered folks like you,
Let Virgil bluſh, and Horace too!"

His death, though it might have been expected, was not lamented by any of his contemporary Poets, till Mr. Maſon made amends by his Muſæus.

Conſidering the debility, deformity, and diſtortion of his bodily frame, it is rather wonderful he lived ſo long. He was protuberant both before and behind; and

and he compared himſelf, in his humorous account of the club of little men, to a ſpider. He was ſo very feeble and weak, as not to be able to dreſs or undreſs himſelf without aſſiſtance; and ſo ſuſceptible of cold, that he was not only wrapt up in fur and flannel, but was alſo obliged to wear boddice made of ſtiff canvaſs, cloſely laced about him. We muſt not wonder, or be diſguſted, that he had much of the irritability, peeviſhneſs, and fretfulneſs of a conſtant valetudinarian.

In the intervals of ſickneſs and head-ach, with which he was ſo frequently afflicted, he too much indulged his appetite, and was too fond of a variety of diſhes highly ſeaſoned, and of the moſt poignant flavour; with which, when his ſtomach was oppreſſed, he had recourſe to ſtrong liquors and drams. His converſation was not remarkably brilliant or pleaſant, and no ſallies of his wit or humour are recorded. It is obſervable, that he never was ſeen to laugh heartily. It is unpleaſant to hear it ſaid, that, in the common intercourſe of life, he delighted in petty ſtratagems and idle artifices, in procuring what he wanted, without plainly and directly mentioning the thing. So that "he played the politician," ſaid Lady Bolingbroke, "about cabbages and turnips."

But whatever might be the imperfections of our great Poet's perſon or temper, yet the vigour, force, and activity of his mind were almoſt unparalleled. His whole life, and every hour of it, in ſickneſs and in health, was devoted ſolely, and with unremitting diligence, to cultivate that one art in which he had

determined

determined to excel. Many other Poets have been unavoidably immerſed in buſineſs, in wars, in politics, and diverted from their favourite bias and purſuits. Of Pope it might truly and ſolely be ſaid, *Verſus amat, hoc ſtudet unum.* His whole thoughts, time, and talents were ſpent on his Works alone: which Works, if we diſpaſſionately and carefully review, we ſhall find, that the largeſt portion of them, for he attempted nothing of the epic or dramatic, is of the didactic, moral, and ſatiric kind; and, conſequently, not of the moſt poetic ſpecies of Poetry. There is nothing in ſo ſublime a ſtyle as the Bard of Gray. This is a matter of *fact*, not of *reaſoning;* and means to point out, what Pope *has actually done*, not what, if he had put out his full ſtrength, he was *capable* of *doing*. No man can poſſibly think, or can hint, that the Author of the *Rape of the Lock*, and the *Eloiſa*, wanted *imagination*, or *ſenſibility*, or *pathetic;* but he certainly did not ſo often indulge and exert thoſe talents, nor give ſo many proofs of them, as he did of ſtrong ſenſe and judgment. This turn of mind led him to admire French models; he ſtudied *Boileau* attentively; formed himſelf upon *him*, as Milton formed himſelf upon the Grecian and Italian Sons of *Fancy*. He ſtuck to deſcribing *modern manners;* but theſe *manners*, becauſe they are *familiar*, *uniform*, *artificial*, and *poliſhed*, are, for theſe *four* reaſons, in their very nature *unfit* for any lofty effort of the Muſe. He gradually became one of the moſt correct, even, and exact Poets that ever wrote; but yet with force and

ſpirit,

ſpirit, finiſhing his pieces with a patience, a care, and aſſiduity, that no buſineſs nor avocation ever interrupted; ſo that if he does not frequently raviſh and tranſport his reader, like his Maſter *Dryden*, yet he does not ſo often diſguſt him, like Dryden, with unexpected inequalities and abſurd improprieties. He is never above or below his ſubject. Whatever poetical enthuſiaſm he actually poſſeſſed, he with-held and ſuppreſſed. The peruſal of him, in moſt of his pieces, affects not our minds with ſuch ſtrong emotions as we feel from *Homer* and *Milton;* ſo that no man, of a true poetical ſpirit, is maſter of himſelf while he reads them. Hence he is a writer fit for univerſal peruſal, and of general utility; adapted to all ages and all ſtations; for the old and for the young; the man of buſineſs and the ſcholar. He who would think, and there are many ſuch, the *Fairy Queen*, *Palamon and Arcite*, the *Tempeſt*, or *Comus*, childiſh and romantic, may reliſh Pope. Surely it is no narrow, nor invidious, nor niggardly encomium to ſay, he is the great Poet of Reaſon; the *Firſt* of *Ethical* Authors in Verſe; which he was by choice, not neceſſity. And this ſpecies of writing is, after all, the ſureſt road to an extenſive and immediate reputation. It lies more level to the general capacities of men, than the higher flights of more exalted and genuine poetry. *Waller* was more applauded than the *Paradiſe Loſt;* and we all remember when *Churchill* was more in vogue than *Gray*.

We live in a reaſoning and proſaic age. The foreſts of Fairy-land have been rooted up and deſtroyed; the caſtles and the palaces of Fancy are in ruins; the magic wand of Proſpero is broken and buried many fathoms in the earth. *Telemachus* was ſo univerſally read and admired in France, not ſo much on account of the poetical images and the fine imitations of Homer which it contained, but for the many artful and ſatirical alluſions to the profligate court of Louis XIV. ſcattered up and down. He that treats of faſhionable follies, and the topics of the day, that deſcribes preſent perſons and recent events, as Dryden did in his Abſalom and Achitophel, finds many readers, whoſe underſtandings and whoſe paſſions he gratifies, and who love politics far more than poetry.

The name of *Cheſterfield* on one hand, and of *Walpole* on the other, failed not to make a Poem bought up, and talked of. And it cannot be doubted, that the Odes of Horace which celebrated, and the Satires which ridiculed, well-known and real characters at Rome, were more eagerly read, and more frequently cited, than the Æneid and the Georgic of Virgil. Malignant and inſenſible muſt be the critic, who ſhould impotently dare to aſſert, that *Pope* wanted *genius* and *imagination*; but perhaps it may ſafely be affirmed, that his *peculiar* and *characteriſtical* excellencies were good ſenſe and judgment. And this was the opinion of Atterbury and Bolingbroke; and it was alſo his own opinion. See in Volume Ninth,

the

the Fifth and the Nineteenth Letters; particularly what he ſaid to Warburton at the end of the latter.

If we conſider him as a man, and examine his moral character impartially, we ſhall find that his predominant virtues ſeem to have been filial piety, and conſtancy in his friendſhips; an ardent love of liberty and of his country, and what ſeemed be to its true intereſt; a manly deteſtation of court-flatterers and ſervility; a frugality, and economy, and order, in his houſe, and at his table; at the ſame time that his private charities were many and great; of which *Dodſley*, whom he honoured with his friendſhip, and who partook of his beneficence, gave me ſeveral inſtances. His revenue was about eight hundred pounds a year.

As to his religious opinions, though he would not publicly renounce the tenets of his family, from the fear of being reckoned an intereſted convert, yet he had too clear and ſolid an underſtanding, not to diſcern the groſs abſurdities, and glaring impieties of Popiſh ſuperſtition; and once owned to Dr. Warburton, that he was convinced the Church of Rome had all the marks and ſigns of that Antichriſtian Power and Apoſtacy, ſo ſtrongly painted and predicted in the New Teſtament. Which opinion Dr. Warburton himſelf was ſo zealous in eſtabliſhing, that he founded a Lecture for Sermons to be annually preached at Lincoln's Inn Chapel, on this very ſubject; perſuaded, like his excellent friend Dr. Balguy,

that

that "Popery is indeed nothing better than a refined "species of Paganism; and that, so far as this ex- "tends, the Gospel has failed of its genuine effect, "and left men as it found them, Polytheists and "Idolaters." The approaching destruction of the Church of Rome, especially in a neighbouring kingdom, was thus remarkably foretold by the King of Prussia, 1777: "Le Pape & les moines finiront sans "doute; leur chute ne sera pas l'ouvrage de la rai- "son; mais ils périeront à mesure que les *Finances* "des grandes potentates se dérangeront. En *France*, "quand on aura epuisé tous les expédiens pour avoir "des espèces, on sera forcé de seculariser des Ab- "bayes & des Convens. Cet example sera imité, "& le nombre des *Cuculati* reduit à peu de chose."

Through the whole course of his life, Pope was firmly and unvariably convinced of the Being of a God, a Providence, and the Immortality of the Soul. Though perhaps, when he was writing under the guidance of Bolingbroke, he entertained some unhappy and ill-founded doubts concerning the truth of the Christian Dispensation.

THE

*THE AUTHOR's PREFACE**.

I AM inclined to think that both the writers of books, and the readers of them, are generally not a little unreaſonable in their expectations. The firſt ſeem to fancy the world muſt approve whatever they produce, and the latter to imagine that authors are obliged to pleaſe them at any rate. Methinks, as on the one hand, no ſingle man is born with a right of controuling the opinions of all the reſt; ſo on the other, the world has no title to demand, that the whole care and time of any particular perſon ſhould be ſacrificed to its entertainment. Therefore I cannot but believe that writers and readers are under equal obligations,

* The clearneſs, the cloſeneſs, and the elegance of ſtyle with which this preface is written, render it one of the beſt pieces of proſe in our language. It abounds in ſtrong good ſenſe, and profound knowledge of life. It is written with ſuch ſimplicity that ſcarcely a ſingle metaphor is to be found in it. Atterbury was ſo delighted with it, that he tells our Author he had read it over twice with pleaſure, and deſired him not to balance a moment about printing it; "always provided there is nothing ſaid there that you may have occaſion to unſay hereafter." Theſe words are remarkable. This preface far excels thoſe of Peliſſon, Vaugelas, and D'Ablancourt, of which the French boaſt ſo highly. May I be allowed juſt to add, that the fineſt prefaces ever written, were, perhaps, that of Thuanus to his Hiſtory, of Calvin to his Inſtitutes, and of Cauſabon to his Polybius.

obligations, for as much fame, or pleasure, as each affords the other.

Every one acknowledges, it would be a wild notion to expect perfection in any work of man: and yet one would think the contrary was taken for granted, by the judgment commonly past upon Poems. A Critic supposes he has done his part, if he proves a writer to have failed in an expression, or erred in any particular point: and can it then be wondered at, if the Poets in general seem resolved not to own themselves in any error? For as long as one side will make no allowances, the other will be brought to no acknowledgments *.

I am afraid this extreme zeal on both sides is ill-placed; Poetry and Criticism being by no means the universal concern of the world, but only the affair of idle men who write in their closets, and of idle men who read there.

Yet sure, upon the whole, a bad Author deserves better usage than a bad Critic: for a Writer's endeavour, for the most part, is to please his Readers, and he fails merely through the misfortune of an ill judgment; but such a Critic's is to put them out of

* In the former editions it was thus—*For as long as one side despises a well-meant endeavour, the other will not be satisfied with a moderate approbation.*——But the Author altered it, as these words were rather a consequence from the conclusion he would draw, than the conclusion itself, which he has now inserted. W.

humour;

humour; a deſign he could never go upon without both that and an ill temper.

I think a good deal may be ſaid to extenuate the fault of bad Poets. What we call a Genius, is hard to be diſtinguiſhed by a man himſelf, from a ſtrong inclination: and if his genius be ever ſo great, he cannot at firſt diſcover it any other way, than by giving way to that prevalent propenſity which renders him the more liable to be miſtaken. The only method he has is to make the experiment by writing, and appealing to the judgment of others: now if he happens to write ill, (which is certainly no ſin in itſelf), he is immediately made an object of ridicule. I wiſh we had the humanity to reflect that even the worſt authors might, in their endeavour to pleaſe us, deſerve ſomething at our hands. We have no cauſe to quarrel with them but for their obſtinacy in perſiſting to write; and this too may admit of alleviating circumſtances. Their particular friends may be either ignorant, or inſincere; and the reſt of the world in general is too well-bred to ſhock them with a truth, which generally their Bookſellers are the firſt that inform them of. This happens not till they have ſpent too much of their time to apply to any profeſſion which might better fit their talents; and till ſuch talents as they have are ſo far diſcredited as to be but of ſmall ſervice to them. For (what is the hardeſt caſe imaginable) the reputation of a man generally depends upon the firſt ſteps he makes in the world; and people will eſtabliſh their opinion of us; from what we do at that ſeaſon when we have leaſt judgment to direct us.

On the other hand, a good Poet no ſooner communicates his works with the ſame deſire of information, but it is imagined he is a vain young creature given up to the ambition of fame; when perhaps the poor man is all the while trembling with the fear of being ridiculous. If he is made to hope he may pleaſe the world, he falls under very unlucky circumſtances: for, from the moment he prints, he muſt expect to hear no more truth, than if he were a Prince, or a Beauty. If he has not very good ſenſe (and indeed there are twenty men of wit for one man of ſenſe) his living thus in a courſe of flattery may put him in no ſmall danger of becoming a Coxcomb: if he has, he will conſequently have ſo much diffidence as not to reap any great ſatisfaction from his praiſe; ſince, if it be given to his face, it can ſcarce be diſtinguiſhed from flattery, and if in his abſence, it is hard to be certain of it. Were he ſure to be commended by the beſt and moſt knowing, he is as ſure of being envied by the worſt and moſt ignorant, which are the majority; for it is with a fine Genius as with a fine faſhion, all thoſe are diſpleaſed at it who are not able to follow it: and it is to be feared that eſteem will ſeldom do any man ſo much good, as ill-will does him harm. Then there is a third claſs of people, who make the largeſt

part

part of mankind, thoſe of ordinary or indifferent capacities; and theſe (to a man) will hate, or ſuſpect him: a hundred honeſt Gentlemen will dread him as a Wit, and a hundred innocent women as a Satiriſt. In a word, whatever be his fate in Poetry, it is ten to one but he muſt give up all the reaſonable aims of life for it. There are indeed ſome advantages accruing from a Genius to Poetry, and they are all I can think of: the agreeable power of ſelf-amuſement when a man is idle or alone; the privilege of being admitted into the beſt company; and the freedom of ſaying as many careleſs things as other people, without being ſo ſeverely remarked upon.

I believe, if any one, early in his life, ſhould contemplate the dangerous fate of authors *, he would ſcarce be of their number on any conſideration. The life of a Wit is a warfare upon earth; and the preſent ſpirit of the learned world is ſuch, that to attempt to ſerve it (any way) one muſt have the conſtancy of a martyr, and a reſolution to ſuffer for its ſake. I could wiſh people would believe, what I am pretty certain they will not, that I have been much leſs concerned about Fame than I durſt declare till this occaſion, when methinks I ſhould find more credit than I could heretofore: ſince my writings

* This fate and theſe dangers have been the ſubject of an ingenious epiſtle by the amiable Mr. Whitehead, The Danger of writing Verſe; one of the happieſt imitations of our Author's didactic manner; in which are many particulars ſuggeſted or borrowed from this preface.

have had their fate already, and it is too late to think of prepoſſeſſing the reader in their favour. I would plead it as ſome merit in me, that the world has never been prepared for theſe Trifles by Prefaces *, byaſſed by recommendation, dazzled with the names of great Patrons, wheedled with fine reaſons and pretences, or troubled with excuſes. I confeſs it was want of conſideration that made me an author; I writ becauſe it amuſed me; I corrected becauſe it was as pleaſant to me to correct as to write; and I publiſhed becauſe I was told, I might pleaſe ſuch as it was a credit to pleaſe. To what degree I have done this, I am really ignorant; I had too much fondneſs for my productions to judge of them at firſt, and too much judgment to be pleaſed with them at laſt. But I have reaſon to think they can have no reputation which will continue long, or which deſerves to do ſo: for they have always fallen ſhort † not only of what I read of others, but even of my own ideas of Poetry.

If any one ſhould imagine I am not in earneſt, I deſire him to reflect, that the Ancients (to ſay the

* As was the practice of his maſter Dryden, who is ſeverely laſhed for this in the Tale of a Tub, and of as great a Genius P. Corneille, whoſe pieces of baſe adulation are a diſgrace to Poetry and Literature. Our Author was accuſtomed to mention Locke's dedication to Lord Pembroke with ſtrong marks of diſapprobation.

† Il n'y a preſque aucun de mes ouvrages dont je ſois content, & il y en a quelques uns que je voudrais n'avoir jamais faits, ſays Voltaire.

least of them) had as much Genius as we: and that to take more pains, and employ more time, cannot fail to produce more complete pieces. They constantly apply'd themselves not only to that art, but to that single branch of an art, to which their talent was most powerfully bent; and it was the business of their lives to correct and finish their works for posterity. If we can pretend to have used the same industry, let us expect the same immortality: Tho' if we took the same care, we should still lie under a further misfortune: they writ in languages that became universal and everlasting, while ours are extremely limited both in extent and in duration. A mighty foundation for our pride! when the utmost we can hope, is but to be read in one Island, and to be thrown aside at the end of one Age.

All that is left us * is to recommend our productions by the imitation of the Ancients: and it will be found true,

* I have frequently heard Dr. Young speak with great disapprobation of the doctrine contained in this passage; with a view to which he wrote his discourse on *Original Composition*: in which he says, "Would not Pope have succeeded better in an *original* attempt? Talents untried are talents unknown. All that I know, is, that, contrary to these sentiments, he was not only an avowed professor of imitation, but a zealous recommender of it also. Nor could he recommend any thing better, except emulation, to those who write. One of these, all writers must call to their aid; but aids they are of unequal repute. Imitation is inferiority confessed; emulation is superiority contested or denied; imitation is servile, emulation generous; that fetters, this fires; that may give a name; this, a name immortal. This made Athens to succeeding ages the rule of taste, and the standard of

true, that in every age, the highest character for sense and learning has been obtained by those who have been most indebted to them. For, to say truth, whatever is very good sense, must have been common sense in all times; and what we call learning, is but the knowledge of the sense of our predecessors. Therefore they who say our thoughts are not our own, because they resemble the Ancients, may as well say our faces are not our own, because they are like our Fathers: And indeed it is very unreasonable,

of perfection. Her men of genius struck fire against each other; and kindled, by conflict, into glories, which no time shall extinguish. We thank Eschylus for Sophocles, and Parrhasius for Zeuxis; *Emulation* for both. That bids us fly the general fault of *imitators*; bids us not be struck with the loud report of former fame, as with a knell, which damps the spirits; but, as with a trumpet, which inspires ardour to rival the renowned. Emulation exhorts us, instead of learning our discipline for ever, like raw troops, under ancient leaders in composition, to put those laurel'd veterans in some hazard of losing their superior posts in glory. Such is Emulation's high-spirited advice, such her immortalizing call. Pope would not hear, pre-engaged with imitation, which blessed him with all her charms. He chose rather, with his namesake of Greece, to triumph in the old world, than to look out for a new. His taste partook the error of his religion: it denied not worship to saints and angels; that is, to writers, who, canonized for ages, have received their apotheosis from established and universal fame." It might, perhaps, have been replied to Young; you, indeed, have given us a considerable number of original thoughts in your works, but they would have been more chaste and correct if you had imitated the ancients more. There are entertaining dissertations on plagiarism and borrowing in Le Motthe le Vayer, tom. ii. 344.

The opinion of Longinus deserves our attention. Ἐςὶ δ' οὐ κλοπὴ το πρᾶγμα, ἀλλ', ὡς ἀπὸ καλῶν ἠθῶν, ἢ πλασμάτων, ἢ δημιουργημάτων ἀπολύπωσις. Sect. 13. p. 88. edit. Pearce. Of this opinion also were Addison and Boileau.

that

that people ſhould expect us to be Scholars, and yet be angry to find us ſo.

I fairly confeſs that I have ſerved myſelf all I could by reading; that I made uſe of the judgment of authors dead and living; that I omitted no means in my power to be informed of my errors, both by my friends and enemies: But the true reaſon theſe pieces are not more correct, is owing to the conſideration how ſhort a time they, and I, have to live: One may be aſhamed to conſume half one's days in bringing ſenſe and rhyme together; and what Critic can be ſo unreaſonable, as not to leave a man time enough for any more ſerious employment, or more agreeable amuſement?

The only plea I ſhall uſe for the favour of the public, is, that I have as great a reſpect for it, as moſt authors have for themſelves; and that I have ſacrificed much of my own ſelf-love for its ſake, in preventing not only many mean things from ſeeing the light, but many which I thought tolerable. I would not be like thoſe Authors, who forgive themſelves ſome particular lines for the ſake of a whole Poem, and vice verſa a whole Poem for the ſake of ſome particular lines. I believe no one qualification is ſo likely to make a good writer, as the power of rejecting his own thoughts; and it muſt be this (if any thing) that can give me a chance to be one. For what I have publiſhed, I can only hope to be pardoned; but for what I have burn'd, I

deſerve

deserve to be prais'd. On this account the world is under some obligation to me, and owes me the justice in return, to look upon no verses as mine that are not inserted in this collection. And perhaps nothing could make it worth my while to own what are really so, but to avoid the imputation of so many dull and immoral things, as partly by malice, and partly by ignorance, have been ascribed to me. I must further acquit myself of the presumption of having lent my name to recommend any Miscellanies, or Works of other men; a thing I never thought becoming a Person who has hardly credit enough to answer for his own.

In this office of collecting my pieces, I am altogether uncertain, whether to look upon myself as a man building a monument, or burying the dead.

If Time shall make it the former, may these Poems (as long as they last) remain as a testimony, that their Author never made his talents subservient to the mean and unworthy ends of Party or Self-interest; the gratification of public prejudices, or private passions; the flattery of the undeserving, or the insult of the unfortunate. If I have written well, let it be considered that 'tis what no man can do without good sense, a quality that not only renders one capable of being a good writer, but a good man. And if I have made any acquisition in the opinion of any one under the notion of the former,

let

let it be continued to me under no other title than that of the latter.

But if this publication be only a more ſolemn funeral of my remains, I deſire it may be known that I die in charity, and in my ſenſes; without any murmurs againſt the juſtice of this age, or any mad appeals to poſterity. I declare I ſhall think the world in the right, and quietly ſubmit to every truth which time ſhall diſcover to the prejudice of theſe writings; not ſo much as wiſhing ſo irrational a thing, as that every body ſhould be deceived merely for my credit. However, I deſire it may then be conſidered, That there are very few things in this collection which were not written under the age of five and twenty: ſo that my youth may be made (as it never fails to be in Executions) a caſe of compaſſion. That I was never ſo concerned about my works as to vindicate them in print, believing, if any thing was good, it would defend itſelf, and what was bad could never be defended. That I uſed no artifice to raiſe or continue a reputation, depreciated no dead author I was obliged to, bribed no living one with unjuſt praiſe, inſulted no adverſary * with ill language; or, when I could not attack a Rival's works, encouraged reports againſt his Morals. To conclude, if this volume periſh, let it ſerve as a warning to the

* This was written in 1716; did our Author recollect this ſentiment in 1729?

Critics,

Critics, not to take too much pains for the future to deſtroy ſuch things as will die of themſelves; and a Memento mori to ſome of my vain contemporaries the Poets, to teach them that, when real merit is wanting, it avails nothing to have been encouraged by the great, commended by the eminent, and favoured by the public in general *.

Nov. 10, 1716.

Variations in the Author's Manuſcript Preface.

AFTER p. 5. l. 13. it followed thus—For my part, I confeſs, had I ſeen things in this view at firſt, the public had never been troubled either with my writings, or with this apology for them. I am ſenſible how difficult it is to ſpeak of one's ſelf with decency: but when a man muſt ſpeak of himſelf, the beſt way is to ſpeak truth of himſelf, or, he may depend upon it, others will do it for him. I'll † therefore make this Preface a general confeſſion of all my thoughts of my own Poetry, reſolving with the ſame freedom to expoſe myſelf, as it is in the power of any other to expoſe them. In the firſt place, I thank God and nature, that I

* I cannot forbear adding how excellently well written is Cowley's preface to his works, folio, 1656; and how much ſuperior it is to Sprat's Life of that amiable author. Both Cowley and Spenſer wrote proſe excellently.

† Johnſon was angry at this abbreviation for *I will.*

was

was born with a love to poetry *; for nothing more conduces to fill up all the intervals of our time, or, if rightly uſed, to make the whole courſe of life entertaining: Cantantes licet uſque (minus via laedet.) 'Tis a vaſt happineſs to poſſeſs the pleaſures of the head, the only pleaſures in which a man is ſufficient to himſelf, and the only part of him which, to his ſatisfaction, he can employ all day long. The Muſes are amicae omnium horarum; and, like our gay acquaintance, the beſt company in the world † as long as one expects no real ſervice from them. I confeſs there was a time when I was in love with myſelf, and my firſt productions were the children of ſelf-love upon innocence. I had made an Epic Poem, and Panegyrics on all the Princes in Europe, and thought myſelf the greateſt genius that ever was. I can't but regret thoſe delightful viſions of my childhood, which, like the fine colours we ſee when our eyes are ſhut, are vaniſhed for ever. Many trials and ſad experience have ſo undeceived me by degrees, that I am utterly at a loſs at what rate to value myſelf. As for fame, I ſhall be glad of any I can get, and not repine at any I miſs; and as for vanity, I have enough to keep me from hanging myſelf, or even from wiſhing thoſe

* But at the concluſion of his tranſlation of the Iliad, he contradicts this ſentiment, by applying to himſelf a paſſage of M. Antoninus.

† Johnſon thought "*in the world*" a vulgariſm, and always avoided the expreſſion.

hanged

hanged who would take it away. It was this that made me write. The ſenſe of my faults made me correct: beſides that it was as pleaſant to me to correct as to write.

At p. 9. l. 2.—In the firſt place I own that I have uſed my beſt endeavours to the finiſhing theſe pieces. That I made what advantage I could of the judgment of authors dead and living; and that I omitted no means in my power to be informed of my errors by my friends and my enemies: And that I expect no favour on account of my youth, buſineſs, want of health, or any ſuch idle excuſes. But the true reaſon they are not yet more correct is owing to the conſideration how ſhort a time they, and I, have to live. A man that can expect but ſixty years may be aſhamed to employ thirty in meaſuring ſyllables and bringing ſenſe and rhyme together. We ſpend our youth in purſuit of riches or fame, in hopes to enjoy them when we are old, and when we are old, we find it is too late to enjoy any thing. I therefore hope the Wits will pardon me, if I reſerve ſome of my time to ſave my ſoul; and that ſome wiſe men will be of my opinion, even if I ſhould think a part of it better ſpent in the enjoyments of life than in pleaſing the critics.

ON MR. POPE AND HIS POEMS,

BY HIS GRACE

JOHN SHEFFIELD,

DUKE OF BUCKINGHAM.

With Age decay'd, with Courts and bus'nefs tir'd,
Caring for nothing but what Eafe requir'd;
Too dully ferious for the Mufe's fport,
And from the Critics fafe arriv'd in Port;
I little thought of launching forth agen,
Amidft advent'rous Rovers of the Pen:
And after fo much undeferv'd fuccefs,
Thus hazarding at laft to make it lefs.
Encomiums fuit not this cenforious time,
Itfelf a fubject for fatiric rhyme;
Ignorance honour'd, Wit and Worth defam'd,
Folly triumphant, and ev'n Homer blam'd!
But to this Genius, join'd with fo much Art,
Such various Learning mix'd in ev'ry part,
Poets are bound a loud applaufe to pay;
Apollo bids it, and they muft obey.
And yet fo wonderful, fublime a thing
As the great Iliad, fcarce could make me fing;

Ver. ii.] This is the common-place cant of men tir'd with bufinefs and courts.

"This is mere moral babble." Comus, p. 806.

Except

Except I juſtly could at once commend
A good Companion, and as firm a Friend.
One moral, or a mere well-natur'd deed
Can all deſert in Sciences exceed.
  'Tis great delight to laugh at ſome mens ways,
But a much greater to give Merit praiſe.

TO MR. POPE.

ON HIS PASTORALS.

In theſe more dull, as more cenſorious days,
  When few dare give, and fewer merit praiſe,
A Muſe ſincere, that never Flatt'ry knew,
Pays what to friendſhip and deſert is due.
Young, yet judicious; in your verſe are found
Art ſtrength'ning Nature, Senſe improv'd by Sound.
Unlike thoſe Wits, whoſe numbers glide along
So ſmooth, no thought e'er interrupts the ſong:
Laboriouſly enervate they appear,
And write not to the head, but to the ear:
Our minds unmov'd and unconcern'd they lull,
And are at beſt moſt muſically dull:
So purling ſtreams with even murmurs creep,
And huſh the heavy hearers into ſleep.
As ſmootheſt ſpeech is moſt deceitful found,
The ſmootheſt numbers oft are empty ſound.
But Wit and Judgment join at once in you,
Sprightly as Youth, as Age conſummate too:

Your

Your ſtrains are regularly bold, and pleaſe
With unforc'd care, and unaffected eaſe,
With proper thoughts, and lively images:
Such as by Nature to the Ancients ſhewn,
Fancy improves, and judgment makes your own:
For great mens faſhions to be follow'd are,
Altho' diſgraceful 'tis their clothes to wear.
Some in a poliſh'd ſtyle write Paſtoral,
Arcadia ſpeaks the language of the Mall;
Like ſome fair Shepherdeſs, the Sylvan Muſe
Should wear thoſe flow'rs her native fields produce;
And the true meaſure of the Shepherd's wit
Should, like his garb, be for the Country fit:
Yet muſt his pure and unaffected thought
More nicely than the common ſwains be wrought.
So, with becoming art, the Players dreſs,
In ſilks the ſhepherd, and the ſhepherdeſs;
Yet ſtill unchang'd the form and mode remain,
Shap'd like the homely ruſſet of the ſwain.
Your rural Muſe appears to juſtify
The long loſt graces of Simplicity:
So rural beauties captivate our ſenſe
With virgin charms, and native excellence.
Yet long her Modeſty thoſe charms conceal'd,
'Till by mens Envy to the world reveal'd;
For Wits induſtrious to their trouble ſeem,
And needs will envy what they muſt eſteem.

VER. 28. *Sylvan Muſe*] From Boileau's Art of Poetry, Chant. 2. l. 1. Pope ſeems to have corrected theſe lines.

Live and enjoy their ſpite! nor mourn that fate,
Which would, if Virgil liv'd, on Virgil wait;
Whoſe Muſe did once, like thine, in plains delight;
Thine ſhall, like his, ſoon take a higher flight;
So Larks, which firſt from lowly fields ariſe,
Mount by degrees, and reach at laſt the ſkies.

W. WYCHERLEY.

TO MR. POPE,

ON HIS WINDSOR-FOREST.

HAIL, ſacred Bard! a Muſe unknown before
Salutes thee from the bleak Atlantic ſhore.
To our dark world thy ſhining page is ſhown,
And Windſor's gay retreat becomes our own.
The Eaſtern pomp had juſt beſpoke our care,
And India pour'd her gaudy treaſures here:
A various ſpoil adorn'd our naked land,
The pride of Perſia glitter'd on our ſtrand,
And China's earth was caſt on common ſand:
Toſs'd up and down the gloſſy fragments lay,
And dreſs'd the rocky ſhelves, and pav'd the painted bay.
Thy treaſures next arriv'd: and now we boaſt
A nobler cargo on our barren coaſt:
From thy luxuriant Foreſt we receive
More laſting glories than the Eaſt can give.

Where-

Where-e'er we dip in thy delightful page,
What pompous ſcenes our buſy thoughts engage!
The pompous ſcenes in all their pride appear,
Freſh in the page, as in the grove they were.
Nor half ſo true the fair Lodona ſhows
The ſylvan ſtate that on her border grows,
While ſhe the wand'ring ſhepherd entertains
With a new Windſor in her wat'ry plains;
Thy juſter lays the lucid wave ſurpaſs,
The living ſcene is in the Muſe's glaſs.
Nor ſweeter notes the echoing foreſt cheer,
When Philomela ſits and warbles there,
Than when you ſing the greens and op'ning glades,
And give us Harmony as well as Shades:
A *Titian*'s hand might draw the grove, but you
Can paint the grove, and add the Muſic too.
With vaſt variety thy pages ſhine;
A new creation ſtarts in ev'ry line.
How ſudden trees riſe to the reader's ſight,
And make a doubtful ſcene of ſhade and light,
And give at once the day, at once the night!
And here again what ſweet confuſion reigns,
In dreary deſerts mix'd with painted plains!
And ſee! the deſerts caſt a pleaſing gloom,
And ſhrubby heaths rejoice in purple bloom:

Ver. 16. *Where-e'er we dip*] There are ſeveral lines in this copy of verſes, which would not be endured in a common monthly magazine. So much is the public ear, and public taſte improved!

Whilſt fruitful crops riſe by their barren ſide,
And bearded groves diſplay their annual pride.
Happy the man, who ſtrings his tuneful lyre,
Where woods, and brooks, and breathing fields inſpire!
Thrice happy thou! and worthy beſt to dwell
Amidſt the rural joys you ſing ſo well.
I in a cold, and in a barren clime,
Cold as my thought, and barren as my rhime,
Here on the Weſtern beach attempt to chime.
O joyleſs flood! O rough tempeſtuous main!
Border'd with weeds, and ſolitudes obſcene!
Snatch me, ye Gods! from theſe *Atlantic* ſhores,
And ſhelter me in *Windſor*'s fragrant bow'rs;
Or to my much lov'd *Iſis'* walks convey,
And on her flow'ry banks for ever lay.
Thence let me view the venerable ſcene,
The awful dome, the groves eternal green:
Where ſacred *Hough* long found his fam'd retreat,
And brought the Muſes to the ſylvan ſeat,
Reform'd the wits, unlock'd the Claſſic ſtore,
And made that Muſic which was noiſe before.
There with illuſtrious Bards I ſpent my days,
Nor free from cenſure, nor unknown to praiſe,
Enjoy'd the bleſſings that his reign beſtow'd,
Nor envy'd *Windſor* in the ſoft abode.
The golden minutes ſmoothly danc'd away,
And tuneful Bards beguil'd the tedious day:

They

They ſung, nor ſung in vain, with numbers fir'd
That *Maro* taught, or *Addiſon* inſpir'd.
Ev'n I eſſay'd to touch the trembling ſtring:
Who could hear them, and not attempt to ſing?

Rouz'd from theſe dreams by thy commanding ſtrain,
I riſe and wander through the field or plain;
Led by thy Muſe from ſport to ſport I run,
Mark the ſtretch'd line, or hear the thund'ring gun.
Ah! how I melt with pity, when I ſpy
On the cold earth the flutt'ring Pheaſant lie;
His gaudy robes in dazzling lines appear,
And every feather ſhines and varies there.

Nor can I paſs the generous courſer by,
But while the prancing ſteed allures my eye,
He ſtarts, he's gone! and now I ſee him fly
O'er hills and dales, and now I loſe the courſe,
Nor can the rapid ſight purſue the flying horſe.
Oh could thy *Virgil* from his orb look down,
He'd view a courſer that might match his own!
Fir'd with the ſport, and eager for the chace,
Lodona's murmurs ſtop me in the race.
Who can refuſe *Lodona*'s melting tale?
The ſoft complaint ſhall over time prevail;
The Tale be told, when ſhades forſake her ſhore,
The Nymph be ſung, when ſhe can flow no more.

Nor ſhall thy ſong, old *Thames!* forbear to ſhine,
At once the ſubject and the ſong divine.

Peace, ſung by thee, ſhall pleaſe ev'n *Britons* more
Than all their ſhouts for Victory before.
Oh! could *Britannia* imitate thy ſtream,
The World ſhould tremble at her awful name:
From various ſprings divided waters glide,
In diff'rent colours roll a diff'rent tide,
Murmur along their crooked banks a while,
At once they murmur and enrich the Iſle;
A while diſtinct through many channels run,
But meet at laſt, and ſweetly flow in one;
There joy to loſe their long-diſtinguiſh'd names,
And make one glorious, and immortal *Thames*.

FR. KNAPP.

TO MR. POPE.

IN IMITATION OF A GREEK EPIGRAM ON HOMER.

WHEN *Phoebus*, and the nine harmonious maids,
Of old aſſembled in the *Theſpian* ſhades;
What theme, they cry'd, what high immortal air,
Befit theſe harps to ſound, and thee to hear?
Reply'd the God; "Your loftieſt notes employ,
"To ſing young *Peleus*, and the fall of *Troy*."

VER. 1. *When Phoebus*] By far the moſt elegant and beſt turned compliment of all addreſſed to our Author; happily borrowed from that fine Greek epigram in the Anthologia, p. 30, and moſt gracefully applied;

Ἤειδον μὲν Ἐγὼν, ἐχάρασσε δὲ θεῖος Ὅμηρος.

Fenton was the beſt Greek ſcholar of all our Author's poetical friends. Boileau alſo imitated this epigram.

The

The wond'rous ſong with rapture they rehearſe;
Then aſk who wrought that miracle of verſe?
He anſwer'd with a frown; "I now reveal
"A truth, that envy bids me not conceal:
"Retiring frequent to this Laureat vale,
"I warbled to the Lyre that fav'rite tale,
"Which, unobſerv'd, a wand'ring *Greek* and blind,
"Heard me repeat, and treaſur'd in his mind;
"And fir'd with thirſt of more than mortal praiſe,
"From me, the God of Wit, uſurp'd the bays.
"But let vain *Greece* indulge her growing fame,
"Proud with celeſtial ſpoils to grace her name;
"Yet when my Arts ſhall triumph in the Weſt,
"And the white Iſle with female pow'r is bleſt;
"Fame, I foreſee, will make repriſals there,
"And the Tranſlator's Palm to me transfer.
"With leſs regret my claim I now decline,
"The World will think his *Engliſh Iliad* mine."

E. FENTON.

TO MR. POPE.

To praiſe, and ſtill with juſt reſpect to praiſe
A Bard triumphant in immortal bays,
The Learn'd to ſhow, the Senſible commend,
Yet ſtill preſerve the Province of the Friend;
What life, what vigour muſt the lines require?
What Muſic tune them, what Affection fire?

O might thy Genius in my bosom shine;
Thou should'st not fail of numbers worthy thine;
The brightest Ancients might at once agree
To sing within my lays, and sing of thee.
Horace himself would own thou dost excell
In candid arts to play the Critic well.
Ovid himself might wish to sing the Dame
Whom Windsor Forest sees a gliding stream:
On silver feet, with annual Osier crown'd,
She runs for ever through Poetic ground.
How flame the glories of Belinda's Hair,
Made by thy Muse the envy of the Fair?
Less shone the tresses Egypt's Princess wore,
Which sweet Callimachus so sung before.
Here courtly trifles set the world at odds;
Belles war with Beaus, and Whims descend for Gods.
The new Machines, in names of ridicule,
Mock the grave phrenzy of the Chemic fool.
But know, ye Fair, a point conceal'd with art,
The Sylphs and Gnomes are but a woman's heart.
The Graces stand in sight; a Satire-train
Peeps o'er their head, and laughs behind the scene.
In Fame's fair Temple, o'er the boldest wits
Inshrin'd on high the sacred Virgil sits;
And sits in measures such as Virgil's Muse
To place thee near him might be fond to chuse.
How might he tune th' alternate reed with thee,
Perhaps a Strephon thou, a Daphnis he;

While ſome old Damon, o'er the vulgar wiſe,
Thinks he deſerves, and thou deſerv'ſt the Prize?
Rapt with the thought, my fancy ſeeks the plains,
And turns me ſhepherd while I hear the ſtrains.
Indulgent nurſe of ev'ry tender gale,
Parent of flowrets, old Arcadia, hail!
Here in the cool my limbs at eaſe I ſpread,
Here let thy poplars whiſper o'er my head:
Still ſlide thy waters, ſoft among the trees,
Thy aſpins quiver in a breathing breeze!
Smile, all ye valleys, in eternal ſpring,
Be huſh'd, ye winds, while Pope and Virgil ſing.
  In Engliſh lays, and all ſublimely great,
Thy Homer warms with all his ancient heat;
He ſhines in Council, thunders in the Fight,
And flames with every ſenſe of great delight.
Long has that Poet reign'd, and long unknown,
Like Monarchs ſparkling on a diſtant throne;
In all the Majeſty of Greek retir'd,
Himſelf unknown, his mighty name admir'd;
His language failing, wrapt him round with night;
Thine, rais'd by thee, recalls the work to light.
So wealthy Mines, that ages long before
Fed the large realms around with golden Ore,
When choak'd by ſinking banks, no more appear,
And Shepherds only ſay, *The mines were here:*
Should ſome rich youth (if nature warm his heart,
And all his projects ſtand inform'd with art)

Ver. 50. *And flames*] A very poor and unmeaning line, and unworthy the ſenſible and elegant Parnell!

Here clear the caves, there ope the leading vein;
The mines detected flame with gold again.
  How vaſt, how copious, are thy new deſigns!
How ev'ry Muſic varies in thy lines!
Still, as I read, I feel my boſom beat,
And riſe in raptures by another's heat.
Thus in the wood, when ſummer dreſs'd the days,
While Windſor lent us tuneful hours of eaſe,
Our ears the lark, the thruſh, the turtle bleſt,
And Philomela ſweeteſt o'er the reſt:
The ſhades reſound with ſong—O ſoftly tread,
While a whole ſeaſon warbles round my head.
  This to my Friend—and when a friend inſpires,
My ſilent harp its maſter's hand requires;
Shakes off the duſt, and makes theſe rocks reſound;
For fortune plac'd me in unfertile ground;
Far from the joys that with my ſoul agree,
From wit, from learning—very far from thee.
Here moſs-grown trees expand the ſmalleſt leaf;
Here half an acre's corn is half a ſheaf;
Here hills with naked heads the tempeſt meet,
Rocks at their ſides, and torrents at their feet;
Or lazy lakes unconſcious of a flood,
Whoſe dull brown Naiads ever ſleep in mud.
Yet here Content can dwell, and learned Eaſe,
A Friend delight me, and an Author pleaſe;
Ev'n here I ſing, when Pope ſupplies the theme,
Shew my own love, tho' not increaſe his fame.

T. PARNELL.

TO MR. POPE.

LET vulgar ſouls triumphal arches raiſe,
Or ſpeaking marbles, to record their praiſe;
And picture (to the voice of Fame unknown)
The mimic Feature on the breathing ſtone;
Mere mortals; ſubject to death's total ſway,
Reptiles of earth, and beings of a day!
'Tis thine, on ev'ry heart to grave thy praiſe,
A monument which Worth alone can raiſe:
Sure to ſurvive, when time ſhall whelm in duſt
The arch, the marble, and the mimic buſt:
Nor till the volumes of th' expanded ſky
Blaze in one flame, ſhalt thou and Homer die:
Then ſink together in the world's laſt fires,
What heav'n created, and what heav'n inſpires.
If aught on earth, when once this breath is fled,
With human tranſport touch the mighty dead,
Shakeſpear, rejoice! his hand thy page refines;
Now ev'ry ſcene with native brightneſs ſhines;
Juſt to thy fame, he gives thy genuine thought;
So Tully publiſh'd what Lucretius wrote;
Prun'd by his care, thy laurels loftier grow,
And bloom afreſh on thy immortal brow.
Thus when thy draughts, O Raphael! time invades,
And the bold figure from the canvas fades,

VER. 17.—*thy page*] This was a compliment our author could not take much pleaſure in reading; for he could not value himſelf on his edition of Shakeſpeare.

A rival hand recalls from every part
Some latent grace, and equals art with art;
Tranſported we ſurvey the dubious ſtrife,
While each fair image ſtarts again to life.
  How long, untun'd, had Homer's ſacred lyre
Jarr'd grating diſcord, all extinct his fire?
This you beheld; and taught by heav'n to ſing,
Call'd the loud muſic from the ſounding ſtring.
Now wak'd from ſlumbers of three thouſand years,
Once more Achilles in dread pomp appears,
Tow'rs o'er the field of death; as fierce he turns,
Keen flaſh his arms, and all the Hero burns;
With martial ſtalk, and more than mortal might,
He ſtrides along, and meets the Gods in fight:
Then the pale Titans, chain'd on burning floors,
Start at the din that rends th' Infernal ſhores,
Tremble the tow'rs of Heav'n, earth rocks her coaſts,
And gloomy Pluto ſhakes with all his ghoſts.
To ev'ry theme reſponds thy various lay;
Here rolls a torrent, there Meanders play;
Sonorous as the ſtorm thy numbers riſe,
Toſs the wild waves, and thunder in the ſkies;
Or ſofter than a yielding virgin's ſigh,
The gentle breezes breathe away and die.
Thus, like the radiant God who ſheds the day,
You paint the vale, or gild the azure way;
And while with ev'ry theme the verſe complies,
Sink without grov'ling, without raſhneſs riſe.

Proceed, great Bard! awake th' harmonious ſtring,
Be ours all Homer! ſtill Ulyſſes ſing.
How long [a] that Hero, by unſkilful hands,
Stripp'd of his robes, a beggar trod our lands?
Such as he wander'd o'er his native coaſt,
Shrunk by the wand, and all the warrior loſt:
O'er his ſmooth ſkin a bark of wrinkles ſpread;
Old age diſgrac'd the honours of his head;
Nor longer in his heavy eye-ball ſhin'd
The glance divine, forth-beaming from the mind.
But you, like Pallas, ev'ry limb infold
With royal robes, and bid him ſhine in gold;
Touch'd by your hand his manly frame improves
With grace divine, and like a God he moves.
Ev'n I, the meaneſt of the Muſes' train,
Inflam'd by thee, attempt a nobler ſtrain;
Advent'rous waken the Maeonian lyre,
Tun'd by your hand, and ſing as you inſpire:
So arm'd by great Achilles for the fight,
Patroclus conquer'd in Achilles' right:
Like theirs, our Friendſhip! and I boaſt my name
To thine united—for thy Friendſhip's Fame.
This labour paſt, of heav'nly ſubjects ſing,
While hov'ring angels liſten on the wing,
To hear from earth ſuch heart-felt raptures riſe,
As, when they ſing, ſuſpended hold the Skies:
Or nobly riſing in fair Virtue's cauſe,
From thy own life tranſcribe th' unerring laws:

[a] Odyſſey, lib. xvi.

Teach

Teach a bad world beneath her ſway to bend:
To verſe like thine fierce ſavages attend,
And men more fierce: when Orpheus tunes the lay
Ev'n fiends relenting hear their rage away.

W. BROOME.

TO MR. POPE,

ON THE PUBLISHING HIS WORKS.

HE comes, he comes! bid ev'ry Bard prepare
The ſong of triumph, and attend his Car.
Great Sheffield's Muſe the long proceſſion heads,
And throws a luſtre o'er the pomp ſhe leads,
Firſt gives the Palm ſhe fir'd him to obtain,
Crowns his gay brow, and ſhews him how to reign.
Thus young Alcides, by old Chiron taught,
Was form'd for all the miracles he wrought:
Thus Chiron did the youth he taught applaud,
Pleas'd to behold the earneſt of a God.
But hark, what ſhouts, what gath'ring crouds rejoice!
Unſtain'd their praiſe by any venal Voice,
Such as th' Ambitious vainly think their due,
When Proſtitutes, or needy Flatt'rers ſue.
And ſee the Chief! before him laurels born;
Trophies from undeſerving temples torn;

VER. 83.—*when Orpheus*] Theſe three laſt verſes are trite and feeble enough!

Here Rage enchain'd reluctant raves, and there
Pale Envy dumb, and sick'ning with despair,
Prone to the earth she bends her loathing eye,
Weak to support the blaze of majesty.
But what are they that turn the sacred page?
Three lovely virgins, and of equal age;
Intent they read, and all enamour'd seem,
As he that met his likeness in the stream:
The GRACES these; and see how they contend,
Who most shall praise, who best shall recommend.
The Chariot now the painful steep ascends,
The Paeans cease; thy glorious labour ends.
Here fix'd, the bright eternal Temple stands,
Its prospect an unbounded view commands:
Say, wond'rous youth, what Column wilt thou chuse,
What laurel'd Arch for thy triumphant Muse?
Tho' each great Ancient court thee to his shrine,
Tho' ev'ry Laurel through the dome be thine,
(From the proud Epic, down to those that shade
The gentler brow of the soft Lesbian maid)
Go to the Good and Just, an awful train,
Thy soul's delight, and glory of the Fane:
While through the earth thy dear remembrance flies,
"Sweet to the World, and grateful to the skies."

SIMON HARCOURT.

TO MR. POPE.

From Rome, 1730.

IMMORTAL Bard! for whom each Muſe has wove
The faireſt garlands of th' Aonian grove;
Preſerv'd, our drooping Genius to reſtore,
When Addiſon and Congreve are no more;
After ſo many ſtars extinct in night,
The darken'd age's laſt remaining light!
To thee from Latian realms this verſe is writ,
Inſpir'd by memory of ancient Wit:
For now no more theſe climes their influence boaſt,
Fall'n is their glory, and their virtue loſt:
From Tyrants, and from Prieſts, the Muſes fly,
Daughters of Reaſon and of Liberty.
Nor Baiae now, nor Umbria's plain they love,
Nor on the banks of Nar, or Mincio rove;
To Thames's flow'ry borders they retire,
And kindle in thy breaſt the Roman fire.
So in the ſhades, where chear'd with ſummer rays
Melodious linnets warbled ſprightly lays,
Soon as the faded, falling leaves complain
Of gloomy winter's unauſpicious reign,
No tuneful voice is heard of joy or love,
But mournful ſilence ſaddens all the grove.
Unhappy Italy! whoſe alter'd ſtate
Has felt the worſt ſeverity of Fate:

Not that Barbarian hands her Faſces broke,
And bow'd her haughty neck beneath their yoke;
Nor that her palaces to earth are thrown,
Her Cities deſert, and her fields unſown;
But that her ancient Spirit is decay'd,
That ſacred Wiſdom from her bounds is fled,
That there the ſource of Science flows no more,
Whence its rich ſtreams ſupply'd the world before.

Illuſtrious Names! that once in Latium ſhin'd,
Born to inſtruct, and to command Mankind;
Chiefs, by whoſe Virtue mighty Rome was rais'd,
And Poets, who thoſe Chiefs ſublimely prais'd!
Oft I the traces you have left explore,
Your aſhes viſit, and your urns adore;
Oft kiſs, with lips devout, ſome mould'ring ſtone,
With ivy's venerable ſhade o'ergrown;
Thoſe hallow'd ruins better pleas'd to ſee
Than all the pomp of modern Luxury.

As late on Virgil's tomb freſh flow'rs I ſtrow'd,
While with th' inſpiring Muſe my boſom glow'd,
Crown'd with eternal bays my raviſh'd eyes
Beheld the Poet's awful Form ariſe:
Stranger, he ſaid, whoſe pious hand has paid
Theſe grateful rites to my attentive ſhade,
When thou ſhalt breathe thy happy native air,
To Pope this meſſage from his Maſter bear:

" Great Bard! whoſe numbers I myſelf inſpire,
To whom I gave my own harmonious lyre,

If high exalted on the Throne of Wit,
Near me and Homer thou aspire to sit,
No more let meaner Satire dim the rays
That flow majestic from thy nobler Bays;
In all the flow'ry paths of Pindus stray,
But shun that thorny, that unpleasing way;
Nor, when each soft engaging Muse is thine,
Address the least attractive of the Nine.
Of thee more worthy were the task to raise
A lasting Column to thy Country's Praise,
To sing the Land, which yet alone can boast
That Liberty corrupted Rome has lost;
Where Science in the arms of Peace is laid;
And plants her Palm beneath the Olive's shade.
Such was the Theme for which my lyre I strung,
Such was the People whose exploits I sung;
Brave, yet refin'd, for Arms and Arts renown'd,
With diff'rent bays by Mars and Phoebus crown'd,
Dauntless opposers of Tyrannic Sway,
But pleas'd, a mild AUGUSTUS to obey."
If these commands submissive thou receive,
Immortal and unblam'd thy name shall live;

VER. 60. *Address the least*] It is to be wished that Pope had attended to this advice, and employed his great genius in the higher species of poetry. The noble and ingenious author of this useful admonition, who honoured me with his friendship, told me, that he frequently, in many conversations, prest it on Pope. He that could write these excellent lines, deserved more praise than Dr. Johnson thought proper to give him in the Lives of the Poets.

Envy

Envy to black Cocytus ſhall retire,
And howl with Furies in tormenting fire;
Approving Time ſhall conſecrate thy Lays,
And join the Patriot's with the Poet's Praiſe.

GEORGE LYTTELTON.

TO MR. POPE,

ON HIS TRANSLATION OF HOMER's ILIAD.

'TIS true, what fam'd Pythagoras maintain'd,
That ſouls departed in new bodies reign'd:
We muſt approve the doctrine, ſince we ſee
The ſoul of god-like Homer breathe in thee.
Old Ennius firſt, then Virgil felt her fires;
But now a Britiſh Poet ſhe inſpires.

To you, O Pope, the lineal right extends,
To you th' hereditary muſe deſcends.
At a vaſt diſtance we of Homer heard,
Till you brought in, and nat'raliz'd the Bard;
Bade him our Engliſh rights and freedom claim,
His voice, his habit, and his air the ſame.
Now in the mighty Stranger we rejoice,
And Britain thanks thee, with a public voice.
See! too the Poet, a majeſtic ſhade,
Lifts up in awful pomp his laurel'd head,

To thank his Succeſſor, who ſets him free
From the vile hands of Hobbs and Ogilby;
Who vext his venerable Aſhes more,
Than his ungrateful Greece, the living Bard before.
While Homer's thoughts in thy bold lines are ſhown,
Tho' worlds contend, we claim him for our own;
Our blooming boys proud Ilion's fate bewail;
Our liſping babes repeat the dreadful tale,
Ev'n in their ſlumbers they purſue the theme,
Start, and enjoy a fight in every dream.
By turns the Chief and Bard their ſouls inflame,
And every little boſom beats for fame.
Thus ſhall they learn (as future times will ſee)
From Him to conquer, or to write from Thee.
In every hand we ſee the glorious ſong,
And Homer is the Theme of every tongue.
Parties in State poetic ſchemes employ,
And Whig and Tory ſide with Greece and Troy;
Neglect their feuds: and ſeem more zealous grown
To puſh thoſe countries Intereſts, than their own.
Our buſieſt Politicians have forgot
How Sommers counſel'd, and how Marlbro' fought;
But o'er their ſettling coffee gravely tell,
What Neſtor ſpoke, and how brave Hector fell.
Our ſofteſt Beaux and Coxcombs you inſpire,
With Glacus' courage, and Achilles' fire.
Now they reſent affronts which once they bore,
And draw thoſe ſwords that ne'er were drawn before;

Nay

Nay ev'n our Belles inform'd how Homer writ,
Learn thence to criticize on modern Wit.
  Let the mad Critics to their ſide engage
The envy, pride, and dulneſs of the age:
In vain they curſe, in vain they pine and mourn,
Back on themſelves, their arrows will return;
Whoe'er would thy eſtabliſh'd fame deface,
Are but immortaliz'd to their diſgrace,
Live, and enjoy their ſpite, and ſhare that fate,
Which would, if Homer liv'd, on Homer wait.
  And lo! his ſecond labour claims thy care,
Ulyſſes' toils, ſucceed Achilles' war.
Haſte to the work; the ladies long to ſee
The pious frauds of chaſte Penelope.
Helen they long have ſeen, whoſe guilty charms
For ten whole years engag'd the world in Arms.
Then, as thy Fame ſhall ſee a length of days,
Some future Bard ſhall thus record thy Praiſe;
" In thoſe bleſt times when ſmiling Heav'n and Fate,
Had rais'd Britannia to her happieſt ſtate,
When wide around ſhe ſaw the World ſubmit,
And own her Sons ſupreme in Arts and Wit;
Then Pope and Dryden brought in triumph home,
The Pride of Greece, and Ornament of Rome;
To the great taſk each bold tranſlator came,
With Virgil's Judgement, and with Homer's Flame.
Here the pleas'd Mantuan ſwan was taught to ſoar,
Where ſcarce the Roman eagles towr'd before:

And Greece no more was Homer's native earth,
Tho' her ſev'n rival cities claim'd his birth;
On her ſev'n cities, he look'd down with ſcorn,
And own'd with pride, he was in Britain born."

CHRISTOPHER PITT.

VOLTAIRE AU ROI DE PRUSSE.

———Horace avec Boileau:
Vous y cherchiez le vrai, vous y goutez le beau;
Quelques traits échappés d'une utile morale,
Dans leurs piquans ecrits brillent par intervalle;
Mais Pope approfondit ce qu'ils ont effleuré;
D'un eſprit plus hardi, d'un pas plus aſſuré,
Il porta le flambeau dans l'abime de l'etre,
Et l'homme avec lui ſeul apprit à ſe connoitre.
L'Art quelquefois frivole, et quelquefois divin,
L'Art des vers eſt dans Pope utile au genre humain.

At Stowe in Buckinghamſhire, the ſeat of Earl Temple, is a building called The Temple of Britiſh Worthies, deſigned by Kent. One of the niches has a buſt of Pope, with the following inſcription:

Alexander Pope,
Who uniting the correctneſs of judgment to the fire of Genius,
by the melody and power of his numbers,
gave ſweetneſs to ſenſe, and grace to philoſophy.
He employed the pointed brilliancy of wit to chaſtiſe the vices,
and the eloquence of poetry to exalt the virtues of human nature;
and being without a rival in his own age,
imitated and tranſlated, with a ſpirit equal to the originals,
the beſt poets of Antiquity.

TO MR. POPE.

To move the ſprings of nature as we pleaſe,
To think with ſpirit, but to write with eaſe:
With living words to warm the conſcious heart,
Or pleaſe the ſoul with nicer charms of art,
For this the Grecian ſoar'd in Epic ſtrains,
And ſofter Maro left the Mantuan plains:
Melodious Spencer felt the lover's fire,
And awful Milton ſtrung his heav'nly lyre.
'Tis yours, like theſe, with curious toil to trace
The pow'rs of language, harmony, and grace,

How nature's ſelf with living luſtre ſhines;
How judgment ſtrengthens, and how art refines;
How to grow bold with conſcious ſenſe of fame,
And force a pleaſure which we dare not blame:
To charm us more thro' negligence than pains,
And give ev'n life and action to the ſtrains:
Led by ſome law, whoſe pow'rful impulſe guides
Each happy ſtroke, and in the ſoul preſides:
Some fairer image of perfection, giv'n
T' inſpire mankind, itſelf deriv'd from heav'n.

O ever worthy, ever crown'd with praiſe;
Bleſt in thy life, and bleſt in all thy lays!
Add that the Siſters ev'ry thought refine;
Or ev'n thy life be faultleſs as thy line;
Yet envy ſtill with fiercer rage purſues,
Obſcures the virtue, and defames the muſe.
A ſoul like thine, in pains, in grief reſign'd,
Views with vain ſcorn the malice of mankind:
Not critics, but their planets prove unjuſt:
And are they blam'd who ſin becauſe they muſt?

Yet ſure not ſo muſt all peruſe thy lays;
I cannot rival——and yet dare to praiſe.
A thouſand charms at once my thoughts engage,
Sappho's ſoft ſweetneſs, Pindar's warmer rage,
Statius' free vigour, Virgil's ſtudious care,
And Homer's force, and Ovid's eaſier air.

So ſeems ſome Picture, where exact deſign,
And curious pains, and ſtrength and ſweetneſs join:
Where

Where the free thought its pleaſing grace beſtows,
And each warm ſtroke with living colour glows:
Soft without weakneſs, without labour fair;
Wrought up at once with happineſs and care!

How bleſt the man that from the world removes
To joys that MORDAUNT, or his POPE approves;
Whoſe taſte exact each author can explore,
And live the preſent and paſt ages o'er:
Who free from pride, from penitence, or ſtriſe,
Move calmly forward to the verge of life:
Such be my days, and ſuch my fortunes be,
To live by reaſon, and to write by thee!

Nor deem this verſe, tho' humble, thy diſgrace;
All are not born the glory of their race:
Yet all are born t' adore the great man's name,
And trace his footſteps in the paths to fame.
The Muſe who now this early homage pays,
Firſt learn'd from thee to animate her lays:
A Muſe as yet unhonour'd, but unſtain'd,
Who prais'd no vices, no preferment gain'd:
Unbyaſs'd, or to cenſure or commend,
Who knows no envy, and who grieves no friend;
Perhaps too fond to make thoſe virtues known,
And fix her fame immortal on thy own.

WALTER HARTE.

PASTORALS,

WITH A DISCOURSE ON PASTORAL.

Written in the Year MDCCIV.

Rura mihi et rigui placeant in vallibus amnes,
Flumina amem, ſylvaſque, inglorius! VIRG.

A DISCOURSE ON PASTORAL POETRY[a].

THERE are not, I believe, a greater number of any ſort of verſes than of thoſe which are called Paſtorals; nor a ſmaller than of thoſe which are truly ſo. It therefore ſeems neceſſary to give ſome account of this kind of Poem, and it is my deſign to comprize in this ſhort paper the ſubſtance of thoſe numerous diſſertations that Critics have made on the ſubject, without omitting any of their rules in my

[a] Written at ſixteen years of age. P.

This ſenſible and judicious diſcourſe, written at ſo early an age, is a more extraordinary production, than the paſtorals that follow it: in which, I hope, it will not be deemed an injurious criticiſm to ſay, there is ſcarcely a ſingle rural image to be found that is new. The ideas of Theocritus, Virgil, and Spencer, are indeed here exhibited in language equally mellifluous and pure; but the deſcriptions and ſentiments are trite and common. To this aſſertion, formerly made, Dr. Johnſon anſwered; "That no invention was intended:" he therefore allows the fact, and the charge. Our author has chiefly drawn his obſervations from Rapin, Fontenelle, and the preface to Dryden's Virgil. A tranſlation of Rapin's Diſcourſe had been ſome years before prefixed to Creech's Tranſlation of Theocritus, and is no extraordinary piece of criticiſm. And though Hume highly praiſes the Diſcourſe of Fontenelle, yet Dr. Hurd thinks it only, rather my own favour. You will alſo find ſome points reconciled, about which they ſeem to differ, and a few remarks, which, I think, have eſcaped their obſervation.

The original of Poetry is aſcribed to that Age which ſucceeded the creation of the world: and as the keeping of flocks ſeems to have been the firſt employment of mankind, the moſt ancient ſort of poetry was probably *paſtoral*[b]. It is natural to imagine, that the leiſure of thoſe ancient ſhepherds admitting and inviting ſome diverſion, none was ſo

rather more tolerable than his Paſtorals. I much wonder our author did not allude to the elegant lines on Paſtoral Poetry at the beginning of the ſecond canto of Boileau's Art of Poetry. The beſt diſſertations on this ſubject, ſeem to be thoſe in the IId and Vth volumes of the Memoirs of the French Academy, that which is prefixed to Heyne's excellent edition of Virgil's Eclogues, and that which is prefixed to the Oxford edition of Theocritus, in two volumes 4to, 1776; in which the reader will find a particular account of the three diſtinct characters and perſonages introduced by Theocritus, namely, the Keepers of Oxen, the Keepers of Sheep, and of Goats; to which diſtinction even Virgil did not attend: and in which he alſo will find ſuch reaſons for preferring the paſtorals of Theocritus to thoſe of Virgil, as will ſerve for a complete confutation of Dr. Johnſon's opinion on this ſubject, delivered with a ſurprizing want of taſte and judgment, in the Life of that great man, vol. ii. p. 329. The truly learned Heyne goes ſo far as to ſay, that if Virgil had written only his Bucolics, vix eum in cenſum principum poetarum venturum fuiſſe arbitror. So competent and able a judge as the ſweet and pathetic Racine, aſſured M. de Longepierre, that he thought the ſecond Idyllium of Theocritus was one of the moſt exquiſite pieces that antiquity had left us, and that it contained the moſt ſtriking and forcible deſcriptions of the paſſion of love he had ever ſeen.

[b] Fontenelle's Diſc. on Paſtorals. P.

proper

proper to that ſolitary and ſedentary life as ſinging; and that in their ſongs they took occaſion to celebrate their own felicity. From hence a Poem was invented, and afterwards improved to a perfect image of that happy time; which, by giving us an eſteem for the virtues of a former age, might recommend them to the preſent. And ſince the life of ſhepherds was attended with more tranquillity than any other rural employment, the Poets choſe to introduce their Perſons, from whom it received the name of Paſtoral.

A Paſtoral is an imitation of the action of a ſhepherd, or one conſidered under that Character. The form of this imitation is dramatic, or narrative, or mixed of both[c]; the fable ſimple, the manners not too polite nor too ruſtic: the thoughts are plain, yet admit a little quickneſs and paſſion, but that ſhort and flowing: the expreſſion humble, yet as pure as the language will afford; neat, but not florid; eaſy, and yet lively. In ſhort, the fable, manners, thoughts, and expreſſions are full of the greateſt ſimplicity in nature.

The complete character of this poem conſiſts in ſimplicity[d], brevity, and delicacy; the two firſt of which render an eclogue natural, and the laſt delightful.

[c] Heinſius in Theocr. P.

[d] Rapin de Carm. Paſt. p. 2. P.

If

If we would copy Nature, it may be uſeful to take this Idea along with us, that Paſtoral is an image of what they call the golden age *. So that we are not to deſcribe our ſhepherds as ſhepherds at this day really are, but as they may be conceived then to have been; when the beſt of men followed the employment. To carry this reſemblance yet further, it would not be amiſs to give theſe ſhepherds ſome ſkill in aſtronomy, as far as it may be uſeful to that ſort of life. And an air of piety to the Gods ſhould ſhine through the poem, which ſo viſibly appears in all the works of antiquity: and it ought to preſerve ſome reliſh of the old way of writing; the connection ſhould be looſe, the narrations and deſcriptions ſhort [e], and the periods conciſe. Yet it is not ſufficient, that the ſentences only be brief, the whole Eclogue ſhould be ſo too. For we cannot ſuppoſe Poetry in thoſe days to have been the buſineſs of men, but their recreation at vacant hours.

But with a reſpect to the preſent age, nothing more conduces to make theſe compoſures natural, than when ſome Knowledge in rural affairs is diſcovered [f]. This may be made to appear rather

* Avoiding, what a ſenſible writer calls, les ſentimens quinteſſencies, les douceurs metaphyſiques. Geſner's Paſtorals are exquiſite; and abound in new ſituations, images, and ſentiments.

[e] Rapin, Reflex. ſur l'Art Poet. d'Ariſt. p. 2. Refl. xxvii. P.

[f] Pref. to Virg. Paſt. in Dryd. Virg. P.

done

done by chance than on deſign, and ſometimes is beſt ſhewn by inference; leſt by too much ſtudy to ſeem natural, we deſtroy that eaſy ſimplicity from whence ariſes the delight. For what is inviting in this ſort of poetry proceeds not ſo much from the Idea of that buſineſs, as of the tranquillity of a country life.

We muſt therefore uſe ſome illuſion to render a Paſtoral delightful; and this conſiſts in expoſing the beſt ſide only of a ſhepherd's life, and in concealing its miſeries[g]. Nor is it enough to introduce ſhepherds diſcourſing together in a natural way; but a regard muſt be had to the ſubject; that it contain ſome particular beauty in itſelf, and that it be different in every Eclogue. Beſides, in each of them a deſign'd ſcene or proſpect is to be preſented to our view, which ſhould likewiſe have its variety[h]. This variety is obtained in a great degree by frequent compariſons, drawn from the moſt agreeable objects of the country; by interrogations to things inanimate; by beautiful digreſſions, but thoſe ſhort; ſometimes by inſiſting a little on circumſtances; and laſtly, by elegant turns on the words, which render the numbers extremely ſweet and pleaſing. As for the numbers themſelves, though they are properly of the heroic meaſure, they ſhould be the ſmootheſt, the moſt eaſy and flowing imaginable.

[g] Fontenelle's Diſc. of Paſtorals. P.

[h] See the forementioned Preface. P.

It is by rules like these that we ought to judge of pastoral. And since the instructions given for any art are to be delivered as that art is in perfection, they must of necessity be derived from those in whom it is acknowledged so to be. It is therefore from the practice of Theocritus and Virgil (the only undisputed authors of Pastoral) that the Critics have drawn the foregoing notions concerning it.

Theocritus * excels all others in nature and simplicity. The subjects of his Idyllia are purely pastoral; but he is not so exact in his persons, having introduced reapers [1] and fishermen as well as shepherds †. He is apt to be too long in his descriptions, of which that of the Cup in the first pastoral is a remarkable instance. In the manners he seems a little defective, for his swains are sometimes abusive and immodest, and perhaps too much inclining to rusticity; for instance, in his fourth and fifth Idyllia. But 'tis enough that all others learnt their excellencies from him, and that his Dialect alone has a secret charm in it, which no other could ever attain.

* Stesichorus, it is said, wrote pastorals also.

[1] ΘΕΡΙΣΤΑΙ, Idyl. x. and ΑΛΙΕΙΣ, Idyl. xxi. P.

† The 10th and 21st Idyll. here alluded to, contain some of the most exquisite strokes of nature and true poetry any where to be met with, as does the beautiful description of the carving on the cup; which, indeed, is not a cup, but a very large pastoral vessel or cauldron. Vas pastorilium amplissimum.

Virgil ‡, who copies Theocritus, refines upon his original: and in all points, where judgment is principally concerned, he is much ſuperior to his maſter. Though ſome of his ſubjects are not paſtoral in themſelves, but only ſeem to be ſuch; they have a wonderful variety in them, which the Greek was a ſtranger to [k]. He exceeds him in regularity and brevity, and falls ſhort of him in nothing but ſimplicity and propriety of ſtyle; the firſt of which perhaps was the fault of his age, and the laſt of his language.

Among the moderns, their ſucceſs has been greateſt who have moſt endeavoured to make theſe ancients their pattern. The moſt conſiderable Genius appears in the famous Taſſo, and our Spenſer. Taſſo § in his Aminta has as far excelled all

‡ He refines indeed ſo much as to make him, on this very account, much inferior to the beautiful ſimplicity of his original.

[k] Rapin, Refl. on Ariſt. part ii. refl. xxvii.—Pref. to the Ecl. in Dryden's Virg. P.

§ The Aminta of Taſſo is here erroneouſly mentioned by Pope as the very firſt paſtoral comedy that appeared in Italy: And Dr. Hurd alſo fell into the ſame miſtake. But it is certain that Il Sacrificio of Agoſtino Beccari was the firſt, who boaſts of it in his prologue, and who died very old in 1590; which drama was acted in the Palace of Franceſco of Eſte. Such a miſtake is very pardonable in ſo young an author, and very different from the groſs and unſcholar-like blunder of Trapp, who tells us in his fourteenth Lecture, that all the eclogues of Calphurnius and Nemeſian, who flouriſhed under Diocletian, were entirely loſt.

all the Paſtoral writers, as in his Gieruſalemme he has out-done the Epic poets of his country. But as this piece ſeems to have been the original of a new ſort of poem, the Paſtoral Comedy, in Italy, it cannot ſo well be conſidered as a copy of the ancients. Spenſer's Calendar, in Mr. Dryden's opinion, is the moſt complete work of this kind which any nation has produced ever ſince the time of Virgil[1]. Not but that he may be thought imperfect in ſome few points. His Eclogues are ſomewhat too long, if we compare them with the ancients. He is ſometimes too allegorical, and treats of Matters of religion in a paſtoral ſtyle, as the Mantuan had done before him. He has employed the Lyric meaſure, which is contrary to the practice of the old Poets. His ſtanza is not ſtill the ſame, nor always well choſen. This laſt may be the reaſon his expreſſion is ſometimes not conciſe enough: for the Tetraſtic has obliged him to extend his ſenſe to the length of four lines, which would have been more cloſely confined in the Couplet.

I will juſt add, that the famous Critic, Jaſon de Nores, who wrote ſo well on Horace's Art of Poetry, condemned the Paſtoral Drama. And that the above-mentioned Il Sacrificio was acted at Ferrara 1550, and the Aminta 1573, and the Paſtor Fido before Cardinal Borgheſe 1590. It is obſervable, that Pope does not mention the Comus of Milton, the moſt exquiſite of all paſtoral dramas.

[1] Dedication to Virg. Ecl. P.

In the manners, thoughts, and characters, he comes near to Theocritus himſelf; tho', notwithſtanding all the care he has taken, he is certainly inferior in his Dialect: For the Doric had its beauty and propriety in the time of Theocritus; it was uſed in part of Greece, and frequent in the mouths of many of the greateſt perſons: whereas the old Engliſh and country phraſes of Spenſer were either entirely obſolete, or ſpoken only by people of the loweſt condition. As there is a difference betwixt ſimplicity and ruſticity, ſo the expreſſion of ſimple thoughts ſhould be plain, but not clowniſh. The addition he has made of a Calendar to his Eclogues, is very beautiful; ſince by this, beſides the general moral of innocence and ſimplicity, which is common to other authors of Paſtoral, he has one peculiar to himſelf; he compares human Life to the ſeveral Seaſons, and at once expoſes to his readers a view of the great and little worlds, in their various changes and aſpects. Yet the ſcrupulous diviſion of his Paſtorals into Months, has obliged him either to repeat the ſame deſcription, in other words, for three months together; or, when it was exhauſted before, entirely to omit it: whence it comes to paſs that ſome of his Eclogues (as the ſixth, eighth, and tenth, for example) have nothing but their Titles to diſtinguiſh them. The reaſon is evident, becauſe the year has not that variety in it to furniſh every month with a particular deſcription, as it may every ſeaſon.

 Of

* Of the following Eclogues I ſhall only ſay, that theſe four comprehend all the ſubjects which the Critics upon Theocritus and Virgil will allow to be fit for paſtoral: That they have as much variety of deſcription, in reſpect of the ſeveral ſeaſons, as Spenſer's: that in order to add to this variety, the ſeveral times of the day are obſerv'd, the rural employments in each ſeaſon or time of day, and

* The ſuperiority of Milton's Lycidas to all paſtoral poems in our language is, I ſhould hope, acknowledged by every man of true claſſical judgment; and Dr. Johnſon's ſtrange animadverſions on it have been thus effectually anſwered. "Lycidas, (ſays he,) is filled with the heathen deities; and a long train of mythological imagery, ſuch as a College eaſily ſupplies.—But it is alſo ſuch as even the Court itſelf could now have eaſily ſupplied. The public diverſions, and books of all ſorts, and from all ſorts of writers, more eſpecially compoſitions in poetry, were at this time over-run with claſſical pedantries. But what writer, of the ſame period, has made theſe obſolete fictions the vehicle of ſo much fancy and poetical deſcription? How beautifully has he applied this ſort of alluſion to the Druidical rocks of Denbighſhire, to Mona, and the fabulous banks of Deva! It is objected, that its paſtoral form is diſguſting. But this was the age of paſtoral; and yet Lycidas has but little of the bucolic cant, now ſo faſhionable. The ſatyrs and fauns are but juſt mentioned. If any trite rural topics occur, how are they heightened!

"Together both, ere the high lawns appear'd
Under the opening eye-lids of the morn,
We drove afield, and both together heard
What time the gray-fly winds her ſultry horn,
Batt'ning our flocks with the freſh dews of night.

"Here the day-break is deſcribed by the faint appearance of the upland lawns under the firſt gleams of light: the ſun-ſet, by the buzzing of the chaffer: and the night ſheds her freſh dews on their flocks. We cannot blame paſtoral imagery and paſtoral allegory, which carry with them ſo much natural painting. In this and the rural ſcenes or places proper to ſuch employments; not without ſome regard to the ſeveral ages of man, and the different paſſions proper to each age.

But after all, if they have any merit, it is to be attributed to ſome good old Authors, whoſe works as I had leiſure to ſtudy, ſo I hope I have not wanted care to imitate.

this piece there is perhaps more poetry than ſorrow. But let us read it for its poetry. It is true, that paſſion plucks no berries from the myrtle and ivy, no calls upon Arethuſe and Mincius, nor tells of rough ſatyrs with cloven heel. But poetry does this; and in the hands of Milton, does it with a peculiar and irreſiſtible charm. Subordinate poets exerciſe no invention, when they tell how a ſhepherd has loſt his companion, and muſt feed his flocks alone without any judge of his ſkill in piping: but Milton dignifies and adorns theſe common artificial incidents with unexpected touches of picturesque beauty, with the graces of ſentiment, and with the novelties of original genius. It is ſaid, "here is no art, for there is nothing new." But this objection will vaniſh, if we conſider the imagery which Milton has raiſed from local circumſtances. Not to repeat the uſe he has made of the mountains of Wales, the Iſle of Man, and the river Dee, near which Lycidas was ſhip-wrecked; let us recollect the introduction of the romantic ſuperſtition of Saint Michael's Mount in Cornwall, which overlooks the Iriſh ſeas, the fatal ſcene of his friend's diſaſter.

"But the poetry is not always unconnected with paſſion. The poet laviſhly deſcribes an ancient ſepulchral rite, but it is made preparatory to a ſtroke of tenderneſs. He calls for a variety of flowers to decorate his friend's hearſe, ſuppoſing that his body was preſent, and forgetting for a while he was drowned; it was ſome conſolation that he was to receive the decencies of burial. This is a pleaſing deception: it is natural and pathetic. But the real cataſtrophe recurs. And this circumſtance again opens a new vein of imagination."

Poems of Milton, ſecond edition, Robinſon, 1791, p. 35.

SPRING:

THE FIRST PASTORAL,

OR,

DAMON.

TO SIR WILLIAM TRUMBAL.

FIRST in theſe fields I try the ſylvan ſtrains,
Nor bluſh to ſport on Windſor's bliſsful plains:
Fair Thames, flow gently from thy ſacred ſpring,
While on thy banks Sicilian Muſes ſing;

Let

REMARKS.

Theſe Paſtorals were written at the age of ſixteen, and then paſt through the hands of Mr. Walſh, Mr. Wycherley, G. Granville afterwards Lord Lanſdown, Sir William Trumbal, Dr. Garth, Lord Hallifax, Lord Somers, Mr. Mainwaring, and others. All theſe gave our Author the greateſt encouragement, and particularly Mr. Walſh, whom Mr. Dryden, in his Poſtſcript to Virgil, calls the beſt Critic of his age. "The Author (ſays he) ſeems to have a particular genius for this kind of Poetry, and a judgment that much exceeds his years. He has taken very freely from the Ancients. But what he has mixed of his own with theirs is no way inferior to what he has taken from them. It is not flattery at all to ſay that Virgil had written nothing ſo good at his Age. His Preface is very judicious and learned." Letter to Mr. Wycherley, Ap. 1705. The Lord Lanſdown about the ſame time, mentioning the youth of our Poet, ſays (in a printed Letter of the Character of Mr. Wycherley), "that if he goes on as he hath begun in the Paſtoral way, as Virgil

firſt

Let vernal airs through trembling osiers play,
And Albion's cliffs resound the rural lay.

You, that too wise for pride, too good for pow'r,
Enjoy the glory to be great no more,
And

REMARKS.

first tried his strength, we may hope to see English Poetry vie with the Roman," &c. Notwithstanding the early time of their production, the Author esteemed these as the most correct in the versification, and musical in the numbers, of all his works. The reason for his labouring them into so much softness, was, doubtless, that this sort of poetry derives almost its whole beauty from a natural ease of thought and smoothness of verse; whereas that of most other kinds consists in the strength and fulness of both. In a letter of his to Mr. Walsh about this time we find an enumeration of several niceties in Versification, which perhaps have never been strictly observed in any English poem, except in these Pastorals. They were not printed till 1709. P.

Sir William Trumbal.] Our Author's friendship with this gentleman commenced at very unequal years; he was under sixteen, but Sir William above sixty, and had lately resign'd his employment of Secretary of State to King William. P.

VER. 7. *You, that too wise*] This amiable old man, who had been a Fellow of All Souls College, Oxford, and Dr. of Civil Law, was sent, by Charles II, Judge Advocate to Tangier, and afterwards in a public character to Florence, to Turin, to Paris; and by James II, Ambassador to Constantinople; to which city he went through the continent on foot. He was afterwards a Lord of the Treasury, and Secretary of State with the Duke of Shrewsbury, which office he resigned 1697, and retiring to East Hampstead, died there in December 1716, aged seventy-seven. Nothing of his writing remains but an elegant character of Archbishop Dolben.

IMITATIONS.

VER. 1. "Prima Syracosio dignata est ludere versu,
Nostra nec erubuit sylvas habitare Thalia."

This is the general exordium and opening of the Pastorals, in imitation of the sixth of Virgil, which some have therefore not improbably thought to have been the first originally. In the beginnings of the other three Pastorals, he imitates expresly those
which

And carrying with you all the world can boaſt,
To all the world illuſtriouſly are loſt!
O let my Muſe her ſlender reed inſpire,
Till in your native ſhades you tune the lyre:
So when the Nightingale to reſt removes,
The Thruſh may chant to the forſaken groves,

REMARKS.

VER. 12. *in your native ſhades*] Sir W. Trumbal was born in Windſor-foreſt, to which he retreated, after he had reſigned the poſt of Secretary of State of King William III. P.

VER. 13. *So when the Nightingale*] This is ſurely a miſtake, for the nightingale does not ſing till other birds are at reſt.

IMITATIONS.

which now ſtand firſt * of the three chief Poets in this kind, Spenſer, Virgil, Theocritus.

A Shepherd's Boy (he ſeeks no better name)—
Beneath the ſhade a ſpreading beach diſplays,—
Thyrſis, the Muſic of that murm'ring Spring,—

are manifeſtly imitations of

"—A Shepherd's Boy (no better do him call)"
"—Tityre, tu patulae recubans ſub tegmine fagi."
"—Ἀδύ τι τὸ ψιθύρισμα καὶ ἁ πίτυς, αἰπόλε, τήνα." P.

VER. 9. *And carrying, &c.*]

Happy is he that from the world retires,
And carries with him what the world admires.
Waller. Maid's Tragedy altered.

* The learned and accurate Heyne, after much inveſtigation, is of opinion, that the following is the order in which the Eclogues of Virgil were written: what is now uſually called the ſecond was firſt; the third, ſecond; the fifth, third; the firſt, fourth; the ninth, fifth; the ſixth, as it was called, to be the ſixth ſtill; the fourth, ſeventh; the eighth ſtill the eighth; the ſeventh the ninth; the tenth and laſt, as it was called, ſtill the tenth. Vol. I. 205.

The collection of paſſages imitated from the Claſſics, marked in the margin with the letter P. was made by the accurate and learned Mr. Bowyer the Printer, and given to Pope at his deſire, as appears from MSS. Notes of Mr. Bowyer now before me.

But charm'd to ſilence, liſtens while ſhe ſings,
And all th' aërial audience clap their wings.

Soon as the flocks ſhook off the nightly dews,
Two Swains, whom Love kept wakeful, and the Muſe,
Pour'd o'er the whit'ning vale their fleecy care,
Freſh as the morn, and as the ſeaſon fair:
The dawn now bluſhing on the mountain's ſide,
Thus Daphnis ſpoke, and Strephon thus reply'd.

DAPHNIS.

Hear how the birds, on ev'ry blooming ſpray,
With joyous muſic wake the dawning day!
Why ſit we mute, when early linnets ſing,
When warbling Philomel ſalutes the ſpring?
Why ſit we ſad, when Phoſphor ſhines ſo clear,
And laviſh Nature paints the purple year?

STREPHON.

Sing then, and Damon ſhall attend the ſtrain,
While yon' ſlow oxen turn the furrow'd plain.
Here the bright crocus and blue vi'let glow,
Here weſtern winds on breathing roſes blow.

REMARKS.

VER. 17, *&c.*] The Scene of this Paſtoral a Valley, the Time the Morning. It ſtood originally thus,

Daphnis and Strephon to the ſhades retir'd,
Both warm'd by love, and by the Muſe inſpir'd,
Freſh as the morn, and as the ſeaſon fair,
In flow'ry vales they fed their fleecy care;
And while Aurora gilds the mountain's ſide,
Thus Daphnis ſpoke, and Strephon thus reply'd.

VER. 28. From Spenſer's Muipotmos.

Purple year?] Gray has adopted the expreſſion of the purple year, in the firſt ſtanza of his exquiſite Ode on Spring.

I'll

I'll ſtake yon' lamb, that near the fountain plays,
And from the brink his dancing ſhade ſurveys.

DAPHNIS.

And I this bowl, where wanton ivy twines,
And ſwelling cluſters bend the curling vines:
Four figures riſing from the work appear,
The various ſeaſons of the rowling year;
And what is that, which binds the radiant ſky,
Where twelve fair ſigns in beauteous order lie?

VARIATIONS.

VER. 34. The firſt reading was,
And his own image from the bank ſurveys. W.

VER. 36. And cluſters lurk beneath the curling vines. P.

REMARKS.

VER. 38. *The various ſeaſons*] The ſubject of theſe Paſtorals engraven on the bowl is not without its propriety. W.

My friend Mr. William Collins, author of the Perſian Eclogues and Odes, aſſured me that Thomſon informed him, that he took the firſt hint and idea of writing his Seaſons, from the titles of Pope's four Paſtorals. So that theſe Paſtorals have not had only the merit of ſetting a pattern for correct and muſical Verſification, but have given riſe to ſome of the trueſt poetry in our language. Mr. Collins wrote his Eclogues when he was about ſeventeen years old, at Wincheſter School, and, as I well remember, had been juſt reading that volume of Salmon's Modern Hiſtory, which deſcribed Perſia; which determined him to lay the ſcene of theſe pieces, as being productive of new images and ſentiments. In his maturer years he was accuſtomed to ſpeak very contemptuouſly of

IMITATIONS.

VER. 35, 36.
"Lenta quibus torno facili ſuperaddita vitis,
Diffuſos edera veſtit pallente corymbos." Virg. P.

The Shepherd's heſitation at the name of the Zodiac imitates that in Virgil,
"Et quis fuit alter,
Deſcripſit radio totum qui gentibus orbem?" P.

Then

DAMON.

Then ſing by turns, by turns the Muſes ſing,
Now hawthorns bloſſom, now the daiſies ſpring,
Now leaves the trees, and flow'rs adorn the ground;
Begin, the vales ſhall ev'ry note rebound.

STREPHON.

Inſpire me, Phoebus, in my Delia's praiſe,
With Waller's ſtrains, or Granville's moving lays!
A milk-white Bull ſhall at your altars ſtand,
That threats a fight, and ſpurns the riſing ſand.

REMARKS.

of them, calling them his Iriſh Eclogues, and ſaying they had not in them one ſpark of Orientaliſm; and deſiring me to eraſe a motto he had prefixed to them in a copy he gave me;

——quos primus equis oriens afflavit anhelis. Virg.

He was greatly mortified that they found more readers and admirers than his Odes.

VER. 41. *ſing by turns,*] Amabæan Verſes, and the cuſtom of vying in extempore verſes, by turns, was a cuſtom derived from the old Sicilian ſhepherds, and ſpread over all Italy; and is, as Mr. Spence obſerves, exactly like the practice of the Improviſatori at preſent in Italy. They are ſurprizingly ready in their anſwers, and go on octave for octave, and ſpeech for ſpeech alternately, for a conſiderable time. At Florence they have even had Improviſo Comedies. It is remarkable that the celebrated Triſſino, Leonardi du Vinci, Bramante, and the charming dramatic poet Metaſtaſio, were all Improviſatori.

VER. 46. *Granville*—] George Granville, afterwards Lord Lanſdown, known for his Poems, moſt of which he compos'd very young, and propos'd Waller as his model. P.

IMITATIONS.

VER. 41. *Then ſing by turns,*] Literally from Virgil,
"Alternis dicetis, amant alterna Camoenae:
Et nunc omnis ager, nunc omnis parturit arbos,
Nunc frondent ſylvae, nunc formoſiſſimus annus." P.

VER. 47. *A milk-white Bull.*] Virg.—"Paſcite taurum,
Qui cornu petat, et pedibus jam ſpargat arenam." P.

O Love!

DAPHNIS.

O Love! for Sylvia let me gain the prize,
And make my tongue victorious as her eyes:
No lambs or sheep for victims I'll impart,
Thy victim, Love, shall be the shepherd's heart.

STREPHON.

Me gentle Delia beckons from the plain,
Then hid in shades, eludes her eager swain;
But feigns a laugh, to see me search around,
And by that laugh the willing fair is found.

DAPHNIS.

The sprightly Sylvia trips along the green,
She runs, but hopes she does not run unseen;
While a kind glance at her pursuer flies,
How much at variance are her feet and eyes!

VARIATIONS.

VER. 49. Originally thus in the MS.
Pan, let my numbers equal Strephon's lays,
Of Parian stone thy statue will I raise;
But if I conquer and augment my fold,
Thy Parian statue shall be chang'd to gold. W.

REMARKS.

VER. 60. *How much at variance*] A very trifling and false conceit, and too witty for the occasion.

IMITATIONS.

VER. 58. *She runs, but hopes*] Imitation of Virgil,
"Malo me Galatea petit, lasciva puella,
Et fugit ad salices, sed se cupit ante videri." P.

O'er

STREPHON.

O'er golden ſands let rich Pactolus flow,
And trees weep amber on the banks of Po;
Bright Thames's ſhores the brighteſt beauties yield,
Feed here my lambs, I'll ſeek no diſtant field.

DAPHNIS.

Celeſtial Venus haunts Idalia's groves;
Diana Cynthus, Ceres Hybla loves;
If Windſor-ſhades delight the matchleſs maid,
Cynthus and Hybla yield to Windſor-ſhade.

STREPHON.

All nature mourns, the ſkies relent in ſhow'rs,
Huſh'd are the birds, and cloſ'd the drooping flow'rs;

VARIATIONS.

VER. 61. It ſtood thus at firſt,
Let rich Iberia golden fleeces boaſt,
Her purple wool the proud Aſſyrian coaſt,
Bleſt Thames's ſhores, &c. P.

VER. 61. Originally thus in the MS.
Go, flow'ry wreath, and let my Sylvia know,
Compar'd to thine how bright her Beauties ſhow;
Then die; and dying teach the lovely Maid
How ſoon the brighteſt beauties are decay'd.

DAPHNIS.

Go, tuneful bird, that pleas'd the woods ſo long,
Of Amaryllis learn a ſweeter ſong;
To Heav'n ariſing then her notes convey,
For Heav'n alone is worthy ſuch a lay. W.

VER. 69, &c. Theſe verſes were thus at firſt:
All nature mourns, the birds their ſongs deny,
Nor waſted brooks the thirſty flow'rs ſupply;
If Delia ſmile the flow'rs begin to ſpring,
The brooks to murmur, and the birds to ſing. P.

IMITATIONS.

VER. 69. *All nature mourns,*]
"Aret ager, vitio moriens ſitit aëris herba," &c.
"Phyllidis adventu noſtrae nemus omne virebit." Virg. P.

If Delia ſmile, the flow'rs begin to ſpring,
The ſkies to brighten, and the birds to ſing.

DAPHNIS.

All nature laughs, the groves are freſh and fair,
The Sun's mild luſtre warms the vital air;
If Sylvia ſmiles new glories gild the ſhore,
And vanquiſh'd nature ſeems to charm no more.

STREPHON.

In ſpring the fields, in autumn hills I love,
At morn the plains, at noon the ſhady grove,
But Delia always; abſent from her ſight,
Nor plains at morn, nor groves at noon delight.

DAPHNIS.

Sylvia's like autumn ripe, yet mild as May,
More bright than noon, yet freſh as early day;
Ev'n ſpring diſpleaſes, when ſhe ſhines not here;
But bleſt with her, 'tis ſpring throughout the year.

STREPHON.

Say, Daphnis, ſay, in what glad ſoil appears,
A wondrous Tree that ſacred Monarchs bears;
Tell me but this, and I'll diſclaim the prize,
And give the conqueſt to thy Sylvia's eyes.

REMARKS.

VER. 86. *A wondrous Tree that ſacred Monarchs bears;*] An alluſion to the Royal Oak, in which Charles II. had been hid from the purſuit after the battle at Worceſter. P.

This is one of the moſt trifling and puerile conceits in any of our author's works; except what follows of the Thiſtle and the Lily.

DAPHNIS.

Nay tell me firſt, in what more happy fields
The Thiſtle ſprings, to which the Lily yields: 90
And then a nobler prize I will reſign;
For Sylvia, charming Sylvia ſhall be thine.

DAMON.

Ceaſe to contend, for, Daphnis, I decree,
The bowl to Strephon, and the lamb to thee:
Bleſt Swains, whoſe Nymphs in ev'ry grace excel;
Bleſt Nymphs, whoſe Swains thoſe graces ſing ſo well!
Now riſe, and haſte to yonder woodbine bow'rs, 97
A ſoft retreat from ſudden vernal ſhow'rs;
The turf with rural dainties ſhall be crown'd,
While op'ning blooms diffuſe their ſweets around.
For ſee! the gath'ring flocks to ſhelter tend, 101
And from the Pleiads fruitful ſhow'rs deſcend.

VARIATIONS.

VER. 99. was originally,

The turf with country dainties ſhall be ſpread,
And trees with twining branches ſhade your head. P.

REMARKS.

VER. 93. *Ceaſe to contend,*] An author of ſtrong ſenſe, but not of equal taſte and feeling, and who preferred the dungeons of the Strand to the valleys of Arcadia, ſays, "That every intelligent reader ſickens at the mention of the crook and the pipe, the ſheep and the kids." This appears to be an unjuſt and harſh condemnation of all Paſtoral Poetry. And the ſame author depreciates and deſpiſes the Amynta of Taſſo, and the Paſtor Fido of Guarini, two pieces of exquiſite poetry, and which have gained a laſting applauſe.

IMITATIONS.

VER. 90. *The Thiſtle ſprings, to which the Lily yields:*] Alludes to the device of the Scots Monarchs, the Thiſtle worn by Queen Anne; and to the arms of France, the Fleur de lys. The two riddles are in imitation of thoſe in Virg. Ecl. iii.

"Dic quibus in terris inſcripti nomina *Regum*
Naſcantur *Flores*, & Phyllida ſolus habeto" P.

A mixture of Britiſh and Grecian ideas may juſtly be deemed a blemiſh in theſe Paſtorals: and propriety is certainly violated, when he couples Pactolus with Thames, and Windſor with Hybla. Complaints of immoderate heat, and wiſhes to be conveyed to cooling caverns, when uttered by the inhabitants of Greece, have a decorum and conſiſtency, which they totally loſe in the character of a Britiſh ſhepherd: and Theocritus, during the ardors of Sirius, muſt have heard the murmurings of a brook, and the whiſpers of a pine, with more home-felt pleaſure, than Pope could poſſibly experience upon the ſame occaſion. We can never completely reliſh, or adequately underſtand any author, eſpecially any ancient, except we keep in our eye, his climate, his country, and his age. Pope himſelf informs us, in a Note, that he judiciouſly omitted the following verſe,

And liſt'ning wolves grow milder as they hear,

on account of the abſurdity, which Spenſer overlooked, of introducing wolves into England. But on this principle, which is certainly a juſt one, may it not be aſked why he ſhould ſpeak, the ſcene lying in Windſor Foreſt, of the ſultry Sirius, of the grateful cluſters of *grapes*, of a *pipe of reeds*, the antique fiſtula, of *thanking Ceres for a plentiful harveſt*, of *the ſacrifice of lambs*, with many other inſtances that might be adduced to this purpoſe. That Pope however was ſenſible of the importance of adapting images to the ſcene of action, is obvious from the following example of his judgment; for in tranſlating

Audiit Eurotas, juſſitque ediſcere Lauros,

he has dexterouſly dropt the *laurels* appropriated to Eurotas, as he is ſpeaking of the river Thames, and has rendered it,

Thames heard the numbers, as he flow'd along,
And bade his *Willows* learn the moving ſong.

In the paſſages which Pope has imitated from Theocritus, and from his Latin Tranſlator Virgil, he has merited but little applauſe. It may not be unentertaining to ſee how coldly and unpoetically Pope has copied the ſubſequent appeal to the Nymphs on the death of Daphnis, in compariſon of Milton on Lycidas, one of his juvenile, but one of his moſt exquiſite pieces.

Where were ye, Nymphs, when the remorſeleſs deep
Clos'd o'er the head of your lov'd Lycidas?

For neither were ye playing on the ſteep
Where your old bards, the famous Druids lie;
Nor on the ſhaggy top of Mona high,
Nor yet where Deva ſpreads her wizard ſtream.

LYCIDAS.

The mention of places remarkably romantic, the ſuppoſed habitations of Druids, Bards, and Wizards, is far more pleaſing to the imagination, than the obvious introduction of Cam and Iſis, as ſeats of the Muſes.

SUMMER:

THE SECOND PASTORAL.[a]

OR,

ALEXIS.

TO DR. GARTH.

A Shepherd's Boy (he ſeeks no better name)
Led forth his flocks along the ſilver Thame,
Where dancing ſun-beams on the waters play'd,
And verdant alders form'd a quiv'ring ſhade.
Soft as he mourn'd, the ſtreams forgot to flow,
The flocks around a dumb compaſſion ſhow,

VARIATIONS.

Ver. 1, 2, 3, 4, were thus printed in the firſt edition:
A faithful ſwain, whom Love had taught to ſing,
Bewail'd his fate beſide a ſilver ſpring;
Where gentle Thames his winding waters leads
Thro' verdant foreſts, and thro' flow'ry meads. P.

Ver. 3. Originally thus in the MS.
There to the winds he plain'd his hapleſs love,
And Amaryllis fill'd the vocal grove. W.

REMARKS.

[a] It is unfortunate that this ſecond paſtoral, the worſt of the four, ſhould be inſcribed to the beſt judge of all his four other friends to whom they were addreſt.

Ver. 2. *Thame,*] An inaccurate word, inſtead of Thames.

Ver. 3. The Scene of this Paſtoral by the river ſide, ſuitable to the heat of the ſeaſon; the Time, noon. P.

The Naïads wept in ev'ry wat'ry bow'r,
And Jove consented in a silent show'r.
Accept, O Garth, the Muse's early lays,
That adds this wreath of ivy to thy bays;
Hear what from Love unpractis'd hearts endure,
From Love, the sole disease thou canst not cure.
Ye shady beeches, and ye cooling streams,
Defence from Phoebus', not from Cupid's beams,
To you I mourn, nor to the deaf I sing,
The woods shall answer, and their echo ring,
The hills and rocks attend my doleful lay,
Why art thou prouder and more hard than they?

REMARKS.

Ver. 9. Dr. Samuel Garth, Author of the Dispensary, was one of the first friends of our Poet, whose acquaintance with him began at fourteen or fifteen. Their friendship continued from the year 1703 to 1718, which was that of his death. P.

He was a man of the sweetest disposition, amiable manners, and universal benevolence. All parties, at a time when party violence was at a great height, joined in praising and loving him. I hope I may be pardoned from speaking of his character *con amore*, from my near connexion with one of his descendants; and yet I trust I shall not be accused of an improper partiality. One of the most exquisite pieces of wit ever written by Addison, is a defence of Garth against the Examiner, 1710.

Ver. 16. *The woods shall answer, and their echo ring,*] Is a line out of Spenser's Epithalamion. P.

Ver. 18. *Why art thou prouder and more hard than they?*] A line unworthy our Author, containing a false and trivial thought; as is also the 22d line.

IMITATIONS.

Ver. 8. *And Jove consented*]
"Jupiter et laeto descendet plurimus imbri." Virg. P.

Ver. 15. *nor to the deaf I sing.*]
"Non canimus surdis, respondent omnia sylvae." Virg. P.

The

The bleating ſheep with my complaints agree,
They parch'd with heat, and I inflam'd by thee.
The ſultry Sirius burns the thirſty plains,
While in thy heart eternal winter reigns.
  Where ſtray ye, Muſes, in what lawn or grove,
While your Alexis pines in hopeleſs love?
In thoſe fair fields where ſacred Iſis glides,
Or elſe where Cam his winding vales divides?
As in the cryſtal ſpring I view my face,
Freſh riſing bluſhes paint the wat'ry glaſs;

VARIATIONS.

VER. 27. Oft in the cryſtal ſpring I caſt a view,
And equal'd Hylas, if the glaſs be true;
But ſince thoſe graces meet my eyes no more,
I ſhun, &c. P.

REMARKS.

VER. 27. *As in the*] This is one of thoſe paſſages in which Virgil, by too cloſely copying Theocritus, has violated propriety; and not attended to the different characters of Cyclops and Corydon. The ſea, which is a proper looking-glaſs for the gigantic ſon of Neptune, who alſo conſtantly dwelt on the ſhore, was certainly not equally adapted to the face of the little Land-ſhepherd. The ſame may be ſaid of the cheeſe and milk, and numerous herds of Polypheme, exactly ſuited to his Sicilian ſituation, and the rude and ſavage ſtate of the ſpeaker, whoſe character is admirably ſupported through the whole eleventh Idyllium of Theocritus.

IMITATIONS.

VER. 23. *Where ſtray ye, Muſes, &c.*]
"Quae nemora, aut qui vos ſaltus habuere, puellae
Naïades, indigno cum Gallus amore periret?
Nam neque Parnaſſi vobis juga, nam neque Pindi
Ulla moram fecere, neque Aonia Aganippe."
Virg. out of Theocr. P.

VER 27. Virgil again, from the Cyclops of Theocritus,
"nuper me in littore vidi,
Cum placidum ventis ſtaret mare; non ego Daphnim,
Judice te, metuam, ſi numquam fallat imago." P.

But ſince thoſe graces pleaſe thy eyes no more,
I ſhun the fountains which I ſought before.
Once I was ſkill'd in ev'ry herb that grew,
And ev'ry plant that drinks the morning dew;
Ah wretched ſhepherd, what avails thy art,
To cure thy lambs, but not to heal thy heart!
Let other ſwains attend the rural care,
Feed fairer flocks, or richer fleeces ſheer:
But nigh yon' mountain let me tune my lays,
Embrace my Love, and bind my brows with bays.
That flute is mine which Colin's tuneful breath
Inſpir'd when living, and bequeath'd in death:
He ſaid; Alexis, take this pipe, the ſame
That taught the groves my Roſolinda's name:

REMARKS.

VER. 35, 36. *Care,*] The only faulty rhymes, *care* and *ſheer*, perhaps in theſe poems, where verſification is in general ſo exact and correct.

VER. 39. *Colin*] The name taken by Spenſer in his Eclogues, where his miſtreſs is celebrated under that of Roſalinda. P.

VER. 42. *Roſalinda's*] This is the Lady with whom Spenſer fell violently in love, as ſoon as he left Cambridge and went into the North; it is uncertain into what family, and in what capacity. Her name is an Anagram, and the letters of which it is compoſed will make out her true name; for Spenſer (ſays the learned and ingenious Mr. Upton, his beſt Editor) is an Anagrammatiſt in many of his names: thus *Algrind* tranſpoſed is Archbiſhop *Grindal*; and Morrel is Biſhop *Elmer*. He is ſuppoſed to hint at the cruelty and coquettery of his Roſalind in B. 6. of the Fairy Queen, in the character of Mirabella.

IMITATIONS.

VER. 40. *bequeath'd in death, &c.*] Virg. Ecl. ii.

"Eſt mihi diſparibus ſeptem compacta cicutis
Fiſtula, Damoetas dono mihi quam dedit olim,
Et dixit moriens, Te nunc habet iſta ſecundum." P.

But

But now the reeds ſhall hang on yonder tree,
For ever ſilent, ſince deſpis'd by thee.
Oh! were I made by ſome transforming pow'r
The captive bird that ſings within thy bow'r!
Then might my voice thy liſt'ning ears employ,
And I thoſe kiſſes he receives enjoy.

And yet my numbers pleaſe the rural throng,
Rough Satyrs dance, and Pan applauds the ſong:
The Nymphs, forſaking ev'ry cave and ſpring,
Their early fruit, and milk-white turtles bring!
Each am'rous nymph prefers her gifts in vain,
On you their gifts are all beſtow'd again.
For you the ſwains their faireſt flow'rs deſign,
And in one garland all their beauties join;
Accept the wreath which you deſerve alone,
In whom all beauties are compriz'd in one.

See what delights in ſylvan ſcenes appear!
Deſcending Gods have found Elyſium here.
In woods bright Venus with Adonis ſtray'd,
And chaſte Diana haunts the foreſt-ſhade.
Come, lovely nymph, and bleſs the ſilent hours,
When ſwains from ſheering ſeek their nightly bow'rs;
When weary reapers quit the ſultry field,
And crown'd with corn their thanks to Ceres yield.

IMITATIONS.

Ver. 60. *Deſcending Gods have found Elyſium here.*]
"Habitarunt Di quoque ſylvas"—Virg.
"Et formoſus oves ad flumina pavit Adonis." Idem. P.

This harmleſs grove no lurking viper hides,
But in my breaſt the ſerpent Love abides.
Here bees from bloſſoms ſip the roſy dew,
But your Alexis knows no ſweets but you.
O deign to viſit our forſaken ſeats,
The moſſy fountains, and the green retreats!
Where'er you walk, cool gales ſhall fan the glade,
Trees, where you ſit, ſhall croud into a ſhade:
Where'er you tread, the bluſhing flow'rs ſhall riſe,
And all things flouriſh where you turn your eyes.
O! how I long with you to paſs my days,
Invoke the Muſes, and reſound your praiſe!
Your praiſe the birds ſhall chant in ev'ry grove,
And winds ſhall waft it to the pow'rs above.
But would you ſing, and rival Orpheus' ſtrain,
The wond'ring foreſts ſoon ſhould dance again,
The moving mountains hear the pow'rful call,
And headlong ſtreams hang liſt'ning in their fall!

VER. 67, 68.] I think theſe two lines would not have paſſed without animadverſion in any of our great ſchools.

VARIATIONS.

VER. 79, 80.
Your praiſe the tuneful birds to heav'n ſhall bear,
And liſt'ning wolves grow milder as they hear.
So the verſes were originally written. But the Author, young as he was, ſoon found the abſurdity which Spenſer himſelf overlooked, of introducing wolves into England. P.

IMITATIONS.

VER. 80. *And winds ſhall waft, &c.*]
"Partem aliquam, venti, divûm referatis ad aures!"
Virg. P.

But see, the shepherds shun the noon-day heat,
The lowing herds to murm'ring brooks retreat,
To closer shades the panting flocks remove;
Ye Gods! and is there no relief for Love?
But soon the sun with milder rays descends
To the cool ocean, where his journey ends:
On me love's fiercer flames for ever prey,
By night he scorches, as he burns by day.

VARIATIONS.

VER. 91. Me love inflames, nor will his fires allay. P.

IMITATIONS.

VER. 88. *Ye Gods, &c.*]
"Me tamen urit amor, quis enim modus adsit amori?"
Idem. P.

Virgil in his Epic, attempted to paint those manners which he had never seen; and in his Pastoral, those rustic manners which he was little acquainted with.

AUTUMN:

THE THIRD PASTORAL.[a]

OR,

HYLAS and *AEGON*.

TO MR. WYCHERLEY. †

BENEATH the ſhade a ſpreading Beech diſplays,
Hylas and Aegon ſung their rural lays;
This mourn'd a faithleſs, that an abſent Love,
And Delia's name and Doris' fill'd the Grove.
Ye Mantuan nymphs, your ſacred ſuccour bring;
Hylas and Aegon's rural lays I ſing.

REMARKS.

[a] This Paſtoral conſiſts of two parts, like the viiith of Virgil: The Scene, a Hill; the Time at Sun-ſet. P.

† His intrigues with the Dutcheſs of Cleveland, his marriage with the Counteſs of Drogheda, Charles the Second's diſpleaſure on this marriage, his debts and diſtreſſes, and other particulars of his life, are well related by Dennis in a Letter to Major Pack, 1720. In Dennis's collection of Letters, publiſhed in two volumes, 1721, to which Mr. Pope ſubſcribed, Lord Lanſdown has drawn his character, as a Writer, in an elegant manner; chiefly with a view of ſhewing the impropriety of an epithet given to him by Lord Rocheſter, who called him Slow Wycherley; for that, notwithſtanding his pointed wit, and forcible expreſſion, he compoſed with facility and haſte.

Thou,

Thou, whom the Nine, with Plautus' wit inſpire,
The art of Terence, and Menander's fire;
Whoſe ſenſe inſtructs us, and whoſe humour charms,
Whoſe judgment ſways us, and whoſe ſpirit warms!
Oh, ſkill'd in Nature! ſee the hearts of Swains, 11
Their artleſs paſſions, and their tender pains.

REMARKS.

VER. 7. *Thou, whom the Nine,*] Mr. Wycherley, a famous author of Comedies; of which the moſt celebrated were the *Plain-Dealer* and *Country-wife*. He was a writer of infinite ſpirit, ſatire, and wit. The only objection made to him was, that he had too much. However, he was followed in the ſame way by Mr. Congreve; tho' with a little more correctneſs. P.

Surely with much more correctneſs, taſte, and judgment.

VER. 8. *The art of Terence, and Menander's fire;*] This line alludes to that famous character given of Terence, by Caeſar:

> " Tu quoque, tu in ſummis, *ô dimidiate Menander,*
> Poneris, et merito, puri ſermonis amator:
> Lenibus atque utinam ſcriptis adjuncta foret *vis Comica.*"

So that the judicious critic ſees he ſhould have ſaid—*with Menander's fire*. For what the Poet meant, was, that his friend had joined to Terence's art, what Caeſar thought wanting in Terence, namely, the *vis comica* of Menander. Beſides,—*and Menander's fire,* is making that the Characteriſtic of Menander which was not. He was diſtinguiſhed for having art and *comic ſpirit* in conjunction, and Terence having only the firſt part, is called the *half of Menander*. W.

VER. 9. *Whoſe ſenſe inſtructs us,*] He was always very careful in his encomiums not to fall into ridicule, the deſerved fate of weak and proſtitute flatterers, and which they rarely eſcape. For *ſenſe*, he would willingly have ſaid *moral*; propriety required it. But this dramatic Poet's moral was remarkably faulty. His plays are all ſhamefully profligate both in the Dialogue and Action. W.

VER. 11. *Oh, ſkill'd*] Few writers have leſs nature in them than Wycherley.

Now

Now ſetting Phoebus ſhone ſerenely bright,
And fleecy clouds were ſtreak'd with purple light;
When tuneful Hylas with melodious moan,
Taught rocks to weep, and made the mountains groan.

Go, gentle gales, and bear my ſighs away!
To Delia's ear the tender notes convey.
As ſome ſad turtle his loſt love deplores,
And with deep murmurs fills the ſounding ſhores;
Thus, far from Delia, to the winds I mourn,
Alike unheard, unpity'd, and forlorn.

Go, gentle gales, and bear my ſighs along!
For her, the feather'd quires neglect their ſong:
For her, the limes their pleaſing ſhades deny;
For her, the lilies hang their heads and die.
Ye flow'rs that droop, forſaken by the ſpring,
Ye birds that, left by ſummer, ceaſe to ſing,
Ye trees that fade when autumn-heats remove,
Say, is not abſence death to thoſe who love?

Go, gentle gales, and bear my ſighs away!
Curs'd be the fields that cauſe my Delia's ſtay;
Fade ev'ry bloſſom, wither ev'ry tree,
Die ev'ry flow'r, and periſh all, but ſhe,
What have I ſaid? where'er my Delia flies,
Let ſpring attend, and ſudden flow'rs ariſe;

REMARKS.

VER. 25.] This rich aſſemblage of very pleaſing paſtoral images, is yet excelled by Shenſtone's beautiful Paſtoral Ballad in four parts.

Let op'ning roſes knotted oaks adorn,
And liquid amber drop from ev'ry thorn.
  Go, gentle gales, and bear my ſighs along!
The birds ſhall ceaſe to tune their ev'ning ſong,
The winds to breathe, the waving woods to move,
And ſtreams to murmur, ere I ceaſe to love.
Not bubbling fountains to the thirſty ſwain,
Not balmy ſleep to lab'rers faint with pain,

REMARKS.

VER. 43. *Not bubbling*] The turn of theſe four lines is evidently borrowed from Drummond of Hawthwarden, a charming but neglected Poet. He was born 1585, and died 1649. His verſes are as ſmooth as Waller's, whom he preceded many years, having written a poem to King James, 1617; whereas Waller's firſt compoſition was to Charles I, 1625. His Sonnets are exquiſitely beautiful and correct. He was one of our firſt, and beſt imitators of the Italian Poets, and Milton had certainly read and admired him, as appears by many paſſages that might be quoted for that purpoſe. The four lines mentioned above follow;

To virgins flow'rs, to ſun-burnt earth the rain,
To mariners fair winds amid the main,
Cool ſhades to pilgrims, whom hot glances burn,
Are not ſo pleaſing as thy bleſt return.

And afterwards again our author borrows in Abelard;

The grief was common, common were the cries.

I will juſt add, that Drayton's Paſtorals, and his Nymphidia, do not ſeem to be attended to ſo much as they deſerve.

IMITATIONS.

VER. 37. "Aurea durae
Mala ferant quercus; narciſſo floreat alnus,
Pinguia corticibus ſudent electra myricae."
Virg. Ecl. viii. P.

VER. 43, &c.]
"Quale ſopor feſſis in gramine, quale per aeſtum
Dulcis aquae ſaliente ſitim reſtinguere rivo."
Ecl. v. P.

Not

Not ſhow'rs to larks, nor ſhun-ſhine to the bee,
Are half ſo charming as thy ſight to me.
Go, gentle gales, and bear my ſighs away!
Come, Delia, come; ah, why this long delay?
Thro' rocks and caves the name of Delia ſounds,
Delia, each cave and echoing rock rebounds.
Ye pow'rs, what pleaſing phrenzy ſooths my mind!
Do lovers dream, or is my Delia kind?
She comes, my Delia comes!—Now ceaſe my lay,
And ceaſe, ye gales, to bear my ſighs away!
Next Aegon ſung, while Windſor groves admir'd;
Rehearſe, ye Muſes, what yourſelves inſpir'd.
Reſound, ye hills, reſound my mournful ſtrain!
Of perjur'd Doris, dying I complain:
Here, where the mountains, leſs'ning as they riſe,
Loſe the low vales, and ſteal into the ſkies:
While lab'ring oxen, ſpent with toil and heat,
In their looſe traces from the field retreat:
While curling ſmoaks from village tops are ſeen,
And the fleet ſhades glide o'er the duſky green.
Reſound, ye hills, reſound my mournful lay!
Beneath yon' poplar oft we paſt the day:

VARIATIONS.

VER. 48. Originally thus in the MS.
With him through Lybia's burning plains I'll go,
On Alpine mountains tread th' eternal ſnow;
Yet feel no heat but what our loves impart,
And dread no coldneſs but in Thyrſis heart. W.

IMITATIONS.

VER. 52. "An qui amant, ipſi ſibi ſomnia fingunt?"
Id. viii. P.

Oft'

Oft' on the rind I carv'd her am'rous vows,
While ſhe with garlands hung the bending boughs:
The garlands fade, the vows are worn away;
So dies her love, and ſo my hopes decay.
 Reſound, ye hills, reſound my mournful ſtrain!
Now bright Arcturus glads the teeming grain,
Now golden fruits on loaded branches ſhine,
And grateful cluſters ſwell with floods of wine;
Now bluſhing berries paint the yellow grove;
Juſt Gods! ſhall all things yield returns but love?
 Reſound, ye hills, reſound my mournful lay!
The ſhepherds cry, "Thy flocks are left a prey"—
Ah! what avails it me, the flocks to keep,
Who loſt my heart while I preſerv'd my ſheep.
Pan came, and aſk'd, what magic caus'd my ſmart
Or what ill eyes malignant glances dart?
What eyes but hers, alas, have pow'r to move!
And is there magic but what dwells in love!
 Reſound, ye hills, reſound my mournful ſtrains!
I'll fly from ſhepherds, flocks, and flow'ry plains,
From ſhepherds, flocks, and plains, I may remove,
Forſake mankind, and all the world—but love!
I know thee, Love! on foreign mountains bred,
Wolves gave thee ſuck, and ſavage tigers fed.

REMARKS.

VER. 82. *dart?*] It ſhould be *darted*; the preſent tenſe is uſed for the ſake of the rhyme.

IMITATIONS.

VER. 82. *Or what ill eyes*]
 "Neſcio quis teneros oculus mihi faſcinat agnos." P.

Thou wert from Aetna's burning entrails torn,
Got by fierce whirlwinds, and in thunder born!
  Reſound, ye hills, reſound my mournful lay!
Farewel, ye woods, adieu the light of day!
One leap from yonder cliff ſhall end my pains,
No more, ye hills, no more reſound my ſtrains!
  Thus ſung the ſhepherds till th' approach of night,
The ſkies yet bluſhing with departing light,
When falling dews with ſpangles deck'd the glade,
And the low ſun had lengthen'd ev'ry ſhade.

REMARKS.

VER. 97. *Thus ſung*] Among the multitude of Engliſh Poets who wrote paſtorals, Fairfax, to whom our Verſification is thought to be ſo much indebted, ought to be mentioned. He wrote ten or twelve Eclogues after the acceſſion of James I. They were like thoſe of Mantuan and Spenſer, allegorical, and alluded to the manners and characters of the times, and contained many ſatyrical ſtrokes againſt the King and his Court. They were loſt in the fire that conſumed the Banquetting Houſe at Whitehall; but it is ſaid that Mr. W. Fairfax, his ſon, recovered them from his father's papers; the fourth of them was publiſhed by Mrs. Cooper in the Muſes Library, 1737.

VER. 98. 100.] There is a little inaccuracy here; the firſt line makes the time after ſun-ſet; the ſecond, before. W.

VER. 100. *And the low ſun*] Mr. Gray's Evening, deſcribed in the two firſt ſtanzas of his excellent Elegy, is far more pictureſque and poetical. I would propoſe to read the two firſt lines of his elegy with a new punctuation, as follows:

The curfew tolls! the knell of parting day!

IMITATIONS.

VER. 89. "Nunc ſcio quid ſit Amor: duris in cotibus illum," &c. P.

This from Virgil is much inferior to the paſſage in Theocritus, from whence it is taken.

WINTER:

THE FOURTH PASTORAL,

OR,

DAPHNE.

TO THE MEMORY OF MRS. TEMPEST.

LYCIDAS.

THYRSIS, the muſic of that murm'ring ſpring
Is not ſo mournful as the ſtrains you ſing.
Nor rivers winding through the vales below,
So ſweetly warble, or ſo ſmoothly flow.

REMARKS.

WINTER.] This was the Poet's favourite Paſtoral.

Mrs. Tempeſt.] This Lady was of an ancient family in Yorkſhire, and particularly admired by the Author's friend Mr. Walſh *, who having celebrated her in a Paſtoral Elegy, deſired his friend to do the ſame, as appears from one of his Letters,

IMITATIONS.

VER. 1. *Thirſis, the muſic, &c.*] Ἁδύ τι, &c. Theocr. Id. i.

---

* On lately reading Mr. Walſh's Preface to Dryden's tranſlation of Virgil's Eclogues, I was convinced he had a greater ſhare of learning than he is uſually allowed to poſſeſs. His ſtrictures on the French language and manners, and on Fontenelle's affected and unnatural eclogues, as well as on his vain attempt to depreciate the Ancients, are very ſolid and judicious. To what he has ſaid of Virgil may be added, that one of the moſt natural ſtrokes in all his eclogues, is the ſhepherd's reckoning his years by the ſucceſſion of his loves;

Poſtquam nos Amaryllis habet——

This paſtoral chronology is much in character.

Now ſleeping flocks on their ſoft fleeces lie,
The moon, ſerene in glory, mounts the ſky,
While ſilent birds forget their tuneful lays,
Oh ſing of Daphne's fate, and Daphne's praiſe!

THYRSIS.

Behold the groves that ſhine with ſilver froſt,
Their beauty wither'd, and their verdure loſt.
Here ſhall I try the ſweet Alexis' ſtrain,
That call'd the liſt'ning Dryads to the plain?
Thames heard the numbers as he flow'd along,
And bade his willows learn the moving ſong.

REMARKS.

Letters, dated Sept. 9, 1706. "Your laſt Eclogue being on the ſame ſubject with mine, on Mrs. Tempeſt's death, I ſhould take it very kindly in you to give it a little turn, as if it were to the memory of the ſame lady." Her death having happened on the night of the great ſtorm in 1703, gave a propriety to this eclogue, which in its general turn alludes to it. The ſcene of the Paſtoral lies in a grove, the time at midnight. P.

I do not find any lines that allude to the great ſtorm of which the Poet ſpeaks.

VER. 9. *ſhine with ſilver froſt,*] The image is a fine one, but improperly placed. The idea he would raiſe is the *deformity* of Winter, as appears by the following line: but this imagery contradicts it. It ſhould have been—*glare with hoary froſt*, or ſome ſuch expreſſion: the ſame inaccuracy in ver. 31, where he uſes *pearls*, when he ſhould have ſaid *tears*. W.

The alteration here propoſed by Warburton, ſeems to be very injudicious and inelegant; and much reſembles an alteration he wiſhed to make in Love's Labour Loſt; which was, to read—

——to paint the meadows *much bedight*,

inſtead of the preſent reading,

——to paint the meadows with delight.

IMITATIONS.

VER. 13. *Thames heard,* &c.]

"Audiit Eurotas, juſſitque ediſcere lauros." Virg. P.

LYCIDAS.

So may kind rains their vital moiſture yield,
And ſwell the future harveſt of the field.
Begin; this charge the dying Daphne gave,
And ſaid, " Ye ſhepherds ſing around my grave!"
Sing, while beſide the ſhaded tomb I mourn,
And with freſh bays her rural ſhrine adorn.

THYRSIS.

Ye gentle Muſes, leave your cryſtal ſpring,
Let Nymphs and Sylvans cypreſs garlands bring;
Ye weeping Loves, the ſtream with myrtles hide,
And break your bows, as when Adonis dy'd;
And with your golden darts, now uſeleſs grown,
Inſcribe a verſe on this relenting ſtone:
" Let nature change, let heav'n and earth deplore,
" Fair Daphne's dead, and love is now no more!"
'Tis done, and nature's various charms decay,
See gloomy clouds obſcure the chearful day!
Now hung with pearls the dropping trees appear,
Their faded honours ſcatter'd on her bier.

VARIATIONS.

VER 29. Originally thus in the MS.
'Tis done, and nature's chang'd ſince you are gone;
Behold the clouds have put their mourning on. W.
Which are very bad lines indeed.

REMARKS.

VER. 29. *'Tis done,*] Thomſon uſes theſe very words at the end of his Winter. *'Tis done! &c.*

IMITATIONS.

VER. 23, 24, 25. " Inducite fontibus umbras——
Et tumulum facite, et tumulo ſuperaddite carmen." P.

 See,

See, where on earth the flow'ry glories lie,
With her they flourish'd, and with her they die.
Ah what avail the beauties nature wore?
Fair Daphne's dead, and beauty is no more!
  For her the flocks refuse their verdant food,
The thirsty heifers shun the gliding flood,
The silver swans her hapless fate bemoan,
In notes more sad than when they sing their own;
In hollow caves sweet echo silent lies,
Silent, or only to her name replies;
Her name with pleasure once she taught the shore,
Now Daphne's dead, and pleasure is no more!
  No grateful dews descend from ev'ning skies,
Nor morning odours from the flow'rs arise;
No rich perfumes refresh the fruitful field,
Nor fragrant herbs their native incense yield.
The balmy Zephyrs, silent since her death,
Lament the ceasing of a sweeter breath;
Th' industrious bees neglect their golden store!
Fair Daphne's dead, and sweetness is no more!
  No more the mounting larks, while Daphne sings,
Shall list'ning in mid-air suspend their wings;
No more the birds shall imitate her lays,
Or hush'd with wonder, hearken from the sprays;
No more the streams their murmurs shall forbear,
A sweeter music than their own to hear,

REMARKS.

VER. 41. *sweet echo*] This expression of *sweet echo* is taken from Comus; as is another expression, *loose traces*, Third Past. v. 62. And he recommends these poems in high terms to Sir W. Trumball (see the Letters) so early as the year 1704.

But

But tell the reeds, and tell the vocal ſhore,
Fair Daphne's dead, and muſic is no more!

Her fate is whiſper'd by the gentle breeze,
And told in ſighs to all the trembling trees;
The trembling trees, in ev'ry plain and wood,
Her fate remurmur to the ſilver flood;
The ſilver flood, ſo lately calm, appears
Swell'd with new paſſion, and o'erflows with tears;
The winds, and trees, and floods, her death deplore,
Daphne, our grief! our glory now no more!

But ſee! where Daphne wond'ring mounts on high
Above the clouds, above the ſtarry ſky!
Eternal beauties grace the ſhining ſcene,
Fields ever freſh, and groves for ever green!
There while you reſt in Amaranthine bow'rs,
Or from thoſe meads ſelect unfading flow'rs,
Behold us kindly, who your name implore,
Daphne, our Goddeſs, and our grief no more!

REMARKS.

VER. 70. *Above the clouds,*] In Spenſer's November, and in Milton's Lycidas, is the ſame beautiful change of circumſtances: in the latter moſt exquiſite, from line 165.

Weep no more, woful ſhepherds, weep no more—
Where other groves and other ſtreams along,
With nectar pure his oozy locks he laves,
And hears the inexpreſſive nuptial ſong
In the bleſt kingdoms meek of joy and love.

IMITATIONS.

VER. 69, 70. "miratur limen Olympi,
Sub pedibuſque videt nubes et ſydera Daphnis." Virg. P.

LYCIDAS.

How all things liſten, while thy Muſe complains!
Such ſilence waits on Philomela's ſtrains,
In ſome ſtill ev'ning, when the whiſp'ring breeze
Pants on the leaves, and dies upon the trees.
To thee, bright goddeſs, oft a lamb ſhall bleed,
If teeming ewes increaſe my fleecy breed.
While plants their ſhade, or flow'rs their odours give,
Thy name, thy honour, and thy praiſe ſhall live!

THYRSIS.

But ſee, Orion ſheds unwholeſome dews;
Ariſe, the pines a noxious ſhade diffuſe;
Sharp Boreas blows, and Nature feels decay,
Time conquers all, and we muſt Time obey.

VARIATIONS.

VER. 83. Originally thus in the MS.
While vapours riſe, and driving ſnows deſcend,
Thy honour, name, and praiſe, ſhall never end.

REMARKS.

VER. 85. *unwholeſome dews*;] Obſerve how the melody of thoſe four verſes is improved, by the pure iambic foot at the end of each line, except the ſecond,

—— unwholeſomĕ dēws
—— dĕcāy
—— ŏbēy.

VER. 87.] If, according to ſome critics, pleaſing images alone are proper to be exhibited in paſtoral poetry, it muſt be unſuitable, to the intent of this ſort of poetry, to lay the ſcene in the ſeverities of winter.

IMITATIONS.

VER. 81. "illius aram
Saepe tener noſtris ab ovilibus imbuet agnus. Virg." P.

VER. 86. "ſolet eſſe gravis cantantibus umbra,
Juniperi gravis umbra." Virg. P.

VER. 88. *Time conquers all, &c.*]
"Omnia vincit amor, et nos cedamus amori."
Vid. etiam Sannazarii Ecl. et Spenſer's Calendar.

Adieu,

Adieu, ye vales, ye mountains, ſtreams and groves,
Adieu, ye ſhepherds' rural lays and loves;
Adieu, my flocks; farewel, ye ſylvan crew;
Daphne, farewel; and all the world adieu!

REMARKS.

VER. 89, &c.] Theſe four laſt lines allude to the ſeveral ſubjects of the four paſtorals, and to the ſeveral ſcenes of them, particularized before in each. P.

The Sycophancy of A. Phillips, who had prejudiced Mr. Addiſon againſt Pope, occaſioned thoſe papers in the Guardian, written by the latter, in which there is an ironical preference given to the Paſtorals of Phillips, above his own; in order to ſupport the profound judgment of thoſe who could not diſtinguiſh between the rural and the ruſtic; and on that account, condemned the Paſtorals of Pope for wanting ſimplicity. Theſe papers were ſent by an unknown hand to Steele, and the irony eſcaping him, he communicated them to Mr. Pope, declaring he would never publiſh any paper, where one of the Club was complimented at the expence of another. Pope told him he was too delicate, and inſiſted that the papers ſhould be publiſhed in the Guardian. They were ſo. And the pleaſantry eſcaped all but Addiſon: who, taking Pope aſide, ſaid to him in his agreeable manner; You have put your friends here in a very ridiculous light, as will be ſeen when it is underſtood, as it muſt ſoon be, that you was only laughing at the admirers of Phillips.

But this ill conduct of Phillips occaſioned a more open ridicule of his Paſtorals, in the mock poem called the *Shepherd's Week*, written by Gay. But tho' more open, the object of it was ill underſtood by thoſe who were ſtrangers to the quarrel. Theſe miſtook the *Shepherd's Week* for a Burleſque of *Virgils Paſtorals*. How far this goes towards a vindication of Phillips's ſimple painting, let others judge. W.

Upon the whole, the principal merit of theſe paſtorals conſiſts, in their muſical and correct verſification; muſical, to a degree of which rhyme could hardly be thought capable; and in giving the trueſt ſpecimen of that harmony in Engliſh verſe, which is now become indiſpenſably neceſſary; and which has ſo forcibly and

universally

universally influenced the public ear, as to have obliged every moderate rhymer to be at least melodious. Ten pastorals written by Dr. Evans, the friend of Pope, are inserted in the Eighth Volume of Nichols's Poems, never before printed, and as early as our Author's. Some of them in the rustic style and manner of Gay. In the same volume, page 208, are fourteen Piscatory Eclogues, entitled Nereides, by Diaper, who was patronized by Swift, and who dedicates them to Congreve.

MESSIAH,

A SACRED ECLOGUE:

IN IMITATION OF

VIRGIL'S POLLIO.

ADVERTISEMENT.

IN reading ſeveral paſſages of the Prophet Iſaiah, which foretel the coming of Chriſt and the felicities attending it, I could not but obſerve a remarkable parity between many of the thoughts, and thoſe in the Pollio of Virgil. This will not ſeem ſurpriſing, when we reflect, that the Eclogue was taken from a Sibylline prophecy on the ſame ſubject. One may judge that Virgil did not copy it line by line, but ſelected ſuch ideas as beſt agreed with the nature of paſtoral poetry, and diſpoſed them in that manner which ſerved moſt to beautify his piece. I have endeavoured the ſame in this imitation of him, though without admitting any thing of my own; ſince it was written with this particular view, that the reader, by comparing the ſeveral thoughts, might ſee how far the images and deſcriptions of the Prophet are ſuperior to thoſe of the Poet. But as I fear I have prejudiced them by my management, I ſhall ſubjoin the paſſages of Iſaiah, and thoſe of Virgil, under the ſame diſadvantage of a literal tranſlation *. P.

* As Pope made uſe of the old tranſlation of Iſaiah in the paſſages which he ſubjoined, it was thought proper to uſe the ſame, and not have recourſe to the more accurate and more animated verſion of Biſhop Lowth.

The ſpuriouſneſs of thoſe Sibylline verſes which have been applied to our Saviour, has been ſo fully demonſtrated by many able and judicious critics, that, I imagine, they will not be again adduced

adduced as proofs of the truth of the Chriſtian Religion by any ſound and concluſive reaſoner. The learned Heyne has diſcuſſed this point in his notes on the ſecond eclogue of Virgil, p. 73. v. 1.; and he adds an opinion about prophecy in general, too remarkable to be omitted, but of too delicate a nature to be quoted in any words but his own. " Scilicet inter omnes populos, magna imprimis calamitate oppreſſos, Vaticinia circumferri ſolent, quæ ſive graviora minari, ſive lætiora ſolent polliceri, eaque, neceſſariâ rerum viciſſitudine, melioribus aliquando ſuccedentibus temporibus, ferè ſemper eventum habent. Nullo tamen tempore vaticiniorum inſanius fuit ſtudium, quàm ſub extrema Reipublicæ Romanæ tempora, primoſque imperatores; cum bellorum civitium calamitates hominum animos terroribus omnis generis agitatos; ad varia portentorum prodigiorum, & vaticiniorum ludibria convertiſſent. Quaſcunque autem hoc in genere deſcriptiones, novæ felicitatis habemus, ſive in Orientis ſive in Græcis & Romanis poetis, omnes inter ſe ſimiles ſunt: beſtiæ ac feræ cicures, ſerpentes innocui, fruges nullo cultû enatæ, mare plaidum, dii preſentes in terris, aliaque ejuſmodi in omnibus memorantur. In contradiction to this opinion the reader is deſired to turn to as remarkable a paſſage at the end of the twenty-firſt of Biſhop Lowth's excellent Lectures on the Hebrew Poetry.

MESSIAH,

A SACRED ECLOGUE.

YE Nymphs of Solyma! begin the ſong:
To heav'nly themes, ſublimer ſtrains belong.
The moſſy fountains, and the ſylvan ſhades,
The dreams of Pindus and th' Aonian maids,
Delight no more—O Thou my voice inſpire
Who touch'd Iſaiah's hallow'd lips with fire!
Rapt into future times, the Bard begun:
A Virgin ſhall conceive, a Virgin bear a Son!

IMITATIONS.

VER. 8. *A Virgin ſhall conceive—All crimes ſhall ceaſe, &c.*] Virg. Ecl. iv. ver. 6.

" Jam redit et Virgo, redeunt Saturnia regna *;
Jam nova progenies coelo demittitur alto.
Te duce, ſi qua manent ſceleris veſtigia noſtri,
Irrita perpetua ſolvent formidine terras——
Pacatumque reget patriis virtutibus orbem."

" Now the Virgin returns, now the kingdom of Saturn returns, now a new progeny is ſent down from high heaven. By means of thee, whatever reliques of our crimes remain, ſhall be wiped away, and free the world from perpetual fears. He ſhall govern the earth in peace, with the virtues of his father."

Iſaiah, Ch. vii. v. 14.—" Behold, a Virgin ſhall conceive and bear a ſon."——Ch. ix. v. 6, 7. " Unto us a Child is born, unto us a Son is given; the Prince of Peace: of the increaſe of his government, and of his peace, there ſhall be no end: Upon the throne of David, and upon his kingdom, to order and to eſtabliſh it, with judgment, and with juſtice, for ever and ever." P.

* Dante ſays, that Statius was made a Chriſtian by reading this paſſage in Virgil. See L. Gyraldus, p. 534.

From [a] Jeſſe's root behold a branch ariſe,
Whoſe ſacred flow'r with fragrance fills the ſkies:
Th' Ethereal Spirit o'er its leaves ſhall move,
And on its top deſcends the myſtic Dove.
Ye [b] heav'ns! from high the dewy nectar pour,
And in ſoft ſilence ſhed the kindly ſhow'r!

REMARKS.

Ver. 10. *with fragrance fills*] Badly tranſlated by Dr. Johnſon;

—— mulcenteſque æthera flores
Cæleſtes lambunt animæ——

Ver. 13. *The heav'ns! from high the dewy nectar pour, And in ſoft ſilence ſhed the kindly ſhow'r!*] His original ſays, "Drop down, ye heavens, from above, and let the ſkies pour down righteouſneſs: let the earth open, and let them bring forth ſalvation, and let righteouſneſs ſpring up together."—This is a very noble deſcription of divine grace ſhed abroad in the hearts of the faithful under the Goſpel diſpenſation. And the poet underſtood all its force, as appears from the two lines preceding theſe,—*Th' Ethereal Spirit, &c.* The prophet deſcribes this under the image of *rain*, which chiefly fits the *firſt age* of the Goſpel: The poet, under the idea of *dew*, which extends it to *every age*. And it was his purpoſe it ſhould be ſo underſtood, as appears from his expreſſion of *ſoft ſilence*, which agrees with the *common*, not the *extraordinary* effuſions of the Holy Spirit. The figurative term is wonderfully happy. He who would moralize the ancient Mythology in the manner of Bacon, would ſay, that by the poetical *nectar*, is meant the *grace* of the Theologiſts. W.

This interpretation of the words *rain* and *dew*, and of the *common* and the *extraordinary* effuſions of the Holy Spirit, is to the laſt degree forced, and fanciful, and far-fetched. Warburton, it muſt be confeſſed, frequently diſgraced his acuteneſs and great talents, by endeavouring to find out and extort new meanings in the authors whom he undertook to criticiſe. This interpretation is near a-kin to that marvellous one which he has given to a ſpeech in the ſecond Act of Hamlet, where he contends, that the words, "if the ſun breeds maggots in a dead dog, being a God, kiſſing carrion," point out the ſupreme cauſe diffuſing its bleſſings on

[a] Iſai. xi. v. 1. [b] Ch. xlv. v. 8.

The

The [c] ſick and weak the healing plant ſhall aid,
From ſtorms a ſhelter, and from heat a ſhade.
All crimes ſhall ceaſe, and ancient fraud ſhall fail;
Returning [d] Juſtice lift aloft her ſcale;
Peace o'er the world her olive wand extend,
And white-rob'd Innocence from heav'n deſcend.
Swift fly the years, and riſe the expected morn!
Oh ſpring to light, auſpicious Babe, be born!
See Nature haſtes her earlieſt wreaths to bring,
With all the incenſe of the breathing ſpring:

REMARKS.

on mankind, who is, as it were, a dead carrion, dead in original ſin, man, inſtead of a proper return of duty, ſhould breed only corruption and vices. Are theſe ſort of interpretations a jot leſs ridiculous than that of Father Harduin's on the twentieth ode of the ſecond book of Horace, who tells us, this ode is a proſopopeia of Chriſt triumphing and addreſſing the Jews after his reſurrection? That biformis vates alludes to his being in formâ dei, and in formâ ſervi. That the ſecond part of the allegory points to the Dominicans, who ſhould preach and diffuſe his goſpel to diſtant nations; that alitem album, meant their white garments; and reſidunt pelles cruribus aſperæ, their boots.

VER. 17. *ancient fraud*] *i. e.* the fraud of the ſerpent. W.

VER. 23. *See Nature*] Perhaps the dignity, the energy, and the ſimplicity of the original, are in a few paſſages weakened and diminiſhed by florid epithets, and uſeleſs circumlocutions.

See Nature haſtes her earlieſt wreaths to bring,
With all the incenſe of the breathing ſpring:

Are

IMITATIONS.

VER. 23. *See Nature haſtes, &c.*]
Virg. Ecl. iv. v. 18.

"At tibi prima, puer, nullo munuſcula cultu,
Errantes hederas paſſim cum baccare tellus,
Mixtaque ridenti colocaſia fundet acantho——
Ipſa tibi blandos fundent cunabula flores."

"For

[c] Iſai. xxv. v. 4. [d] Ch. ix. v. 7.

 See

See lofty Lebanon[e] his head advance,
See nodding foreſts on the mountains dance:
See ſpicy clouds from lowly Saron riſe,
And Carmel's flow'ry top perfumes the ſkies!
Hark! a glad voice the lonely deſert cheers;
Prepare the [f] way! a God, a God appears:

REMARKS.

Are lines which have too much prettineſs, and too modern an air. The judicious addition of circumſtances and adjuncts is what renders poeſy a more lively imitation of nature than proſe. Pope has been happy in introducing the following circumſtance: the prophet ſays, "The parched ground ſhall become a pool;" our Author expreſſes this idea by ſaying, that the ſhepherd

—— ſhall ſtart amid the thirſty wild to hear
New falls of water murm'ring in his ear *.

A ſtriking example of a ſimilar beauty may be added from Thomſon. Meliſander, in the Tragedy of Agamemnon, after telling us he was conveyed in a veſſel, at midnight, to the wildeſt of the Cyclades, adds, when the pitileſs mariners had left him in that dreadful ſolitude,

———————— I never heard
A ſound ſo diſmal as their parting oars!

On

IMITATIONS.

"For thee, O Child, ſhall the earth, without being tilled, produce her early offerings; winding ivy, mixed with *Baccar*, and *Colocaſia* with ſmiling *Acanthus*. Thy cradle ſhall pour forth pleaſing flowers about thee."

Iſaiah, Ch. xxxv. v. 1. "The wilderneſs and the ſolitary place ſhall be glad, and the deſert ſhall rejoice and bloſſom as the roſe."—Ch. lx. v. 13. "The glory of *Lebanon* ſhall come unto thee, the fir-tree, the pine-tree, and the box together, to beautify the place of thy ſanctuary." P.

VER. 29. *Hark! a glad voice, etc.*]
Virg. Ecl. iv. v. 46.

"Aggredere ô magnos, aderit jam tempus, honores,
Cara deûm ſoboles, magnum Jovis incrementum—

Ipſi

[e] Iſai. xxxv. v. 2. [f] Ch. xl. v. 3, 4.

* Meſſ. v. 70.

A God,

A God, a God! the vocal hills reply,
The rocks proclaim th' approaching Deity.
Lo, earth receives him from the bending ſkies!
Sink down, ye mountains, and, ye valleys, riſe;
With heads declin'd, ye cedars, homage pay;
Be ſmooth, ye rocks; ye rapid floods, give way!

REMARKS.

On the other hand, the prophet has been ſometimes particular, when Pope has been only general. "Lift up thine eyes round about, and ſee; all they gather themſelves together, they come to thee:——The multitude of camels ſhall cover thee, the dromedaries of Midian and Ephah: all they from Sheba ſhall come: they ſhall bring gold and incenſe, and they ſhall ſhew forth the praiſes of the Lord. All the flocks of Kedar ſhall be gathered together unto thee; the rams of Nebaioth ſhall miniſter unto thee †." In imitating this paſſage, Pope has omitted the different beaſts that in ſo picturefque a manner characteriſe the different countries which were to be gathered together on this important event; and ſays, only in undiſtinguiſhing terms,

> See barbarous nations at thy gates attend,
> Walk in thy light, and in thy temple bend;
> See thy bright altars throng'd with proſtrate kings;
> And heap'd with products of Sabæan ſprings ‡.

VER. 26.] An improper and burleſque image!

VER. 35. *With heads declin'd,*] All is here uniformly ſolemn, and majeſtic; not debaſed by any of thoſe mean images that Cowley has ſo unaccountably introduced into his imitation of the 34th

IMITATIONS.

> Ipſi laetitia voces ad ſydera jactant
> Intonſi montes, ipſae jam carmina rupes,
> Ipſa ſonant arbuſta, Deus, deus ille Menalca!"
>
> Ecl. v. ver. 62.

"Oh come and receive the mighty honours: the time draws nigh, O beloved offspring of the Gods, O great encreaſe of Jove! The

† Iſaiah, ch. lx. v. 4, 6, 7. ‡ Meſſ. v. 94.

 The

The Saviour comes! by ancient bards foretold!
Hear [g] him, ye deaf, and all ye blind, behold!
He from thick films ſhall purge the viſual ray,
And on the ſightleſs eye-ball pour the day:

REMARKS.

34th chapter of this ſublime prophet. The ſword of God is called the Scarlet Glutton. And ſee the marvellous burleſque in the following lines;

> The lion then ſhall to the leopard ſay,
> Brother leopard come away!
> The vultures ſhall find the bus'neſs done!
> Th' unbury'd ghoſts ſhall ſadly moan,
> The ſatyrs laugh to hear them groan!

VER. 39. *He from thick films ſhall purge the viſual ray,*] The ſenſe and language ſhew, that by *viſual ray,* the poet meant the *ſight,* or, as Milton calls it, indeed ſomething leſs boldly, tho' more exactly, *the viſual nerve.* However, no critic would quarrel with the figure which calls the *inſtrument* of viſion by the name of the *cauſe.* But tho' the term be noble and ſublime, yet the expreſſion of *thick films* is faulty; and he fell into it by a common neglect of the following rule of good writing, "That when a figurative word is uſed, whatſoever is predicated of it ought not only to agree in terms to the thing to which the figure is applied, but likewiſe to that from which the figure is taken." *Thick films* agree only with the thing to which it is applied, namely, to the *ſight* or eye; and not to that from which it is taken, namely, a *ray of light* coming to the eye. He ſhould have ſaid *thick clouds,* which would have agreed with both. But theſe inaccuracies are not to found in his later poems. W.

It

IMITATIONS.

The uncultivated mountains ſend ſhouts of joy to the ſtars, the very rocks ſing in verſe, the very ſhrubs cry out, A God, a God!"

Iſaiah, ch. xl. v. 3, 4. "The voice of him that crieth in the wilderneſs, Prepare ye the way of the Lord! make ſtraight in the deſert a high way for our God! Every valley ſhall be exalted, and every mountain and hill ſhall be made low, and the crooked ſhall be made ſtraight, and the rough places plain." Ch. iv. v. 23. "Break forth into ſinging, ye mountains! O foreſt, and every tree therein! for the Lord hath redeemed Iſrael." P.

[g] Iſai. xliii. v. 18. Ch. xxxv. v. 5, 6.

'Tis

'Tis he th' obſtructed paths of ſound ſhall clear,
And bid new muſic charm th' unfolding ear:
The dumb ſhall ſing, the lame his crutch forego,
And leap exulting like the bounding roe.
No ſigh, no murmur the wide world ſhall hear,
From ev'ry face he wipes off ev'ry tear.
In [h] adamantine chains ſhall death be bound,
And Hell's grim tyrant feel th' eternal wound.
As the good ſhepherd [i] tends his fleecy care,
Seeks freſheſt paſture and the pureſt air,
Explores the loſt, the wand'ring ſheep directs,
By day o'erſees them, and by night protects,
The tender lambs he raiſes in his arms,
Feeds from his hand, and in his boſom warms;
Thus ſhall mankind his guardian care engage,
The promis'd [k] father of the future age.
No more ſhall [l] nation againſt nation riſe,
Nor ardent warriors meet with hateful eyes,

REMARKS.

It is remarkable, that this obſervation bears a cloſe reſemblance to what Concanen ſays of this paſſage, p. 23. of his Supplement to the Profund. 1728.

VER. 46. This line was thus altered by Steele.

VER. 53. HE, is redundant.

VER. 56. *The promis'd father of the future age.*] In Iſaiah ix. it is the everlaſting Father; which the LXX render, *The Father of the world to come*; agreeably to the ſtyle of the New Teſtament, in which the kingdom of the Meſſiah is called the age of the world to come; Mr. Pope, therefore, has, with great judgment, adopted the ſenſe of the LXX, which, it is ſtrange, his commentator, who is a divine, has not obſerved.

[h] Iſai. xxv. v. 8. [i] Ch. xl. v. 11. [k] Ch. ix. v. 6. [l] Ch. ii. v. 4.

Nor fields with gleaming ſteel be cover'd o'er,
The brazen trumpets kindle rage no more;
But uſeleſs lances into ſcythes ſhall bend,
And the broad faulchion in a plow-ſhare end.
Then palaces ſhall riſe; the joyful [m] Son
Shall finiſh what his ſhort-liv'd Sire begun;
Their vines a ſhadow to their race ſhall yield,
And the ſame hand that ſow'd, ſhall reap the field.
The ſwain in barren [n] deſerts with ſurpriſe
See lilies ſpring, and ſudden verdure riſe;
And ſtarts, amidſt the thirſty wilds to hear
New falls of water murm'ring in his ear.
On rifted rocks, the dragon's late abodes,
The green reed trembles, and the bulruſh nods.
Waſte ſandy [o] valleys, once perplex'd with thorn,
The ſpiry fir and ſhapely box adorn;
To leafleſs ſhrubs the flow'ring palms ſucceed,
And od'rous myrtle to the noiſom weed.

IMITATIONS.

VER. 67. *The ſwain in barren deſerts*] Virg. Ecl. iv. ver. 28.

"Molli paulatim flaveſcet campus ariſta,
Incultiſque rubens pendebit ſentibus uva,
Et durae quercus ſudabunt roſcida mella."

"The fields ſhall grow yellow with ripen'd ears, and the red grape ſhall hang upon the wild brambles, and the hard oaks ſhall diſtil honey like dew."

Iſaiah, Ch. xxxv. v. 7. "The parched ground ſhall become a pool, and the thirſty lands ſprings of water: In the habitation where dragons lay, ſhall be graſs, and reeds and ruſhes."—Ch. lv. v. 13. "Inſtead of the thorn ſhall come up the fir-tree, and inſtead of the briar ſhall come up the myrtle-tree." P.

[m] Iſai. lxv. v. 21, 22. [n] Ch. xxxv. v. 1, 7.
[o] Ch. xli. v. 19. and Ch. lv. v. 13.

The [p] lambs with wolves ſhall graze the verdant mead,
And boys in flow'ry banks the tiger lead;
The ſteer and lion at one crib ſhall meet,
And harmleſs [q] ſerpents lick the pilgrim's feet.
The ſmiling infant in his hand ſhall take
The creſted baſiliſk and ſpeckled ſnake,
Pleas'd the green luſtre of the ſcales ſurvey,
And with their forky tongue ſhall innocently play.
Riſe, crown'd with light, imperial [r] Salem, riſe!
Exalt thy tow'ry head, and lift thy eyes!

IMITATIONS.

VER. 77. *The lambs with wolves, &c.*] Virg. Ecl. iv. ver. 21.

"Ipſae lacte domum referent diſtenta capellae
Ubera, nec magnos metuent armenta leones—
Occidet et ſerpens, et fallax herba veneni
Occidet."—

"The goats ſhall bear to the fold their udders diſtended with milk: nor ſhall the herds be afraid of the greateſt lions. The ſerpent ſhall die, and the herb that conceals poiſon ſhall die."

Iſaiah, Ch. xi. v. 16, &c. "The wolf ſhall dwell with the lamb, and the leopard ſhall lie down with the kid, and the calf and the young lion and the fatling together: and a little child ſhall lead them.—And the lion ſhall eat ſtraw like the ox. And the ſucking child ſhall play on the hole of the aſp, and the weaned child ſhall put his hand on the den of the cockatrice." P.

VER. 80. From the words occidet & ſerpens, it was idly concluded the old ſerpent, Satan, was meant.

VER. 85. *Riſe, crown'd with light, imperial Salem, riſe!*] The thoughts of Iſaiah, which compoſe the latter part of the poem, are wonderfully elevated, and much above thoſe general exclamations of Virgil, which make the loftieſt parts of his Pollio.

"Magnus

[p] Iſai. xi. v. 6, 7, 8. [q] Ch. lvi. v. 25. [r] Ch. lx. v. 1.

See, a long [s] race thy ſpacious courts adorn;
See future ſons, and daughters yet unborn,
In crouding ranks on ev'ry ſide ariſe,
Demanding life, impatient for the ſkies!
See barb'rous [t] nations at thy gates attend,
Walk in thy light, and in thy temple bend;
See thy bright altars throng'd with proſtrate kings,
And heap'd with products of [u] Sabaean ſprings!
For thee Idume's ſpicy foreſts blow,
And ſeeds of gold in Ophir's mountains glow.
See heav'n its ſparkling portals wide diſplay,
And break upon thee in a flood of day.
No more the riſing [w] Sun ſhall gild the morn,
Nor ev'ning Cynthia fill her ſilver horn;
But loſt, diſſolv'd in thy ſuperior rays,
One tide of glory, one unclouded blaze

REMARKS.

VER. 87. See the very animated prophecy of Joad, in the ſeventh ſcene of Racine's Athaliah, perhaps the moſt ſublime piece of poetry in the French language, and a chief ornament of that which is one of the beſt of their tragedies. In ſpeaking of theſe paraphraſes from the ſacred ſcriptures, I cannot forbear mentioning Dr. Young's nervous and noble paraphraſe of the book of Job, and Mr. Pitt's of the third and twenty-fifth chapters of the ſame book, and alſo of the fifteenth chapter of Exodus.

VER. 100. Cynthia is an improper becauſe a claſſical word.

IMITATIONS.

"Magnus ab integro ſaeclorum naſcitur ordo!
—toto ſurget gens aurea mundo!
—incipient magni procedere menſes!
Aſpice, venturo laetentur ut omnia ſaeclo!" &c.

The reader needs only to turn to the paſſages of Iſaiah, here cited. P.

[s] Iſai. lx. v. 4. [t] Ch. lx. v. 3. [u] Ch. lx. v. 6.
[w] Ch. lx. v. 19, 20.

O'erflow thy courts: the Light himself shall shine
Reveal'd, and God's eternal day be thine!
The [x] seas shall waste, the skies in smoke decay,
Rocks fall to dust, and mountains melt away; 106
But fix'd his word, his saving pow'r remains:
Thy realm for ever lasts, thy own MESSIAH reigns!

[x] Isai. li. v. 6. and Ch. liv. v. 10.

THIS is certainly the most animated and sublime of all our Author's compositions, and it is manifestly owing to the great original which he copied. Isaiah abounds in striking and magnificent imagery. See Mr. Mason's paraphrase of the 14th chapter of this exalted prophet. Dr. Johnson, in his youth, gave a translation of this piece, which has been praised and magnified beyond its merits. It may justly be said, (with all due respect to the great talents of this writer), that in this translation of the Messiah are many hard and unclassical expressions, a great want of harmony, and many unequal and Un-virgilian lines. I was once present at a dispute, on this subject, betwixt a person of great political talents, and a scholar who had spent his life among the Greek and Roman classics. Both were intimate friends of Johnson. The former, after many objections had been made to this translation by the latter, quoted a line which he thought equal to any he ever had read.

——juncique tremit variabilis umbra.

The green reed trembles——

The Scholar (Pedant if you will) said, there is no such word as variabilis in any classical writer. Surely, said the other, in Virgil; variabile semper fœmina.——You forget, said the oppouent, it is varium & mutabile.

In two men of superior talents it was certainly no disgrace to the one not to have written pure Virgilian verses, nor to the other to have misquoted a line of the Æneid. They only who are such idolaters of the Rambler, as to think he could do every thing equally well, can alone be mortified at hearing that the following lines in his Messiah are reprehensible;

——Cœlum mihi carminis alta materies——

——dignos accende furores——

Mittit

Mittit aromaticas vallis ſaronica nubes—
Ille cutim ſpiſſam viſus habetare vetabit—
—— furat horrida membris—
——juncique tremit variabilis umbra—
—— Buxique ſequaces
Artificis frondent dextræ—
—— feſſa colubri
Membra viatoris recreabunt frigore linguæ.

Boileau deſpiſed the writers of modern Latin poetry. Jortin ſaid he was no extraordinary claſſical ſcholar, and that he tranſlated Longinus from the Latin. Of all the celebrated French writers Racine appears to be the beſt, if not the only Greek ſcholar, except Fenelon. The reſt, Corneille, Moliere, La Motte, Fontenelle, Crebillon, Voltaire, knew little of that language.

I find and feel it impoſſible to conclude theſe remarks on Pope's Meſſiah, without mentioning another poem taken alſo from Iſaiah, the noble and magnificent ode on the Deſtruction of Babylon, which Dr. Lowth hath given us in the thirteenth of his Prelections on the Poetry of the Hebrews; and which, the ſcene, the actors, the ſentiments, and diction, all contribute to place in the firſt rank of the ſublime; theſe Prelections, abounding in remarks entirely new, delivered in the pureſt and moſt expreſſive language, have been received and read with almoſt univerſal approbation, both at home and abroad, as being the richeſt augmentation literature has in our times received, and as tending to illuſtrate and recommend the Holy Scriptures in an uncommon degree. It has been conſequently a matter of ſurprize to hear an eminent prelate pronouncing lately, with a dogmatical air, that theſe Prelections, "are in a vein of criticiſm not above the common." Notwithſtanding which deciſion, it may ſafely be affirmed, that they will long ſurvive, after the commentaries on Horace's Art of Poetry, and on the Eſſay on Man, are loſt and forgotten.

WINDSOR-FOREST.

TO THE RIGHT HONOURABLE

GEORGE LORD LANSDOWN.

Non injuſſa cano: Te noſtrae, *Vare*, myricae,
Te *Nemus* omne canet; nec Phoebo gratior ulla eſt,
Quam ſibi quae *Vari* praeſcripſit pagina nomen. VIRG.

WINDSOR-FOREST.

TO THE RIGHT HONOURABLE

GEORGE LORD LANSDOWN.[a]

THY foreſt, Windſor! and thy green retreats,
At once the Monarch's and the Muſe's ſeats,
Invite my lays. Be preſent, ſylvan maids!
Unlock your ſprings, and open all your ſhades.

GRANVILLE

VARIATIONS.

VER. 3, &c. Originally thus, (and indeed much better;)

Chaſte Goddeſs of the woods,
Nymphs of the vales, and Naïads of the floods,
Lead me through arching bow'rs, and glimm'ring glades,
Unlock your ſprings— P.

NOTES.

This Poem was written at two different times: the firſt part of it, which relates to the country, in the year 1704, at the ſame time with the Paſtorals; the latter part was not added till the year 1713, in which it was publiſhed. P.

[a] Notwithſtanding the many praiſes laviſhed on this celebrated nobleman as a poet, by Dryden, by Addiſon, by Bolingbroke, by our Author, and others, yet candid criticiſm muſt oblige us to confeſs, that he was but a feeble imitator of the feebleſt parts of Waller. In his tragedy of Heroic Love, he ſeems not to have had a true reliſh for Homer whom he copied; and in the Britiſh Enchanters, very little fancy is to be found in a ſubject fruitful of romantic imagery. It was fortunate for him, ſays Mr. Walpole in his Anecdotes, that in an age when perſecution raged ſo fiercely againſt lukewarm authors, that he had an intimacy with the Inquiſitor General; how elſe would ſuch lines as theſe eſcape the Bathos; they are in his Heroic Love;

—— Why thy Gods
Enlighten thee to ſpeak their *dark* decrees.

His Progreſs of Beauty, and his Eſſay on Unnatural Flights in Poetry, ſeem to be the beſt of his pieces; in the latter are many good critical remarks and precepts, and it is accompanied with

notes

GRANVILLE commands; your aid, O Muses, bring!
What Muse for GRANVILLE can refuse to sing? 6

The Groves of Eden, vanish'd now so long,
Live in description, and look green in song:

NOTES.

notes that contain much agreeable instruction. For it may be added, his prose is better than his verse. Witness a Letter to a Young Man on his taking Orders, his Observations on Burnet, and his Defence of his relation Sir Richard Grenville, and a Translation of some parts of Demosthenes, and a Letter to his Father on the Revolution, written in October 1688. After having been Secretary at War 1710, Controller and Treasurer to the Household, and of her Majesty's Privy Council, and created a Peer 1711, he was seized as a suspected person, at the accession of King George the First, and confined in the Tower, in the very chamber that had before been occupied by Sir Robert Walpole. But whatever may be thought of Lord Lansdown as a poet, his character as a man, was highly valuable. His conversation was most pleasing and polite; his affability, and universal benevolence and gentleness, captivating; he was a firm friend, and a sincere lover of his country. This is the character I received of him from his near relation, and descendant, the late excellent Mrs. Delany; who was herself a true judge of merit and worth; of which she possessed so great a degree. Lord Lansdown was frequently the subject of those entertaining conversations at which I had the honour and advantage of being sometimes present, both in London and Windsor; in both which places, she was enabled to pass the remainder of a most well-spent life, with great ease and comfort, by the kindness of royal munificence, bestowed on her with equal delicacy and generosity.

VER. 7. A feeble and niggardly encomium on the Paradise Lost, which in truth was not much read when our young poet wrote this passage. There is an inaccuracy in the ninth line, in making the flame equal to a grove. It might have been Milton's flame. In a great writer we can pardon nothing, least his blemishes should be copied.

IMITATIONS.

VER. 6. "neget quis carmina Gallo?" Virg.

These,

These, were my breaſt inſpir'd with equal flame,
Like them in beauty, ſhould be like in fame.
Here hills and vales, the woodland and the plain,
Here earth and water ſeem to ſtrive again;
Not Chaos-like together cruſh'd and bruis'd,
But, as the world, harmoniouſly confus'd:
Where order in variety we ſee,
And where, tho' all things differ, all agree.
Here waving groves a chequer'd ſcene diſplay,
And part admit, and part exclude the day;
As ſome coy nymph her lover's warm addreſs
Nor quite indulges, nor can quite repreſs.
There, interſpers'd in lawns and op'ning glades,
Thin trees ariſe that ſhun each other's ſhades.
Here in full light the ruſſet plains extend:
There wrapt in clouds the blueiſh hills aſcend.
Ev'n the wild heath diſplays her purple dyes,
And 'midſt the deſert fruitful fields ariſe,
That crown'd with tufted trees and ſpringing corn,
Like verdant iſles the ſable waſte adorn.

VARIATIONS.

VER. 25. Originally thus;
Why ſhould I ſing our better ſuns or air,
Whoſe vital draughts prevent the leach's care,
While through freſh fields th' enliv'ning odours breathe,
Or ſpread with vernal blooms the purple heath? P.

NOTES.

VER. 15.] Evidently from Cooper's Hill;
Such was the diſcord which did firſt diſperſe
Form, order, beauty, thro' the univerſe.

VER. 19.] It is a falſe thought, and gives, as it were, ſentiment to the groves.

Let

Let India boaſt her plants, nor envy we
The weeping amber or the balmy tree,
While by our oaks the precious loads are born,
And realms commanded which thoſe trees adorn.
Not proud Olympus yields a nobler ſight,
Tho' gods aſſembled grace his tow'ring height,
Than what more humble mountains offer here,
Where, in their bleſſings, all thoſe Gods appear.
See Pan with flocks, with fruits Pomona crown'd,
Here bluſhing Flora paints th' enamel'd ground,
Here Ceres' gifts in waving proſpect ſtand,
And nodding tempt the joyful reaper's hand;
Rich Induſtry ſits ſmiling on the plains,
And peace and plenty tell, a STUART reigns.
  Not thus the land appear'd in ages paſt,
A dreary deſert, and a gloomy waſte,
To ſavage beaſts and ſavage laws a prey,
And kings more furious and ſevere than they;

NOTES.

VER. 33. *Not proud Olympus, &c.*] Sir J. Denham, in his Cooper's Hill, had ſaid,

"Than which a nobler weight no mountain bears,
But Atlas only, which ſupports the ſpheres."

The compariſon is childiſh, as the taking it from fabulous hiſtory deſtroys the compliment. Our Poet has ſhewn more judgment: he has made a manly uſe of as fabulous a circumſtance by the artful application of the mythology,

"Where, in their bleſſings, all thoſe Gods appear," &c.

Making the nobility of the hills of Windſor-foreſt to conſiſt in ſupporting the inhabitants in plenty. W.

This appears an idle play on the word "ſupporting."

VER. 37.] The word *crown'd* is exceptionable; it makes Pan crowned with flocks.

VER. 45. *ſavage laws*] The Foreſt Laws. See the account of them in Blackſtone's excellent Lectures; the killing a deer, boar, or hare, was puniſhed with the loſs of the delinquent's eyes.

Who

Who claim'd the ſkies, diſpeopled air and floods,
The lonely lords of empty wilds and woods:
Cities laid waſte, they ſtorm'd the dens and caves,
(For wiſer brutes were backward to be ſlaves)
What could be free, when lawleſs beaſts obey'd,
And ev'n the elements a Tyrant ſway'd?
In vain kind ſeaſons ſwell'd the teeming grain,
Soft ſhow'rs diſtill'd, and ſuns grew warm in vain;
The ſwain with tears his fruſtrate labour yields,
And famiſh'd dies amidſt his ripen'd fields.
What wonder then, a beaſt or ſubject ſlain
Were equal crimes in a deſpotic reign?
Both doom'd alike, for ſportive Tyrants bled,
But while the ſubject ſtarv'd, the beaſt was fed.
Proud Nimrod firſt the bloody chace began,
A mighty hunter, and his prey was man:
Our haughty Norman boaſts that barb'rous name,
And makes his trembling ſlaves the royal game.

VARIATIONS.

Ver. 49. Originally thus in the MS.

From towns laid waſte, to dens and caves they ran
(For who firſt ſtoop'd to be a ſlave was man.)

Ver. 57, &c.

No wonder ſavages or ſubjects ſlain——
But ſubjects ſtarv'd, while ſavages were fed.

It was originally thus, but the word "ſavages" is not properly applied to beaſts, but to men; which occaſioned the alteration. P.

The fields are raviſh'd from th' induſtrious ſwains,
From men their cities, and from Gods their fanes:
The levell'd towns with weeds lie cover'd o'er;
The hollow winds through naked temples roar;
Round broken columns claſping ivy twin'd;
O'er heaps of ruin ſtalk'd the ſtately hind;
The fox obſcene to gaping tombs retires,
And ſavage howlings fill the ſacred quires.

VARIATIONS.

VER. 72. And wolves with howling fill, &c.] The author thought this an error, wolves not being common in England at the time of the Conqueror. P.

NOTES.

VER. 65. *The fields are raviſh'd, &c.*] Alluding to the deſtruction made in the New Foreſt, and the tyrannies exerciſed there by William I. P.

I have the authority of three or four of our beſt antiquarians to ſay, that the common tradition of villages and pariſhes, within the compaſs of thirty miles, being deſtroyed, in the New Foreſt, is abſolutely groundleſs, no traces or veſtiges of ſuch being to be diſcovered, nor any other pariſh named in Doomſday Book, but what now remains. Of late years, ſome minute enquiries have been made on this ſubject, by accurate and well-inform'd judges, who are clearly of this opinion. The Preſident Henault has given us a more amiable idea of our Norman Conqueror than is here exhibited.

VER. 71.] This image of the fox is in the poems aſcribed to Oſſian.

IMITATIONS.

VER. 65. *The fields are raviſh'd from th' induſtrious ſwains,*
From men their cities, and from Gods their fanes:]
Tranſlated from

" Templa adimit divis, fora civibus, arva colonis,"

an old monkiſh writer, I forget who. P.

In Camden's Britannia, firſt edition, in the account of Somerſetſhire it is ſaid of Edgar,

Templa Deo, Templis Monachos, Monachis dedit agros.

Aw'd by his Nobles, by his Commons curſt,
Th' Oppreſſor rul'd tyrannic where he durſt,
Stretch'd o'er the Poor and Church his iron rod,
And ſerv'd alike his Vaſſals and his God.
Whom ev'n the Saxon ſpar'd, and bloody Dane,
The wanton victims of his ſport remain.
But ſee, the man, who ſpacious regions gave
A waſte for beaſts, himſelf deny'd a grave!
Stretch'd on the lawn his ſecond hope ſurvey,
At once the chaſer, and at once the prey:

NOTES.

Ver. 74.] A fine remain of ancient art and ancient cuſtoms, a piece of tapeſtry, ſaid to be the work of Queen Matilda, is annually exhibited in the cathedral church of Bayeux, in Normandy, repreſenting the expedition of William the Conqueror, and containing a moſt minute picture of every part of that event, from his landing in England to the battle of Haſtings. An engraving of it is given in the tenth volume of the Memoirs of the Academy of Belles Lettres.

Ver. 80.] In St. Foix's entertaining hiſtorical Eſſays on Paris, it is related, p. 95. tom. 5. that juſt as the body of William I. was going to be put into the grave, a voice cried aloud, "I forbid his interment. When William was only Duke of Normandy, he ſeized this piece of Land from my father, on which he built this abbey of St. Stephen, without making me a recompence, which I now demand." Prince Henry, who was preſent, called out the man, who was only a common farrier, and agreed to give him an hundred crowns for this burial place. Except the former conqueſt of England by the Saxons, (ſays Hume, vol. i.), who were induced, by peculiar circumſtances, to proceed even to the extermination of the natives, it would be difficult to find in all hiſtory, a revolution more deſtructive, or attended with a more complete ſubjection of the ancient inhabitants.

Ver. 81. *ſecond hope*] Richard, ſecond ſon of William the Conqueror. W.

Lo Rufus, tugging at the deadly dart,
Bleeds in the foreſt like a wounded hart.
Succeeding monarchs heard the ſubjects cries,
Nor ſaw diſpleas'd the peaceful cottage riſe:
Then gath'ring flocks on unknown mountains fed,
O'er ſandy wilds were yellow harveſts ſpread,
The foreſt wonder'd at th' unuſual grain,
And ſecret tranſports touch'd the conſcious ſwain.
Fair Liberty, Britannia's Goddeſs, rears
Her chearful head, and leads the golden years.
  Ye vig'rous ſwains! while youth ferments your blood,
And purer ſpirits ſwell the ſprightly flood,

VARIATIONS.

VER. 91.

O may no more a foreign maſter's rage,
With wrongs yet legal, curſe a future age!
Still ſpread, fair Liberty! thy heav'nly wings,
Breathe plenty on the fields, and fragrance on the ſprings. P.

NOTES.

VER. 83. The moment Walter Tyrrel had ſhot him, without ſpeaking of the accident, he inſtantly haſtened to the ſea ſhore and embarked for France, and from thence hurried to Jeruſalem to do penance for his involuntary crime. The body of Rufus was found in the foreſt by a countryman, whoſe family are ſtill ſaid to be living near the ſpot, and was buried, without any pomp, before the altar of Wincheſter cathedral, where the monument ſtill remains. Though the Monkiſh hiſtorians, who hated him, may perhaps have exaggerated his vices, yet he ſeems really to have been a violent, prodigal, proud, perfidious, ungenerous, and tyrannical prince. There was however ſomething of magnificence in his building the Tower, Weſtminſter-hall, and London-bridge.

IMITATIONS.

VER. 89. "Miraturque novas frondes et non ſua poma." Virg.

Now range the hills, the gameful woods beſet,
Wind the ſhrill horn, or ſpread the waving net.
When milder autumn ſummer's heat ſucceeds,
And in the new-ſhorn field the partridge feeds,
Before his lord the ready ſpaniel bounds,
Panting with hope, he tries the furrow'd grounds;
But when the tainted gales the game betray,
Couch'd cloſe he lies, and meditates the prey;
Secure they truſt th' unfaithful field beſet,
'Till hov'ring o'er 'em ſweeps the ſwelling net.
Thus (if ſmall things we may with great compare)
When Albion ſends her eager ſons to war,
Some thoughtleſs Town, with eaſe and plenty bleſt,
Near, and more near, the cloſing lines inveſt;

VARIATIONS.

VER. 97.

When yellow autumn ſummer's heat ſucceeds,
And into wine the purple harveſt bleeds [a],
The partridge feeding in the new-ſhorn fields,
Both morning ſports and ev'ning pleaſures yields.

VER. 107. It ſtood thus in the firſt Editions:

Pleas'd in the Gen'ral's ſight, the hoſt lie down
Sudden before ſome unſuſpecting town;
The young, the old, one inſtant makes our prize,
And o'er their captive heads Britannia's ſtandard flies.

NOTES.

VER. 93.] Theſe rural ſports of ſetting, ſhooting, and fiſhing, are not, it muſt be allowed, ſufficiently appropriated, and are ſuited as much to any other place as to the foreſt of Windſor. The ſtag chaſe is by no means ſo full, ſo animated, and ſo circumſtantial, as that of Somerville.

[a] Perhaps the Author thought it not allowable to deſcribe the ſeaſon by a circumſtance not proper to our climate, the vintage. P.

Sudden they ſeize th' amaz'd, defenceleſs prize,
And high in air Britannia's ſtandard flies.

See! from the brake the whirring pheaſant ſprings,
And mounts exulting on triumphant wings:
Short is his joy; he feels the fiery wound,
Flutters in blood, and panting beats the ground.
Ah! what avail his gloſſy, varying dyes,
His purple creſt, and ſcarlet-circled eyes,
The vivid green his ſhining plumes unfold,
His painted wings, and breaſt that flames with gold?

Nor yet, when moiſt Arcturus clouds the ſky,
The woods and fields their pleaſing toils deny.
To plains with well-breath'd beagles we repair,
And trace the mazes of the circling hare:
(Beaſts, urg'd by us, their fellow-beaſts purſue,
And learn of man each other to undo.)
With ſlaught'ring guns th' unwearied fowler roves,
When froſts have whiten'd all the naked groves;

VARIATIONS.

VER. 126. O'er ruſtling leaves around the naked groves.
This is a better line.

NOTES.

VER. 115.] In the art of inſerting reflections, moral or pathetic, in deſcriptive poems, no writer has excelled Gray, in his enchanting Elegy written in a country church-yard; one of the chief beauties in any piece of local poetry, when ſuch reflections naturally riſe out of the ſcene and ſubject before us.

VER. 124. The philoſophy, and the ſentiment, and the expreſſions of this line, and of line 50, *beaſts were backward to be ſlaves*, are all blameable.

IMITATIONS.

VER. 115. "nec te tua plurima, Pantheu,
Labentem pietas, vel Apollinis infula texit." Virg. W.

Certainly not an imitation of this paſſage in Virgil.

Where doves in flocks the leafleſs trees o'erſhade,
And lonely woodcocks haunt the wat'ry glade.
He lifts the tube, and levels with his eye;
Straight a ſhort thunder breaks the frozen ſky:
Oft, as in airy rings they ſkim the heath,
The clam'rous lapwings feel the leaden death:
Oft, as the mounting larks their notes prepare,
They fall, and leave their little lives in air.

In genial ſpring, beneath the quiv'ring ſhade,
Where cooling vapours breathe along the mead,
The patient fiſher takes his ſilent ſtand,
Intent, his angle trembling in his hand:
With looks unmov'd, he hopes the ſcaly breed,
And eyes the dancing cork, and bending reed.
Our plenteous ſtreams a various race ſupply,
The bright-ey'd perch with fins of Tyrian dye,
The ſilver eel, in ſhining volumes roll'd,
The yellow carp, in ſcales bedrop'd with gold,
Swift trouts, diverſify'd with crimſon ſtains,
And pykes, the tyrants of the watry plains.

Now Cancer glows with Phoebus' fiery car:
The youth ruſh eager to the ſylvan war,
Swarm o'er the lawns, the foreſt walks ſurround,
Rouze the fleet hart, and cheer the opening hound.

VARIATIONS.

VER. 129. The fowler lifts his levell'd tube on high. P.

IMITATIONS.

VER. 134. "Praecipites alta vitam ſub nube relinquunt."
Virg.

Th' impatient courſer pants in ev'ry vein, 151
And pawing, ſeems to beat the diſtant plain:
Hills, vales, and floods appear already croſs'd,
And ere he ſtarts, a thouſand ſteps are loſt. 154
See the bold youth ſtrain up the threat'ning ſteep,
Ruſh through the thickets, down the valleys ſweep,
Hang o'er their courſers heads with eager ſpeed,
And earth rolls back beneath the flying ſteed.
Let old Arcadia boaſt her ample plain,
Th' immortal huntreſs, and her virgin train;
Nor envy, Windſor! ſince thy ſhades have ſeen
As bright a Goddeſs, and as chaſte a Queen;
Whoſe care, like hers, protects the ſylvan reign,
The Earth's fair light, and Empreſs of the Main.

Here too, 'tis ſung, of old Diana ſtray'd,
And Cynthus' top forſook for Windſor ſhade;
Here was ſhe ſeen o'er airy waſtes to rove,
Seek the clear ſpring, or haunt the pathleſs grove;

NOTES.

VER. 162. Queen Anne.

IMITATIONS.

VER. 151. *Th' impatient courſer, &c.*] Tranſlated from Statius,

"Stare adeo miſerum eſt, pereunt veſtigia mille
Ante fugam, abſentemque ferit gravis ungula campum."

Theſe lines Mr. Dryden, in his preface to his tranſlation of Freſnoy's Art of Painting, calls *wonderfully fine*, and ſays, "they would coſt him an hour, if he had the leiſure, to tranſlate them, there is ſo much of beauty in the original;" which was the reaſon, I ſuppoſe, why Mr. P. tried his ſtrength with them. W.

The ſecond line in Statius, ſays Jortin, is bombaſtic.

VER. 158. *and earth rolls back*] He has improv'd his original,

"terraeque urbeſque recedunt." Virg. W.

But no imitation of Virgil was here intended.

Here

Here arm'd with ſilver bows, in early dawn,
Her buſkin'd Virgins trac'd the dewy lawn.
Above the reſt a rural nymph was fam'd,
Thy offspring, Thames! the fair Lodona nam'd;
(Lodona's fate, in long oblivion caſt,
The Muſe ſhall ſing, and what ſhe ſings ſhall laſt.)
Scarce could the Goddeſs from her nymph be known,
But by the creſcent and the golden zone.
She ſcorn'd the praiſe of beauty, and the care;
A belt her waiſt, a fillet binds her hair;
A painted quiver on her ſhoulder ſounds,
And with her dart the flying deer ſhe wounds.
It chanc'd, as eager of the chace, the maid
Beyond the foreſt's verdant limits ſtray'd,
Pan ſaw and lov'd, and burning with deſire
Purſu'd her flight, her flight increas'd his fire.

NOTES.

VER. 171.] Dr. Johnſon ſeems to have paſſed too ſevere a cenſure on this epiſode of Lodona. A tale in a deſcriptive poet has certainly a good effect. See Thomſon's Lavinia; and the many beautiful tales interwoven in the Loves of the Plants.

VER. 179.] From the fourth book of Virgil, who copied it from Homer's beautiful figure of Apollo. Iliad, b. i. v. 76. But, as Dr. Clark finely and acutely obſerves, even Virgil has loſt the beauty and the propriety of the original. Homer ſays, the arrows ſounded in the quiver becauſe the ſtep of the God was haſty and irregular, as of an angry perſon. Irati deſcribitur inceſſus, paulo utique inæquebilior.

IMITATIONS.

VER. 175.

"Nec poſitu variare comas; ubi fibula veſtem,
Vitta coërcuerat neglectos alba capillos." Ovid.

Not

Not half ſo ſwift the trembling doves can fly
When the fierce eagle cleaves the liquid ſky;
Not half ſo ſwiftly the fierce eagle moves,
When through the clouds he drives the trembling doves;
As from the God ſhe flew with furious pace,
Or as the God, more furious, urg'd the chace.
Now fainting, ſinking, pale, the nymph appears;
Now cloſe behind, his ſounding ſteps ſhe hears;
And now his ſhadow reach'd her as ſhe run,
His ſhadow lengthen'd by the ſetting ſun;
And now his ſhorter breath, with ſultry air,
Pants on her neck, and fans her parting hair.
In vain on father Thames ſhe calls for aid,
Nor could Diana help her injur'd maid.
Faint, breathleſs, thus ſhe pray'd, nor pray'd in vain;
" Ah Cynthia! ah—tho' baniſh'd from thy train,
" Let me, O let me, to the ſhades repair,
" My native ſhades—there weep, and murmur there."
She ſaid, and melting as in tears ſhe lay,
In a ſoft, ſilver ſtream diſſolv'd away.
The ſilver ſtream her virgin coldneſs keeps,
For ever murmurs, and for ever weeps;

IMITATIONS.

VER. 185, 186.

" Ut fugere accipitrem penna trepidante columbae,
Ut ſolet accipiter trepidas agitare columbas." Ovid.

VER. 193, 196.

" Sol erat a tergo: vidi praecedere longam
Ante pedes umbram: niſi ſi timor illa videbat.
Sed certe ſonituque pedum terrebar; et ingens
Crinales vittas afflabat anhelitus oris."

Moſt of the circumſtances in this tale are from Ovid.

Still

Still bears the name the hapleſs virgin bore,
And bathes the foreſt where ſhe rang'd before.
In her chaſte current oft the Goddeſs laves,
And with celeſtial tears augments the waves.
Oft in her glaſs the muſing ſhepherd ſpies
The headlong mountains and the downward ſkies.
The wat'ry landſkip of the pendant woods,
And abſent trees that tremble in the floods;
In the clear azure gleam the flocks are ſeen,
And floating foreſts paint the waves with green,
Through the fair ſcene roll ſlow the ling'ring ſtreams,
Then foaming pour along, and ruſh into the Thames.
  Thou, too, great father of the Britiſh floods!
With joyful pride ſurvey'ſt our lofty woods;
Where tow'ring oaks their growing honours rear,
And future navies on thy ſhores appear.
Not Neptune's ſelf from all her ſtreams receives
A wealthier tribute than to thine he gives.
No ſeas ſo rich, ſo gay no banks appear,
No lake ſo gentle, and no ſpring ſo clear.
Nor Po ſo ſwells the fabling Poet's lays,
While led along the ſkies his current ſtrays,
As thine, which viſits Windſor's fam'd abodes,
To grace the manſion of our earthly Gods:

NOTES.

VER. 207. *Still bears the name*] The River Loddon.

VER. 211. *Oft in her glaſs, &c.*] Theſe ſix lines were added after the firſt writing of this poem. P.

And in truth they are but puerile and redundant.

VER. 227.] Very ill expreſſed; eſpecially the river's filling the lays.

Nor

Nor all his ſtars above a luſtre ſhow,
Like the bright beauties on thy banks below;
Where Jove, ſubdu'd by mortal paſſion ſtill,
Might change Olympus for a nobler hill.

Happy the man whom this bright Court approves,
His Sov'reign favours, and his country loves:
Happy next him, who to theſe ſhades retires,
Whom Nature charms, and whom the Muſe inſpires:
Whom humbler joys of home-felt quiet pleaſe,
Succeſſive ſtudy, exerciſe, and eaſe.
He gathers health from herbs the foreſt yields,
And of their fragrant phyſic ſpoils the fields:
With chemic art exalts the min'ral pow'rs,
And draws the aromatic ſouls of flow'rs:
Now marks the courſe of rolling orbs on high;
O'er figur'd worlds now travels with his eye;
Of ancient writ unlocks the learned ſtore,
Conſults the dead, and lives paſt ages o'er:
Or wand'ring thoughtful in the ſilent wood,
Attends the duties of the wiſe and good,

VARIATIONS.

VER. 233. It ſtood thus in the MS.

And force great Jove, if Jove's a lover ſtill,
To change Olympus, &c.

VER. 235.

Happy the man, who to theſe ſhades retires,
But doubly happy, if the Muſe inſpires!
Bleſt whom the ſweets of home-felt quiet pleaſe;
But far more bleſt, who ſtudy joins with eaſe. P.

NOTES.

VER. 236.] All this paſſage clearly reſembles one in Philips's Cyder, Book i. towards the end.

T' obſerve

T' obſerve a mean, be to himſelf a friend,
To follow nature, and regard his end;
Or looks on heav'n with more than mortal eyes,
Bids his free ſoul expatiate in the ſkies,
Amid her kindred ſtars familiar roam,
Survey the region, and confeſs her home!
Such was the life great Scipio once admir'd,
Thus Atticus, and TRUMBAL thus retir'd.

Ye ſacred Nine! that all my ſoul poſſeſs,
Whoſe raptures fire me, and whoſe viſions bleſs,
Bear me, oh bear me to ſequeſter'd ſcenes,
The bow'ry mazes, and ſurrounding greens;
To Thames's banks which fragrant breezes fill,
Or where ye Muſes ſport on COOPER'S HILL.

(On

NOTES.

VER. 251. *T' obſerve a mean*] This is marked as an imitation of Lucretius in the firſt, and all editions of Warburton; but erroneouſly; the paſſage is in the ſecond book of Lucan, v. 381.

VER. 259.] "Here, you cannot but be ſenſible (ſays the ingenious Mr. Webb) how the enthuſiaſm is tamed by the preciſion of the couplet, and the conſequent littleneſs of the ſcenery. How different from Milton?

"——Yet not the more
Ceaſe I to wander," &c. Par. Loſt. 3d B.

The following four lines, v. 267, are far more poetical, but theſe again muſt yield to an enchanting paſſage in Thomſon's Summer, p. 39, of the firſt edition, and which is altered for the worſe in the later editions.

VER. 263.] Denham, ſays Dr. Johnſon, ſeems to have been, at leaſt among us, the author of a ſpecies of compoſition that may be denominated *Local Poetry*, of which the fundamental ſubject is ſome particular landſcape, to be poetically deſcribed, with the addition of ſuch embelliſhments as may be ſupplied by hiſtorical retroſpection, or incidental meditation. Cooper's Hill,

if

(On COOPER's HILL eternal wreathes ſhall grow
While laſts the mountain, or while Thames ſhall flow)
I ſeem through conſecrated walks to rove,
I hear ſoft muſic die along the grove:
Led by the ſound, I roam from ſhade to ſhade,
By god-like Poets venerable made:
Here his firſt lays majeſtic DENHAM ſung;
There the laſt numbers flow'd from COWLEY's tongue.

VARIATIONS.

VER. 267. It ſtood thus in the MS.

Methinks around your holy ſcenes I rove,
And hear your muſic echoing through the grove:
With tranſport viſit each inſpiring ſhade,
By God-like Poets venerable made.

NOTES.

if it be maliciouſly inſpected, will not be found without its faults; the digreſſions are too long, the morality too frequent, and the ſentiments ſuch as will not bear a rigorous enquiry. It was firſt printed at Oxford, in 1633.

VER. 271. *majeſtic Denham*] In the Memoirs of Count Grammont, 4to edition, p. 200, Sir John Denham is charged with the atrocious crime of poiſoning his young and beautiful wife. The populace in his neighbourhood ſaid they would tear him in pieces for this abominable act, as ſoon as he ſhould come abroad. In the year 1667 he appeared to have been diſordered in his intellects. And in Temple's Works a very depretiating account of his behaviour is given, vol. i. p. 484. In Butler's Poſthumous Works is a ſatire, entitled, A Panegyric on Denham's Recovery from Madneſs.

VER. 272. *There the laſt numbers flow'd from Cowley's tongue.*] Mr. Cowley died at Chertſey on the borders of the Foreſt, and was from thence convey'd to Weſtminſter. P.

Diſguſted with the buſineſs and buſtle of the world, and the intrigues of courts, Cowley thought to have found an exemption of all cares in retiring to Chertſey. Dr. Johnſon wrote a Rambler to ridicule his wiſh to retire to America, and has publiſhed a Letter, vol. i. of his Lives, p. 29, which he recommends to the peruſal of all who pant for ſolitude. His Houſe at Chertſey now belongs to Mr. Alderman Clarke.

O early

O early loſt! what tears the river ſhed,
When the ſad pomp along his banks was led?
His drooping ſwans on every note expire,
And on his willows hung each Muſe's lyre.
Since fate relentleſs ſtop'd their heav'nly voice,
No more the foreſts ring, or groves rejoice;
Who now ſhall charm the ſhades, where COWLEY ſtrung
His living harp, and lofty DENHAM ſung?
But hark! the groves rejoice, the foreſt rings!
Are theſe reviv'd? or is it GRANVILLE ſings!
'Tis yours, my Lord, to bleſs our ſoft retreats,
And call the Muſes to their ancient ſeats;
To paint anew the flow'ry ſylvan ſcenes,
To crown the foreſts with immortal greens,
Make Windſor-hills in lofty numbers riſe,
And lift her turrets nearer to the ſkies!
To ſing thoſe honours you deſerve to wear,
And add new luſtre to her ſilver ſtar.

VARIATIONS.

VER. 275.
What ſighs, what murmurs, fill'd the vocal ſhore!
His tuneful ſwans were heard to ſing no more. P.

VER. 290. *Her ſilver ſtar.*] All the lines that follow were not added to the poem till the year 1710. What immediately followed this, and made the concluſion, were theſe,
My humble Muſe in unambitious ſtrains
Paints the green foreſts and the flow'ry plains;

Where

NOTES.

VER. 280.] *Living* is from Cowley.

VER. 282.] The Mira of Granville was the Counteſs of Newburgh. Towards the end of her life Dr. King, of Oxford, wrote a very ſevere ſatire againſt her, in three books, 4to, called The Toaſt.

Here

Here noble SURREY felt the ſacred rage,
SURREY, the GRANVILLE of a former age:
Matchleſs his pen, victorious was his lance,
Bold in the liſts, and graceful in the dance:
In the ſame ſhades the Cupids tun'd his lyre,
To the ſame notes, of love, and ſoft deſire:
Fair Geraldine, bright object of his vow,
Then fill'd the groves, as heav'nly Mira now.

O would'ſt

VARIATIONS.

Where I obſcurely paſs my careleſs days,
Pleas'd in the ſilent ſhade with empty praiſe,
Enough for me that to the liſt'ning ſwains
Firſt in theſe fields I ſung the ſylvan ſtrains. P.

NOTES.

VER. 291. *Here noble Surrey*] Henry Howard Earl of Surrey, one of the firſt refiners of the Engliſh poetry; who flouriſh'd in the time of Henry VIII. P.

VER. 297. *Fair Geraldine*] "The Fair Geraldine, (ſays Mr. Warton in his Hiſt. of Engliſh Poetry, vol. iii.) the general object of Lord Surrey's paſſionate ſonnets, is commonly ſaid to have lived at Florence, and to have been of the family of the Geraldi of that city. This is a miſapprehenſion of an expreſſion in one of our poet's odes, and a paſſage in Drayton's Heroic Epiſtles. She was, undoubtedly, one of the daughters of Gerald Fitzgerald, Earl of Kildare.

"It is not preciſely known at what period the Earl of Surrey began his travels. They have the air of a romance. He made the tour of Europe in the true ſpirit of chivalry, and with the ideas of an Amadis; proclaiming the unparalleled charms of his miſtreſs, and prepared to defend the cauſe of her beauty with the weapons of knight-errantry; nor was this adventurous journey performed without the intervention of an enchanter. The firſt city in Italy which he propoſed to viſit was Florence, the capital of Tuſcany, and the original ſeat of the anceſtors of his Geraldine. In his way thither, he paſſed a few days at the Emperor's court; where he became acquainted with Cornelius Agrippa, a celebrated adept

in

O would'st thou sing what heroes Windsor bore,
What kings first breath'd upon her winding shore,
Or raise old warriours, whose ador'd remains
In weeping vaults her hallow'd earth contains!

With

NOTES.

in natural magic. This visionary philosopher shewed our hero, in a mirror of glass, a living image of Geraldine, reclining on a couch, sick, and reading one of his most tender sonnets by a waxen taper. His imagination, which wanted not the flattering representations and artificial incentives of illusion, was heated anew by this interesting and affecting spectacle. Inflamed with every enthusiasm of the most romantic passion, he hastened to Florence; and, on his arrival, immediately published a defiance against any person who could handle a lance and was in love, whether Christian, Jew, Turk, Saracen, or Canibal, who should presume to dispute the superiority of Geraldine's beauty. As the lady was pretended to be of Tuscan extraction, the pride of the Florentines was flattered on this occasion: and the Grand Duke of Tuscany permitted a general and unmolested ingress into his dominions of the combatants of all countries, till this important trial should be decided. The challenge was accepted, and the Earl victorious. The shield which he presented to the Duke before the tournament began, is exhibited in Vertue's valuable plate of the Arundel family, and was actually in the possession of the late Duke of Norfolk.

" These heroic vanities did not, however, so totally engross the time which Surrey spent in Italy, as to alienate his mind from letters: he studied, with the greatest success, a critical knowledge of the Italian tongue; and, that he might give new lustre to the name of Geraldine, attained a just taste for the peculiar graces of the Italian poetry.

" He was recalled to England for some idle reason by the King, much sooner than he expected: and he returned home, the most elegant traveller, the most polite lover, the most learned nobleman, and the most accomplished gentleman, of his age. Dexterity in tilting, and gracefulness in managing a horse under arms, were excellencies now viewed with a critical eye, and practised with a high degree of emulation. In 1540, at a tournament held in presence of the court at Westminster, and in which the principal of the nobility were engaged, Surrey was

 distinguished

With Edward's acts adorn the shining page,
Stretch his long triumphs down through ev'ry age,
Draw monarchs chain'd, and Cressi's glorious field,
The lilies blazing on the regal shield:
Then, from her roofs when Verrio's colours fall,
And leave inanimate the naked wall,

Still

VARIATIONS.

Ver. 307. Originally thus in the MS.

When Brass decays, when Trophies lie o'er-thrown,
And mould'ring into dust *drops the proud stone.*

NOTES.

distinguished above the rest for his address in the use and exercise of arms."

In the History of English Poetry, vol. iii. p. 12. is a poem of the elegiac kind, in which he laments his imprisonment in Windsor Castle.

Ver. 303. *Edward's acts*] Edward III. born here. P.

In what an exquisite strain does Gray speak of this monarch! and his son!

Mighty victor, mighty lord,
Low on his funeral couch he lies!
No pitying heart, no eye,
Afford a tear to grace his obsequies.

Which is followed by that striking question,—

Is the sable warrior fled?——
Thy son is gone. He rests among the dead.
The swarm, that in thy noontide beam were born,
Gone to salute the rising morn.

The Bard, strophe 2.

I have sometimes wondered that Pope did not mention the building of Windsor Castle by Edward III. His architect was William of Wykeham, whose name, it must not be wondered at, if I seize every opportunity of mentioning with veneration and gratitude. Yet, perhaps, he was rather the supervisor and comptroller of the work, than the actual architect, as he had singular talents for business, activity, and management of affairs.

Ver. 307.] "Without much invention, (says Mr. Walpole, vol. iii. p. 59.) and with less taste, Verrio's exuberant pencil was

ready

Still in thy ſong ſhould vanquiſh'd France appear,
And bleed for ever under Britain's ſpear.
Let ſofter ſtrains ill-fated Henry mourn,
And palms eternal flouriſh round his urn.
Here o'er the Martyr-King the marble weeps,
And, faſt beſide him, once-fear'd Edward ſleeps:
Whom not th' extended Albion could contain,
From old Belerium to the northern main,
The grave unites; where e'en the Great find reſt,
And blended lie th' oppreſſor and th' oppreſt!
Make ſacred Charles's tomb for ever known,
(Obſcure the place, and uninſcrib'd the ſtone)
Oh

NOTES.

ready at pouring out gods, goddeſſes, kings, emperors, and triumphs, over thoſe public ſurfaces, on which the eye never reſts long enough to criticiſe, and where one ſhould be ſorry to place the works of a better maſter, I mean, ceilings and ſtaircaſes. He received, in all, for his various works, the ſum of £. 6,845."

VER. 311. *Henry mourn*] Henry VI. P.

How could he here omit the mention of Eton College, founded by this unfortunate King, and the Chapel of King's College in Cambridge. But Gray has made ample amends for this omiſſion, by his moſt beautiful ode on the proſpect of this neighbouring college, from which ſo many ornaments and ſupports of ſtate and church have proceeded.

VER. 314. *once-fear'd Edward ſleeps:*] Edward IV. P.

VER. 316.] See an account of Belerium, ſo called from Bellerus a Corniſh giant, that part of Cornwall called the Lands End, in Warton's edition of Milton's Poems, p. 28.

VER. 319. *Make ſacred Charles's*] Vigneal-Marville, v. 1. p. 152. relates a fact concerning this unhappy Monarch that I do not find mentioned in any hiſtory; which, he ſays, Lord Clarendon uſed to mention when he retired to Rouen in Normandy; that one of the firſt circumſtances that gave diſguſt to the people of England, and to ſome of the nobility, was a hint

Oh fact accurſt! what tears has Albion ſhed,
Heav'ns, what new wounds! and how her old have bled!
She ſaw her ſons with purple death expire,
Her ſacred domes involv'd in rolling fire,
A dreadful ſeries of inteſtine wars,
Inglorious triumphs and diſhoneſt ſcars.
At length great ANNA ſaid—"Let diſcord ceaſe!"
She ſaid, the world obey'd, and all was Peace!
In that bleſt moment from his oozy bed 329
Old father Thames advanc'd his rev'rend head;

His

VARIATIONS.

VER. 321. Originally thus in the MS.

Oh fact accurſt! oh ſacrilegious brood,
Sworn to Rebellion, principled in blood!
Since that dire morn what tears has Albion ſhed,
Gods! what new wounds, &c.

VER. 327. Thus in the MS.

Till Anna roſe and bade the Furies ceaſe;
Let there be peace—ſhe ſaid, and all was *Peace*.

NOTES.

hint thrown out by Charles I. at the beginning of his reign, that he thought all the eccleſiaſtical revenues that had been ſeized and diſtributed by Henry VIII. ought to be reſtored to the church.

VER. 322.] To ſay that the plague in London, and its conſumption by fire, were judgments inflicted by Heaven for the murder of Charles I. is a very extraordinary ſtretch of Tory principles indeed.

VER 329.] It may gratify a curious reader to ſee an extract of a letter of Prior to Lord Bolingbroke, written from Paris, May 18, 1713, concerning a medal that was to be ſtruck on the Peace of Utrecht, ſo highly celebrated in this paſſage: communicated to me by the favor of the late Dutcheſs Dowager of Portland.

" I diſlike

His treſſes drop'd with dews, and o'er the ſtream
His ſhining horns diffus'd a golden gleam;
Grav'd on his urn appear'd the moon, that guides
His ſwelling waters, and alternate tides;
The figur'd ſtreams in waves of ſilver roll'd,
And on her banks Auguſta roſe in gold.
Around his throne the ſea-born brothers ſtood,
Who ſwell with tributary urns his flood:
Firſt the fam'd authors of his ancient name,
The winding Iſis and the fruitful Thame:

VARIATIONS.

Between Verſe 330 and 331, originally ſtood theſe lines,

From ſhore to ſhore exulting ſhouts he heard,
O'er all his banks a lambent light appear'd,
With ſparkling flames heav'n's glowing concave ſhone,
Fictitious ſtars, and glories not her own.
He ſaw, and gently roſe above the ſtream;
His ſhining horns diffuſe a golden gleam:
With pearl and gold his tow'ry front was dreſt,
The tributes of the diſtant Eaſt and Weſt. P.

NOTES.

" I diſlike your medal, with the motto,

—— COMPOSITIS VENERANTUR ARMIS——

I will have one of my own deſign; the Queen's buſt ſurrounded with laurel, and with this motto,

ANNÆ AUG.

FELICI, PACIFICÆ:

Peace in a triumphal car, and the words,

PAX MISSA PER ORBEM.

This is ancient, this is ſimple, this is ſenſe.

Roſier ſhall execute it, in a manner not ſeen in England ſince Simonds's time."

VER. 337.] He has copied, and equalled, the Rivers of Spenſer, Drayton, and Milton.

The Kennet swift, for silver eels renown'd;
The Lodden slow, with verdant alders crown'd;
Cole, whose dark streams his flow'ry islands lave;
And chalky Wey, that rolls a milky wave:
The blue transparent Vandalis appears;
The gulphy Lee his sedgy tresses rears;
And sullen Mole, that hides his diving flood;
And silent Darent, stain'd with Danish blood.
High in the midst, upon his urn reclin'd,
(His sea-green mantle waving with the wind)
The

NOTES.

VER. 341.] The word *renown'd*, says a true poet, Dr. Darwin, does not present the idea of a visible object to the mind, and is thence prosaic.

VER. 350.] Whenever the river Thames is mentioned, I am afraid the disgraceful and impotent criticism of Dr. Johnson on a passage in Gray's Odes, will recur to the mind of the reader. I heartily wish, for the sake of its author, who had more strong sense than a just relish for true poetry, that this strange and unwarrantable remark of his, could be sunk into oblivion.

Our poet was not deterred, from the censure which Addison passed in his Campaign, on raising and personifying river-gods, from giving us this fine description, in which Thames appears and speaks with suitable dignity and importance. How much superior is this picture to that of Boileau's Rhine; who represents the Naids as alarming the God with an account of the march of the French Monarch; upon which the River God assumes the appearance of an old experienced commander, flies to a Dutch fort, and exhorts the garrison to dispute the intended passage. The Rhine, marching at their head, and observing Mars and Bellona on the side of the enemy, is so terrified with the view of these superior divinities, that he most gallantly runs away, and leaves the great hero Louis XIV. in quiet possession of his banks.—So much for a true court poet, who would not have dared to write the eight last lines of this speech of Thames, from v. 415. The lines of Addison in the Campaign were;

Gods

The God appear'd: he turn'd his azure eyes
Where Windſor-domes and pompous turrets riſe;
Then bow'd and ſpoke; the winds forget to roar,
And the huſh'd waves glide ſoftly to the ſhore.
" Hail, ſacred Peace! hail long-expected days,
That Thames's glory to the ſtars ſhall raiſe!
Tho' Tyber's ſtreams immortal Rome behold,
Tho' foaming Hermus ſwells with tides of gold,
From heav'n itſelf, tho' ſev'nfold Nilus flows,
And harveſts on a hundred realms beſtows;
Theſe now no more ſhall be the Muſe's themes,
Loſt in my fame, as in the ſea their ſtreams.
Let Volga's banks with iron ſquadrons ſhine,
And groves of lances glitter on the Rhine,
Let barb'rous Ganges arm a ſervile train;
Be mine the bleſſings of a peaceful reign.
No more my ſons ſhall dye with Britiſh blood
Red Iber's ſands, or Iſter's foaming flood:

VARIATIONS.

VER. 363. Originally thus in the MS.
Let Venice boaſt her Tow'rs amidſt the Main,
Where the rough Adrian ſwells and roars in vain;
Here not a Town, but ſpacious Realm ſhall have
A ſure foundation on the rolling wave.

NOTES.

Gods may deſcend in factions from the ſkies,
And rivers from their oozy beds ariſe.

I cannot forbear mentioning, that the very firſt compoſition that made the young Racine known at Paris was his Ode from the Nymph of the Seine to the Queen, which ode, by the way, was corrected by Chapelain, at that time in high vogue as a critic, and by him recommended to the court.

Safe on my ſhore each unmoleſted ſwain
Shall tend the flocks, or reap the bearded grain;
The ſhady empire ſhall retain no trace
Of war or blood, but in the ſylvan chace;
The trumpet ſleep, while chearful horns are blown,
And arms employ'd on birds and beaſts alone.
Behold! th' aſcending Villas on my ſide,
Project long ſhadows o'er the cryſtal tide;
Behold! Auguſta's glitt'ring ſpires increaſe,
And Temples riſe, the beauteous works of Peace.
I ſee, I ſee, where two fair cities bend
Their ample bow, a new Whitehall aſcend!
There mighty Nations ſhall enquire their doom,
The World's great Oracle in times to come;
There Kings ſhall ſue, and ſuppliant States be ſeen
Once more to bend before a BRITISH QUEEN.
Thy trees, fair Windſor! now ſhall leave their woods,
And half thy foreſts ruſh into thy floods,

Bear

VARIATIONS.

VER. 385, &c. were originally thus,

Now ſhall our fleets the bloody Croſs diſplay
To the rich regions of the riſing day,
Or thoſe green iſles, where headlong Titan ſteeps
His hiſſing axle in th' Atlantic deeps;
Tempt icy ſeas, &c. P.

NOTES.

VER. 378. *And Temples riſe,*] The fifty new churches. P.

VER. 380, *A new Whitehall*] "Several plates (ſays Mr. Walpole) of the intended palace of Whitehall have been given, but, I believe, from no finiſhed deſign of Inigo Jones. The four great

Bear Britain's thunder, and her Crofs difplay,
To the bright regions of the rifing day;
Tempt icy feas, where fcarce the waters roll,
Where clearer flames glow round the frozen Pole;
Or under fouthern fkies exalt their fails,
Led by new ftars, and borne by fpicy gales!
For me the balm fhall bleed, and amber flow,
The coral redden, and the ruby glow,
The pearly fhell its lucid globe infold,
And Phoebus warm the rip'ning ore to gold.
The time fhall come, when free as feas or wind
Unbounded Thames fhall flow for all mankind,
Whole nations enter with each fwelling tide,
And feas but join the regions they divide;
Earth's diftant ends our glory fhall behold,
And the new world launch forth to feek the old.
Then fhips of uncouth form fhall ftem the tide,
And feather'd people croud my wealthy fide,

NOTES.

great fheets are evidently made up from general hints, nor could fuch a fource of invention and tafte, as the mind of Inigo, ever produce fo much famenefs. The ftrange kind of cherubims on the towers at the end are prepofterous ornaments, and whether of Inigo or not, bear no relation to the reft. The great towers in the front are too near, and evidently borrowed from what he had feen in Gothic, not in Roman buildings. The circular court is a picturefque thought, but without meaning or utility.

VER. 391.] Here is almoft a prophecy of thofe difcoveries of new iflands and continents which this country of late years has had the honour to make.

VER. 398. *Unbounded Thames, &c.*] A wifh that London may be made a FREE PORT. P.

And

And naked youths and painted chiefs admire
Our ſpeech, our colour, and our ſtrange attire!
Oh ſtretch thy reign, fair Peace! from ſhore to ſhore,
'Till Conqueſt ceaſe; and Slav'ry be no more;
'Till the freed Indians in their native groves
Reap their own fruits, and woo their ſable loves,
Peru once more a race of Kings behold,
And other Mexico's be roof'd with gold.
Exil'd by thee from earth to deepeſt hell,
In brazen bonds, ſhall barb'rous Diſcord dwell:
Gigantic pride, pale Terror, gloomy Care,
And mad Ambition ſhall attend her there:
There purple Vengeance bath'd in gore retires,
Her weapons blunted, and extinct her fires:
There hated Envy her own ſnakes ſhall feel,
And Perſecution mourn her broken wheel:
There Faction roar, Rebellion bite her chain,
And gaſping Furies thirſt for blood in vain."
Here ceaſe thy flight, nor with unhallow'd lays
Touch the fair fame of Albion's golden days:

NOTES.

VER. 409.]
To hear the ſavage youth repeat
In looſe numbers wildly ſweet,
Their feather-cinctured chiefs, and duſky loves,
ſays Mr. Gray, moſt beautifully in his ode; *duſky* loves is more accurate than *ſable*; they are not negroes.

VER. 422. *in vain.*] This concluſion both of Horace and of Pope is feeble and flat. The whole ſhould have ended with this ſpeech of Thames at this line, 422.

IMITATIONS.

VER. 423.
"Quo, Muſa, tendis? deſine pervicax
Referre ſermones Deorum et
Magna modis tenuare parvis." Hor.

The

The thoughts of Gods let GRANVILLE's verſe recite,
And bring the ſcenes of op'ning fate to light.
My humble Muſe, in unambitious ſtrains,
Paints the green foreſts and the flow'ry plains,
Where Peace deſcending bids her olive ſpring,
And ſcatters bleſſings from her dove-like wing.
Ev'n I more ſweetly paſs my careleſs days,
Pleas'd in the ſilent ſhade with empty praiſe;
Enough for me, that to the liſt'ning ſwains
Firſt in theſe fields I ſung the ſylvan ſtrains.

Several elegant imitations have been given of this ſpecies of local poetry; the principal ſeem to be, Grongar Hill; the Ruins of Rome; Claremont, by Garth; Kymber, by Mr. Potter; Kenſington Gardens; Catharine Hill; Faringdon Hill; Newdwood Foreſt; Leweſdon Hill; the Deſerted Village, and Traveller, of Goldſmith; and the Ode on the diſtant Proſpect of Eton College.

Pope, it ſeems, was of opinion, that deſcriptive poetry is a compoſition as abſurd as a feaſt made up of ſauces: and I know many other perſons that think meanly of it. I will not preſume to ſay it is equal, either in dignity or utility, to thoſe compoſitions that lay open the internal conſtitution of man, and that imitate characters, manners, and ſentiments. I may however remind ſuch contemners of it, that, in a ſiſter art, landſcape-painting claims the very next rank to hiſtory-painting, being ever preferred to ſingle portraits, to pieces of ſtill-life, to droll figures, to fruit and flower-pieces; that Titian thought it no diminution of his genius, to ſpend much of his time in works of the former ſpecies; and that, if their principles lead them to condemn Thomſon, they muſt alſo condemn the Georgics of Virgil, and the greateſt part of the nobleſt deſcriptive poem extant; I mean that of Lucretius.

O D E

ON ST. CECILIA'S DAY,

MDCCVIII.

AND OTHER PIECES FOR MUSIC.

ODE FOR MUSIC

ON ST. CECILIA'S DAY*.

I.

DESCEND, ye Nine! descend and sing;
The breathing instruments inspire,
Wake into voice each silent string,
And sweep the sounding lyre!
In a sadly-pleasing strain
Let the warbling lute complain:
Let the loud trumpet sound,
'Till the roofs all around
The shrill echos rebound:
While

NOTES.

* Our Author, as Mr. Harte told me, frequently and earnestly declared, that if Dryden had finished a translation of the Iliad, he would not have attempted one, after so great a master; he might have said, with even more propriety, I will not write a music ode after Alexander's Feast; which the variety and harmony of its numbers, and the beauty, force, and energy of its images, have conspired to place at the head of modern Lyric compositions: always excepting The Bard of Gray, which, being of a more exalted strain than the moral poetry we had been accustomed to, was not, at its first appearance, so much relished as it deserved; but which, I will presume to say, will, in every succeeding year, gain more and more admiration and applause, notwithstanding the unjust, and I may say tasteless, animadversions which Dr. Johnson degraded himself by throwing out upon it, in the Lives of the Poets. The subject of Dryden's ode is superior to this of Pope's, because the former is historical, and the latter merely mythological. Dryden's is also more perfect in the unity of the action; for Pope's is not the recital of one great action, but a description of many of the adventures of Orpheus. We all know, and have felt, the effects of Handel's having set Dryden's ode to music. Mr. Smith, a worthy pupil of Handel, (as Mr. Mason informs us), intended to have set Mr. Gray's ode to music,

While in more lengthen'd notes and ſlow,
The deep, majeſtic, ſolemn organs blow.
Hark! the numbers ſoft and clear
Gently ſteal upon the ear;
Now louder, and yet louder riſe,
And fill with ſpreading ſounds the ſkies;
Exulting in triumph now ſwell the bold notes,
In broken air, trembling, the wild muſic floats;
'Till, by degrees, remote and ſmall,
The ſtrains decay,
And melt away,
In a dying, dying fall.

By

NOTES.

muſic, and Mr. Gray, whoſe muſical feelings were exquiſite, with a knowledge of the art, gave him an idea for the overture, which ſeemed equally proper and ſtriking. In this reſpect, as well as many others, he reſembled Milton.

The name and the genius of Cowley gave, for many years, a currency and vogue to irregular odes, called Pindaric. One of the beſt of which ſpecies is that of Cobb, called, the Female Reign; and two of the worſt, Sprat's Plague of Athens, and Bolingbroke's Almahide. Congreve is thought to be the firſt writer that gave a ſpecimen of a legitimate Pindaric ode, with ſtrophe, antiſtrophe, and ode, elucidated with a ſenſible and judicious preface on the ſubject. But it does not ſeem to have been obſerved, that, long before, Ben Johnſon had given a model of this very ſpecies of a regular Pindaric ode, addreſt to Sir Lucius Cary and Sir H. Morriſon, page 233 of his works, folio, in which he entitles each ſtanza the turne, the counter-turne, and the ſtand. Though Congreve's ode is not extraordinary, yet the diſcourſe prefixed to it has a great deal of learning. Dr. Akenſide frequently mentioned to me, as one of the beſt of the regular Pindaric odes, Fenton's to Lord Gower, 1716. Mr. Gray was of opinion, that the ſtanzas of theſe regular odes ought not to conſiſt of above nine lines each, at the moſt.

VER. 7. *Let the loud trumpet ſound, &c.*] Our Author, in his rules for good writing, had ſaid, that *the ſound ſhould be an echo*

to

II.

By Music, minds an equal temper know,
Nor swell too high, nor sink too low.
If in the breast tumultuous joys arise,
Music her soft, assuasive voice applies;
Or, when the soul is press'd with cares,
Exalts her in enliv'ning airs.
Warriors she fires with animated sounds;
Pours balm into the bleeding lover's wounds:
Melancholy lifts her head,
Morpheus rouzes from his bed,
Sloth unfolds her arms and wakes,
List'ning Envy drops her snakes;
Intestine war no more our Passions wage,
And giddy Factions hear away their rage.

But

NOTES.

to the sense. The graces it adds to the harmony are obvious. But we should never have seen all the advantages arising from this rule, had this ode not been written. In which, one may venture to say, is found all the harmony that poetic sound, when it comes in aid of sense, is capable of producing. W.

This panegyric is certainly carried too high: this ode is not the consummation of true poetic harmony.

VER. 22.] This stanza much resembles the fifth of Congreve's music ode; the second of which, by the way, is uncommonly good. It is remarkable that Pope knew nothing of music, and had no ear for it; as had Milton, Gray, and Mason: the last of whom is an excellent performer and composer.

VER. 35. Dr. Greene set this ode to music, in 1730, as an exercise for his Doctor's Degree at Cambridge, on which occasion Pope made considerable alteration in it, and added the following stanza in this place.

Amphion thus bade wild dissension cease,
And soften'd mortals learn'd the arts of peace,

 Amphion

III.

But when our Country's cauſe provokes to Arms,
How martial muſic ev'ry boſom warms!
So when the firſt bold veſſel dar'd the ſeas,
High on the ſtern the Thracian rais'd his ſtrain,
While Argo ſaw her kindred trees
Deſcend from Pelion to the main.
Tranſported demi-gods ſtood round,
And men grew heroes at the ſound,
Enflam'd with glory's charms:

NOTES.

Amphion taught contending kings,
From various diſcords, to create
The muſic of a well-tun'd ſtate;
Nor ſlack, nor ſtrain the tender ſtrings,
Thoſe uſeful touches to impart,
That ſtrike the ſubject's anſwering heart,
And the ſoft ſilent harmony that ſprings
From ſacred union and conſent of things.

And he made another alteration, at the ſame time, in ſtanza iv. v. 51, and wrote it thus;

Sad Orpheus ſought his conſort loſt;
The adamantine gates were barr'd,
And nought was ſeen and nought was heard,
Around the dreary coaſt;
But dreadful gleams, &c.

VER. 39.] He might have added a beautiful deſcription of the Argo in Apollonius Rhodius; and if he had been a reader of Pindar, he might have looked into the fourth Pythian ode, particularly verſe 315 of Orpheus. Oxford edition, folio, 1697.

VER. 40. *While Argo*] Few images in any poet, ancient or modern, are more ſtriking than that in Apollonius, where he ſays, that when the Argo was ſailing near the coaſt where the Centaur Chiron dwelt, he came down to the very margin of the ſea, bringing his wife with the young Achilles in her arms, that he might ſhew the child to his father Peleus, who was on his voyage with the other Argonauts. Apollonius Rhodius, Lib. v. ver. 553.

Each

Each chief his ſev'nfold ſhield diſplay'd,
And half unſheath'd the ſhining blade:
And ſeas, and rocks, and ſkies rebound
To arms, to arms, to arms!

IV.

But when through all th' infernal bounds,
Which flaming Phlegeton ſurrounds,
Love, ſtrong as Death, the Poet led
To the pale nations of the dead,

What

NOTES.

VER. 48. *To arms, to arms,*] Which effects of the ſong, however lively, do not equal the force and ſpirit of what Dryden aſcribes to the ſong of his Grecian artiſt; whoſe imagery in this paſſage is ſo alive, ſo ſublime, and ſo animated, that the poet himſelf appears to be ſtrongly poſſeſſed of the action deſcribed, and conſequently places it fully before the eyes of the reader.

Mr. St. John, afterwards Lord Bolingbroke, happening to pay a morning viſit to Dryden, whom he always reſpected, found him in an unuſual agitation of ſpirits, even to a trembling. On enquiring the cauſe, "I have been up all night, (replied the old bard); my muſical friends made me promiſe to write them an ode for their Feaſt of St. Cæcilia: I have been ſo ſtruck with the ſubject which occurred to me, that I could not leave it till I had completed it: here it is, finiſhed at one ſitting." And immediately he ſhewed him this ode, which places the Britiſh lyric poetry above that of any other nation. This anecdote, as true as it is curious, was imparted by Lord Bolingbroke to Pope, by Pope to Mr. Gilbert Weſt, by him to my ingenious friend Mr. Berenger, who communicated it to me. The rapidity, and yet the perſpicuity of the thoughts, the glow and the expreſſiveneſs of the images, thoſe certain marks of the firſt ſketch of a maſter, conſpire to corroborate the fact. It is not to be underſtood, that this piece was not afterwards reconſidered, retouched, and corrected.

VER. 49. *But when*] See Divine Legation, Book ii. ſect. 1. Where Orpheus is conſidered as a Philoſopher, a Legiſlator, and a Myſtagogue. In vol. v. of the Memoirs of Inſcriptions, &c.

p. 117.

What ſounds were heard,
What ſcenes appear'd,
O'er all the dreary coaſt!
Dreadful gleams,
Diſmal ſcreams,
Fires that glow,
Shrieks of woe,
Sullen moans,
Hollow groans,
And cries of tortur'd ghoſts!
But hark! he ſtrikes the golden lyre;
And ſee! the tortur'd ghoſts reſpire,
See, ſhady forms advance!
Thy ſtone, O Siſyphus, ſtands ſtill,
Ixion reſts upon his wheel,
And the pale ſpectres dance;
The Furies ſink upon their iron beds,
And ſnakes uncurl'd hang liſt'ning round their heads.

V.

By the ſtreams that ever flow,
By the fragrant winds that blow
O'er the Elyſian flow'rs;

NOTES.

p. 117, is a very curious diſſertation upon the Orphic Life, by the Abbé Fraguier. He was the firſt critic who rightly interpreted the words of Horace, Cædibus & fædo victû, as meaning an abolition of eating human fleſh.

Though the Hymns that remain are not the work of the real Orpheus, yet are they extremely ancient, certainly older than the Expedition of Xerxes againſt Greece.

Ver. 66.] This line is taken from an ode of Cobb.

Ver. 68. *Dance*;] A moſt improper, becauſe ludicrous image.

By

By those happy souls who dwell
In yellow meads of Asphodel,
Or Amaranthine bow'rs;
By the heroes armed shades,
Glitt'ring through the gloomy glades;
By the youths that dy'd for love,
Wand'ring in the myrtle grove,
Restore, restore Eurydice to life:
Oh take the husband, or return the wife!

He sung, and hell consented
To hear the Poet's prayer:
Stern Proserpine relented,
And gave him back the fair.
Thus song could prevail
O'er death, and o'er hell,
A conquest how hard and how glorious!
Tho' fate had fast bound her
With Styx nine times round her
Yet music and love were victorious.

But

NOTES.

VER. 77.] These images are picturesque and appropriated, and are such notes as might,

Draw iron tears down Pluto's cheek,
And make hell grant what love did seek.

Pope being insensible of the effects of music, enquired of Dr. Arbuthnot whether Handel really deserved the applause he met with. The Dutchess of Queensberry told me that Gay could play on the flute, and that this enabled him to adapt so happily some airs in the Beggars Opera.

VER. 83.] This measure is unsuited to the subject.

VER. 87.] These numbers are of so burlesque, so low, and ridiculous a kind, and have so much the air of a vulgar drinking

 song,

VI.

But ſoon, too ſoon, the lover turns his eyes:
Again ſhe falls, again ſhe dies, ſhe dies!
How wilt thou now the fatal ſiſters move?
No crime was thine, if 'tis no crime to love.
 Now under hanging mountains,
 Beſide the falls of fountains,
 Or where Hebrus wanders,
 Rolling in Maeanders,
  All alone,
  Unheard, unknown,
  He makes his moan;
  And calls her ghoſt,
 For ever, ever, ever loſt!

NOTES.

ſong, that one is amazed and concerned to find them in a ſerious ode; and in an ode of a writer eminently ſkilled, in general, in accommodating his ſounds to his ſentiments. Addiſon thought this meaſure exactly ſuited to the comic character of Sir Truſty in his Roſamond, by the introduction of which he has ſo ſtrangely debaſed that very elegant opera. It is obſervable that this ludicrous meaſure is uſed by Dryden, in a ſong of evil ſpirits, in the fourth act of the State of Innocence.

VER. 97.] Theſe ſcenes, in which Orpheus is introduced as making his lamentations, are not ſo wild, ſo ſavage, and diſmal, as thoſe mentioned by Virgil; and convey not ſuch images of deſolation and deep deſpair, as the caverns on the banks of Strymon and Tanais, the Hyperborean deſerts, and the Riphæan ſolitudes. And to ſay of Hebrus, only, that it rolls in meanders, is flat and feeble, and does not heighten the melancholy of the place. He that would have a complete idea of Orpheus's anguiſh and ſituation, muſt look at the exquiſite figure of him (now in the poſſeſſion of Sir Watkin Williams Wynne) painted by Mr. Dance, a work that does honor to the true genius of the artiſt, and to the age in which it was produced.

Now

Now with Furies ſurrounded,
Deſpairing, confounded,
He trembles, he glows,
Amidſt Rhodope's ſnows:
See, wild as the winds, o'er the deſert he flies;
Hark! Haemus reſounds with the Bacchanals cries—
Ah ſee, he dies!
Yet ev'n in death Eurydice he ſung,
Eurydice ſtill trembled on his tongue,
Eurydice the woods,
Eurydice the floods,
Eurydice the rocks, and hollow mountains rung.

VII.

Muſic the fierceſt grief can charm,
And fate's ſevereſt rage diſarm:
Muſic can ſoften pain to eaſe,
And make deſpair and madneſs pleaſe:
Our joys below it can improve,
And antedate the bliſs above.

NOTES.

VER. 108.] I am afraid there is a trivial antitheſis in theſe lines betwixt the words *ſnows* and *glows*, unworthy our author.

VER. 112.] The death is expreſſed with a brevity and abruptneſs ſuitable to the nature of the ode. Inſtead of *he ſung*, Virgil ſays, *vocabat*, which is more natural and tender, and adds a moving epithet, that he called *miſeram* Eurydicen. The repetition of Eurydice in two very ſhort lines hurts the ear, which Virgil eſcaped by interpoſing ſeveral other words; and the name itſelf happens not to be harmonious enough to ſuffer ſuch repetition.

VER. 118. *Muſic the fierceſt*] This is ſuch a cloſe repetition of the ſubject of the ſecond ſtanza, that it muſt be thought a blameable tautology.

This the divine Cecilia found,
And to her Maker's praiſe confin'd the ſound.
When the full organ joins the tuneful quire,
Th' immortal pow'rs incline their ear;
Borne on the ſwelling notes our ſouls aſpire,
While ſolemn airs improve the ſacred fire;
And Angels lean from heav'n to hear.
Of Orpheus now no more let Poets tell,
To bright Cecilia greater pow'r is giv'n;
His numbers rais'd a ſhade from hell,
Her's lift the ſoul to heav'n.

NOTES.

VER. 131. It is obſervable that this ode, as well as that of Dryden, concludes with an epigram of four lines; a ſpecies of witty writing as flagrantly unſuitable to the dignity, and as foreign to the nature of the lyric, as it is of the epic muſe.

IF we caſt a tranſient view over the moſt celebrated of the modern lyrics, we may obſerve that the ſtanza of Petrarch, which has been adopted by all his ſucceſſors, diſpleaſes the ear, by its tedious uniformity, and by the number of identical cadences, And, indeed, to ſpeak truth, there appears to be little valuable in Petrarch, except the purity of his diction. His ſentiments, even of love, are metaphyſical and far-fetched, Neither is there much variety in his ſubjects, or fancy in his method of treating them. Fulvio Teſti, Chiabrera, and Metaſtaſio, are much better lyric poets. When Boileau attempted an ode, he exhibited a glaring proof of what will frequently be hinted in the courſe of theſe notes, that the writer, whoſe grand characteriſtical talent is ſatiric or moral poetry, will never ſucceed, with equal merit, in the higher branches of his art. In his ode on the taking Namur, are inſtances of the bombaſtic, of the proſaic, and of the puerile; and it is no ſmall confirmation of the ruling paſſion of this author, that he could not conclude his ode, but with a ſevere ſtroke on his old

old antagonist Perrault, though the majesty of this species of composition is so much injured by descending to personal satire. The name of Malherbe is respectable, as he was the first reformer of the French poesy, and the first who gave his countrymen any idea of a legitimate ode, though his own pieces have hardly any thing but harmony to recommend them. The odes of La Motte, though so highly praised by Sanadon, and by Fontenelle, are fuller of delicate sentiment, and philosophical reflection, than of imagery, figures, and poetry. There are particular stanzas eminently good, but not one intire ode. Some of Rousseau's, particularly that to Fortune, and some of his Psalms; and one or two of Voltaire's, particularly, to the King of Prussia on his accession to the throne, and on Maeupertuis's travels to the North, to measure the degrees of the meridian toward the equator, seem to rise above that exact mediocrity which distinguishes the lyric poetry of the French.

"We have had (says Mr. Gray) in our language, no other odes of the sublime kind, than that of Dryden on St. Cecilia's Day: for Cowley, who had his merit, yet wanted judgment, style, and harmony, for such a task. That of Pope is not worthy of so great a master. Mr. Mason, indeed of late days, has touched the true chords, and with a masterly hand, in some of his choruses; above all in the last of Caractacus;

"Hark! heard ye not yon footstep dread?" &c.

Gray's Works, 4to. page 25.

TWO CHORUS'S

TO THE TRAGEDY OF BRUTUS[a].

CHORUS OF ATHENIANS.

STROPHE I.

YE ſhades, where ſacred truth is ſought;
Groves, where immortal Sages taught:
Where heav'nly viſions Plato fir'd,
And Epicurus lay inſpir'd!
In vain your guiltleſs laurels ſtood
Unſpotted long with human blood.
War, horrid war, your thoughtful Walks invades,
And ſteel now glitters in the Muſes ſhades.

NOTES.

[a] Altered from Shakeſpear by the Duke of Buckingham, at whoſe deſire theſe two Chorus's were compoſed to ſupply as many, wanting in his play. They were ſet many years afterward by the famous Bononcini, and performed at Buckingham-houſe. P.

VER. 3. *Where heav'nly viſions Plato fir'd, And Epicurus lay inſpir'd!*] The propriety of theſe lines ariſes from hence, that Brutus, one of the Heroes of this play, was of the Old Academy; and Caſſius, the other, was an Epicurean. W.

I cannot be perſuaded that Pope thought of Brutus and Caſſius, as being followers of different ſects of philoſophy.

Oh

ANTISTROPHE I.

Oh heav'n-born ſiſters! ſource of art!
Who charm the ſenſe, or mend the heart;
Who lead fair Virtue's train along,
Moral Truth, and myſtic Song!
To what new clime, what diſtant ſky,
Forſaken, friendleſs, ſhall ye fly?
Say, will ye bleſs the bleak Atlantic ſhore?
Or bid the furious Gaul be rude no more?

STROPHE II.

When Athens ſinks by fates unjuſt,
When wild Barbarians ſpurn her duſt;
Perhaps ev'n Britain's utmoſt ſhore
Shall ceaſe to bluſh with ſtranger's gore,
See Arts her ſavage ſons controul,
And Athens riſing near the pole!
Till ſome new Tyrant lifts his purple hand,
And civil madneſs tears them from the land.

NOTES.

VER. 12. *Moral Truth, and myſtic Song!*] The conſtruction is dubious. Does the poet addreſs Moral Truth and Myſtic Song, as being the Heaven-born Siſters; or does he addreſs himſelf to the Muſes, mentioned in the preceding line, and ſo make Moral Truth and Myſtic Song to be a part of Virtue's train? As Heſiod begins his poem,

Dr. Warburton's propoſed correction is not conſiſtent with either conſtruction, when he ſays, the poet had expreſſed himſelf better had he ſaid Moral Truth in Myſtic Song. Moral Truth, a ſingle perſon, can neither be the Heaven-born Siſters, nor yet, alone, the train of Virtue. If it could, the emendation might have been ſpared, becauſe this is no uncommon figure in poetry.

The metre is unſkilfully broken by the want of a ſyllable in this line.

Ye

ANTISTROPHE II.

Ye Gods! what juſtice rules the ball?
Freedom and Arts together fall;
Fools grant whate'er Ambition craves,
And men, once ignorant, are ſlaves.
Oh curs'd effects of civil hate,
In ev'ry age, in ev'ry ſtate!
Still, when the luſt of tyrant pow'r ſucceeds,
Some Athens periſhes, ſome Tully bleeds.

NOTES.

VER. 26. *Freedom and Arts*] A ſentiment worthy of Alcæus! Throughout all his works our author conſtantly ſhews himſelf a true lover of true liberty.

VER. 32. *Some Athens*]

——— Where the muſes haunt,
The marble porch where wiſdom wont to talk
With Socrates or Tully, hears no more,
Save the hoarſe jargon of contentious monks;
Or female ſuperſtition's midnight prayer;
——— When brutal force
Uſurps the throne of juſtice, turns the pomp
Of guardian power, the majeſty of rule,
The ſword, the laurel, and the purple robe,
To poor diſhoneſt pageants!

Pleaſures of Imagination, B. ii. p. 663.

This ode is of the kind which M. D'Alembert, judging like a mathematician, prefers to odes that abound with imagery and figures, namely, what he calls the Didactic ode; and then proceeds to give reaſons for preferring Horace to Pindar as a lyric poet. Marmontel in his Poetic oppoſes him.

Theſe choruſes are elegant and harmonious; but are they not chargeable with the fault, which Ariſtotle imputes to many of Euripides, that they are foreign and adventitious to the ſubject, and

and contribute nothing towards the advancement of the main action? Whereas the chorus ought,

"Μοριον ειναι τȣ ὁλȣ, και συναγωνιζεσθαι,"

to be a part or member of the one whole, co-operate with, and help to accelerate the intended event; as is constantly, adds the philosopher, the practice of Sophocles. Whereas these reflections of Pope on the baneful influences of war, on the arts and learning, and on the universal power of love, seem to be too general, are not sufficiently appropriated, do not rise from the subject and occasion, and might be inserted with equal propriety in twenty other tragedies. This remark of Aristotle, though he does not himself produce any examples, may be verified from the following, among many others. In the Phœnicians of Euripides, they sing a long and very beautiful, but ill placed, hymn to Mars; I speak of that which begins so nobly, ver. 793,

"Ω πολυμοχθος Αρης,"

"O direful Mars! why art thou still delighted with blood and with death, and why an enemy to the feasts of Bacchus?" And a still more glaring instance may be brought from the end of the third act of the Troades, in which the story of Ganymede is introduced not very artificially. To these may be added that exquisite ode in praise of Apollo, descriptive of his birth and victories, which we find in the Iphigenia in Tauris.

On the other hand, the choruses of Sophocles, never desert the subject of each particular drama, and all their sentiments and reflections are drawn from the situation of the principal personage of the fable. Nay Sophocles hath artfully found a method of making those poetical descriptions, with which the choruses of the ancients abound, carry on the chief design of the piece; and has by these means accomplished what is a great difficulty in writing tragedy, united poetry with propriety.

In the Philoctetes the chorus takes a natural occasion, at verse 694, to give a minute and moving picture of the solitary life of that unfortunate hero; and when afterwards, at verse 855, pain has totally exhausted the strength and spirits of Philoctetes, and it is necessary for the plot of the tragedy that he should fall asleep, it is then, that the chorus breaks out into an exquisite ode to sleep. As in the Antigone, with equal beauty and decorum in an address to the God of Love, at verse 791 of that play. And thus lastly, when the birth of Edipus is doubtful, and his parents unknown, the chorus suddenly exclaims,

"Τις σε, τεκνον,"

"From which, O my son, of the immortal gods, didst thou spring? Was it some nymph, a favourite of Pan, that haunts the mountains

mountains; or ſome daughter of Apollo; for this god loves the remote rocks and caverns, who bore you? Or was it Mercury who reigns in Cyllene, or did Bacchus,

"Θεος ναιων επ' ακρων ορεων," ver. 1118.

a god who dwells on the tops of the mountains, beget you, on any of the nymphs, that poſſeſs Helicon, with whom he frequently ſports?"

But what ſhall we ſay to the ſtrong objections lately made by ſome very able and learned critics to the uſe of the chorus at all? The critics I have in view, are Metaſtaſio, Twining, Pye, Colman, and Johnſon; who have brought forward ſuch powerful arguments againſt this ſo important a part of the ancient drama, as to ſhake our conviction of its utility and propriety, founded on what Hurd, Maſon, and Brumoy, have ſo earneſtly and elegantly urged on the ſubject.

CHORUS OF YOUTHS AND VIRGINS*.

SEMICHORUS.

OH Tyrant Love! haſt thou poſſeſt
The prudent, learn'd, and virtuous breaſt?
Wiſdom and wit in vain reclaim,
And Arts but ſoften us to feel thy flame.
Love, ſoft intruder, enters here,
But entring learns to be ſincere.
Marcus with bluſhes owns he loves,
And Brutus tenderly reproves.

NOTES.

* Some of Dryden's ſhort lyrical odes and ſongs are wonderfully harmonious; and not ſufficiently noticed; particularly in King Arthur, Act III.

"O ſight! the mother of deſire," &c.

The ſong alſo of the Syrens in Act IV: and the Incantations in the Third Act of Œdipus, put in the mouth of Tireſias;

"Chuſe the darkeſt part o'th' grove,
Such as ghoſts at noon-day love," &c.

Nor muſt his firſt ode for St. Cecilia's Day be forgotten, in which are paſſages almoſt equal to any of the ſecond: eſpecially its opening, and the ſecond ſtanza that deſcribes Tubal and his brethren. It is, methinks, impoſſible to read, without aſtoniſhment and regret, ſuch taſteleſs commendations and unmerited applauſes as ſuch a man as Dr. Johnſon has beſtowed on the ode to Mrs. Killigrew, and the ſtrange preference he gives it, eſpecially the firſt ſtanza, to any compoſition in our language; which ſtanza is really unintelligible, and full of abſurd bombaſt, and nearly approaching the realm of nonſenſe.

Why, Virtue, doſt thou blame deſire,
Which Nature has impreſt?
Why, Nature, doſt thou ſooneſt fire
The mild and gen'rous breaſt?

CHORUS.

Love's purer flames the Gods approve;
The Gods and Brutus bend to love:
Brutus for abſent Portia ſighs,
And ſterner Caſſius melts at Junia's eyes.
What is looſe love? a tranſient guſt,
Spent in a ſudden ſtorm of luſt,
A vapour fed from wild deſire,
A wand'ring, ſelf-conſuming fire.
But Hymen's kinder flames unite,
And burn for ever one;
Chaſte as cold Cynthia's virgin light,
Productive as the Sun.

SEMICHORUS.

Oh ſource of ev'ry ſocial tye,
United wiſh, and mutual joy!
What various joys on one attend,
As ſon, as father, brother, huſband, friend?
Whether his hoary ſire he ſpies,
While thouſand grateful thoughts ariſe;

NOTES.

VER. 9. *Why, Virtue, &c.*] In alluſion to that famous conceit of Guarini,

"Se il peccare è sì dolce," &c. W.

Bayle is fond of ſaying that Manicheiſm probably aroſe from a ſtrong meditation on this deplorable ſtate of man.

Or

Or meets his ſpouſe's fonder eye;
Or views his ſmiling progeny;
What tender paſſions take their turns,
What home-felt raptures move?
His heart now melts, now leaps, now burns,
With rev'rence, hope, and love.

CHORUS.

Hence guilty joys, diſtaſtes, ſurmiſes,
Hence falſe tears, deceits, diſguiſes,
Dangers, doubts, delays, ſurprizes;
Fires that ſcorch, yet dare not ſhine:
Pureſt love's unwaſting treaſure,
Conſtant faith, fair hope, long leiſure,
Days of eaſe, and nights of pleaſure;
Sacred Hymen! theſe are thine [a].

NOTES.

VER. 31. *Or meets*] Recalling to our minds that pathetic ſtroke in Lucretius;

—— "dulces occurrunt oſcula nati
Præripere, & tacitâ pectus dulcedine tangunt."
Lib. iii. 909.

VER. 42.] Not to the purpoſe; *long leiſure.*

[a] Theſe two Chorus's are enough to ſhew us his great talents for this ſpecies of Poetry, and to make us lament he did not proſecute his purpoſe in executing ſome plans he had chalked out; but the Character of the Managers of Playhouſes at that time, was what (he ſaid) ſoon determined him to lay aſide all thoughts of that nature. Nor did his morals, leſs than the juſt ſenſe of his own importance, deter him from having any thing to do with the Theatre. He remembered that an ancient Author hath acquainted us with this extraordinary circumſtance; that, in the conſtruction of Pompey's magnificent Theatre, the ſeats of it were ſo contrived, as to ſerve, at the ſame time, for ſteps to a

temple of Venus, which he had joined to his Theatre. The moral Poet could not but be struck with a story where the λόγος and the μῦθος of it ran as imperceptibly into one another, as the Theatre and the Temple. W.

How lamentable is it, that a writer of great talents, should misemploy them in striving to discover new meanings, and analogies, in things not alike, and not founded on plain truth and reason! Thus, the Vine in Lycidas is called gadding, because, though married to the Elm, like bad wives she goes abroad. Thus, in Shakespear, the flower called Love-in-idleness intimates that this passion has its chief power when people are idle. Thus, in Macbeth, screams of death and prophesying, should be read, Aunts, prophesying, old women. And thus, in Midsummer Night's Dream, instead of Cupid all-arm'd, read Cupid alarm'd; that is, alarmed at the chastity of Lady Elizabeth, which lessened his power.

ODE ON SOLITUDE[a].

HAPPY the man, whofe wifh and care
  A few paternal acres bound,
Content to breathe his native air,
          In his own ground.

Whofe herds with milk, whofe fields with bread,
  Whofe flocks fupply him with attire,
Whofe trees in fummer yield him fhade,
          In winter fire.

Bleft, who can unconcern'dly find
  Hours, days, and years flide foft away,
In health of body, peace of mind,
          Quiet by day,

Sound fleep by night; ftudy and eafe,
  Together mixt; fweet recreation:
And innocence, which moft does pleafe
          With meditation.

Thus let me live, unfeen, unknown,
  Thus unlamented let me die,
Steal from the world, and not a ftone
          Tell where I lie.

[a] This was a very early production of our Author, written at about twelve years old. P.

Scaliger, Voltaire, and Grotius, were but eighteen years old when they produced, the two firſt their Œdipuſes, and the laſt his Adamus Exul. But the moſt extraordinary inſtance of early excellence is The Old Batchelor of Congreve, written at nineteen only; as comedy implies and requires a knowledge of life and characters, which are here diſplayed with accuracy and truth. Mr. Spence informed me that Pope once ſaid to him, "I wrote things, I am aſhamed to ſay how ſoon; part of my epic poem Alcander when about twelve. The ſcene of it lay in Rhodes, and ſome of the neighbouring iſlands; and the poem opened under the water, with a deſcription of the court of Neptune; that couplet on the circulation of the blood, which I afterwards inſerted in the Dunciad,

As man's mæanders, to the vital ſpring
Roll all their tides, then back their circles bring,

was originally in this poem, word for word." After he had burnt this very early compoſition, Atterbury told him, he much wiſhed ſome parts of it, as a ſpecimen, had been more carefully preſerved.

Quintilian, whoſe knowledge of human nature was conſummate, has obſerved, that nothing quite correct and faultleſs is to be expected in very early years, from a truly elevated genius: that a generous extravagance and exuberance are its proper marks, and that a premature exactneſs is a certain evidence of future flatneſs and ſterility. His words are incomparable, and worthy conſideration. "Audeat hæc ætas plura, et inveniat, et inventis gaudeat, ſint licet illa non ſatis interim ſicca et ſevera. Facile remedium eſt ubertatis, ſterilia nullo labore vincuntur. Illa mihi in pueris natura nimium ſpei dabit, in quâ ingenium judicio præſumitur.—Materiam eſſe primum volo vel abundantiorem, atque ultra quam oportet fuſam. Multum inde decoquant anni, multum ratio limabit, aliquid velut uſu ipſo deteretur, ſit modo unde excidi poſſit & quod exculpi:—erit autem, ſi non ab initio tenuem laminam duxerimus, et quam cælatura altior rumpat.—Quare mihi ne maturitas quidem ipſa feſtinet, nec muſta in lacu ſtatim auſtera ſint; ſic et annos ferent, et veſtuſtate proficient." This is very ſtrong and maſculine ſenſe, expreſſed and enlivened by a train of metaphors, all of them elegant, and well preſerved. Whether theſe early productions of Pope, would not have appeared

to

to Quintilian to be rather too finiſhed, correct, and pure, and what he would have inferred concerning them, is too delicate a ſubject for me to enlarge upon. Let me rather add an entertaining anecdote. When Guido and Dominichino had each of them painted a picture in the church of Saint Andrew, Annibal Carrache, their maſter, was preſſed to declare which of his two pupils had excelled. The picture of Guido repreſented Saint Andrew on his knees before the croſs; that of Dominichino repreſented the flagellation of the ſame Apoſtle. Both of them in their different kinds were capital pieces, and were painted in freſco, oppoſite each other, to eternize, as it were, their rivalſhip and contention. "Guido (ſaid Carrache) has performed as a maſter, and Dominichino as a ſcholar. But (added he) the work of the ſcholar is more valuable than that of the maſter. In truth, one may perceive faults in the picture of Dominichino that Guido has avoided, but then there are noble ſtrokes, not to be found in that of his rival." It was eaſy to diſcern a genius that promiſed to produce beauties, to which the ſweet, the gentle, and the graceful Guido would never aſpire.

The firſt ſketches of ſuch an artiſt ought highly to be prized. Different geniuſes unfold themſelves at different periods of life. In ſome minds the one is a long time in ripening. Not only inclination, but opportunity and encouragement, a proper ſubject, or a proper patron, influence the exertion or the ſuppreſſion of genius. Theſe ſtanzas on Solitude are a ſtrong inſtance of that contemplation and moral turn, which was the diſtinguiſhing characteriſtic of our Poet's mind. An ode of Cowley, which he produced at the age of thirteen years, is of the ſame caſt, and perhaps not in the leaſt inferior to this of Pope. The voluminous Lopez de Vega is commonly, but perhaps incredibly, reported by the Spaniards to have compoſed verſes when he was five years old; and Torquato Taſſo, the ſecond or third of the Italian poets, for that wonderful original Dante is the firſt, is ſaid to have recited poems and orations of his own writing, when he was ſeven. It is however certain, which is more extraordinary, that he produced his Rinaldo in his eighteenth year, no bad precurſor to the Geruſalemma Liberata, and no ſmall effort of that genius, which was in due time to ſhew, how fine an epic poem the Italian language, notwithſtanding the vulgar imputation of effeminacy, was capable of ſupporting.

THE DYING CHRISTIAN TO HIS SOUL.

ODE.

I.

VITAL ſpark of heav'nly flame!
Quit, oh quit this mortal frame:
Trembling, hoping, ling'ring, flying;
Oh the pain, the bliſs of dying!
Ceaſe, fond Nature, ceaſe thy ſtrife,
And let me languiſh into life.

II.

Hark! they whiſper; Angels ſay,
Siſter Spirit, come away.
What is this abſorbs me quite?
Steals my ſenſes, ſhuts my ſight,
Drowns my ſpirits, draws my breath?
Tell me, my Soul, can this be death?

III.

The world recedes; it diſappears!
Heav'n opens on my eyes! my ears
With ſounds ſeraphic ring;
Lend, lend your wings! I mount! I fly!
O Grave! where is thy Victory?
O Death! where is thy Sting?

This Ode was written, we find, at the desire of Steele; and our Poet, in a letter to him on that occasion, says,—"You have it, as Cowley calls it, just warm from the brain; it came to me the first moment I waked this morning; yet you'll see, it was not so absolutely inspiration, but that I had in my head, not only the verses of Hadrian, but the fine fragment of Sappho."

It is possible, however, that our Author might have had another composition in his head, besides those he here refers to: for there is a close and surprising resemblance between this ode of Pope, and one of an obscure and forgotten rhymer of the age of Charles the Second, namely Thomas Flatman; from whose dunghill, as well as from the dregs of Crashaw, of Carew, of Herbert, and others, (for it is well known he was a great reader of all those poets), Pope has very judiciously collected gold. And the following stanza is, perhaps, the only valuable one Flatman has produced.

When on my sick bed I languish;
Full of sorrow, full of anguish,
Fainting, gasping, trembling, crying,
Panting, groaning, speechless, dying;
Methinks I hear some gentle spirit say,
Be not fearful, come away!

The third and fourth lines are eminently good and pathetic, and the climax well preserved, the very turn of them is closely copied by Pope; as is likewise the striking circumstance of the dying man's imagining he hears a voice calling him away.

Vital spark of heavenly flame
Quit, O quit, this mortal frame;
Trembling, hoping, ling'ring, flying,
O the pain, the bliss of dying!
Hark! they whisper! angels say,
Sister spirit come away!

AN

E S S A Y

ON

CRITICISM.

Written in the Year MDCCIX *.

---

* First advertised in the Spectator, N° 65. May 15, 1711.

CONTENTS.

PART I.

PART II. Ver. 203, &c.

PART

PART III. Ver. 560, &c.

AN
ESSAY
ON
CRITICISM.

'Tis hard to ſay, if greater want of ſkill
Appear in writing or in judging ill;
But, of the two, leſs dang'rous is th' offence
To tire our patience, than miſlead our ſenſe.

Some

NOTES.

An Eſſay] For a perſon of only twenty years old to have produced ſuch an Eſſay, ſo replete with a knowledge of life and manners, ſuch accurate obſervations on men and books, ſuch variety of literature, ſuch ſtrong good ſenſe, and refined taſte and judgment, has been the ſubject of frequent, and of juſt admiration. It may fairly entitle him to the character of being one of the firſt of critics, though ſurely not of poets, as Dr. Johnſon aſſerts. For Didactic poetry being, from its nature, inferior to Lyric, Tragic, and Epic poetry, we ſhould confound and invert all literary rank and order if we compared and preferred the Georgics of Virgil to the Æneid, the Epiſtle to the Piſos, to the Qualem Miniſtrum of Horace, and Boileau's Art of Poetry to the Iphigenie of Racine. But Johnſon's mind was formed for the Didactic, the Moral, and the Satyric; and he had no true reliſh for the higher and more genuine ſpecies of poetry. Strong couplets, modern manners, preſent life, moral ſententious writings alone pleaſed him. Hence his taſteleſs and groundleſs objections to The Lycidas of Milton, and to The Bard of Gray. Hence his own Irene is ſo frigid and unintereſting a tragedy; while his imitations of Juvenal are ſo forcible and pointed. His Lives of the Poets are unhappily tinctured with this narrow prejudice, and confined notion of poetry, which has occaſioned many falſe

and

Some few in that, but numbers err in this,
Ten cenſure wrong for one who writes amiſs;
A fool might once himſelf alone expoſe,
Now one in verſe makes many more in proſe.

'Tis

NOTES.

and ſpurious remarks, and many ill-grounded opinions, in a work that might have been, and was intended to have been, a manual of good taſte and judgment.

Dr. Warburton, endeavouring to demonſtrate, what Addiſon could not diſcover, nor what Pope himſelf, according to the teſtimony of his intimate friend Richardſon, ever thought of or intended, that this eſſay was written with a methodical and ſyſtematical regularity, has accompanied the whole with a long and laboured commentary, in which he has tortured many paſſages to ſupport this groundleſs opinion. Warburton had certainly wit, genius, and much miſcellaneous learning; but, was perpetually dazzled and miſled, by the eager deſire of ſeeing every thing in a new light unobſerved before, into perverſe interpretations and forced comments. His paſſion being (as Longinus expreſſes it) τυ ξενας νοησεις αιει κινει. It is painful to ſee ſuch abilities waſted on ſuch unſubſtantial objects. Accordingly his notes on Shakeſpear have been totally demoliſhed by Edwards and Malone; and Gibbon has torn up by the roots his fanciful and viſionary interpretation of the ſixth Book of Virgil. And but few readers, I believe, will be found, that will cordially ſubſcribe to an opinion lately delivered, that his notes on Pope's Works are the very beſt ever given on any claſſic whatever. For to inſtance no other, ſurely the attempt to reconcile the doctrines of the Eſſay on Man to the doctrines of Revelation, is the raſheſt adventure in which ever critic yet engaged. This is, in truth, to divine, rather than to explain an author's meaning.

For theſe reaſons, it is not thought proper to accompany this eſſay with a perpetual commentary. A poem, as hath been well obſerved, that conſiſts of precepts, is ſo far arbitrary and immethodical, that many of the paragraphs may change places with no apparent inconvenience; for of two or more poſitions depending on ſome remote principle, there is ſeldom any cogent reaſon, why one ſhould precede the other.

VER. 6. *Ten cenſure*] Readers more eaſily perceive blemiſhes than beauties. Adeſt ferè nemo, ſays Tully, De Orator. i. quin acutiùs

'Tis with our judgments as our watches, none
Go juſt alike, yet each believes his own.
In Poets as true Genius is but rare,
True Taſte as ſeldom is the Critic's ſhare;
Both

NOTES.

acutiùs atque acriùs vitia in dicendo, quàm recta videant. Ita quidquid eſt in quo offenditur, id etiam illa quæ laudanda ſunt obruit. La critique, ſays the ſenſible Abbé de S. Pierre, d'un ouvrage doit etre telle, que l'auteur critiqué ſoit bien aiſe, a tout prendre, qu'on l'ait donnée au public.

Every one of Racine's tragedies were attacked by malignant critics. And Racine uſed to ſay, that theſe paltry critics gave him more pain than all his applauders had given him pleaſure.

VER. 11. *In poets as true Genius is but rare,*] It is indeed ſo extremely rare, that no country, in the ſucceſſion of many ages, has produced above three or four perſons that deſerve the title. The "man of rhymes" may be eaſily found; but the genuine poet, of a lively plaſtic imagination, the true Maker or Creator, is ſo uncommon a prodigy, that one is almoſt tempted to ſubſcribe to the opinion of Sir William Temple, where he ſays, "That of all the numbers of mankind that live within the compaſs of a thouſand years, for one man that is born capable of making a great poet, there may be a thouſand born capable of making as great generals, or miniſters of ſtate, as the moſt renowned in ſtory." There are indeed more cauſes required to concur to the formation of the former, than of the latter; which neceſſarily render its production more difficult.

VER. 12. *True Taſte as ſeldom*] The firſt piece of criticiſm in our language, worthy our attention, for little can be gathered from Webbe and Puttenham, was Sir Philip Sydney's Defence of Poeſie. Spenſer is ſaid to have written a critical diſcourſe, called The Poet; the loſs of which, conſidering the exquiſite taſte and extenſive learning of Spenſer, is much to be regretted. Next came Daniel's Apology; then Ben Jonſon's Diſcoveries, the Preface to Gondibert, and Hobbes's Letter to D'Avenant, the Preface and Notes of Cowley, (whoſe proſe ſtyle, by the way, is admirable), Temple's Eſſays, Dryden's Eſſay on Dramatic Poetry, and his various Prefaces and Prologues, Rhymer's Preface to Rapin, and Letter on Tragedy, and Dennis's Reformation of Poetry, and the Eſſays of Roſcommon and Buckingham.

Both muſt alike from Heav'n derive their light,
Theſe born to judge, as well as thoſe to write.
Let ſuch teach others who themſelves excel,
And cenſure freely who have written well.

Authors

NOTES.

Buckingham. Theſe were the critical pieces that preceded our Author's Eſſay, which was publiſhed without his name, May 1711, about the ſame time with Fenton's Epiſtle to Southerne; and did not, as Lewis the bookſeller told me, ſell at firſt, till our Author ſent copies, as preſents, to ſeveral eminent perſons.

It is ſaid, very ſenſibly, by La Bruyere, "I will allow that good writers are ſcarce enough; but then I aſk, where are the people that know to read and judge? An union of theſe qualities, which are ſeldom found in the ſame perſon, ſeem to be indiſpenſably neceſſary to form an able critic; he ought to poſſeſs ſtrong good ſenſe, lively imagination, and exquiſite ſenſibility. And of theſe three qualities, the laſt is the moſt important; ſince, after all that can be ſaid on the utility or neceſſity of rules and precepts, it muſt be confeſſed, that the merit of all works of genius, muſt be determined by taſte and ſentiment. "Why do you ſo much admire the Helen of Zeuxis?" ſaid one to Nicoſtratus; "You would not wonder why I ſo much admired it, (replied the painter), if you had my eyes." Of the three requiſites to make a juſt critic, mentioned above, Ariſtotle ſeems to have poſſeſſed the firſt, in the higheſt degree; Longinus the ſecond; and Addiſon the third; on whom, however, a celebrated writer has paſſed the following cenſure: "It muſt not be diſſembled that criticiſm was by no means the talent of Addiſon. His taſte was truly elegant; but he had neither that vigour of underſtanding, nor chaſtiſed philoſophical ſpirit, which are ſo eſſential to this character, and which we find in hardly any of the ancients, beſides Ariſtotle, and but in a very few of the moderns. For what concerns his criticiſm on Milton, in particular, there was this accidental benefit ariſing from it, that it occaſioned an admirable poet to be read, and his excellencies to be obſerved. But, for the merit of the work itſelf, if there be any thing juſt in the plan, it was becauſe Ariſtotle and Boſſu had taken the ſame route before him. And as to his own proper obſervations, they are for the moſt part ſo general and indeterminate, as to afford but little inſtruction to the reader, and are not unfrequently altogether frivolous. They

are

Authors are partial to their wit, 'tis true,
But are not Critics to their judgment too?

Yet

NOTES.

are of a kind with those, which the French critics (for I rather instance in the defects of foreign writers than our own) so much abound; and which good judges agree to rank in the worst sort of criticism." Thus far Dr. Hurd, Notes on the Epistle to Augustus, v. 210.

To this censure on Addison Dr. Johnson replied in the following excellent words: "It is not uncommon for those who have grown wise by the labour of others, to add a little of their own, and overlook their masters. Addison is now despised by some, who, perhaps, would never have seen his defects, but by the lights which he afforded them. That he always wrote, as he would think it necessary to write now, cannot be affirmed; his instructions were such as the character of his readers made proper. That general knowledge which now circulates in common talk, was in his time rarely to be found. Men not professing learning, were not ashamed of ignorance; and in the female world, any acquaintance with books, was distinguished only to be censured. His purpose was to infuse literary curiosity, by gentle and unsuspected conveyance, into the gay, the idle, and the wealthy; he therefore presented knowledge in the most alluring form; not lofty and austere, but accessible and familiar. When he shewed them their defects, he shewed them likewise that they might be easily supplied; his attempt succeeded, enquiry was awakened, and comprehension expanded. An emulation of intellectual elegance was excited, and from his time to our own, life has been gradually exalted, and conversation purified and enlarged. Before the profound observers of the present race repose too securely on the consciousness of their superiority to Addison, let them consider his Remarks on Ovid, in which may be found specimens of criticism, sufficiently subtle and refined; let them peruse likewise his Essays on Wit, and on The Pleasures of Imagination, in which he founds art on the base of nature, and draws the principles of invention, from dispositions inherent in the mind of man, with skill and elegance, such as his contemners will not easily attain." Lives of the Poets, vol. ii. page 442.

Many men are to be found who can judge truly, though they may want the power of execution. And it was a proper answer

Yet if we look more cloſely, we ſhall find
Moſt have the ſeeds of judgment in their mind:
Nature

NOTES.

of the Miſanthrope, in Moliere, who had blamed ſome bad verſes, to the poet who defied him to make better;

"J'en pourrois par malheur faire d'auſſi mechans,
Mais je me garderois de les montrer aux gens."

VER. 15. *Let ſuch teach others,*] "Qui ſcribit artificioſe, ab aliis commode ſcripta facile intelligere poterit." Cic. ad Herenn. lib. iv. "De pictore, ſculptore, fictore, niſi artifex, judicare non poteſt." Pliny. P.

"Publiſh ſome work of your own (ſaid a certain angry author to a critic) before you cenſure mine.

Cum tua non edas, carpis mea carmina;
You print nothing for fear of repriſals."

Regnier, the predeceſſor of Boileau, in his ninth ſatire, calls on his cenſors to publiſh ſomething; and adds a ludicrous tale of a peaſant who applied to the Pope, and begged he would ſuffer prieſts to marry; "that we laymen (ſaid he) may careſs their wives, as well as they careſs ours."

"In the large city of Paris, (ſays Voltaire), containing ſix hundred thouſand inhabitants, there are not three thouſand who have any true taſte for literature and the arts."

It is remarked by Dryden, I think, that none but a poet is qualified to judge of a poet. The maxim is however contradicted by experience. Ariſtotle is ſaid indeed to have written one ode; but neither Boſſu nor Hurd are poets. The penetrating author of The Reflections on Poetry, Painting, and Muſic, will for ever be read with delight, and with profit, by all ingenious artiſts; "neverthelefs (ſays Voltaire) he did not underſtand muſic, could never make verſes, and was not poſſeſſed of a ſingle picture; but he had read, ſeen, heard, and reflected a great deal." And Lord Shafteſbury ſpeaks with ſome indignation on this ſubject; "If a muſician performs his part well in the hardeſt ſymphonies, he muſt neceſſarily know the notes, and underſtand the rules of harmony and muſic. But muſt a man, therefore, who has an ear, and has ſtudied the rules of muſic, of neceſſity have a voice, or hand? Can no one poſſibly judge a fiddle, but who is himſelf a fiddler? Can no one judge a picture, but who is himſelf a layer of colours?" Quintilian and Pliny, who ſpeak of the works

Nature affords at leaſt a glimm'ring light;
The lines, tho' touch'd but faintly, are drawn right.
But as the ſlighteſt ſketch, if juſtly trac'd,
Is by ill-colouring but the more diſgrac'd,
So by falſe learning is good ſenſe defac'd:

VARIATIONS.

Between ver. 25 and 26 were theſe lines, ſince omitted by the author.

Many are ſpoil'd by that pedantic throng,
Who with great pains teach youth to reaſon wrong.
Tutors, like Virtuoſo's, oft inclin'd
By ſtrange transfuſion to improve the mind,
Draw off the ſenſe we have, to pour in new;
Which yet, with all their ſkill, they ne'er could do. P.

NOTES.

works of the ancient painters and ſtatuaries with ſo much taſte and ſentiment, handled not themſelves either the pencil or the chiſſel, nor Longinus and Dionyſius the harp. But although ſuch as have actually performed nothing in the art itſelf, may not, on that account, be totally diſqualified to judge with accuracy of any piece of workmanſhip, yet, perhaps, a judgement will come with more authority and force from an artiſt himſelf. Hence the connoiſſeurs highly prize the treatiſe of Ruben's concerning the Imitation of Antique Statues, the Art of Painting by Leonardo da Vinci, and the Lives of the Painters by Vaſari. As, for the ſame reaſons, Rameau's Diſſertation on The Thorough Baſs; and The Introduction to a Good Taſte in Muſic, by the excellent, but neglected, Geminiani, demand a particular regard. The prefaces of Dryden would be equally valuable, if he did not ſo frequently contradict himſelf, and advance opinions diametrically oppoſite to each other. Some of Corneille's diſcourſes on his own tragedies are admirably juſt. And one of the beſt pieces of modern criticiſm, The Academy's Obſervations on the Cid, was, we know, the work of perſons who had themſelves written well. And our Author's own excellent preface to his tranſlation of the Iliad, one of the beſt pieces of proſe in the Engliſh language, is an example how well poets are qualified to be critics.

Some are bewilder'd in the maze of ſchools,
And ſome made coxcombs Nature meant but fools.

NOTES.

VER. 20. *Moſt have the ſeeds*] "Omnes tacito quodam ſenſu, ſine ulla arte, aut ratione, quæ ſint in artibus, ac rationibus recta et prava disjudicant." Cic. de Orat. lib. iii. P.

VER. 25. *So by falſe learning*] "Plus ſine doctrina prudentia, quam ſine prudentia valet doctrina." Quint. P.

VER. 27. *Made coxcombs*] It is hardly poſſible to find an example of an affected critic ſo ridiculous as the following, taken from Spence's Anecdotes.

"The famous Lord Halifax was rather a pretender to taſte than really poſſeſſed of it. When I had finiſhed the two or three firſt books of my tranſlation of the Iliad, that Lord deſired to have the pleaſure of hearing them read at his houſe. Addiſon, Congreve, and Garth, were there at the reading. In four or five places Lord Halifax ſtopt me very civilly, and with a ſpeech each time, much of the ſame kind, "I beg your pardon Mr. Pope, but there is ſomething in that paſſage which does not quite pleaſe me;—be ſo good as to mark the place, and conſider it a little at your leiſure;—I am ſure you can give it a little turn." I returned from Lord Halifax's with Dr. Garth in his chariot; and, as we were going along, was ſaying to the Doctor, that my Lord had laid me under a good deal of difficulty by ſuch looſe and general obſervations; that I had been thinking over the paſſages almoſt ever ſince, and could not gueſs at what it was that had offended his Lordſhip in either of them. Garth laughed heartily at my embarraſſment; ſaid, I had not been long enough acquainted with Lord Halifax to know his way yet; that I need not puzzle myſelf about looking thoſe places over and over when I got home. "All you need do (ſays he) is to leave them juſt as they are; call on Lord Halifax two or three months hence, thank him for his kind obſervations on thoſe paſſages, and then read them to him, as altered. I have known him much longer than you have, and will be anſwerable for the event." I followed his advice, waited on Lord Halifax ſome time after; ſaid, I hoped he would find his objections to thoſe paſſages removed; read them to him, exactly as they were at firſt: and then his Lordſhip was extremely pleaſed with them, and cried out, "Aye, now they are perfectly right; nothing can be better."

In

In ſearch of wit theſe loſe their common ſenſe,
And then turn Critics in their own defence:
Each burns alike, who can, or cannot write,
Or with a Rival's, or an Eunuch's ſpite.
All fools have ſtill an itching to deride,
And fain would be upon the laughing ſide.
If Maevius ſcribble in Apollo's ſpight,
There are, who judge ſtill worſe than he can write.

Some have at firſt for Wits, then Poets paſt,
Turn'd Critics next, and prov'd plain fools at laſt.
Some neither can for Wits nor Critics paſs,
As heavy mules are neither horſe nor aſs.

Thoſe

NOTES.

VER. 28. *In ſearch of wit theſe loſe their common ſenſe,*] This obſervation is extremely juſt. Search of Wit is not only the occaſion, but the efficient cauſe of the loſs of common ſenſe. For Wit conſiſting in chuſing out, and ſetting together ſuch Ideas from whoſe aſſemblage pleaſant pictures may be drawn on the Fancy; the Judgment, through an habitual ſearch of Wit, loſes, by degrees, its faculty of ſeeing the true relation of things; in which conſiſts the exerciſe of common ſenſe. W.

VER. 35. *Who judge ſtill worſe*] " Le plus grand malheur (ſays Voltaire) d'un homme des lettres, n'eſt peutetre pas d'etre objet de la jalouſie de ſes confreres, la victime de la cabale, le mepris de puiſſans du monde, c'eſt d'etre jugé par des ſots. L'homme de lettres, (ſi on lui fait injuſtice), eſt ſans ſecours; il reſemble au poiſſons volantes; s'il s'éleve un peu, les oiſeaux le devorent; s'il ſe plonge, les poiſſons le mangent. Tout homme public paye tribut à la malignité; mais il eſt payé en deniers & en honneurs." Queſtions ſur L'Encycl. 7 T. 323.

VER. 38. *Some neither can for Wits nor Critics paſs,*] Theſe lines, and thoſe preceding and following them, are excellently ſatirical; and were, I think, the firſt we find in his works, that give an indication of that ſpecies of poetry to which his talent was moſt powerfully bent, and in which, though not as we ſhall ſee in others, he excelled all mankind. The ſimile of the mule

N 3 heightens

Thoſe half-learn'd witlings, numerous in our iſle,
As half-form'd inſects on the banks of Nile;
Unfiniſh'd things, one knows not what to call,
Their generation's ſo equivocal:
To tell 'em would an hundred tongues require,
Or one vain wit's, that might a hundred tire.
 But you who ſeek to give and merit fame,
And juſtly bear a Critic's noble name,
Be ſure yourſelf and your own reach to know,
How far your genius, taſte, and learning go;
Launch not beyond your depth, but be diſcreet,
And mark that point where ſenſe and dullneſs meet.
Nature to all things fix'd the limits fit,
And wiſely curb'd proud man's pretending wit.
As on the land while here the ocean gains,
In other parts it leaves wide ſandy plains;
Thus in the Soul while memory prevails,
The ſolid pow'r of underſtanding fails;

Where

NOTES.

heightens the ſatire, and is new; as is the application of the inſects of the Nile. Pope never ſhines ſo brightly as when he is proſcribing bad authors.

"The Nile (ſays Fenton on Waller) has been as fruitful of Engliſh ſimiles as the ſun; from both which it would be as ſevere to reſtrain a young poet, as forbidding the uſe of fire and water was eſteemed among the Romans."

VER. 56. *Thus in the Soul*] The beauty of imagery in theſe lines ſhould not make us blind to the want of juſtneſs in the thought. To repreſent ſtrength of memory as incompatible with ſolidity of underſtanding, is ſo obviouſly contrary to fact, that I preſume the author had in his eye only the caſe of extraordinary memory for names, dates, and things, which offer no ideas to the mind; which has, indeed, been often diſplayed in great

perfection

Where beams of warm imagination play,
The memory's ſoft figures melt away.
One ſcience only will one genius fit;
So vaſt is art, ſo narrow human wit:

Not

NOTES.

perfection by mere idiots. For, it is difficult to conceive how the faculty of judgment, which conſiſts in the compariſon of different ideas, can at all be exerciſed without the power of ſtoring up ideas in the mind, and calling them forth when required. From the ſecond couplet, apparently meant to be the converſe of the firſt, one would ſuppoſe that he conſulted the underſtanding and the imagination as the ſame faculty, elſe the counterpart is defective. Further, ſo far is it from being true, that imagination obliterates the figures of memory, that the circumſtance which cauſes a thing to be remembered is principally its being aſſociated with other ideas by the agency of the imagination. If the poet only meant, that thoſe ideas about which imagination is occupied, are apt to exclude ideas of a different kind, the remark is true, but it ſhould have been differently expreſſed.

Voltaire ſays well, " He that retains the greateſt number of images in the magazine of memory, has the beſt imagination." Encycl. v. xxxi. p. 187. And alſo in another place; " The faculty of imagination depends entirely on the memory. We ſee men, animals, horſes, gardens, and other ſenſible objects; theſe perceptions enter our minds by the ſenſes; the memory retains them; the imagination combines them; and this is the reaſon why the Greeks called the Muſes the Daughters of Memory."

VER. 60. *One ſcience only will one genius fit*;] When Tully attempted poetry, he became as ridiculous as Bolingbroke when he attempted philoſophy and divinity. We look in vain for that genius which produced The Diſſertation on Parties, in his tedious philoſophical works; of which it is no exaggerated ſatire to ſay, that the reaſoning of them is ſophiſtical and inconcluſive, the ſtyle diffuſe and verboſe, and the learning ſeemingly contained in them not drawn from the originals, but picked up and purloined from French critics and tranſlations; and particularly from Bayle, Rapin, and Thomaſſin, (as perhaps may be one day minutely ſhewn), together with the aſſiſtances which our Cudworth and Stanley

Not only bounded to peculiar arts,
But oft in thoſe confin'd to ſingle parts.
Like Kings we loſe the conqueſts gain'd before,
By vain ambition ſtill to make them more:

Each

NOTES.

happily afforded a writer confeſſedly ignorant of the Greek tongue, who has yet the inſufferable arrogance to vilify and cenſure, and to think he can confute, the beſt writers in that beſt language.

When Fontaine, whoſe Tales indicated a truly comic genius, brought a comedy on the ſtage, it was received with a contempt equally unexpected and deſerved. Terence has left us no tragedy; and the Mourning Bride of Congreve, notwithſtanding the praiſes beſtowed on it by Pope, in the Dunciad, is certainly a deſpicable performance; the plot is unnaturally intricate, and overcharged with incidents, the ſentiments trite, and the language turgid and bombaſt. The Biter of Rowe is wretched. Heemſkirk and Teniers could not ſucceed in a ſerious and ſublime ſubject of hiſtory painting. The latter, it is well known, deſigned cartoons for tapeſtry, repreſenting the hiſtory of the Turriani of Lombardy. Both the compoſition and the expreſſion are extremely indifferent; and certain nicer virtuoſi have remarked, that in the ſerious pieces of Titian himſelf, even in one of his Laſt Suppers, a circumſtance of the ridiculous and the familiar is introduced, which ſuits not with the dignity of his ſubject. Hogarth's Sigiſmonda diſgraced his pencil.

The modeſty and good ſenſe of the ancients is, in this particular, as in others, remarkable. The ſame writer never preſumed to undertake more than one kind of dramatic poetry, if we except the Cyclops of Euripides. A poet never preſumed to plead in public, or to write hiſtory, or indeed any conſiderable work in proſe. The ſame actors never recited tragedy and comedy: this was obſerved long ago, by Plato, in the third book of his Republic. They ſeem to have held that diverſity, nay univerſality, of excellence, at which the moderns frequently aim, to be a gift unattainable by man. We therefore, of Great Britain, have, perhaps, more reaſon to congratulate ourſelves, on two great phenomena; I mean Shakeſpear's being able to pourtray characters ſo very different as Falſtaff and Macbeth; and Garrick's being able to perſonate ſo inimitably a Lear, or an

Abel

Each might his sev'ral province well command,
Would all but stoop to what they understand.
First follow Nature, and your judgment frame
By her just standard, which is still the same:
Unerring

NOTES.

Abel Drugger. Nothing can more fully demonstrate the extent and versatility of these two original geniuses. Corneille, whom the French are so fond of opposing to Shakespear, produced very contemptible comedies; and the Plaideures of Racine is so close a resemblance of Aristophanes, that it ought not to be here urged. The most universal of authors seems to be Voltaire, who has written almost equally well, both in prose and verse; and whom either the tragedies of Merope and Mahomet, or the history of Louis XIV. or Charles XII. would alone have immortalized. It might have been expected that the author of Candide would have been able to produce a good comedy; and that a writer who draws characters, and plans a fable so inimitably well, as Fielding in Tom Jones, would have done the same; but both these authors have failed in the attempt.

VER. 66. *His sev'ral province*] A clear head and strong sense were the characteristical qualities of our Author; and every man soonest and best displays his radical excellencies. If his predominant talent be warmth and vigor of imagination, it will break out in fanciful and luxuriant descriptions, the colouring of which will perhaps be too rich and glowing. If his chief force lies in the understanding rather than in the imagination, it will soon appear by solid and manly observations on life or learning, expressed in a more chaste and subdued style. The former will frequently be hurried into obscurity or turgidity, and a false grandeur of diction; the latter will seldom hazard a figure, whose usage is not already established, or an image beyond common life; will always be perspicuous, if not elevated; will never disgust, if not transport, his readers; will avoid the grosser faults, if not arrive at the greater beauties of composition. The "eloquentiæ genus," for which he will be distinguished, will not be the "plenum, et erectum, et audax, et præcelsum," but the "pressum, et mite, et limatum." In the earliest letters of Pope to Wycherley, to Walsh, and Cromwell, we find many admirable and acute judgments of men and books, and an intimate acquaintance, not only

Unerring NATURE, ſtill divinely bright,
One clear, unchang'd, and univerſal light,
Life, force, and beauty, muſt to all impart,
At once the ſource, and end, and teſt of Art.
Art from that fund each juſt ſupply provides;
Works without ſhow, and without pomp preſides:
In ſome fair body thus th' informing ſoul
With ſpirits feeds, with vigor fills the whole,
Each motion guides, and ev'ry nerve ſuſtains;
Itſelf unſeen, but in th' effects remains.

NOTES.

only with ſome of the beſt Greek and Roman, particularly the latter, but the moſt celebrated French and Italian claſſics.

Du Bos fixes the period of time, at which, generally ſpeaking, the poets and the painters have arrived at as high a pitch of perfection, as their geniuſſes will permit, to be the age of thirty years, or a few years more or leſs. Virgil was near thirty when he compoſed his firſt eclogue. Horace was a grown man when he began to be talked of at Rome as a poet, having been formerly engaged in a buſy military life. Racine was about the ſame age when his Andromache, which may be regarded as his firſt good tragedy, was played. Corneille was more than thirty when his Cid appeared. Deſpereaux was full thirty when he publiſhed his Satires, ſuch as we now have them. Moliere was full forty when he wrote the firſt of thoſe comedies, on which his reputation is founded. But to excel in this ſpecies of compoſition, it was not ſufficient for Moliere to be only a great poet; it was rather neceſſary for him to gain a thorough knowledge of men and the world, which is ſeldom attained ſo early in life; but without which, the beſt poet would be able to write but very indifferent comedies. Congreve however was but nineteen when he wrote his Old Bachelor. Raphael was about thirty years old when he diſplayed the beauty and ſublimity of his genius in the Vatican, for it is there we behold the firſt of his works, that are worthy the great name he at preſent ſo deſervedly poſſeſſes. When Shakeſpear wrote his Lear, Milton his Paradiſe Loſt, Spenſer his Fairy Queen, and Dryden his Muſic Ode, they had all exceeded the middle age of man.

Some,

Some, to whom Heav'n in wit has been profuse,
Want as much more, to turn it to its use;
For wit and judgment often are at strife,
Tho' meant each other's aid, like man and wife.

NOTES.

VER. 80. *Some, to whom Heav'n, &c.*] Here the Poet (in a sense he was not, at first, aware of) has given an example of the truth of his observation, in the observation itself. The two lines stood originally thus,

> " There are whom Heav'n has blest with store of Wit,
> Yet want as much again to manage it."

In the first line, *wit* is used, in the modern sense, for the effort of Fancy; in the second line it is used, in the ancient sense, for the result of Judgment. This trick, play'd the Reader, he endeavoured to keep out of sight, by altering the lines as they now stand,

> " Some, to whom Heav'n in Wit has been profuse,
> Want as much more, to turn it to its use."

For the words, *to manage it*, as the lines were at first, too plainly discovered the change put upon the Reader, in the use of the word, *wit*. This is now a little covered by the latter expression of—*turn it to its use*. But then the alteration, in the preceding line, from—*store of wit*, to *profuse*, was an unlucky change. For though he who has *store of wit* may want more, yet he to whom it was given in *profusion* could hardly be said to want more. The truth is, the Poet had said a lively thing, and would, at all hazards, preserve the reputation of it, though the very topic he is upon obliged him to detect the imposition, in the very next lines, which shew he meant two very different things, by the same term, in the two preceding,

> " For wit and judgment often are at strife,
> Tho' meant each other's aid, like man and wife." W.

VER. 82. *Wit*] " If all wisdom be science, and it be the business of science, as well to compound as to separate, may we not say, that those philosophers took half of wisdom for the whole, who distinguished it from wit, as if wisdom only separated, and wit only brought it together? Yet, so held the Philosopher of Malmesbury, and Author of the Essay on the Human Understanding." Harris's Hermes, page 368.

'Tis

'Tis more to guide, than ſpur the Muſe's ſteed;
Reſtrain his fury, than provoke his ſpeed;
The winged courſer, like a gen'rous horſe,
Shews moſt true mettle when you check his courſe.

Thoſe RULES of old diſcover'd, not deviſ'd,
Are Nature ſtill, but Nature methodiz'd;

Nature,

NOTES.

VER. 88. *Thoſe Rules of old, &c.*] Cicero has, beſt of any one I know, explained what that thing is which reduces the wild and ſcattered parts of human knowledge into arts.—"Nihil eſt quod ad artem redigi poſſit, niſi ille prius, qui illa tenet, quorum artem inſtituere vult, habeat illam ſcientiam, ut ex iis rebus, quarum ars nondum ſit, artem efficere poſſit.—Omnia fere, quae ſunt concluſa nunc artibus, diſperſa et diſſipata quondam fuerunt, ut in Muſicis, etc. Adhibita eſt igitur ars quaedam extrinſecus ex alio genere quodam, quod ſibi totum PHILOSOPHI aſſumunt, quae rem diſſolutam divulſamque conglutinaret, et ratione quadam conſtringeret." De Orat. l. i. c. 41, 2. W.

The precepts of the art of poeſy were poſterior to practice; the rules of the Epopea were all drawn from the Iliad, and the Odyſſey; and of Tragedy, from the Oedipus of Sophocles. A petulant rejection, and an implicit veneration, of the rules of the ancient critics, are equally deſtructive of true taſte. "It ought to be the firſt endeavour of a writer (ſays the Rambler, Nº 156.) to diſtinguiſh nature from cuſtom; or that which is eſtabliſhed becauſe it is right, from that which is right only becauſe it is eſtabliſhed; that he may neither violate eſſential principles by a deſire of novelty, nor debar himſelf from the attainment of any beauties within his view, by a needleſs fear of breaking rules, which no literary dictator had authority to preſcribe."

This liberal and manly cenſure of critical bigotry, extends not to thoſe fundamental and indiſpenſable rules, which nature and neceſſity dictate, and demand to be obſerved; ſuch, for inſtance, as in the higher kinds of poetry, that the action of the epopea, be one, great, and entire; that the hero be eminently diſtinguiſhed, move our concern, and deeply intereſt us; that the epiſodes ariſe eaſily out of the main fable; that the action commence as near the

cataſtrophe

Nature, like Liberty, is but reſtrain'd
By the ſame Laws which firſt herſelf ordain'd.

Hear

NOTES.

cataſtrophe as poſſible; and, in the drama, that no more events be crowded together, than can be juſtly ſuppoſed to happen during the time of repreſentation, or to be tranſacted on one individual ſpot, and the like. But the abſurdity here animadverted on, is the ſcrupulous nicety of thoſe who bind themſelves to obey frivolous and unimportant laws; ſuch as, that an epic poem ſhould conſiſt not of leſs than twelve books; that it ſhould end fortunately; that in the firſt book there ſhould be no ſimile; that the exordium ſhould be very ſimple and unadorned; that in a tragedy, only three perſonages ſhould appear at once upon the ſtage; and that every tragedy ſhould conſiſt of five acts; by the rigid obſervation of which laſt unneceſſary precept, the poet is deprived of uſing many a moving ſtory, that would furniſh matter enough for three perhaps, but not for five acts; with other rules of the like indifferent nature. For the reſt, as Voltaire obſerves, whether the action of an epopea be ſimple or complex, completed in a month, or a year, or a longer time, whether the ſcene be fixed on one ſpot, as in the Iliad; or that the hero voyages from ſea to ſea, as in the Odyſſey; whether he be furious like Achilles, or pious like Eneas; whether the action paſs on land or ſea; on the coaſt of Africa, as in the Luziada of Camoens; in America, as in the Araucana of Alonzo D'Ercilla; in Heaven, in Hell, beyond the limits of our world, as in the Paradiſe Loſt; all theſe circumſtances are of no conſequence: the poem will be for ever an epic poem, an heroic poem; at leaſt, till another new title be found proportioned to its merit. " If you ſcruple (ſays Addiſon) to give the title of an Epic Poem to the Paradiſe Loſt of Milton, call it, if you chooſe, a Divine Poem; give it whatever name you pleaſe; provided you confeſs, that it is a work as admirable in its kind as the Iliad.

It has become a faſhionable attempt of late, to cenſure and decry an obedience to the rules laid down by ancient critics; while one party, loudly and frequently exclaim,

—— Vos exemplaria Græca
Nocturnâ verſate manû, verſate diurnâ;

Another, inſtantly anſwers,

—— O imitatores ſervum pecus!

One

Hear how learn'd Greece her uſeful rules indites,
When to repreſs, and when indulge our flights:

High

NOTES.

One of the ableſt defenders of literary liberty expreſſes himſelf thus;

" From the time of Homer, epic poetry became an artificial compoſition, whoſe rules were, in reality, drawn from the practice of the Grecian Bard, rather than from the principles of Nature. Lyric and dramatic poetry were in like manner fixed, though at a later period, by Grecian models; ſo that the Roman writers of ſimilar performances could not be ſaid to bring any thing of their own to their works. The ſame ſhackles of imitation have hung upon the poetry of modern Europe; whence a fair compariſon of the powers and genius of different periods is rendered ſcarcely practicable. The leading ſpecies of poetry, like the orders of architecture, have come down to us ſubject to certain proportions, and requiring certain ornamental accompaniments, which, perhaps, have had no foundation whatever but the caſual practice of the earlieſt maſters; nay, poſſibly, the whole exiſtence of ſome of the ſpecies has had the ſame accidental origin.

" Meantime, the veneration for the ancients has been raiſed to the higheſt pitch by this perpetual reference to them as models; and it has been concluded, that works which have engaged the ſtudy, and called forth the imitation of ſo many ſucceeding ages, muſt poſſeſs a ſuperior degree of excellence. But after all, their reputation may have been much more owing to accident than is commonly ſuppoſed. That the Grecian poets, continually recording the deeds of their countrymen, and offering incenſe to the national vanity, ſhould have been held in high eſteem at home, was natural. That the Romans, receiving all their literature from Greece, ſhould adopt its principles and prejudices, was alſo to be expected. But that they ſhould tranſmit them to ſo large a portion of the civilized world, and this, not only during the period of their domination, but to new races of men, ſo many centuries after the downfall of their empire, muſt be reckoned accident, as far as any thing in human affairs can be called accidental. Had not the Chriſtian religion eſtabliſhed a kind of ſecond Roman empire, even more capable of ſwaying the opinions of mankind than the firſt, it is highly improbable that we ſhould at this day have been commenting upon the claſſical

writers

High on Parnaſſus' top her ſons ſhe ſhow'd,
And pointed out thoſe arduous paths they trod;
Held

NOTES.

writers of Greece and Rome. It is, indeed, aſtoniſhing to reflect, by what a ſtrange concatenation of cauſe and effect, the youth of Chriſtian Europe ſhould be inſtructed in the fables of Greek and Latin Mythology, which were fallen into contempt even before Rome ceaſed to be heathen.

"It certainly has not been on account of their wiſdom and beauty that they have ſurvived the wreck of ſo many better things. They have been embalmed in the languages which contained them, and which, by becoming likewiſe the depoſitaries of Chriſtian doctrine, have been rendered ſacred languages."

To this ſort of reaſoning, the imitators of the ancients, by way of anſwer, muſt ſay, that all they mean in adhering to rules, is to adopt, "that method of treating any ſubject, that may render it moſt intereſting to a reader." This, for inſtance, was the reaſon why Ariſtotle gives the preference to thoſe tragedies, where there is a diſcovery and peripetic. And hence, they will ſay, the Edipus of Sophocles is as perfect a model of dramatic, as the Mediccan Venus is of female, beauty.

The learned and ingenious tranſlator of Ariſtotle's Treatiſe on Poetry, with whoſe words I conclude this long note, is of a different opinion. "When we ſpeak (ſays he) of the Greek tragedies, as perfect and correct models, we ſeem merely to conform to the eſtabliſhed language of prejudice, and content ourſelves with echoing, without reflection or examination, what has been ſaid before us. I ſhould be ſorry to be ranked in the claſs of thoſe critics, who prefer that poetry which has the feweſt faults, to that which has the greateſt beauties. I mean only to combat that conventional and hearſay kind of praiſe, which has ſo often held out the tragedies of the Greek poets, as elaborate and perfect models, ſuch as had received the laſt poliſh of art and meditation. The true praiſe of Eſchylus, Sophocles, and Euripides, is (in kind at leaſt, if not in degree,) the praiſe of Shakeſpeare; that of ſtrong, but irregular, unequal, and haſty genius. Every thing which this genius, and the feeling of the moment could produce, in an early period of the art, before time and long experience, and criticiſm, had cultivated and refined it, theſe

Held from afar, aloft, th' immortal prize,
And urg'd the rest by equal steps to rise.

Just

NOTES.

these writers possess in great abundance: what meditation, and the labour and delay of the file only can effect, they too often want. Of Shakespeare, however, compared with the Greek poets, it may justly, I think, be pronounced, that he has much more both of this want, and of that abundance." Twining's Aristotle, p. 207.

VER. 92. *Hear how learn'd Greece*] In the second part of Shaftesbury's Advice to an Author, is a judicious and elegant account of the rise and progress of arts and sciences, in ancient Greece; to subjects of which sort it were to be wished this author had always confined himself, as he indisputably understood them well, rather than have blemished and belied his patriotism, by writing against the religion of his country.

I shall give the reader a passage that relates to the origin of criticism, which is curious and just. "When the persuasive arts, which were necessary to be cultivated among a people that were to be convinced before they acted, were grown thus in repute; and the power of moving the affections become the study and emulation of the forward wits and aspiring geniuses of the times; it would necessarily happen, that many geniuses of equal size and strength, though less covetous of public applause, of power, or of influence over mankind, would content themselves with the contemplation, merely, of these enchanting arts. These they would the better enjoy, the more they refined their taste and cultivated their ear. Hence was the origin of Critics; who, as arts and sciences advanced, would necessarily come withal into repute; and being heard with satisfaction in their turn, were at length tempted to become authors, and appear in public. These were honoured with the name of Sophists; a character which in early times was highly respected. Nor did the gravest philosophers, who were censors of manners, and critics of a higher degree, disdain to exert their criticism on the inferior arts; especially in those relating to speech, and the power of argument and persuasion. When such a race as this was once risen, it was no longer possible to impose on mankind, by what was specious and pretending. The public would be paid in no false wit, or jingling eloquence.

Where

Juſt precepts thus from great examples giv'n,
She drew from them what they deriv'd from Heav'n.
The gen'rous Critic fann'd the Poet's fire,
And taught the world with reaſon to admire.
Then Criticiſm the Muſe's handmaid prov'd,
To dreſs her charms, and make her more belov'd:

But

NOTES.

Where the learned critics were ſo well received, and philoſophers themſelves diſdained not to be of the number, there could not fail to ariſe critics of an inferior order, who would ſubdivide the ſeveral provinces of this empire." Characteriſtics, vol. i. 12mo. p. 163.

Our author might have profited much by reading Shafteſbury's Advice to an Author; but his eſſay preceded it.

Ver. 98. *Juſt Precepts*] "Nec enim artibus editis factum eſt ut argumenta inveniremus, ſed dicta ſunt omnia antequam praeciperentur; mox ea ſcriptores obſervata et collecta ediderunt." Quintil. P.

Ver. 103. *To dreſs her charms,*] What a dreadful picture has Swift drawn of the evil demon of criticiſm.

"Momus fearing the worſt, and calling to mind an ancient prophecy, which bore no very good face to his children the moderns; bent his flight to the region of a malignant deity, called Criticiſm. She dwelt on the top of a ſnowy mountain in Nova Zembla; there Momus found her extended in her den, upon the ſpoils of numberleſs volumes half devoured. At her right hand ſat Ignorance, her father and huſband, blind with age; at her left, Pride, her mother, dreſſing her up in the ſcraps of paper herſelf had torn. There, was Opinion, her ſiſter, light of foot, hoodwinked, and headſtrong, yet giddy and perpetually turning. About her played her children, Noiſe and Impudence, Dulneſs and Vanity, Poſitiveneſs, Pedantry, and Ill-manners. The goddeſs herſelf had claws like a cat; her head, and ears, and voice, reſembled thoſe of an aſs; her teeth fallen out before; her eyes turned inward, as if ſhe looked only upon herſelf; her diet was the overflowing of her own gall; her ſpleen was ſo large, as

But following wits from that intention ſtray'd,
Who could not win the miſtreſs, woo'd the maid;
Againſt the Poets their own arms they turn'd,
Sure to hate moſt the men from whom they learn'd.
So modern 'Pothecaries, taught the art
By Doctors' bills to play the Doctor's part,
Bold in the practice of miſtaken rules,
Preſcribe, apply, and call their maſters fools.
Some on the leaves of ancient authors prey,
Nor time nor moths e'er ſpoil ſo much as they.
Some drily plain, without invention's aid,
Write dull receipts how poems may be made.

NOTES.

to ſtand prominent like a dug of the firſt rate, nor wanted excreſcencies in form of teats, at which a crew of ugly monſters were greedily ſucking; and, what is wonderful to conceive, the bulk of ſpleen encreaſed faſter than the ſucking could diminiſh it." Tale of a Tub, p. 200.

Ver. 107. *Sure to hate*] A feeble line of monoſyllables, conſiſting of ten low words.

Ver. 112. *Some on the leaves*] He has too frequently expreſſed an idle contempt of the Heinſius's, Burmans, Gronovius's, Reiſkius's, Marklands, and Geſners; and other ſearchers into various readings, who have done ſo much towards ſettling the texts of ancient authors.

Ver. 115. *Write dull*] Perhaps he glanced at Boſſu's famous Treatiſe on Epic Poetry; which may have been too much praiſed. D'Aubignac, under the patronage of Richlieu, wrote a treatiſe on the drama; and Mambrun on the epopée; but the tragedy of the one, aud the Conſtantine, an epic poem, of the other, were deſpicable performances, which induced the great Condé to ſay, " Je ſcais bon gré, à l'Abbé D'Aubignac d'avoir ſuivi les regles d'Ariſtote, mais je ne pardonne pas aux regles, d'Ariſtote d'avoir fait faire une ſi mauvaiſe tragedie à l' Abbé D'Aubignac."

These

These leave the ſenſe, their learning to diſplay,
And thoſe explain the meaning quite away.
You then whoſe judgment the right courſe would ſteer,
Know well each ANCIENT's proper character;
His

NOTES.

VER. 119. *Know well each Ancient's proper character*;] From their inattention to theſe particulars, many critics, and particularly the French, have been guilty of great abſurdities. When Perrault impotently attempted to ridicule the firſt ſtanza of the firſt Olympic of Pindar, he was ignorant that the poet, in beginning with the praiſes of water, alluded to the philoſophy of Thales, who taught, that water was the principle of all things; and which philoſophy, Empedocles the Sicilian, a cotemporary of Pindar, and a ſubject of Hiero, to whom Pindar wrote, had adopted in his beautiful poem. Homer and the Greek tragedians have been likewiſe cenſured, the former for protracting the Iliad after the death of Hector; and the latter, for continuing the Ajax and Phoeniſſæ, after the deaths of their reſpective heroes. But the cenſurers did not conſider the importance of burial among the ancients; and that the action of the Iliad would have been imperfect without a deſcription of the funeral rites of Hector and Patroclus; as the two tragedies, without thoſe of Polynices and Eteocles; for the ancients eſteemed a deprivation of ſepulture to be a more ſevere calamity than death itſelf. It is obſervable, that this circumſtance did not occur to Pope, when he endeavoured to juſtify this conduct of Homer, by only ſaying, that as the anger of Achilles does not die with Hector, but perſecutes his very remains, the poet ſtill keeps up to his ſubject, by deſcribing the many effects of his anger, till it is fully ſatisfied; and that for this reaſon, the two laſt books of the Iliad may be thought not to be excreſcencies, but eſſential to the poem. I will only add, that I do not know an author whoſe capital excellence ſuffers more from the reader's not regarding his climate and country, than the incomparable Cervantes. There is a ſtriking propriety in the madneſs of Don Quixote, not frequently taken notice of; for Thuanus informs us, that madneſs is a common diſorder

 among

His Fable, Subject, scope in ev'ry page;
Religion, Country, genius of his Age:
Without all these at once before your eyes,
Cavil you may, but never criticize.
Be Homer's works your study and delight,
Read them by day, and meditate by night;
Thence form your judgment, thence your maxims bring,
And trace the Muses upward to their spring.
Still with itself compar'd, his text peruse;
And let your comment be the Mantuan Muse.

When

VARIATIONS.

Ver. 123. *Cavil you may, but never criticize.*] The author after this verse originally inserted the following, which he has however omitted in all the editions:

Zoilus, had these been known, without a Name
Had dy'd, and Perault ne'er been dam'd to fame;
The sense of sound Antiquity had reign'd,
And sacred Homer yet been unprophan'd.
None e'er had thought his comprehensive mind
To modern customs, modern rules confin'd;
Who for all ages writ, and all mankind. P.

NOTES.

among the Spaniards at the latter part of life, about the age of which the knight is represented. "Sur la fin de ses jours Mendozza devint furieux, comme sont d'ordinaire les Espagnols."

Ver. 128. *Still with itself compar'd, &c.*] Although perhaps it may seem impossible to produce any new observations on Homer and Virgil, after so many volumes of criticism as have been spent upon them, yet the following remarks have a novelty and penetration in them that may entertain; especially, as the little treatise from which they are taken is extremely scarce.

" Quæ

When first young Maro in his boundless mind
A work t' outlast immortal Rome design'd, 131

Perhaps

VARIATIONS.

VER. 130.]

When first young Maro sung of Kings and Wars,
Ere warning Phoebus touch'd his trembling ears.

NOTES.

" Quæ variæ inter se notæ atque imagines animorum, a principibus utriusque populi poetis, Homero et Virgilio, mirificè exprimuntur. Siquidem Homeri duces et reges rapacitate, libidine, atque anilibus questibus, lacrymisque puerilibus, Græcam levitatem et inconstantiam referunt. Virgiliani vero principes, ab eximio poeta, qui Romanæ severitatis fastidium, et Latinum supercilium verebatur, et ad heroum populum loquebatur, ita componuntur ad majestatum consularem ut quamvis ab Asiatica mollitie luxuque venerint, inter Furios atque Claudios nati educatique videantur. Neque suam, ullo actu, Æneas originem prodidisset, nisi, a præfactiore aliquanto pietate, fudisset crebro copiam lacrymarum. Qua meliorem expressione morum hac ætate, non modo Virgilius Latinorum poetarum princeps, sed quivis inflatissimus vernaculorum, Homero præfertur: cum hic animos proceribus indurit suos, ille vero alienos. Quamobrem varietas morum, qui carmine reddebantur, et hominum ad quos ea dirigebantur, inter Latinam Græcamque poesin, non inventionis tantum attulit, sed et elocutionis discrimen illud, quod præcipue inter Homerum et Virgilium deprehenditur; cum sententias et oramenta quæ Homeras sparserat, Virgilius, Romanorum arium causa, contraxerit; atque ad mores et ingenia retulerit eorum, qui a poesi non petebant publicam aut privatem institutionem, quam ipsi Marte suo invenerant; sed tantum delectationem *. Blackwell, in his excellent Enquiry into the Life and Writings of Homer, has taken many observations from this valuable book, particularly in his twelfth section.

VER. 130. *When first young Maro, &c.*] Virg. Eclog. vi.

" Cum canerem reges et proelia, Cynthius aurum
Vellit."

* J. Vincentii Gravinæ de Poesi, ad S. Maffeinno Epist. added to his treatise entitled Della Rasion Poetica. In Napoli, 1716, page 239. 250.

Perhaps he ſeem'd above the Critic's law,
And but from Nature's fountain ſcorn'd to draw:

NOTES.

It is a tradition preſerved by Servius, that Virgil began with writing a poem of the Alban and Roman affairs; which he found above his years, and deſcended firſt to imitate Theocritus on rural ſubjects, and afterwards to copy Homer in Heroic poetry. P.

That Virgil, not only in his general plan, but in moſt of the ſubordinate parts, was a cloſe copyiſt of Homer, is undeniable, whatever be thought of the ſuppoſition that he ſet out with a deſign of drawing from the ſources of nature, and was diverted from it by the diſcovery that "Nature and Homer were the ſame." The modern idolatry of Shakeſpear has elevated him to the ſame degree of authority among us; and critics have not been wanting, who have confidently drawn from his characters the proofs and illuſtrations of their theories on the human mind. But what can be more unworthy of the true critic and philoſopher, than ſuch an implicit reliance on any man, how exalted ſoever his genius, eſpecially on thoſe who lived in the infancy of their art? If an epic poem be a repreſentation of nature in a courſe of heroic action, it muſt be ſuſceptible of as much variety as nature herſelf; and ſurely it is more deſirable that a poet of original genius ſhould give full ſcope to his inventive powers, under the reſtriction of ſuch laws only as are founded on nature, than that he ſhould fetter himſelf with rules derived from the practice of a predeceſſor. When Pope praiſes the ancient rules for compoſition on the ground that they were "diſcover'd not deviſ'd," and were only "nature methodized," he gives a juſt notion of what they ought to be. But when he ſuppoſes Virgil to have properly "checked in his bold deſign of drawing from Nature's fountains," and in conſequence, to have confined his work within rules as ſtrict,

"As if the Stagyrite o'erlook'd each line;"

how can he avoid the force of his own ridicule, where a little further, in this very piece, he laughs at Dennis for

"Concluding all were deſperate ſots and fools
Who durſt depart from Ariſtotle's rules?"

Such are the inconſiſtencies of a writer who ſometimes utters notions derived from reading and education; ſometimes the ſuggeſtions of native good ſenſe!" Dr. Aikin to his Son.

But

But when t' examine ev'ry part he came,
Nature and Homer were, he found, the ſame.
Convinc'd, amaz'd, he checks the bold deſign:
And rules as ſtrict his labour'd work confine,
As if the Stagirite o'erlook'd each line.
Learn hence for ancient rules a juſt eſteem;
To copy nature is to copy them.

Some

NOTES.

VER. 138. *As if the Stagyrite*] According to a fine precept in the fourteenth ſection of Longinus, who exhorts us, when we aim at any thing elevated and ſublime, to aſk ourſelves while we are compoſing, " how would Homer, or Plato, or Demoſthenes, have exerted and expreſſed themſelves on this ſubject? And ſtill more, if we ſhould continue to aſk ourſelves; what would Homer or Demoſthenes, if they had been preſent, and had heard this paſſage, have thought of it, and how would they have been affected by it?"

VER. 140. *To copy Nature*] It may not be unuſeful or unpleaſant to ſee the very different opinion of a writer, who, perhaps, had done better if he had followed this rule.

" A ſpirit of imitation hath many ill effects, (ſays Dr. Young); I ſhall confine myſelf to three. Firſt, It deprives the liberal and politer arts of an advantage which the mechanic enjoy; in theſe, men are ever endeavouring to go beyond their predeceſſors; in the former, to follow them. And ſince copies ſurpaſs not their originals, as ſtreams riſe not higher than their ſpring, rarely ſo high; hence, while arts mechanic are in perpetual progreſs, and increaſe, the liberal are in retrogradation, and decay. Theſe reſemble pyramids, are broad at bottom, but leſſen exceedingly as they riſe; thoſe reſemble rivers which, from a ſmall fountain-head, are ſpreading ever wider and wider, as they run. Hence it is evident, that different portions of underſtanding are not (as ſome imagine) allotted to different periods of time; for we ſee, in the ſame period, underſtanding riſing in one ſet of artiſts, and declining in another. Therefore nature ſtands abſolved, and our inferiority in compoſition muſt be charged on ourſelves.

" Nay, ſo far are we from complying with a neceſſity, which nature lays us under, that, ſecondly, by a ſpirit of imitation we

 counteract

Some beauties yet no Precepts can declare,
For there's a happineſs as well as care.

Muſic

NOTES.

counteract nature, and thwart her deſign. She brings us into the world all originals. No two faces, no two minds, are juſt alike; but all bear Nature's evident mark of ſeparation on them. Born originals, how comes it to paſs that we die copies? That meddling ape, Imitation, as ſoon as we come to years of indiſcretion, (ſo let me ſpeak), ſnatches the pen, and blots out Nature's mark of ſeparation, cancels her kind intention, deſtroys all mental individuality; the lettered world no longer conſiſts of ſingulars, it is a medley, a maſs; and a hundred books, at bottom, are but one. Why are monkies ſuch maſters of mimickry? Why receive they ſuch a talent at imitation? Is it not as the Spartan ſlaves received a licence for ebriety; that their betters might be aſhamed of it?

"The third fault to be found with a ſpirit of imitation is, that with great incongruity it makes us poor, and proud; makes us think little, and write much; gives us huge folios, which are little better than more reputable cuſhions to promote our repoſe. Have not ſome ſeven-fold volumes put us in mind of Ovid's ſeven-fold channels of the Nile at the conflagration?

"Oſtia ſeptem
Pulverulenta vacant ſeptem ſine flumine valles."

Such leaden labours are like Lycurgus's iron money, which was ſo much leſs in value than in bulk, that it required barns for ſtrong boxes, and a yoke of oxen to draw five hundred pounds."

VER. 141. *Some beauties yet no precepts*] Pope in this paſſage ſeems to have remembered one of the eſſays of Bacon, of which he is known to have been remarkably fond. "There is no excellent beauty that hath not ſome ſtrangeneſs in the proportion. A man cannot tell whether Apelles, or Abel Durer, were the more trifler; whereof the one would make a perſonage by geometrical proportions; the other, by taking the beſt parts out of divers faces to make one excellent. Such perſonages, I think, would pleaſe nobody, but the painter that made them. Not but I think, a painter may make a better face than ever was; but he muſt do it by a kind of felicity, as a muſician that maketh an excellent air in muſic, and not by rule. A man ſhall ſee faces, that if you examine them, part by part, you ſhall find never a good one; and yet altogether do well."

"Non

Music resembles Poetry, in each
Are nameless graces which no methods teach,
And which a master-hand alone can reach.
If, where the rules not far enough extend,
(Since rules were made but to promote their end)
Some lucky licence answer to the full
Th' intent propos'd, that Licence is a rule.
Thus Pegasus, a nearer way to take,
May boldly deviate from the common track.
Great Wits sometimes may gloriously offend,
And rise to faults true Critics dare not mend;
From vulgar bounds with brave disorder part,
And snatch a grace beyond the reach of art,

NOTES.

" Non ratione aliquâ (says Quintilian finely) sed motû nescio an inerrabili judicatur. Neque ab hoc ullo satis explicari puto, licet multi tentaverint." Quintil. Inst. L. vi. In short, in poetry, we must judge by taste and sentiment, not by rules and reasoning. Different theories of philosophy, and different systems of theology, are maintained and exploded in different ages; but true and genuine pictures of nature and passion, are not subject to such revolutions and changes. The doctrines of Plato, Epicurus, and Zeno; of Descartes, Hobbes, and Malebranche, and Gassendi, yield in succession to each other; but Homer, Sophocles, Terence, and Virgil, being felt and relished by all men, still retain and preserve, unaltered and undisputed, admiration and applause.

VER. 143. *Music resembles*] I am informed by one of the best musicians of the age that this observation is not accurate, nor agreeable to the rules of that art.

VER. 146. *If, where the rules, &c.*] " Neque enim rogationibus plebisve scitis sancta sunt ista praecepta, sed hoc, quicquid est, Utilitas excogitavit. Non negabo autem sic utile esse plerumque; verum si eadem illa nobis aliud suadebit Utilitas, hanc, relictis magistrorum autoritatibus, sequemur." Quintil. lib. cap. 13. P.

Which

Which without paſſing through the judgment gains
The heart, and all its end at once attains.
In proſpects thus, ſome objects pleaſe our eyes,
Which out of nature's common order riſe,
The ſhapeleſs rock, or hanging precipice.
But tho' the Ancients thus their rules invade,
(As Kings diſpenſe with laws themſelves have made)
Moderns, beware! or if you muſt offend
Againſt the precept, ne'er tranſgreſs its End;
Let it be ſeldom, and compell'd by need;
And have, at leaſt, their precedent to plead.
The Critic elſe proceeds without remorſe,
Seizes your fame, and puts his laws in force.

I know there are, to whoſe preſumptuous thoughts
Thoſe freer beauties, ev'n in them, ſeem faults.
Some figures monſtrous and mis-ſhap'd appear,
Conſider'd ſingly, or beheld too near,
Which, but proportion'd to their light, or place,
Due diſtance reconciles to form and grace.
A prudent chief not always muſt diſplay
His pow'rs, in equal ranks, and fair array,

But

NOTES.

VER. 161.] *Their* means *their own.*

VER. 175. *A prudent chief, &c.*] Οἷόν τι ποιοῦσιν οἱ φρόνιμοι στρατηλάται κατὰ τὰς τάξεις τῶν στρατευμάτων—Dion. Hal. De ſtruct. orat. P.

The ſame may be ſaid of muſic; concerning which, a diſcerning judge has lately made the following obſervation. "I do not mean to affirm, that in this extenſive work (of Marcello) every recitative air, or chorus, is of equal excellence. A continued elevation of this kind no author ever came up to. Nay, if we conſider that variety, which in all arts is neceſſary to keep up attention,

But with th' occaſion and the place comply,
Conceal his force, nay ſeem ſometimes to fly.
Thoſe oft are ſtratagems which errors ſeem,
Nor is it Homer nods, but we that dream.
Still green with bays each ancient Altar ſtands,
Above the reach of ſacrilegious hands;

Secure

NOTES.

attention, we may perhaps affirm with truth, that inequality makes a part of the character of excellence; that ſomething ought to be thrown into ſhades, in order to make the lights more ſtriking. And, in this reſpect, Marcello is truly excellent; if ever he ſeems to fall, it is only to riſe with more aſtoniſhing majeſty and greatneſs *."

It may be pertinent to ſubjoin Roſcommon's remark on the ſame ſubject.

——— " Far the greateſt part
Of what ſome call neglect, is ſtudy'd art.
When Virgil ſeems to trifle in a line,
'Tis but a warning-piece which gives the ſign
To wake your fancy, and prepare your ſight
To reach the noble height of ſome unuſual flight."

VER. 180. *Nor is it Homer nods, but we that dream.*] " Modeſte, et circumſpecto judicio de tantis viris pronunciandum eſt, ne (quod pleriſque accidit) damnent quod non intelligunt. Ac ſi neceſſe eſt in alteram errare partem, omnia eorum legentibus placere, quam multa diſplicere maluerim." Quint. P.

Racine applied this fine paſſage to Perrault and La Motte when they ſo much undervalued the ancients, in their famous controverſy.

How well Fontenelle, who was at the head of the French wits, that attacked and depreciated Homer, was qualified to judge of our divine old Bard, may be gathered from what the preſent Lord Mansfield told me; that of all the Iliad, the following was the favourite line of this champion of the moderns;

Τισειαν Δαναοι εμα δακρυα σοισι βελεσσιν.

VER. 181. *Each ancient Altar*] " All the inventions and thoughts of the ancients, whether conveyed to us in ſtatues, bas-reliefs,

* Aviſon on Muſical Expreſſion, page 103.

intaglio's

Secure from Flames, from Envy's fiercer rage,
Destructive War, and all-involving Age.

See

NOTES.

intaglio's, cameo's, or coins, are to be sought after, and carefully studied. The genius that hovers over these venerable reliques, may be called the Father of Modern Art.

" From the remains of the works of the antients the modern arts were revived, and it is by their means that they must be restored a second time. However it may mortify our vanity, we must be forced to allow them our masters; and we may venture to prophecy, that when they shall cease to be studied, arts will no longer flourish, and we shall again relapse into barbarism.

" The fire of the artist's own genius operating upon these materials, which have been thus diligently collected, will enable him to make new combinations, perhaps, superior to what had ever before been in the possession of the art. As in the mixture of the variety of metals, which are said to have been melted and run together in the burning of Corinth, a new, and till then unknown, metal was produced, equal in value to any of those that had contributed to its composition. And though a curious refiner may come with his crucibles, analyse and separate its various component parts, yet Corinthian brass would still hold its rank amongst the most beautiful and valuable of metals.

" We have hitherto considered the advantages of imitation, as it tends to form the taste, and as a practice by which a spark of that genius may be caught, which illumines these noble works, that ought always to be present to our thoughts.

" We come now to speak of another kind of imitation; the borrowing a particular thought, an action, attitude, or figure, and transplanting it into your own work; this will either come under the charge of plagiarism, or be warrantable, and deserve commendation, according to the address with which it is performed. There is some difference likewise whether it is upon the ancients or the moderns that these depredations are made. It it generally allowed, that no man need be ashamed of copying the ancients; their works are considered as a magazine of common property, always open to the Public, whence every man has a right to what materials he pleases; and if he has the art of using them, they are supposed to become, to all intents and purposes, his own property.

" The

See from each clime the learn'd their incenſe bring!
Hear, in all tongues conſenting Paeans ring!
In praiſe ſo juſt let ev'ry voice be join'd,
And fill the gen'ral chorus of mankind.
Hail, Bards triumphant! born in happier days;
Immortal heirs of univerſal praiſe!
Whoſe honours with increaſe of ages grow,
As ſtreams roll down, enlarging as they flow;
Nations unborn your mighty names ſhall ſound,
And worlds applaud that muſt not yet be found!
O may ſome ſpark of your celeſtial fire,
The laſt, the meaneſt of your ſons inſpire,
(That on weak wings, from far, purſues your flights;
Glows while he reads, but trembles as he writes)
To teach vain Wits a ſcience little known,
T' admire ſuperior ſenſe, and doubt their own!

II.

Of all the cauſes which conſpire to blind
Man's erring judgment, and miſguide the mind,
What the weak head with ſtrongeſt bias rules,
Is *Pride*, the never-failing vice of fools.
Whatever Nature has in worth deny'd,
She gives in large recruits of needful Pride;

NOTES.

" The collection which Raffaelle made of the thoughts of the ancients with ſo much trouble, is a proof of his opinion on this ſubject. Such collections may be made with much more eaſe, by means of an art ſcarce known in his time, I mean that of engraving; by which, at an eaſy rate, every man may avail himſelf of the inventions of antiquity." Reynolds.

For as in bodies, thus in ſouls, we find
What wants in blood and ſpirits, ſwell'd with wind:
Pride, where Wit fails, ſteps in to our defence,
And fills up all the mighty void of ſenſe.
If once right reaſon drives that cloud away,
Truth breaks upon us with reſiſtleſs day.
Truſt not yourſelf; but your defects to know,
Make uſe of ev'ry friend—and ev'ry foe.

A *little*

NOTES.

VER. 209. *Pride, where Wit fails, ſteps in to our defence,*
And fills up all the mighty void of ſenſe.]

A very ſenſible French writer makes the following remark on this ſpecies of *pride*. "Un homme qui ſçait pluſieurs Langues, qui entend les Auteurs Grecs et Latins, qui s'eleve même juſqu' à la dignité de SCHOLIASTE; ſi cet homme venoit à peſer ſon véritable mérite, il trouveroit ſouvent qu'il ſe réduit, avoir eu des yeux et de la mémoire; il ſe garderoit bien de donner le nom reſpectable de ſcience à *une erudition ſans lumiere*. Il y a une grande difference entre s'enrichir des mots ou des choſes, entre alleguer des autorités ou des raiſons. Si un homme pouvoit ſe ſurprendre à n'avoir que cette ſorte de mérite, il en rougiroit plûtôt que d'en être vain." W.

VER. 213. *Your defects to know,*] Correction is one of the moſt difficult taſks impoſed on an author. It is hard to know how far it ought to be carried. Quintilian has many juſt and uſeful obſervations on this ſubject. Perhaps the exceſs of it is productive of as many miſchiefs, as the total neglect of it. The file ſometimes, inſtead of poliſhing, eats away the ſubſtance to which it is applied. Akenſide much injured his poem by too much correction. Arioſto, as eaſy and familiar as he ſeems to be, made many and great alterations in his enchanting poem. Some of Rocheſocault's Maxims were corrected and new written more than thirty times. The Provincial Letters of Paſcal, the model of good ſtyle in the French language, were ſubmitted to the judgement of twelve members of the Port Royal, who made many corrections in them. Voltaire ſays, "That in all the books of Fenelon's Telemaque, of which he had ſeen the original, there were not ten raſures and alterations. All that can

be

A *little learning* is a dang'rous thing;
Drink deep, or taſte not the Pierian ſpring:
There ſhallow draughts intoxicate the brain,
And drinking largely ſobers us again.
Fir'd at firſt ſight with what the Muſe imparts,
In fearleſs youth we tempt the heights of Arts,
While from the bounded level of our mind,
Short views we take, nor ſee the lengths behind;
But more advanc'd, behold with ſtrange ſurprize
New diſtant ſcenes of endleſs ſcience riſe!
So pleas'd at firſt the tow'ring Alps we try,
Mount o'er the vales, and ſeem to tread the ſky,

Th'

VARIATIONS.

VER. 225.

So pleas'd at firſt the tow'ring Alps to try,
Fill'd with ideas of fair Italy,
The Traveller beholds with chearful eyes
The leſs'ning vales, and ſeems to tread the ſkies.

NOTES.

be ſaid about correction, is contained in theſe few incomparable words of Quintilian. "Hujus operis eſt, adjicere, detrahere, mutare. Sed facilius in his ſimpliciuſque judicium, quæ replenda vel dejicienda ſunt; premere verò tumentia, humilia extollere, luxuriantia aſtringere, inordinata dirigere, ſoluta componere, exultantia coercere, duplicis operæ." Quint. Lib. x. c. 3.

VER. 225. *So pleas'd*] Dr. Johnſon thinks this ſimile the moſt apt, the moſt proper, moſt ſublime, of any in the Engliſh language. I will own I am not of this opinion. It appears evidently to have been ſuggeſted by the following one in the Works of Drummond, p. 38. 4to.

"Ah! as a pilgrim who the Alpes doth paſſe,
Or Atlas' temples crown'd with winter's glaſſe,
The airy Caucaſus, the Apennine,
Pyrene's cliffes where ſunne doth never ſhine,

When

Th' eternal ſnows appear already paſt,
And the firſt clouds and mountains ſeem the laſt:
But, thoſe attain'd, we tremble to ſurvey
The growing labours of the lengthen'd way,
Th' increaſing proſpect tires our wand'ring eyes,
Hills peep o'er hills, and Alps on Alps ariſe!

A perfect Judge will read each work of Wit
With the ſame ſpirit that its author writ:
Survey the WHOLE, nor ſeek ſlight faults to find
Where nature moves, and rapture warms the mind;

Nor

NOTES.

When he ſome heapes of hills hath overwent,
Beginnes to think on reſt, his journey ſpent,
Till mounting ſome tall mountaine he doth finde
More hights before him thann he left behiud."

See alſo Silias Italicus, Lib. iii. 528.

VER. 233. *A perfect Judge, &c.*] "Diligenter legendum eſt ac paene ad ſcribendi ſollicitudinem: Nec per partes modo ſcrutanda ſunt omnia, ſed perlectus liber utique ex integro reſumendus." Quint. P.

It is obſervable that our Author makes it almoſt the neceſſary conſequence of judging by parts, to find fault: And this not without much diſcernment: For the ſeveral parts of a complete Whole, when ſeen only ſingly, and known only independently, muſt always have the appearance of irregularity; often of deformity: becauſe the Poet's deſign being to create a reſultive beauty from the artful aſſemblage of ſeveral various parts into one natural whole; thoſe parts muſt be faſhioned with regard to their mutual relations in the ſtations they occupy in that whole, from whence, the beauty required is to ariſe: But that regard will occaſion ſo unreducible a form in each part, when conſidered ſingly, as to preſent a very mis-ſhapen Form. W.

VER. 235. *Survey the Whole, nor ſeek ſlight faults to find*
Where nature moves, and rapture warms the mind;]
The ſecond line, in apologizing for thoſe faults which the firſt

ſays

Nor loſe for that malignant dull delight,
The gen'rous pleaſure to be charm'd with wit.
But in ſuch lays as neither ebb nor flow,
Correctly cold, and regularly low,
That ſhunning faults, one quiet tenour keep;
We cannot blame indeed—but we may ſleep.
In Wit, as Nature, what affects our hearts
Is not th' exactneſs of peculiar parts;
'Tis not a lip, or eye, we beauty call,
But the joint force and full reſult of all.
Thus when we view ſome well-proportion'd dome,
(The world's juſt wonder, and ev'n thine, O Rome!)
No

NOTES.

ſays ſhould be overlooked, gives the reaſon of the precept. For when a great writer's attention is fixed on a general view of Nature, and his imagination become warmed with the contemplation of great ideas, it can hardly be, but that there muſt be ſmall irregularities in the diſpoſition both of matter and ſtyle, becauſe the avoiding theſe requires a coolneſs of recollection, which a writer ſo qualified and ſo buſied is not maſter of. W.

According to a moſt juſt and judicious obſervation in the firſt book of Strabo, "Καθαπερ γε εν τοις κολοσσικοις εργοις, ȣ το καθ' ὁλȣ ἑκαςον ακριβες ζητȣμεν, αλλα τοις καθ' ὁλȣ προσεχομεν μαλλον ει καλως το ολον· ȣτως κ' αν τȣτοις ποιεισθαι δει την κρισιν." As in great coloſſal works, we do not ſeek for exactneſs and accuracy in every part, but rather attend to the general effect, and beauty of the whole; ſo ought we to judge of compoſitions. And, as Quintilian ſays, Ungues polire, & capillum reponere, is an uſeleſs and ill-placed care.

VER. 239. *But in ſuch lays*] Theſe four lines are ſuperior to Horace's,

"Serpit humi tutus nimium," &c.

VER. 247. *Thus when we view*] This is juſtly and elegantly expreſſed; and though it may ſeem difficult to ſpeak of the ſame ſubject after ſuch a deſcription, yet Akenſide has ventured, and nobly ſucceeded:

 "Mark,

No ſingle parts unequally ſurprize,
All comes united to th' admiring eyes;
No monſtrous height, or breadth, or length appear;
The Whole at once is bold and regular.
  Whoever thinks a faultleſs piece to ſee,
Thinks what ne'er was, nor is, nor e'er ſhall be.

In

NOTES.

" Mark, how the dread Pantheon ſtands,
Amid the domes of modern hands!
Amid the toys of ſimple ſtate,
How ſimply, how ſeverely great!
  Then pauſe!——

VER. 248. *The world's juſt wonder, and ev'n thine, O Rome!*] The Pantheon, I would ſuppoſe; perhaps St. Peter's; no matter which; the obſervation is true of both. There is ſomething very Gothic in the taſte and judgment of a learned man, who deſpiſes this maſter-piece of Art, the Pantheon, for thoſe very qualities which deſerve our admiration.——" Nous eſmerveillons comme l'on fait ſi grand cas de ce Pantheon, veu que ſon edifice n'eſt de ſi grande induſtrie comme l'on crie: car chaque petit Maſſon peut bien concevoir la maniere de ſe façon tout en un inſtant: car eſtant la baſe ſi maſſive, et les murailles ſi eſpaiſſes, ne nous a ſemblé difficile d'y adjouſter la voute à claire voye." Pierre Belon's Obſervations, &c. The nature of the Gothic ſtructures apparently led him into this miſtake of the Architectonic art in general; that the excellency of it conſiſts in raiſing the greateſt weight on the leaſt aſſignable ſupport, ſo that the edifice ſhould have ſtrength without the appearance of it, in order to excite admiration. But to a judicious eye ſuch a building would have a contrary effect, the Appearance (as our poet expreſſes it) of a monſtrous height, or breadth, or length. Indeed did the juſt proportions in regular Architecture take off from the grandeur of a building, by all the ſingle parts coming united to the eye, as this learned traveller ſeems to inſinuate, it would be a reaſonable objection to thoſe rules on which this Maſter-piece of Art was conſtructed. But it is not ſo. The Poet tells us truly,

" The Whole at once is bold and regular." W.

VER. 253. *Whoever thinks a faultleſs piece to ſee,*] He ſhews next [from ver. 252 to 263.] that to fix our cenſure on ſingle

parts,

In ev'ry work regard the writer's End,
Since none can compaſs more than they intend;
And if the means be juſt, the conduct true,
Applauſe, in ſpite of trivial faults, is due.
As men of breeding, ſometimes men of wit,
T' avoid great errors, muſt the leſs commit:
Neglect the rules each verbal Critic lays,
For not to know ſome trifles, is a praiſe.
Moſt Critics, fond of ſome ſubſervient art,
Still make the Whole depend upon a Part:
They talk of principles, but notions prize,
And all to one lov'd Folly ſacrifice.

NOTES.

parts, though they happen to want an exactneſs conſiſtent enough with their relation to the reſt, is even then very unjuſt: And for theſe reaſons, 1. Becauſe it implies an expectation of a faultleſs piece, which is a vain fancy. 2. Becauſe no more is to be expected of any work than that it fairly attains its end: But the end may be attained, and yet theſe trivial faults committed: Therefore, in ſpight of ſuch faults, the work will merit that praiſe that is due to every thing which attains its end. 3. Becauſe ſometimes a great beauty is not to be procured, nor a notorious blemiſh to be avoided, but by ſuffering one of theſe minute and trivial errors. 4. And laſtly, becauſe the general neglect of them is a praiſe; as it is the indication of a Genius, attentive to greater matters. W.

VER. 258. *In ſpite of trivial*] As if one was to condemn the divine Paradiſe Loſt, on account of ſome low puns there introduced; or ſome paſſages in Arioſto, on account of vulgar and familiar images and expreſſions, that have crept unaccountably into that enchanting and original Poem.

VER. 261. *Critic lays,*] The word *lays* is very exceptionable: in an inferior and common Writer it would not be worth while to mark ſuch improper expreſſions.

Once on a time, La Mancha's Knight they ſay,
A certain Bard encount'ring on the way,
Diſcours'd in terms as juſt, with looks as ſage,
As e'er could Dennis, of the Grecian ſtage;

NOTES.

VER. 267. *Once on a time, La Mancha's Knight they ſay*] By this ſhort tale Pope has ſhewed us, how much he could have excelled in telling a ſtory of humour. The incident is taken from the Second Part of Don Quixote, firſt written by Don Alonzo Fernandez de Avellanada, and afterwards tranſlated, or rather imitated and new-modelled, by no leſs an Author than the celebrated Le Sage. The Book is not ſo contemptible as ſome authors inſinuate; it was well received in France, and abounds in many ſtrokes of humour and character worthy of Cervantes himſelf. The brevity to which Pope's narration was confined, would not permit him to inſert the following humourous dialogue at length. "I am ſatisfied you'll compaſs your deſign (ſaid the ſcholar) provided you omit the combat in the liſts. Let him have a care of that, ſaid Don Quixote, interrupting him, that is the beſt part of the plot. But, Sir, quoth the Bachelor, if you would have me adhere to Ariſtotle's rules, I muſt omit the combat. Ariſtotle, replied the Knight, I grant was a man of ſome parts; but his capacity was not unbounded: and, give me leave to tell you, his authority does not extend over combats in the liſt, which are far above his narrow rules. Would you ſuffer the chaſte queen of Bohemia to periſh? For how can you clear her innocence? Believe me, combat is the moſt honourable method you can purſue; and beſides, it will add ſuch grace to your play, that all the rules in the univerſe muſt not ſtand in competition with it. Well, Sir Knight, replied the Bachelor, for your ſake, and for the honour of chivalry, I will not leave out the combat; and that it may appear the more glorious, all the court of Bohemia ſhall be preſent at it, from the Princes of the blood, to the very footmen. But ſtill one difficulty remains, which is, that our common theatres are not large enough for it. There muſt be one erected on purpoſe, anſwered the Knight; and in a word, rather than leave out the combat, the play had better be acted in a field or plain."

It may be obſerved, that there is but one Tale in this eſſay, nor in Boileau's art, nor Roſcommon's eſſay, and this is ſuperior to the other two.

Concluding

Concluding all were deſperate ſots and fools,
Who durſt depart from Ariſtotle's rules.
Our Author, happy in a judge ſo nice,
Produc'd his Play, and begg'd the Knight's advice;
Made him obſerve the ſubject, and the plot,
The manners, paſſions, unities; what not?
All which, exact to rule, were brought about,
Were but a Combat in the liſts left out.
"What leave the Combat out?" exclaims the Knight;
Yes, or we muſt renounce the Stagirite.
"Not ſo, by Heav'n!" (he anſwers in a rage)
"Knights, ſquires, and ſteeds, muſt enter on the ſtage."
So vaſt a throng the ſtage can ne'er contain.
"Then build a new, or act it in a plain."
Thus Critics of leſs judgment than caprice,
Curious not knowing, not exact but nice,

NOTES.

VER. 276. *Unities; what not?*] The two unities of time and place have been ſo powerfully and irreſiſtibly combated by Dr. Johnſon, (in his Preface to Shakeſpeare), that I do not think a critic will be found hardy enough to undertake a defence of them?

——— Non quiſquam ex agmine tanto
Audet adire virum!———

That theſe unities have, in fact, never been obſerved by the three Greek writers of tragedy, is demonſtrated, at large, in the fifth chapter of Metaſtaſio's very judicious work, entitled, Eſtratto della Poetica D'Ariſtotile, from page 93 to 119, a work full of taſte and judgment, and which comes with double weight from ſo long and able a practitioner in the dramatic art, many of whoſe plays are planned with the greateſt ſkill, and who is, on the whole, one of the fineſt and trueſt poets Italy has produced. Whoever would thoroughly underſtand Ariſtotle, ſhould, in my opinion, very attentively peruſe his Eſtratto.

Form ſhort Ideas; and offend in arts
(As moſt in manners) by a love to parts.
  Some to *Conceit* alone their taſte confine,
And glitt'ring thoughts ſtruck out at ev'ry line;
Pleas'd with a work where nothing's juſt or fit;
One glaring Chaos and wild heap of wit.
Poets, like painters, thus, unſkill'd to trace
The naked nature and the living grace,
With gold and jewels cover ev'ry part,
And hide with ornaments their want of art.
True Wit is Nature to advantage dreſs'd;
What oft was thought, but ne'er ſo well expreſs'd;
Something,

NOTES.

VER. 290. *And glitt'ring thoughts*] A rage that infected Marino, Donne, and his diſciple Cowley. See Dr. Johnſon's excellent Diſſertation on Cowley, and his fantaſtic ſtyle, in the firſt volume of Lives of the Poets. Little can be added to his diſcuſſion on falſe and unnatural thoughts. It is, beyond compariſon, the beſt of all his criticiſms.

VER. 296. *Hide with ornaments*] Nothing can excel the fine obſervation of Tully on this ſubject, in the 3d Book de Oratore; "Voluptatibus maximis, faſtidium finitimum eſt in rebus omnibus; quo hoc minus in oratione miremur. In quâ, vel ex poetis, vel oratoribus poſſumus judicare, concinnam, ornatam, feſtivam, ſine intermiſſione, quamvis claris ſit coloribus picta, vel poeſis, vel oratio, non poſſe in delectatione eſſe diuturnâ. Quare bene & præclarè, quamvis nobis ſæpe dicatur, bellè & feſtivè nimium ſæpe nolo."

VER. 297. *True Wit is Nature to advantage dreſs'd, &c.*] This definition is very exact. Mr. Locke had defined wit to conſiſt "in the aſſemblage of ideas, and putting thoſe together, with quickneſs and variety, wherein can be found any reſemblance or congruity, whereby to make up pleaſant pictures and agreeable viſions in the fancy." But that great philoſopher, in ſeparating wit from judgment, as he does in this place, has given us (and he could therefore give us no other) only an account of Wit in general

Something, whoſe truth convinc'd at ſight we ſind,
That gives us back the image of our mind.

As

NOTES.

general: In which falſe wit, tho' not every ſpecies of it, is included. A ſtriking image therefore of Nature is, as Mr. Locke obſerves, certainly Wit: But this image may ſtrike on ſeveral other accounts, as well as for its truth and beauty; and the philoſopher has explained the manner how. But it never becomes that Wit which is the ornament of true poeſy, whoſe end is to repreſent nature, but when it dreſſes that nature to advantage, and preſents her to us in the brighteſt and moſt amiable light. And to know when the Fancy has done its office truly, the poet ſubjoins this admirable teſt, viz. When we perceive that it gives us back the image of our mind. When it does that, we may be ſure it plays no tricks with us: For this image is the creature of the Judgment; and whenever Wit correſponds with Judgment, we may ſafely pronounce it to be true. "Naturam intueamur, hanc ſequamur: id facillime accipiunt animi quod agnoſcunt." Quint. lib. viii. c. 3. W.

"The poet in cenſuring the narrow and partial taſtes of ſome critics, begins with that for *conceit*, or a glitter of dazzling thoughts riſing one after another, without meaning or connection. This is *falſe wit*; as a contraſt to which, he gives a definition of the *true*, in the preceding lines. But he evidently, by this purpoſe of contraſting the two kinds, has been led to a deſcription which exhibits none of the peculiar features of wit, as other writers have repreſented it. By this definition, any juſt moral ſentiment, any exact picture of a natural object, if clothed in good expreſſion, would be wit. Its teſt being an agreement with images previouſly exiſting in our own minds, no other quality is requiſite to it but truth. Even uncommonneſs is not taken into the character: for we muſt often have thought it, and be able to recognize it at ſight. Nor has he given any diſtinct idea of that advantageous dreſs which makes a natural thought witty.

"No dreſs can ſuit ſome thoughts ſo well, as the moſt ſimple. Exalted ſentiments of the heart, and ſublime objects in nature, generally ſtrike moſt when preſented in language the leaſt ſtudied. Indeed, he uſes, within a few lines, the very ſame metaphor of dreſs, in expoſing the finical taſte of thoſe who value a work for the ſtyle rather than the ſenſe; and the fact certainly is, that the

As ſhades more ſweetly recommend the light,
So modeſt plainneſs ſets off ſprightly wit.

NOTES.

moſt confeſſedly witty writers have been often little ſolicitous as to the manner of expreſſing their notions.

"Pope evidently entertains a different conception of wit, from that of the definition above quoted, in the lines immediately following:

> As ſhades more ſweetly recommend the light,
> So modeſt plainneſs ſets off ſprightly wit.
> For works may have more wit than does them good,
> As bodies periſh thro' exceſs of blood.

"Now "modeſt plainneſs" is no foil or contraſt to wit, as characteriſed in the definition, becauſe it may be the moſt "advantageous dreſs" for a thought. Again, that wit which may ſuperabound in a work, muſt be a different thing from "natural imagery joined to good expreſſion," for in theſe, what danger can there be of exceſs? He was certainly now recurring in his mind to thoſe brilliant flaſhes, which, though often introduced with falſe judgment, are not, however, falſe wit.

"The two characters of *bad critic* and *bad poet* are groſsly confounded in the paſſage relating to poetical numbers; for though it be true, that vulgar readers of poetry are chiefly attentive to the melody of the verſe, yet it is not they who admire, but the paltry verſifier who employs monotonous ſyllables, feeble expletives, and a dull routine of unvaried rhymes. Again, an ordinary ear is capable of perceiving the beauty ariſing from the ſound being made an echo to the ſenſe; indeed it is one of the moſt obvious beauties in poetry; but it is no eaſy taſk for the poet to ſucceed in his attempts to render it ſo, as Pope has ſufficiently proved by the miſerable failure of ſome of his examples in illuſtration of the precept." Eſſays Hiſtorical and Critical.

VER. 297. *True Wit is Nature,*] Immediately after this the poet adds,

> For works may have more wit than does 'em good.

"Now (ſays a very acute and judicious critic) let us ſubſtitute the definition in the place of the thing, and it will ſtand thus; A work may have more of Nature dreſs'd to advantage than will do it good. This is impoſſible; and it is evident that the confuſion ariſes from the poet's having annexed two different ideas to the ſame word." Webb's Remarks on the Beauties of Poetry, p. 68.

For

For works may have more wit than does 'em good,
As bodies perifh through excefs of blood.

NOTES.

VER. 298. *What oft was thought,*] In Dr. Johnfon's remarks on thefe poets, whom, after Dryden, he calls the metaphyfical poets, he fays, very finely; "Pope's account of wit is undoubtedly erroneous; he depreffes it below its natural dignity, and reduces it from ftrength of thought to happinefs of language.

"If by a more noble and more adequate conception that be confidered as wit, which is at once natural and new, that which, though not obvious, is, upon its firft production, acknowledged to be juft; if it be that, which he that never found it, wonders how he miffed; to wit of this kind the metaphyfical poets have feldom rifen. Their thoughts are often new, but feldom natural; they are not obvious, but neither are they juft; and the reader, far from wondering that he miffed them, wonders more frequently by what perverfenefs they were ever found.

"But wit, abftracted from its effects upon the hearer, may be more vigoroufly and philofophically confidered as a kind of difcordia concors; a combination of diffimilar images, or difcovery of occult refemblances in things apparently unlike. Of wit, thus defined, they have more than enough. The moft heterogeneous ideas are yoked by violence together; nature and art are ranfacked for illuftrations, comparifons, and allufions; their learning inftructs, and their fubtilty furprifes; but the reader commonly thinks his improvement dearly bought, and, though he fometimes admires, is feldom pleafed.

"From this account of their compofitions it will be readily inferred, that they were not fuccefsful in reprefenting or moving the affections. As they were wholly employed on fomething unexpected and furprizing, they had no regard to that uniformity of fentiment which enables us to conceive and to excite the pains and the pleafures of other minds; they never enquired what, on any occafion, they fhould have faid or done; but wrote rather as beholders than partakers of human nature; as beings looking upon good and evil, impaffive and at leifure, as Epicurean deities, making remarks on the actions of men, and the viciffitudes of life, without intereft and without emotion. Their courtfhip was void of fondnefs, and their lamentation of forrow. Their wifh was only to fay what they hoped had never been faid before."

Others

Others for *Language* all their care expreſs,
And value books, as women men, for dreſs:
Their praiſe is ſtill,—The Style is excellent;
The Senſe, they humbly take upon content.
Words are like leaves; and where they moſt abound,
Much fruit of ſenſe beneath is rarely found:
Falſe eloquence, like the priſmatic glaſs,
Its gaudy colours ſpreads on ev'ry place;

The

NOTES.

Ver. 302. *Modeſt plainneſs.*] Xenophon in Greek, and Cæſar in Latin are the unrivalled maſters of the beautiful ſimplicity here recommended. We have no Engliſh, French, or Italian Writer, that can be placed in the ſame rank with them, for this uncommon excellence.

Ver. 311. *Falſe eloquence,*] The nauſeous affectation of expreſſing every thing pompouſly and poetically, is no where more viſible than in a poem by Mallet, entitled Amyntor and Theodora. The following inſtance may be alleged among many others. Amyntor having a pathetic tale to diſcover, being choaked with ſorrow, and at a loſs for utterance, uſes theſe ornamental and unnatural images.

"—— O could I ſteal
From Harmony her ſofteſt warbled ſtrain
Of melting air! or Zephyr's vernal voice!
Or Philomela's ſong, when love diſſolves
To liquid blandiſhments his evening lay,
All nature ſmiling round."

Voltaire has given a comprehenſive rule with reſpect to every ſpecies of compoſition. "Il ne faut rechercher, ni les penſées, ni les tours, ni les expreſſions, et que l'art, dans tous les grands ouvrages, eſt de bien raiſonner, ſans trop faire d'argument; de bien peindre, ſans voiloir tout peindre, d'émouvoir, ſans vouloir toujours exciter les paſſions."

In a word, true eloquence, a juſt ſtyle, conſiſts in the number, the propriety, and the placing of words; is content with a natural and ſimple beauty; hunts not after foreign figures, diſdains far-ſought and meretricious ornaments. Juſt as the ſtrength of

an

The face of Nature we no more ſurvey,
All glares alike, without diſtinction gay:
But true Expreſſion, like th' unchanging Sun,
Clears and improves whate'er it ſhines upon,
It gilds all objects, but it alters none.
Expreſſion is the dreſs of thought, and ſtill
Appears more decent, as more ſuitable;
A vile conceit in pompous words expreſs'd
Is like a clown in regal purple dreſs'd:
For diff'rent ſtyles with diff'rent ſubjects ſort,
As ſev'ral garbs with country, town, and court.
Some by old words to fame have made pretence,
Ancients in phraſe, meer moderns in their ſenſe;
Such

NOTES.

an army, ſays Algarotti, conſiſts in well-diſciplined men, not in a number of camels, elephants, ſcythed chariots, and Aſiatic encumbrances. Among many excellencies, this is the chief blemiſh of the Rambler; every object, every ſubject, is treated with an equal degree of dignity; he never ſoftens and ſubdues his tints, but paints and adorns every image which he touches, with perpetual pomp, and unremitted ſplendor.

VER. 324. *Some by old words, &c.*] "Abolita et abrogata retinere, inſolentiae cujuſdam eſt, et frivolae in parvis jactantiae." Quint. lib. i. c. 6. P.

"Opus eſt, ut verba à vetuſtate repetita neque crebra ſint, neque manifeſta, quia nil eſt odioſius affectatione, nec utique ab ultimis repetita temporibus. Oratio cujus ſumma virtus eſt perſpicuitas quam ſit vitioſa, ſi egeat interprete? Ergo ut novorum optima erunt maxime vetera, ita veterum maxime nova." Idem. P.

Quintilian's advice on this ſubject is as follows: "Cum ſint autem verba propria, ficta, tranſlata; propriis dignitatem dat antiquitas. Namque et ſanctiorem, et magis admirabilem reddunt orationem, quibus non quilibet fuit uſurus: eoque ornamento acerrimi judicii Virgilius unice eſt uſus. Olli enim, et quianam, et mis, et pone, pellucent, et aſpergunt illam, quae etiam in picturis

Such labour'd nothings, in ſo ſtrange a ſtyle,
Amaze th' unlearn'd, and make the learned ſmile.
Unlucky, as Fungoſo in the Play,
Theſe ſparks with aukward vanity diſplay
What the fine gentleman wore yeſterday;

NOTES.

picturis eſt gratiſſima, vetuſtatis inimitabilem arti auctoritatem. Sed utendum modo, nec ex ultimis tenebris repetenda."

"The language of the age (ſays Mr. Gray, admirably well,) is never the language of poetry; except among the French, whoſe verſe, where the thought or image does not ſupport it, differs in nothing from proſe. Our poetry, on the contrary, has a language peculiar to itſelf; to which almoſt every one that has written, has added ſomething by enriching it with foreign idioms and derivatives: nay, ſometimes words of their own compoſitions or invention. Shakeſpeare and Milton have been great creators this way; and no one more licentious than Pope or Dryden, who perpetually borrow expreſſions from the former. Let me give you ſome inſtances from Dryden, whom every body reckons a great maſter of our poetical tongue. Full of muſeful mopings,—unlike the trim of love,—a pleaſant beverage,—a roundelay of love,—ſtood ſilent in his mood,—with knots and knaves deformed,—his ireful mood,—in proud array,—his boon was granted,—and diſarray and ſhameful rout,—wayward but wiſe,—furbiſhed for the field,—the foiled dodderd oaks, diſherited,—ſmouldring flames,—retchleſs of laws,—crones old and ugly,—the beldam at his ſide,—the grandam hag,—villanize his father's fame.—But they are infinite; and our language not being a ſettled thing, (like the French), has an undoubted right to words of an hundred years old, provided antiquity have not rendered them unintelligible. In truth, Shakeſpeare's language is one of his principal beauties; and he has no leſs advantage over your Addiſons and Rowes in this, than in thoſe great excellencies you mention. Every word in him is a picture. Pray put me in the following lines, into the tongue of our modern dramatics."

VER. 328. *Unlucky, as Fungoſo, &c.*] See Ben. Jonſon's Every Man out of his Humour. P.

And

And but ſo mimic ancient wits at beſt,
As apes our grandſires, in their doublets dreſt,
In words, as faſhions, the ſame rule will hold;
Alike fantaſtic, if too new, or old:
Be not the firſt by whom the new are try'd
Nor yet the laſt to lay the old aſide.
  But moſt by Numbers judge a Poet's ſong,
And ſmooth or rough, with them, is right or wrong:
In the bright Muſe, tho' thouſand charms conſpire,
Her voice is all theſe tuneful fools admire;
Who haunt Parnaſſus but to pleaſe their ear,
Not mend their minds; as ſome to church repair,
Not for the doctrine, but the muſic there.
Theſe equal ſyllables alone require,
Tho' oft the ear the open vowels tire;
While expletives their feeble aid do join;
And ten low words oft creep in one dull line:

NOTES.

Ver. 337. *But moſt by Numbers, &c.*]
"Quis populi ſermo eſt? quis enim? niſi carmine molli
Nunc demum numero fluere, ut per laeve ſeveros
Effundat junctura ungues: ſcit tendere verſum
Non ſecus ac ſi oculo rubricam dirigat uno."
Perſ. Sat. i. P.

Ver. 345. *Tho' oft the ear, &c.*] "Fugiemus crebras vocalium concurſiones, quae vaſtam atque hiantem orationem reddunt." Cic ad Heren. lib. iv. Vide etiam Quintil. lib. ix. c. 4. P.

"Non tamen (ſays the ſenſible Quintilian) id ut crimen ingens expaveſcendum eſt; ac neſcio negligentia in hoc, an ſolicitudo ſit major; nimioſque non immeritò in hâc curâ putant omnes Iſocratem ſecutos, præcipuèque Theopompum. At Demoſthenes & Cicero modicè reſpexerunt ad hanc partem." Quintil. lib. ix. c. 9.

While they ring round the ſame unvary'd chimes,
With ſure returns of ſtill expected rhymes;
Where-e'er you find "the cooling weſtern breeze,"
In the next line, it "whiſpers through the trees:"
If cryſtal ſtreams "with pleaſing murmurs creep,"
The reader's threaten'd (not in vain) with "ſleep:"
Then, at the laſt and only couplet fraught
With ſome unmeaning thing they call a thought,
A needleſs Alexandrine ends the ſong,
That, like a wounded ſnake, drags its ſlow length along.
Leave ſuch to tune their own dull rhymes, and know
What's roundly ſmooth, or languiſhingly ſlow;
And praiſe the eaſy vigour of a line,
Where Denham's ſtrength, and Waller's ſweetneſs join.

NOTES.

VER. 347. *Ten low words*] Our language is thought to be overloaded with monoſyllables; Shafteſbury, we are told, limited their number to nine in any ſentence; Quintilian condemns too great a concourſe of them; etiam monoſyllaba, ſi plura ſunt, malè continuabuntur; quia neceſſe eſt compoſitio, multis clauſulis conciſa, ſubſultet. Inſt. lib. ix. c. 4.

VER. 360. *And praiſe the eaſy vigour*] Fenton, in his entertaining obſervations on Waller, has given us a curious anecdote concerning the

IMITATIONS.

VER. 346. *Where expletives their feeble aid do join,*
And ten low words oft creep in one dull line:]
From Dryden. "He creeps along with ten little words in every line, and helps out his numbers with [for] [to] and [unto] and all the pretty expletives he can find, while the ſenſe is left half tired behind it." Eſſay on Dram. Poetry.

But there are many lines of monoſyllables that have much force and energy; in our author himſelf, as well as Dryden.

True

True ease in writing comes from art, not chance,
As those move easiest who have learn'd to dance.

NOTES.

the great industry and exactness with which Waller polished even his smallest compositions. "When the court was at Windsor, these verses were writ in the Tasso of her Royal Highness, at Mr. Waller's request, by the late Duke of Buckinghamshire; and I very well remember to have heard his Grace say, that the author employed the greatest part of a summer in composing and correcting them." So that, however he is generally reputed the parent of those swarms of insect wits, who affect to be thought easy writers, it is evident that he bestowed much time and care on his poems, before he ventured them out of his hands.

Ver. 361. *Denham's strength,*] Sufficient justice is not done to Sandys, who did more to polish and tune the English versification, by his Psalms and his Job, than those two writers, who are usually applauded on this subject.

Ver. 362. *True ease*] Writers who seem to have composed with the greatest ease, have exerted much labour in attaining this facility. Virgil took more pains than Lucan, though the style of the former appears so natural; and Guarini and Ariosto spent much time in making their poems so seemingly natural and easy. Even Voiture wrote with extreme difficulty, though apparently without any effort; what Tasso says of one of his heroines may be applied to such writers;

"Non so ben dire s'adorna, o se negletta,
Se caso, od arte, il bel volto compose,
Di natura, d'amor, del cielo amici
Le negligenze sue sono artifici."

It is well known, that the writings of Voiture, of Sarassin, and La Fontaine, were laboured into that facility for which they are so famous, with repeated alterations and many rasures. Moliere is reported to have past whole days, in fixing upon a proper epithet or rhyme, although his verses have all the flow and freedom of conversation. "This happy facility (said a man of wit) may be compared to garden-terraces, the expence of which does not appear; and which, after the cost of several millions, yet seem to be a mere work of chance and nature." I have been informed, that Addison was so extremely nice in polishing his prose compositions, that when almost a whole impression of a spectator was worked off, he would stop the press, to insert a new preposition or conjunction.

'Tis

'Tis not enough no harſhneſs gives offence,
The ſound muſt ſeem an Echo to the ſenſe:
Soft is the ſtrain when Zephyr gently blows,
And the ſmooth ſtream in ſmoother numbers flows;

NOTES.

VER. 364. *No harſhneſs gives offence,*] We are ſurpriſed to ſee the conſtant attention of the ancients, to give melody to their periods, both in proſe and verſe; of which ſo many inſtances are given in Tully De Oratore, in Dionyſius, and Quintilian. Plato many times altered the order of the four firſt words of his Republic. Cicero records the approbation he met with for finiſhing a ſentence with the word cōmprŏbāvit, being a dichorcè. Had he finiſhed it otherwiſe, he ſays, it might have been animo ſatis, auribus non ſatis. We may be equally mortified in finding Quintilian condemning the inharmoniouſneſs of many letters with which our language abounds; particularly the letters F, M, B, D, and Dionyſius reprobates the letter S.

VER. 365. *The ſound muſt ſeem an echo to the ſenſe.*] Lord Roſcommon ſays,

"The ſound is ſtill a *comment* to the ſenſe."

They are both well expreſſed, although ſo differently; for Lord R. is ſhewing how the ſenſe is aſſiſted by the ſound; Mr. P. how the ſound is aſſiſted by the ſenſe.

VER. 366. *Soft is the ſtrain*] See examples in Clarke's Homer, Iliad i. v. 430; ii. v. 102; iii. v. 357; vi. v. 510; vii. v. 157; viii. v. 210, 551; xi. v. 687, 697, 766; and many others. The judicious Heyne, in his Virgil, thinks this beauty of ſtyle, as it is called, very fantaſtical, and not intended by either Homer or Virgil, ſo often as hath been imagined.

Theſe lines are uſually cited as fine examples of adapting the ſound to the ſenſe. But that Pope has failed in this endeavour has been clearly demonſtrated by the Rambler. "The verſe intended to repreſent the whiſper of the vernal breeze muſt ſurely be confeſſed not much to excel in ſoftneſs or volubility; and the ſmooth ſtream runs with a perpetual claſh of jarring conſonants.

The

IMITATIONS.

VER. 366. *Soft is the ſtrain, &c.*]
"Tum ſi laeta canunt," &c. Vida, Poet. l. iii. ver. 403.

But

But when loud ſurges laſh the ſounding ſhoar,
The hoarſe, rough verſe ſhould like the torrent roar:
When Ajax ſtrives ſome rock's vaſt weight to throw,
The line too labours, and the words move ſlow:
Not ſo, when ſwift Camilla ſcours the plain,
Flies o'er th' unbending corn, and ſkims along the
main.

NOTES.

The noiſe and turbulence of the torrent is, indeed, diſtinctly imaged; for it requires very little ſkill to make our language rough. But in the lines which mention the effort of Ajax, there is no particular heavineſs or delay. The ſwiftneſs of Camilla, is rather contraſted than exemplified. Why the verſe ſhould be lengthened to expreſs ſpeed, will not eaſily be diſcovered. In the dactyls, uſed for that purpoſe by the ancients, two ſhort ſyllables were pronounced with ſuch rapidity, as to be equal only to one long; they therefore naturally exhibit the act of paſſing through a long ſpace in a ſhort time. But the Alexandrine, by its pauſe in the midſt, is a tardy and ſtately meaſure; and the word *unbending*, one of the moſt ſluggiſh and ſlow which our language affords, cannot much accelerate its motion." Aaron Hill, long before this was publiſhed by the Rambler, wrote a letter to Pope, pointing out the many inſtances in which he had failed to accommodate the ſound to the ſenſe, in this famous paſſage. This rule of making the ſound an echo to the ſenſe, as well as alliteration, has been carried to a ridiculous extreme by ſeveral late writers. It is worth obſerving, that it is treated of at length, and recommended by Taſſo, page 168 of his Diſcorſi del Poema Eroico.

IMITATIONS.

VER. 368. *But when loud ſurges, &c.*]
" Tum longe ſale ſaxa ſonant," &c. Vida, Poet. l. iii. v. 388.

VER. 370. *When Ajax ſtrives, &c.*]
" Atque ideo ſi quid geritur molimine magno," &c.
Vida, ib. 417.

VER. 372. *Not ſo, when ſwift Camilla, &c.*]
" At mora ſi fuerit damno, properare jubebo," &c.
Vida, ib. 420.

Hear how Timotheus' vary'd lays ſurprize,
And bid alternate paſſions fall and riſe!
While at each change, the ſon of Libyan Jove
Now burns with glory, and then melts with love;
Now his fierce eyes with ſparkling fury glow,
Now ſighs ſteal out, and tears begin to flow:
Perſians and Greeks like turns of nature found,
And the world's victor ſtood ſubdu'd by Sound!
The pow'r of Muſic all our hearts allow,
And what Timotheus was, is DRYDEN now.
  Avoid extremes; and ſhun the fault of ſuch,
Who ſtill are pleas'd too little or too much.
At ev'ry trifle ſcorn to take offence,
That always ſhews great pride, or little ſenſe:
Thoſe heads, as ſtomachs, are not ſure the beſt,
Which nauſeate all, and nothing can digeſt.
Yet let not each gay Turn thy rapture move;
For fools admire, but men of ſenſe approve:

As

NOTES.

VER. 374. *Hear how Timotheus, &c.*] See Alexander's Feaſt, or the Power of Muſic; an Ode by Mr. Dryden. P.

"Some of the lines (ſays Dr. Johnſon) are without correſpondent rhymes; a defect which the enthuſiaſm of the writer might hinder him from perceiving."

VER. 391. *Fools admire, but men of ſenſe approve:*] "This prudiſh ſentence has probably made as many formal coxcombs in literature, as Lord Cheſterfield's opinion on the vulgarity of laughter, has among men of high breeding. As a general maxim, it has no foundation whatever in truth.

"Proneneſs to admiration is a quality rather of temper than of underſtanding; and if it often attends light minds, it is alſo inſeparable from that warmth of imagination which is requiſite for the ſtrong perception of what is excellent in art or nature. Innumerable inſtances might be produced of the rapturous admiration

As things ſeem large which we through miſts deſcry,
Dulneſs is ever apt to magnify.

NOTES.

admiration with which men of genius have been ſtruck at the view of great performances. It is enough here to mention the poet's favourite critic, Longinus, who is far from being contented with cool approbation, but gives free ſcope to the moſt enraptured praiſe. Few things indicate a mind more unfavourably conſtituted for the fine arts, than a ſlowneſs in being moved to the admiration of excellence; and it is certainly better that this paſſion ſhould at firſt be excited by objects rather inadequate, than that it ſhould not be excited at all." Theſe are the words of a ſenſible obſerver on this eſſay, Dr. Aikin, in Letters to his Son.

"What I diſlike is, the pedantry of appealing to ſpeculative principles in oppoſition to the deciſions of taſte; and what I deſpiſe is, the ridiculous vanity of attempting to demonſtrate, by argument, that men ought to admire, when experience proves that no one does or can admire; and, on the other hand, that men are in the wrong to be pleaſed, when experience proves that it is impoſſible to avoid it. In a word, of all kind of literary affectation, that which is moſt diſguſting is, the affectation of judging in matters of taſte by rule, and not by feeling; and this appears to me the fundamental defect of the work to which I have before alluded; I mean the Elements of Criticiſm. Lord Kaims was no leſs remarkable for delicacy of taſte than acuteneſs of underſtanding; and he evidently ſeems to have thought it much below the dignity of a critic to embrace any opinion even in a mere matter of taſte, which was not ſupported by ſome rule. Where the rule was not already eſtabliſhed, therefore, he was obliged to have recourſe to his invention, which did not always ſupply him with ſuch as were of the moſt ſatisfactory kind; and he ſeems, through the whole of his elaborate work, to entertain much too high an idea of the importance of thoſe rules; for he ſeems to conſider them as founded in reaſon, and as laws by which taſte ought to be regulated; whereas they are properly founded in taſte, and the moſt judicious and beſt eſtabliſhed rules are really nothing more than the different principles by which experience ſhews that the deciſions of taſte are governed."

Eſſays Philoſophical and Literary.

The turn and manner of many paſſages in our author are much like Dryden's prologues; and particularly the famous prologue and epilogue to All for Love.

 Some

Some foreign writers, ſome our own deſpiſe;
The Ancients only, or the Moderns prize.
Thus Wit, like Faith, by each man is apply'd
To one ſmall ſect, and all are damn'd beſide.
Meanly they ſeek the bleſſing to confine,
And force that ſun but on a part to ſhine,
Which not alone the ſouthern wit ſublimes,
But ripens ſpirits in cold northern climes;
Which from the firſt has ſhone on ages paſt,
Enlights the preſent, and ſhall warm the laſt;

NOTES.

VER. 394. *Our own deſpiſe;*] If any proof was wanting how little the Paradiſe Loſt was read and attended to, at this time, our author's total ſilence on the ſubject would be ſufficient to ſhew it. That an Eſſay on Criticiſm could be written, without a ſingle mention of Milton, appears truly ſtrange and incredible; if we did not know that our author ſeems to have had no idea of any merit ſuperior to that of Dryden! and had no reliſh for an author, who,

" Omnes exſtinxit ſtellas, exortus uti ætherius ſol."
Lucret.

VER. 395. *The Antients only,*] A very ſenſible Frenchman ſays, " En un mot, touchez comme Euripide, etonnez comme Sophocle, peignez comme Homere, & compoſez d' apres vous. Ces maitres n'ont point eu de regles; ils n'en ont eté que plus grands; & ils n'ont acquis le droit de commander, que parce qu'ils n'ont jamais obei. Il en eſt tout autrement en literature qu'en politique; le talent qui a beſoin de ſubir des loix, n'en donnera jamais."

VER. 402. *Which from the firſt, &c.*] Genius is the ſame in all ages; but its fruits are various; and more or leſs excellent as they are checked or matured by the influence of government or religion upon them. Hence in ſome parts of literature the Ancients excel; in others, the Moderns; juſt as thoſe accidental circumſtances occurred. W.

VER. 403. *Enlights*] An improper word for *enlightens.*

Tho'

Tho' each may feel encreaſes and decays,
And ſee now clearer and now darker days.
Regard not then if Wit be old or new,
But blame the falſe, and value ſtill the true.

Some ne'er advance a judgment of their own,
But catch the ſpreading notion of the Town;
They reaſon and conclude by precedent,
And own ſtale nonſenſe which they ne'er invent.
Some judge of authors names, not works, and then
Nor praiſe nor blame the writings, but the men.
Of all this ſervile herd, the worſt is he
That in proud dulneſs joins with Quality.
A conſtant Critic at the great man's board,
To fetch and carry nonſenſe for my Lord.
What woful ſtuff this madrigal would be,
In ſome ſtarv'd hackney ſonneteer, or me?
But let a Lord once own the happy lines,
How the wit brightens! how the ſtile refines!
Before his ſacred name flies ev'ry fault,
And each exalted ſtanza teems with thought!

NOTES.

VER. 408. *Some ne'er*] There is very little poetical expreſſion from this line to ver. 450. It is only mere proſe, fringed with rhyme. Good ſenſe in a very proſaic ſtyle. Reaſoning, not poetry.

VER. 420. *Let a Lord*] "You ought not to write verſes, (ſaid George the Second, who had little taſte, to Lord Hervey,) 'tis beneath your rank; leave ſuch work to little Mr. Pope; it is his trade." But this Lord Hervey wrote ſome that were above the level of thoſe deſcribed here by our author.

The Vulgar thus through Imitation err;
As oft the Learn'd by being singular;
So much they scorn the croud, that if the throng
By chance go right, they purposely go wrong:
So Schismatics the plain believers quit,
And are but damn'd for having too much wit.
Some praise at morning what they blame at night;
But always think the last opinion right.
A Muse by these is like a mistress us'd,
This hour she's idoliz'd, the next abus'd;
While their weak heads, like towns unfortify'd,
'Twixt sense and nonsense daily change their side.
Ask them the cause; they're wiser still they say;
And still to-morrow's wiser than to-day.
We think our fathers fools, so wise we grow;
Our wiser sons, no doubt, will think us so.
Once School-divines this zealous isle o'er-spread;
Who knew most Sentences, was deepest read;
Faith, Gospel, all, seem'd made to be disputed,
And none had sense enough to be confuted:
Scotists and Thomists, now, in peace remain,
Amidst their kindred cobwebs in Duck-lane.

If

NOTES.

VER. 425. *By being singular;*] Of which truth there cannot be a stronger example than the learned commentator on our author; "Who (to use his own excellent words on the character of Bayle) struck into the province of paradox, as an exercise for the restless vigour of his mind."

VER. 444. *Scotists*] So denominated from Johannes Duns Scotus. Erasmus tells us, an eminent Scotist assured him, that it was impossible to understand one single proposition of this famous Duns,

If Faith itſelf has diff'rent dreſſes worn,
What wonder modes in Wit ſhould take their turn?
Oft'

NOTES.

Duns, unleſs you had his whole metaphyſics by heart. This hero of incomprehenſible fame ſuffered a miſerable reverſe at Oxford in the time of Henry VIII. That grave antiquary, Mr. Antony Wood, (in the Vindication of himſelf and his writings from the reproaches of the Biſhop of Saliſbury), ſadly laments the *deformation*, as he calls it, of that Univerſity by the King's Commiſſioners; and even records the blaſphemous ſpeeches of one of them, in his own words—"We have ſet Duns in Boccardo, with all his blind gloſſers, faſt nailed up upon poſts in all common houſes of eaſement." Upon which our venerable antiquary thus exclaims: "If ſo be, the commiſſioners had ſuch diſreſpect for that moſt famous author J. Duns, who was ſo much admired by our predeceſſors, and ſo difficult to be underſtood, that the Doctors of thoſe times, namely, Dr. William Roper, Dr. John Keynton, Dr. William Mowſe, &c. profeſſed, that, in twenty-eight years ſtudy, they could not underſtand him rightly, what then had they for others of inferior note?"—What indeed! But they, If ſo be, that moſt famous J. Duns was ſo difficult to be underſtood, (for that this is a moſt theologic proof of his great worth, is paſt all doubt), I ſhould conceive our good old Antiquary to be a little miſtaken. And that the nailing up his Proteus of the Schools was done by the commiſſioners in honour of the moſt famous Duns: There being no other way of catching the ſenſe of ſo ſlippery and dodging an author, who had eluded the purſuit of three of their moſt renowned doctors in full cry after him, for eight and twenty years together. And this boccardo in which he was confined, ſeemed very fit for the purpoſe; it being obſerved, that men are never more ſerious and thoughtful than in that place of retirement. Scribl.

VER. 444. *Thomiſts*] From Thomas Aquinas, a truly great genius, who, in thoſe blind ages, was the ſame in theology, that our Friar Bacon was in natural philoſophy; leſs happy than our countryman in this, that he ſoon became ſurrounded with a number of dark gloſſers, who never left him till they had extinguiſhed the radiance of that light, which had pierced through the thickeſt night of Monkery, the thirteenth century, when the Waldenſes were ſuppreſſed, and Wickliffe not yet riſen. W.

 Thomiſts]

Oft, leaving what is natural and fit,
The current folly proves the ready wit;

And

VARIATIONS.

Ver. 447. Between this and ver. 452.

The rhyming clowns that gladded Shakespear's age,
No more with crambo entertain the stage.
Who now in anagrams their patron praise,
Or sing their mistress in acrostic lays?
Ev'n pulpits pleas'd with merry puns of yore;
Now all are banish'd to th' Hibernian shore!
Thus leaving what was natural and fit,
The current folly prov'd their ready wit;
And authors thought their reputation safe,
Which liv'd as long as fools were pleas'd to laugh.

NOTES.

Ver. 444. *Thomists*] The Summa summæ, &c. of Thomas Aquinas, is a treatise well deserving a most attentive perusal, and contains an admirable view of Aristotle's Ethics.

Aquinas did not understand Greek; what he knew of Aristotle he got from Averroes, an Arabian, whom the Spanish Jews first translated into Hebrew, and from Hebrew into Latin.

Ver. 445. *Amidst their kindred cobwebs*] Were common sense disposed to credit any of the Monkish miracles of the dark and blind ages of the church, it would certainly be one of the seventh century recorded by honest Bale. "In the sixth general council (says he) holden at Constantinople, Anno Dom. 680, contra Monothelitas, where the Latin Mass was first approved, and the Latin ministers deprived of their lawfull wives, spiders webbs, in wonderfull copye were seen falling down from above, upon the heads of the people, to the marvelous astonishment of many."—The justest emblem and prototype of School Metaphysics, the divinity of Scotists and Thomists, which afterwards fell, in wonderfull copye on the heads of the people, in support of Transubstantiation, to the marvellous astonishment of many, as it continues to do to this day. W.

This is very forced and far-fetched.

Ver. 445. *Duck-lane.*] A place where old and second-hand books were sold formerly, near Smithfield. P.

Ver. 448. *Oft, leaving what is natural*] Ita comparatum est humanum ingenium, ut optimarum rerum satietate defatigetur.

Unde

And authors think their reputation ſafe,
Which lives as long as fools are pleas'd to laugh.
 Some valuing thoſe of their own ſide or mind,
Still make themſelves the meaſure of mankind:

NOTES.

Unde fit, artes, neceſſitatis vi quâdam creſcere, aut decreſcere ſemper, & ad ſummum faſtigium evectas, ibi non diu poſſe conſiſtere. Thus muſic, deſerting ſimple and pathetic expreſſion, is taken up with tricks of execution, and a ſort of ſlight of hand. Thus Borromini, to be new and original, has, as Mr. Walpole expreſſes it, twiſted and curled architecture, by inverting the volutes of the Ionic order. L'ennui du Beau, amene le gout du Singulier. This will happen in every country, every art, and every age.

VER. 450. *And authors think their reputation ſafe,*
Which lives as long as fools are pleas'd to laugh.]
This is an admirable ſatire on thoſe called Authors in faſhion; the men who get the laugh on their ſide. He ſhews, on how pitiful a baſis their reputation ſtands, the changling diſpoſition of fools to laugh, who are always carried away with the laſt joke. W.

Another forced interpretation!

VER. 451. *As long as fools*] "Mirabile eſt (ſays Tully) De Oratore, lib. iii. quum plurimum in faciendo inter doctum & rudem, quàm non multum differant in judicando."

Horace and Milton declare againſt general approbation, and wiſh for fit audience though few. And Tully relates, in his Brutus, the ſtory of Antimachus, who, when his numerous auditors all gradually left him, except Plato, ſaid, I ſtill continue reading my work; Plato, enim mihi unus inſtar eſt omnium. The noble confidence and ſtrength of mind, in Milton, is not in any circumſtance more viſible and more admirable, than his writing a poem in a ſtyle and manner that he was ſure would not be reliſhed or regarded by his corrupt contemporaries.

He was different in this reſpect from Bernardo Taſſo, the father of his beloved Torquato, who, to ſatisfy the vulgar taſte and current opinions of his country, new-modelled his epic poem Amadigi, to make it more wild and romantic, and leſs ſuited to the rules of Ariſtotle.

VER. 452. *Side or mind,*] Are two vulgar words, unworthy of our author.

Fondly

Fondly we think we honour merit then,
When we but praiſe ourſelves in other men.
Parties in Wit attend on thoſe of State,
And public faction doubles private hate.
Pride, Malice, Folly, againſt Dryden roſe,
In various ſhapes of Parſons, Critics, Beaus;
But ſenſe ſurviv'd when merry jeſts were paſt;
For riſing merit will buoy up at laſt.
Might he return, and bleſs once more our eyes,
New Blackmores and new Milbourns muſt ariſe:
Nay ſhould great Homer lift his awful head,
Zoilus again would ſtart up from the dead.

Envy

NOTES.

VER. 458. *Pride, Malice,*] "Many perſons of high quality (ſays Voltaire,) protected Pradon againſt Racine; Duke Zoilus, Le Comte Bavius, Marquis Mævius."

VER. 459. *Shapes of Parſons, Critics,*] The Parſon alluded to was Jeremy Collier; the Critic was the Duke of Buckingham; the firſt of whom very powerfully attacked the profligacy, and the latter the irregularity and bombaſt of ſome of Dryden's plays. Theſe attacks were much more than merry jeſts.

VER. 463. *Milbourn*] The Rev. Mr. Luke Milbourn. Dennis ſerved Mr. Pope in the ſame office. But theſe men are of all times, and riſe up on all occaſions. Sir Walter Raleigh had Alexander Roſs; Chillingworth had Cheynel; Milton a firſt Edwards; and Locke a ſecond; neither of them related to the third Edwards of Lincoln's-Inn. They were divines of parts and learning; this a critic without one or the other. Yet (as Mr. Pope ſays of Luke Milbourn) the faireſt of all critics; for having written againſt the Editor's remarks on Shakeſpear, he did him juſtice in printing, at the ſame time, ſome of his own. W.

But all impartial critics allow the remarks to have been deciſive and judicious; and his Canons of Criticiſm remain unrefuted and unanſwerable.

VER. 465. *Zoilus again*] In the fifth book of Vitruvius is an account of Zoilus's coming to the court of Ptolemy at Alexandria,

and

Envy will merit, as its ſhade, purſue;
But like a ſhadow, proves the ſubſtance true:
For envy'd Wit, like Sol eclips'd, makes known,
Th' oppoſing body's groſſneſs, not its own.
When firſt that ſun too pow'rful beams diſplays,
It draws up vapours which obſcure its rays;
But ev'n thoſe clouds at laſt adorn its way,
Reflect new glories, and augment the day.

Be thou the firſt true merit to befriend;
His praiſe is loſt, who ſtays till all commend.

NOTES.

and preſenting to him his virulent and brutal cenſures of Homer, and begging to be rewarded for his work; inſtead of which, it is ſaid, the king ordered him to be crucified, or, as ſome ſaid, ſtoned alive. His perſon is minutely deſcribed in the 11th book of Ælian's various Hiſtory.

VER. 468. *For envy'd Wit, like Sol eclips'd, &c.*] This ſimilitude implies a fact too often verified; and of which we need not ſeek abroad for examples. It is this, that frequently, thoſe very authors, who have at firſt done all they could to obſcure and depreſs a riſing genius, have at length been reduced to borrow from him, imitate his manner, and reflect what they could of his ſplendor; merely to keep themſelves in ſome little credit. Nor hath the poet been leſs artful, to inſinuate alſo what is ſometimes the cauſe. A youthful genius, like the ſun riſing towards the meridian, diſplays too ſtrong and powerful beams for the dirty temper of inferior writers, which occaſions their gathering, condenſing, and blackening. But as he deſcends from the meridian (the time when the ſun gives its gilding to the ſurrounding clouds) his rays grow milder, his heat more benign, and then

"——ev'n thoſe clouds at laſt adorn its way,
Reflect new glories, and augment the day." W.

All the latter part of this note is in the true manner of our Commentator's extorting meanings never meant, and alluſions incongruous and unnatural.

Short

Short is the date, alas, of modern rhymes, 476
And 'tis but just to let them live betimes.

No

NOTES.

VER. 474. *Be thou the first true merit to befriend;*
His praise is lost, who stays till all commend.]

When Thomson published his Winter, 1726, it lay a long time neglected, till Mr. Spence made honourable mention of it in his Essay on the Odyssey; which becoming a popular book, made the poem universally known. Thomson always acknowledged the use of this recommendation; and from this circumstance an intimacy commenced between the critic and the poet, which lasted till the lamented death of the latter, who was of a most amiable and benevolent temper. I have before me a letter of Mr. Spence to Pitt, earnestly begging him to subscribe to the quarto edition of Thomson's Seasons, and mentioning a design which Thomson had formed of writing a descriptive poem on Blenheim; a subject that would have shone in his hands. It was some time after publication, before the Odes of Gray were relished and admired. They were even burlesqued by two men of wit and genius, who, however, once owned to me, that they repented of the attempt. The Hecyra of Terence, the Misanthrope of Moliere, the Phædra of Racine, the Way of the World of Congreve, the Silent Woman of Ben Jonson, were ill received on their first exhibitions. Out of an hundred comedies written by Menander, eight only obtained the prize; and only five of Euripides out of the seventy tragedies he wrote. Our author seems to be eminently fortunate, who never, from his early youth, published a piece that did not meet with immediate approbation, except, perhaps, the first Epistle of the Essay on Man, which Mallet, not knowing the author, told him he thought it a mean performance. The confusion and shame of Mallet may be easily imagined, when Pope informed him that he was the author.

VER. 476. *Short is the date,*] Dr. Beattie has a good commentary on these words:

" All living languages are liable to change. The Greek and Latin, though composed of more durable materials than ours, were subject to perpetual vicissitude, till they ceased to be spoken. The former is, with reason, believed to have been more stationary than any other; and indeed a very particular attention was paid to the preservation of it; yet, between Spenser and Pope, Hooker

and

No longer now that golden age appears,
When Patriarch-wits furviv'd a thoufand years:
Now length of Fame (our fecond life) is loft,
And bare threefcore is all ev'n that can boaft;
Our fons their fathers' failing language fee,
And fuch as Chaucer is fhall Dryden be.

So

NOTES.

and Sherlock, Raleigh and Smollet, a difference of dialect is not more perceptible, than between Homer and Appollonius, Xenophon and Plutarch, Ariftotle and Antoninus. In the Roman authors, the change of language is ftill more remarkable. How different, in this refpect, is Ennius from Virgil, Lucilius from Horace, Cato from Columella, and even Catullus from Ovid! The Laws of the Twelve Tables, though ftudied by every Roman of condition, were not perfectly underftood, even by antiquarians, in the time of Cicero, when they were not quite four hundred years old. Cicero himfelf, as well as Lucretius, made feveral improvements in the Latin tongue; Virgil introduced fome new words; and Horace afferts his right to the fame privilege; and from his remarks upon it, appears to have confidered the immutability of living language as an impoffible thing. It were vain then to flatter ourfelves with the hope of permanency to any of the modern tongues of Europe; which, being more ungrammatical, than the Latin and Greek, are expofed to more dangerous, becaufe lefs difcernible, innovations. Our want of tenfes and cafes makes a multitude of auxiliary verbs neceffary; and to thefe the unlearned are not attentive, becaufe they look upon them as the leaft important parts of language; and hence they come to be omitted or mifapplied in converfation, and afterwards in writing. Befides the fpirit of commerce, manufacture, and naval enterprize, fo honourable to modern Europe, and to Great Britain in particular, and the free circulation of arts, fciences, and opinions, owing, in part, to the ufe of printing, and to our improvements in navigation, muft render the modern tongues, and efpecially the Englifh, more variable than the Greek or Latin."

VER. 482. *Failing language*] "In England (fays an ingenious Italian) the Tranflation of the Bible is the ftandard of their

language;

So when the faithful pencil has deſign'd
Some bright Idea of the maſter's mind,
Where a new world leaps out at his command,
And ready nature waits upon his hand:
When the ripe colours ſoften and unite,
And ſweetly melt into juſt ſhade and light;
When mellowing years their full perfection give,
And each bold figure juſt begins to live,
The treach'rous colours the fair art betray,
And all the bright creation fades away!

NOTES.

language; in Italy the ſtandard is, the Decamerone of Boccacio. Thoſe tales have been ſo highly applauded, and ſo univerſally read, that they ſeem to have overwhelmed his other works, which are ſeldom ſpoken of. It is only within a few years that the Teſeide of Boccacio was known, or talked of, even among profeſſed critics, though this epic poem was frequently quoted by Taſſo in his Diſcorſi del Poema Eroico. Voltaire calls the languages of modern Europe, Enfans boſſus & boiteaux d'un grand homme de belle taille, meaning Latin."

Ver. 484. *So when the faithful pencil, &c.*] This ſimilitude from painting, in which our author diſcovers (as he always does on that ſubject) real ſcience, has ſtill a more peculiar beauty, as at the ſame time that it confeſſes the juſt ſuperiority of ancient writings, it inſinuates one advantage the modern have above them; which is this, that in theſe latter, our more intimate acqaintance with the occaſion of writing, and with the manners deſcribed, lets us into thoſe living and ſtriking graces which may be well compared to that perfection of imitation given only by the pencil. While the ravages of time, amongſt the monuments of former ages, have left us but the groſs ſubſtance of ancient wit; ſo much only of the form and faſhion of bodies as may be expreſſed in braſs or marble. W.

The ſame may be ſaid of this paſſage, as of that which relates to verſe 468, above mentioned.

Unhappy

Unhappy Wit, like moſt miſtaken things,
Atones not for that envy which it brings.
In youth alone its empty praiſe we boaſt,
But ſoon the ſhort-liv'd vanity is loſt:
Like ſome fair flow'r the early ſpring ſupplies,
That gaily blooms, but e'en in blooming dies.
What is this Wit, which muſt our cares employ?
The owner's wife, that other men enjoy;
Then moſt our trouble ſtill when moſt admir'd,
And ſtill the more we give, the more requir'd;
Whoſe fame with pains we guard, but loſe with eaſe,
Sure ſome to vex, but never all to pleaſe;
'Tis what the vicious fear, the virtuous ſhun,
By fools 'tis hated, and by knaves undone!
If Wit ſo much from Ign'rance undergo,
Ah let not learning too commence its foe!

Of

NOTES.

VER. 494. *Unhappy Wit,*] "Ceux qui manient le plomb & le mercure, (ſays Voltaire with his uſual pleaſantry), ſont ſujets à des coliques dangereuſes, & à des tremblemens de nerfs très facheux. Ceux qui ſe ſervent de plumes & d'encre, ſont attaqués d'une vermine, qu'il faut continuellement ſécouer."

VER. 507.——*by knaves undone!*] By which the poet would inſinuate, a common but ſhameful truth, That men in power, if they got into it by illiberal arts, generally left Wit and Science to ſtarve. W.

VER. 508. *If Wit ſo much from Ign'rance undergo,*] The inconveniences that attend wit are well enumerated in this excellent paſſage. "Poets, who imagine they are known and admired, are frequently mortified, and humbled. Boileau going one day to receive his penſion, and the treaſurer reading theſe words in his order; "the penſion we have granted to Boileau, on account of the ſatisfaction his works have given us," aſked

him

Of old, thoſe met rewards who could excell,
And ſuch were prais'd who but endeavour'd well:
Though triumphs were to gen'rals only due,
Crowns were reſerv'd to grace the ſoldiers too.
Now, they who reach Parnaſſus' lofty crown,
Employ their pains to ſpurn ſome others down;
And while ſelf-love each jealous writer rules,
Contending wits become the ſport of fools:
But ſtill the worſt with moſt regret commend,
For each ill Author is as bad a Friend.

NOTES.

him of what kind were his works; "Of maſonry (replied the poet), I am a builder." Racine always reckoned the praiſes of the ignorant among the chief ſources of chagrin; and uſed to relate, that an old magiſtrate, who had never been at a play, was carried, one day, to his Andromaque. This magiſtrate was very attentive to the tragedy, to which was added the Plaideurs; and going out of the theatre, he ſaid to the author, "I am extremely pleaſed, Sir, with your Andromaque: I am only amazed that it ends ſo gaily; j'avois d'abord eu quelque envie de pleurer, mais la vue des petits chiens m'a fait rire.

VER. 519. *Each ill Author*] This might be expected. But how mortifying, that geniuſes of a higher rank ſhould malign and haraſs each other. What ſhall we ſay of the diſgraceful diſſenſions betwixt Sophocles and Euripides; Plato and Ariſtotle; Boſſuet and Fenelon; Boileau and Quinault; Racine and Moliere; Taſſo and the La Cruſca Academicians; Corneille, Scudery, and Cardinal Richlieu; Bayle and Le Clerc; Voltaire and Crebillon; Bentley and Boyle; Clarke and Atterbury; Locke and Stillingfleet; and many others! Mr. Harte related to me, that being with Mr. Pope when he received the news of Swift's death, Harte ſaid to him, he thought it a fortunate circumſtance for their friendſhip, that they had lived ſo diſtant from each other; Pope reſented the reflection, but yet, ſaid Harte, I am convinced it was true.

To

To what baſe ends, and by what abject ways,
Are mortals urg'd through ſacred luſt of praiſe!
Ah ne'er ſo dire a thirſt of glory boaſt,
Nor in the Critic let the Man be loſt.
Good-nature and good ſenſe muſt ever join;
To err is human, to forgive, divine.
  But if in noble minds ſome dregs remain
Not yet purg'd off, of ſpleen and ſour diſdain;
Diſcharge that rage on more provoking crimes,
Nor fear a dearth in theſe flagitious times.

NOTES.

VER. 526. *But if in noble minds ſome dregs remain, &c.*] So far as to what ought to be the true critic's principal ſtudy and employment. But if the ſour critical humour abounds, and muſt therefore needs have vent, he directs to its proper object; and ſhews [from ver. 525 to 556.] how it may be innocently and uſefully pointed. This is very obſervable; our author had made ſpleen and diſdain the characteriſtic of the falſe critic, and yet here ſuppoſes them inherent in the true. But it is done with judgment, and a knowledge of Nature. For as bitterneſs and aſtringency in unripe fruits of the beſt kind are the foundation and capacity of that high ſpirit, race, and flavour, which we find in them when perfectly concocted by the warmth and influence of the ſun, and which, without thoſe qualities, would gain no more by that influence than only a mellow inſipidity: ſo ſpleen and diſdain in the true critic, when improved by long ſtudy and experience, ripen into an exactneſs of judgment and an elegance of taſte: altho', in the falſe critic, lying remote from the influence of good letters, they remain in all their firſt offenſive harſhneſs and acerbity. The poet therefore ſhews how, after the exaltation of theſe qualities into their ſtate of perfection, the very dregs (which, though precipitated, may poſſibly, on ſome occaſions, riſe and ferment even in a noble mind) may be uſefully employed, that is to ſay, in branding obſcenity and impiety. W.

I have preſerved this remark, to juſtify the cenſure I have preſumed to paſs on Warburton's manner of criticiſing.

No pardon vile Obſcenity ſhould find,
Tho' wit and art conſpire to move your mind;
But Dulneſs with Obſcenity muſt prove
As ſhameful ſure as Impotence in love.
In the fat age of pleaſure, wealth, and eaſe,
Sprung the rank weed, and thriv'd with large increaſe:
When love was all an eaſy Monarch's care;
Seldom at council, never in a war:
Jilts rul'd the ſtate, and ſtateſmen farces writ:
Nay wits had penſions, and young Lords had wit:
The Fair ſate panting at a Courtier's play,
And not a Maſk went unimprov'd away:
The modeſt fan was lifted up no more,
And Virgins ſmil'd at what they bluſh'd before.
The following licence of a foreign reign
Did all the dregs of bold Socinus drain;

Then

NOTES.

VER. 545. ——*bold Socinus*] "This author (ſays Dr. Jortin) ſeems to have had two particular antipathies; one to grammatical and verbal criticiſm, the other to falſe doctrine and hereſy. To the firſt we may aſcribe his treating Bentley, Burman, Kuſter, and Waſſe, with a contempt which recoiled upon himſelf. To the ſecond, we will impute his pious zeal againſt thoſe divines of King William's time, whom he ſuppoſed to be infected with the Infidel, or the Socinian, or the Latitudinarian ſpirit, and not ſo orthodox as himſelf, and his friends Swift, Bolingbroke, &c. Thus he laid about him, and cenſured men, of whoſe literary, or of whoſe theological merits or defects, he was no more a judge than his footman, John Searle. He ſays,

"The following licence of a foreign reign,
Did all the dregs of bold Socinus drain;
Then unbelieving Prieſts reform'd the nation,
And taught more pleaſant methods of ſalvation."

In

Then unbelieving Priests reform'd the nation,
And taught more pleasant methods of salvation;
Where Heav'n's free subjects might their rights dispute,
Lest God himself should seem too absolute:
Pulpits their sacred satire learn'd to spare,
And Vice admir'd to find a flatt'rer there!
Encourag'd thus, Wit's Titans brav'd the skies,
And the press groan'd with licens'd blasphemies.
These monsters, Critics! with your darts engage,
Here point your thunder, and exhaust your rage!
Yet shun their fault, who, scandalously nice,
Will needs mistake an author into vice;
All seems infected that th' infected spy,
As all looks yellow to the jaundic'd eye.

NOTES.

"In the third of these lines he had Burnet in view, and his History of the Reformation; and in the fourth, Kennet; who was accused of having said, in a funeral sermon on some nobleman, that converted sinners, if they were men of parts, repented more speedily and effectually than dull rascals. If his witty friend Swift had consulted the rules of prosody, he would not have begun an epigram with,

Vertiginosus, inops, surdus, malè gratus amicis;

and have made a false quantity in the first word. But writing Latin, either prose or verse, was not his talent, any more than making sermons. As to the knowledge which he is said to have acquired of the learned languages,——Cràs credo, hodiè nihil."

VER. 547. The author has omitted two lines which stood here, as containing a National Reflection, which in his stricter judgment he could not but disapprove on any people whatever. P.

VER. 559. *Jaundic'd*] Borrowed from an old comedy.

III.

Learn then what Morals Critics ought to ſhow,
For 'tis but half a Judge's taſk, to know.
'Tis not enough, taſte, judgment, learning, join;
In all you ſpeak, let truth and candour ſhine:
That not alone what to your ſenſe is due,
All may allow; but ſeek your friendſhip too.
Be ſilent always, when you doubt your ſenſe;
And ſpeak, tho' ſure, with ſeeming diffidence:
Some poſitive, perſiſting fops we know,
Who, if once wrong, will needs be always ſo;
But you, with pleaſure own your errors paſt,
And make each day a Critique on the laſt.

'Tis

NOTES.

Ver. 560. *Learn then, &c.*] We enter now on the third part, the *Morals* of the critic; included in candour, modeſty, and good-breeding. This third and laſt part is in two diviſions. In the firſt of which [from ver. 559 to 631.] our author inculcates theſe morals by precept: In the ſecond [from ver. 630 to the end] by example. His firſt precept [from ver. 561 to 566.] recommends candour, for its uſe to the critic, and to the writer criticiſed. W.

Ver. 570. *Your errors paſt,*] Theſe few following words of Quintilian, (whom Pope himſelf has, with propriety, ſo frequently quoted), contain almoſt every thing that can be ſaid on the ſubject of correcting and emendation. "Hujus autem operis eſt, adjicere, detrahere, mutare. Sed facilius in his ſimpliciuſque judicium, quæ replenda, vel dejicienda ſunt; premere verò tumentia, humilia extollere, luxuriantia aſtringere, inordinata digerere, ſoluta componere, exultantia coercere, duplicis operæ." Suffer me to add another paſſage of equal taſte and utility; "Et ipſa emendatio habet finem; ſunt enim qui ad omnia ſcripta, tanquam vitioſa redeunt; & quaſi nihil fas ſit rectum eſſe quod primum eſt, melius exiſtiment quidquid eſt aliud; idque faciunt quoties librum in manus reſumpſerint; ſimiles medicis, etiam integra ſecantibus.

Accidit

'Tis not enough your counfel ftill be true;
Blunt truths more mifchief than nice falfhoods do;
Men muft be taught as if you taught them not,
And things unknown propos'd as things forgot.
Without Good-Breeding, truth is difapprov'd;
That only makes fuperior fenfe belov'd.
Be niggards of advice on no pretence:
For the worft avarice is that of fenfe.
With mean complacence ne'er betray your truft,
Nor be fo civil as to prove unjuft.
Fear not the anger of the wife to raife;
Thofe beft can bear reproof, who merit praife.
'Twere

NOTES.

Accidit itaque ut cicatricofa fint, & exanguia, & curâ pejora. Sit aliquando quod placeat; aut certè quod fufficiat: ut plus poliat lima, non exterat." Quintil. lib. 10. Thefe cautions and reftrictions, in the bufinefs of emendation, are excellent indeed.

VER. 580. *With mean complacence ne'er betray your truft,*
Nor be fo civil as to prove unjuft.]

Our poet practifed this excellent precept in his conduct towards Wycherley, whofe pieces he corrected with equal freedom and judgment. But Wycherley, who had a bad heart, and an infufferable fhare of vanity, and who was one of the profeffed wits of the laft age, was foon difgufted at this candour and ingenuity of Pope; infomuch, that he came to an open and ungenerous rupture with him.

VER. 582. *Fear not the anger of the wife to raife;*] The freedom and unrefervednefs with which Boileau and Racine communicated their works to each other, is hardly to be paralleled; of which many amiable inftances appear in their letters lately publifhed by a fon of the latter; particularly in the following: " J'ai trouvé que la Trompette & les Sourds etoient trop joués, & qu'il ne falloit point trop appuyer fur votre incommodité, moins encore chercher de l'efprit fur ce fujet." Boileau communicated to his friend the firft fketch of his Ode on the Taking Namur. It is entertaining to

'Twere well might Critics ſtill this freedom take,
But Appius reddens at each word you ſpeak,
And ſtares, tremendous, with a threat'ning eye,
Like ſome fierce tyrant in old tapeſtry.

NOTES.

to contemplate a rude draught by ſuch a maſter; and is no leſs pleaſing to obſerve the temper, with which he receives the objections of Racine. "J'ai deja retouché à tout cela; mais je ne veux point l'achever que je n'aie reçu vos remarques, qui ſurément m'éclaireront encore l'eſprit." The ſame volume informs us of a curious anecdote, that Boileau generally made the ſecond verſe of a couplet before the firſt; that he declared it was one of the grand ſecrets of poetry to give, by this means, a greater energy and meaning to his verſes; that he adviſed Racine to follow the ſame method, and ſaid on this occaſion, "I have taught him to rhyme with difficulty."

VER. 584. *'Twere well might Critics, &c.*] The poet having thus recommended, in his general rules of conduct for the Judgment, theſe three critical virtues to the Heart; ſhews next [from ver. 583 to 631.] upon what three ſorts of writers theſe virtues, together with the advice conveyed under them, would be thrown away; and which is worſe, be repaid with obloquy and ſcorn. Theſe are the falſe Critic, the dull Man of Quality, and the bad Poet; each of which ſpecies of incorrigible writers he hath very exactly painted. But having drawn the laſt of them at full length, and being always attentive to the two main branches of his ſubject, which are, of writing and judging well, he re-aſſumes the character of the bad Critic (whom he had touched upon before) to contraſt him with the other; and makes the characteriſtic common to both, to be a never-ceaſing repetition of their own impertinence.
The Poet—ſtill runs on in a raging vein, &c. ver. 606, &c.
The Critic—with his own tongue ſtill edifies his ears, 614, &c. W.

VER. 586. *And ſtares, tremendous, &c.*] This picture was taken to himſelf by John Dennis, a furious old critic by profeſſion, who, upon no other provocation, wrote againſt this eſſay and its author, in a manner perfectly lunatic: For, as to the mention made of him in ver. 270, he took it as a compliment, and ſaid it was treacherouſly meant to cauſe him to overlook this abuſe of his perſon. P.

Fear

Fear moſt to tax an Honourable fool,
Whoſe right it is, uncenſur'd, to be dull;
Such, without wit, are Poets when they pleaſe,
As without learning they can take Degrees.
Leave dang'rous truths to unſucceſsful Satires,
And flattery to fulſome Dedicators,
Whom, when they praiſe, the world believes no more,
Than when they promiſe to give ſcribling o'er.
'Tis beſt ſometimes your cenſure to reſtrain,
And charitably let the dull be vain:
Your ſilence there is better than your ſpite,
For who can rail ſo long as they can write?
Still humming on, their drouzy courſe they keep,
And laſh'd ſo long, like tops, are laſh'd aſleep.
Falſe ſteps but help them to renew the race,
As, after ſtumbling, Jades will mend their pace.
What crouds of theſe, impenitently bold,
In ſounds and jingling ſyllables grown old,

NOTES.

VER. 593. *Fulſome Dedicators,*] "To ſee a diſcourſe on the ten predicaments (ſays Warburton pleaſantly) addreſſed to a leader of armies, or a ſyſtem of caſuiſtry to a miniſter of ſtate, always appeared to me a high abſurdity." Might we not ſay the ſame of addreſſing a diſcourſe on fataliſm and free-will to the worthy, but illiterate, Mr. Allen of Bath?

VER. 597. *Be vain:*] This was a favourite maxim and practice of Addiſon, as it is related by Swift; he never contradicted a ſelf-ſufficient affected coxcomb.

VER. 604. *Impenitently bold,*] *Bold* is but a poor epithet in this place,

Still run on Poets in a raging vein,
Ev'n to the dregs and ſqueezing of the brain,
Strain out the laſt dull droppings of their ſenſe,
And rhyme with all the rage of Impotence.
  Such ſhameleſs Bards we have; and yet 'tis true,
There are as mad, abandon'd Critics too.
The bookful blockhead ignorantly read,
With loads of learned lumber in his head,
With his own tongue ſtill edifies his ears,
And always liſt'ning to himſelf appears.
All books he reads, and all he reads aſſails,
From Dryden's Fables down to Durfey's Tales.
With him moſt authors ſteal their works, or buy;
Garth did not write his own Diſpenſary.
Name a new play, and he's the Poet's friend,
Nay ſhow'd his faults—but when would Poets mend?
No place ſo ſacred from ſuch fops is barr'd,
Nor is Paul's church more ſafe than Paul's church yard:

Nay,

NOTES.

VER. 607. *Squeezing of the brain,*] It has been ſuggeſted that he alludes to Wycherley, who had quarrelled with him for correcting his rough and harſh verſes, and for ſaying, he had better put his thoughts into proſe, like Rochfoucault's maxims.

VER. 619. *Garth did not write, &c.*] A common ſlander at that time in prejudice of that deſerving author. Our Poet did him this juſtice, when that ſlander moſt prevailed; and it is now (perhaps the ſooner for this very verſe) dead and forgotten. P.

VER. 622. *No place ſo ſacred*] This ſtroke of ſatire is literally taken from Boileau.

" Gardez vous d'imiter ce rimeur furieux,
Qui de ſes vains écrits lecteur harmonieux
Aborde en récitant quiconque le ſalue,
Et pourſuit de ſes vers les paſſans dans le ruë,

Il

Nay, fly to Altars; there they'll talk you dead;
For fools ruſh in where Angels fear to tread.
Diſtruſtful ſenſe with modeſt caution ſpeaks,
It ſtill looks home, and ſhort excurſions makes;
But rattling nonſenſe in full vollies breaks,

VARIATIONS.

VER. 623. Between this and ver. 624.

In vain you ſhrug and ſweat and ſtrive to fly:
Theſe know no Manners but of poetry.
They'll ſtop a hungry chaplain in his grace,
To treat of unities of time and place.

NOTES.

Il n'eſt Temple ſi ſaint, des Anges reſpecté,
Qui ſoit contre ſa muſe un lieu du ſûreté."

Which lines allude to the impertinence of a French poet called Du Perrier, who finding Boileau one day at church, inſiſted upon repeating to him an ode, during the elevation of the hoſt; and deſired his opinion, whether or not it was in the manner of Malherbe. Without this anecdote the pleaſantry of the ſatire would be overlooked. It may here be occaſionally obſerved, how many beauties in this ſpecies of writing are loſt, for want of knowing the facts to which they allude. The following paſſage may be produced as a proof. Boileau, in his excellent epiſtle to his gardener, at Anteuil, ſays,

" Mon maître, dirois-tu, paſſe pour un Docteur,
Et parle quelquefois mieux qu'un Prédicateur."

It ſeems our author and Racine returned one day, in high ſpirits, from Verſailles, with two honeſt citizens of Paris. As their converſation was full of gaiety and humour, the two citizens were greatly delighted; and one of them, at parting, ſtopt Boileau with this compliment, " I have travelled with Doctors of the Sorbonne, and even with the religious; but I never heard ſo many fine things ſaid before; en verite vous parlez cent fois mieux qu'un Predicateur."

It is but juſtice to add, that the fourteen ſucceeding verſes in the poem before us, containing the character of a True Critic, are ſuperior to any thing in Boileau's Art of Poetry; from which, however, Pope has borrowed many obſervations.

And

And never ſhock'd, and never turn'd aſide,
Burſts out, reſiſtleſs, with a thund'ring tide.

But where's the man, who counſel can beſtow,
Still pleas'd to teach, and yet not proud to know?
Unbiaſs'd, or by favour, or by ſpite;
Not dully prepoſſeſs'd, nor blindly right;
Tho' learn'd, well-bred; and tho' well-bred, ſincere;
Modeſtly bold, and humanly ſevere;

NOTES.

VER. 631. *But where's the man, &c.*] The poet, by his manner of aſking after this character, and telling us, when he had deſcribed it, that ſuch once were critics, does not encourage us to ſearch for it amongſt modern writers. And indeed the diſcovery of him, if it could be made, would be but an invidious affair. However, I will venture to name the piece of criticiſm in which all theſe marks may be found. It is entitled, Q. Hor. Fl. Ars Poetica, et ejuſd. Ep. ad Aug. with an Engliſh commentary and notes. W.

This commentary is founded on the idea that Horace writes, in his Art of Poetry, with ſyſtematic order, and the ſtricteſt method. An idea to which ſeveral capable critics will not accede, and which is directly contrary to Pope's own opinion. But it may be added, that Dr. Hurd was not the firſt who entertained this idea. A French writer, M. de Brueys, gave a paraphraſe on this epiſtle of Horace, in 1683, totally grounded on this ſuppoſition. If my partiality to my lamented friend Mr. Colman does not miſlead me, I ſhould think his account of the matter the moſt judicious of any yet publiſhed. He conceives that the elder Piſo had written or meditated a poetical work, probably a tragedy; and had communicated his piece, in confidence, to Horace; but Horace, either diſapproving of the work, or doubting of the poetical faculties of the elder Piſo, or both, wiſhed to diſſuade him from all thoughts of publication. With this view he wrote his epiſtle, addreſſing it with a courtlineſs and delicacy, perfectly agreeable to his acknowledged character, indifferently to the whole family, the father and his two ſons. Epiſtle to the Piſo's, with Notes by George Colman, 4to. 1783, p. 6.

Who to a friend his faults can freely ſhow,
And gladly praiſe the merit of a foe?
Bleſt with a taſte exact, yet unconfin'd;
A knowledge both of books and human kind;
Gen'rous converſe; a ſoul exempt from pride;
And love to praiſe, with reaſon on his ſide?
  Such once were Critics; ſuch the happy few,
Athens and Rome in better ages knew.
The mighty Stagirite firſt left the ſhore,
Spread all his ſails, and durſt the deeps explore;

He

VARIATIONS.

Between ver. 646 and 649. I have found the following lines, ſince ſuppreſt by the author:

That bold Columbus of the realms of wit,
Whoſe firſt diſcovery's not exceeded yet.
Led by the Light of the Maeonian Star,
He ſteer'd ſecurely, and diſcover'd far.
He, when all Nature was ſubdu'd before,
Like his great Pupil, ſigh'd and long'd for more:
Fancy's wild regions yet unvanquiſh'd lay,
A boundleſs empire, and that own'd no ſway.
Poets, &c. W.

NOTES.

Ver. 642. *With reaſon on his ſide, &c.*] Not only on his ſide, but in actual employment. The critic makes but a mean figure, who, when he has found out the beauties of his author, contents himſelf with ſhewing them to the world in only empty exclamations. His office is to explain their nature, ſhew from whence they ariſe, and what effects they produce; or in the better and fuller expreſſion of the poet,

"To teach the world with reaſon to admire." W.

Ver. 645. *The mighty Stagirite*] A noble and juſt character of the firſt and the beſt of critics! and ſufficient to repreſs the faſhionable and nauſeous petulance of ſeveral impertinent moderns, who have attempted to diſcredit this great and uſeful writer.

Whoever

He ſteer'd ſecurely, and diſcover'd far,
Led by the light of the Maeonian ſtar.

Poets,

NOTES.

Whoever ſurveys the variety and perfection of his productions, all delivered in the chaſteſt ſtyle, in the cleareſt order, and the moſt pregnant brevity, is amazed at the immenſity of his genius. His logic, however at preſent neglected for thoſe rudiments and verboſe ſyſtems, which took their riſe from Locke's Eſſay on the Human Underſtanding, is a mighty effort of the mind; in which are diſcovered the principal ſources of the art of reaſoning, and the dependencies of one thought on another; and where, by the different combinations he hath made of all the forms the underſtanding can aſſume in reaſoning, which he hath traced for it, he hath ſo cloſely confined it, that it cannot depart from them, without arguing inconſequentially. His Phyſics contain many uſeful obſervations, particularly his Hiſtory of Animals, which Buffon highly praiſes; to aſſiſt him in which, Alexander gave orders, that creatures of different climates and countries ſhould, at a great expence, be brought to him, to paſs under his inſpection. His Morals are, perhaps, the pureſt ſyſtem of antiquity. His Politics are a moſt valuable monument of the civil wiſdom of the ancients; as they preſerve to us the deſcription of ſeveral governments, and particularly of Crete and Carthage, that otherwiſe would have been unknown. But of all his compoſitions, his Rhetoric and Poetics are moſt excellent. No writer has ſhewn a greater penetration into the receſſes of the human heart, than this philoſopher, in the ſecond book of his Rhetoric; where he treats of the different manners and paſſions that diſtinguiſh each different age and condition of man; and from whence Horace plainly took his famous deſcription, in the Art of Poetry (ver. 157). La Bruyere, La Rochefoucault, and Montaigne himſelf, are not to be compared to him in this reſpect. No ſucceeding writer on eloquence, not even Tully, has added any thing new or important on this ſubject. His Poetics, which, I ſuppoſe, are here by Pope chiefly referred to, ſeem to have been written for the uſe of that prince, with whoſe education Ariſtotle was honoured, to give him a juſt taſte in reading Homer and the tragedians; to judge properly of which, was then thought no unneceſſary accompliſhment in the character of a prince. To attempt to underſtand poetry without having diligently digeſted this treatiſe, would

Poets, a race long unconfin'd, and free,
Still fond and proud of ſavage liberty,
Receiv'd his laws; and ſtood convinc'd 'twas fit,
Who conquer'd Nature, ſhould preſide o'er Wit.
Horace ſtill charms with graceful negligence,
And without method talks us into ſenſe,
Will, like a friend, familiarly convey
The trueſt notions in the eaſieſt way.
He, who ſupreme in judgment, as in wit,
Might boldly cenſure, as he boldly writ,
Yet judg'd with coolneſs, tho' he ſung with fire;
His Precepts teach but what his works inſpire.
Our Critics take a contrary extreme,
They judge with fury, but they write with flegm:
Nor ſuffers Horace more in wrong tranſlations
By Wits, than Critics in as wrong Quotations.

NOTES.

would be as abſurd and impoſſible, as to pretend to a ſkill in geometry, without having ſtudied Euclid. The fourteenth, fifteenth, and ſixteenth chapters, wherein he has pointed out the propereſt methods of exciting terror and pity, convince us, that he was intimately acquainted with thoſe objects which moſt forcibly affect the heart. The prime excellence of this precious treatiſe is the ſcholaſtic preciſion, and philoſophical cloſeneſs, with which the ſubject is handled, without any addreſs to the paſſions, or imagination. It is to be lamented, that the part of the Poetics in which he had given precepts for comedy, did not likewiſe deſcend to poſterity.

VER. 652. *Who conquer'd*] By conquering nature, our poet certainly meant, was a perfect maſter of all natural philoſophy, as far as it was then underſtood; in his own manuſcript lines quoted above he uſes the expreſſion in the very ſame ſenſe;

He, when all nature was ſubdu'd before.

See

See Dionyſius Homer's thoughts refine,
And call new beauties forth from ev'ry line!

Fancy

NOTES.

VER. 665. *See Dionyſius*] Of Halicarnaſſus. P.

VER. 665. *See Dionyſius*] Theſe proſaic lines, this ſpiritleſs eulogy, are much below the merit of the critic whom they are intended to celebrate. Pope ſeems here rather to have conſidered Dionyſius as the author only of reflections concerning Homer; and to have, in ſome meaſure, overlooked, or at leaſt not to have ſufficiently inſiſted on, his moſt excellent book ΠΕΡΙ ΣΥΝΘΕΣΕΩΣ ΟΝΟΜΑΤΩΝ, in which he has unfolded all the ſecret arts that render compoſition harmonious. One part of this diſcourſe, I mean from the beginning of the twenty-firſt to the end of the twenty-fourth ſection, is, perhaps, one of the moſt uſeful pieces of criticiſm extant. He there diſcuſſes the three different ſpecies of compoſition; which he divides into the Nervous and Auſtere, the Smooth and Florid, and the Middle, which partakes of the nature of the two others. As examples of the firſt ſpecies, he mentions Antimachus and Empedocles in heroics, Pindar in lyric, Æſchylus in tragic poetry, and Thucydides in hiſtory. As examples of the ſecond, he produces Heſiod as a writer in heroics; Sappho, Anacreon, and Simonides, in lyric; Euripides only among tragic writers; among the hiſtorians, Ephorus and Theopompus; and Iſocrates among the rhetoricians; all theſe, ſays he, have uſed words that are ΛΕΙΑ, και ΜΑΛΑΚΑ, και ΠΑΡΘΕΝΩΠΑ. The writers which he alleges as inſtances of the third ſpecies, who have happily blended the two other ſpecies of compoſition, and who are the moſt complete models of ſtyle, are Homer in epic poetry; Steſichorus and Alcæus in lyric; in tragic, Sophocles; in hiſtory, Herodotus; in eloquence, Demoſthenes; in philoſophy, Democritus, Plato, and Ariſtotle. Numberleſs are the paſſages which Quintilian has borrowed from this writer; who has lately been brought forward, and perhaps will be more read by being ſo often referred to, by the learned Lord Monboddo. The treatiſe, De Structurâ, was admirably well publiſhed by Mr. Upton, the editor alſo of Ariſtotle's Poetics, printed at Cambridge, under the inſpection of Dr. Hare, in the year 1706, and alſo of Extracts from Ælian, Polyanus, and Herodotus, and of Aſcham's Schoolmaſter. Let me indulge myſelf by adding, that his ſon, Mr. John Upton, Prebendary of Rocheſter, was alſo a man of taſte and ability, author of Obſervations on Shakeſpear,

Fancy and art in gay Petronius pleaſe,
The ſcholar's learning, with the courtier's eaſe.
In grave Quintilian's copious work, we find
The juſteſt rules, and cleareſt method join'd:

NOTES.

Shakeſpear, of a moſt accurate edition of Arrian's Epictetus, and of the beſt edition of Spencer's Fairy Queen, ever given to the public. This amiable and learned man, was unjuſtly and uncandidly depreciated by Dr. Warburton, but, as a full equivalent, was honoured with the conſtant friendſhip and regard of the excellent author of Hermes.

VER. 666. *And call new*] Racine, in one of his letters, ſays, accidentally, and without any affectation, that he had that day read over, in Greek, the whole of Dionyſius's treatiſe De Structura Orationis. I believe few modern poets could, with truth, have ſaid the ſame thing. But he, as well as Boileau, was an excellent Greek ſcholar, which cannot be ſaid of any of their ſucceſſors in France, not even their celebrated Voltaire.

VER. 667. *Petronius pleaſe,*] This diſſolute and effeminate writer little deſerved a place among good critics, for only two or three pages on the ſubject of criticiſm. His fragment on the Civil War is far below Lucan, whom he endeavoured to blame and to excel. Sir George Wheeler, eſteemed an accurate traveller, informs us, that he ſaw at Trau, in the hands of a Doctor Statelius, a fragment of Petronius, in which the account of the Supper of Trimalcion was entire. Yet this fragment has been judged to be ſpurious.

VER. 669. *In grave Quintilian's copious work,*] To commend Quintilian barely for his method, and to inſiſt merely on this excellence, is below the merit of one of the moſt rational and elegant of Roman writers. Conſidering the nature of Quintilian's ſubject, he afforded copious matter for a more appropriated and poetical character. No author ever adorned a ſcientifical treatiſe with ſo many beautiful metaphors. Quintilian was found in the bottom of a tower of the monaſtery of St. Gal, by Poggius; as appears by one of his letters dated 1417, written from Conſtance, where the council was then ſitting. The monaſtery was about twenty miles from that city. Silius Italicus, and Valerius Flaccus, were found at the ſame time and place. A hiſtory of the manner in which the manuſcripts of ancient authors were found, would be an entertaining work to perſons of literary curioſity. See Life of Lorenzo di Medici.

Thus uſeful arms in magazines we place,
All rang'd in order, and diſpos'd with grace,
But leſs to pleaſe the eye, than arm the hand,
Still fit for uſe, and ready at command.
  Thee, bold Longinus! all the Nine inſpire,
And bleſs their Critic with a Poet's fire.
An ardent Judge, who, zealous in his truſt,
With warmth gives ſentence, yet is always juſt:
Whoſe own example ſtrengthens all his laws;
And is himſelf that great ſublime he draws.

NOTES.

VER. 675. *Thee, bold Longinus!*] This abrupt addreſs to Longinus is more ſpirited and ſtriking, and more ſuitable to the character of the perſon addreſſed, than if he had coldly ſpoken of him in the third perſon, as it ſtood in the firſt edition. The taſte and ſenſibility of Longinus were exquiſite; but his obſervations are too general, and his method too looſe. The preciſion of the true philoſophical critic is loſt in the declamation of the florid rhetorician. Inſtead of ſhewing for what reaſon a ſentiment or image is ſublime, and diſcovering the ſecret power by which they affect a reader with pleaſure, he is ever intent on producing ſomething ſublime himſelf, and ſtrokes of his own eloquence. Inſtead of pointing out the foundation of the grandeur of Homer's imagery, where he deſcribes the motion of Neptune, the critic is endeavouring to rival the poet, by ſaying that, " there was not room enough in the whole earth to take ſuch another ſtep." He ſhould have ſhewn why the ſpeech of Phaeton to his ſon, in a fragment of Euripides, was ſo lively and picturesque; inſtead of which, he ardently exclaims, " Would not you ſay, that the ſoul of the writer aſcended the chariot with the driver, and was whirled along in the ſame flight and danger with the rapid horſes?" We have lately ſeen a juſt ſpecimen of the genuine method of criticiſing, in Mr. Harris's accurate Diſcourſe on Poetry, Painting, and Muſic. I have frequently wondered, that Longinus, who mentions Tully, ſhould have taken no notice of Virgil or Horace. I ſuppoſe he thought them only ſervile copiers of the Greeks. Neither Herodotus nor Thucidydes ever once mention the Romans.

Thus

Thus long ſucceeding Critics juſtly reign'd,
Licence repreſs'd, and uſeful laws ordain'd.
Learning and Rome alike in empire grew;
And arts ſtill follow'd where her eagles flew; 684
From the ſame Foes, at laſt, both felt their doom,
And the ſame age ſaw Learning fall and Rome.

With

NOTES.

VER. 685. *From the ſame Foes,*] "'Twas the fate of Rome to have ſcarce an intermediate age, or ſingle period of time, between the riſe of arts and fall of liberty. No ſooner had that nation begun to loſe the roughneſs and barbarity of their manners, and learn of Greece to form their heroes, their orators, and poets, on a right model, than on their unjuſt attempt upon the liberty of the world, they juſtly loſt their own. With their liberty, they loſt not only their force of eloquence, but even their ſtyle and language itſelf. The poets who afterwards aroſe among them, were mere unnatural and forced plants. Their two moſt finiſhed, who came laſt, and cloſed the ſcene, were plainly ſuch as had ſeen the days of liberty, and felt the ſad effects of its departure."

Shafteſbury proceeds to obſerve, that when deſpotiſm was fully eſtabliſhed, not a ſtatue, picture, or medal, not a tolerable piece of architecture, afterwards appeared.—And it was, I may add, the opinion of Longinus, and Addiſon, who adopted it from him, that arbitrary governments were pernicious to the fine arts, as well as to the ſciences. Modern hiſtory, however, has afforded an example to the contrary. Painting, ſculpture, and muſic, have been ſeen to arrive to a high perfection in Rome, notwithſtanding the ſlavery and ſuperſtition that reign there; nay, ſuperſtition itſelf has been highly productive of theſe fine arts; for with what enthuſiaſm muſt a popiſh painter work for an altar-piece? There have been inſtances of painters who, before they began to work, have always received the ſacrament. Neither Dante, Arioſto, nor Taſſo, flouriſhed in free governments; and it ſeems chimerical to aſſert, that Milton would never have written his Paradiſe Loſt if he had not ſeen monarchy deſtroyed, and the ſtate thrown into diſorder. Michael Angelo, Raphael, and Julio Romano, lived in deſpotic ſtates. The fine arts, in ſhort, are naturally attendant upon power and luxury. But the ſciences require unlimited

 freedom,

With Tyranny, then Superſtition join'd,
As that the body, this enſlav'd the mind;
Much was believ'd, but little underſtood,
And to be dull was conſtru'd to be good;
A ſecond deluge Learning thus o'er-run,
And the Monks finiſh'd what the Goths begun.

At

VARIATIONS.

Between ver. 690 and 691, the author omitted theſe two,

Vain Wits and Critics were no more allow'd,
When none but Saints had licence to be proud. P.

NOTES.

freedom, to raiſe them to their full vigour and growth. In a monarchy, there may be poets, painters, and muſicians; but orators, hiſtorians, and philoſophers, can exiſt, in their full force, in a well-ordered republic alone.

VER. 686. *Saw Learning fall*] Literature and the arts, which flouriſhed to ſo great a degree about the time of Auguſtus, gradually felt a decline, from many concurrent cauſes; from the vaſt extent of the Roman empire, and its conſequent deſpotiſm, which cruſhed every noble effort of the mind; from the military government, which rendered life and property precarious, and therefore deſtroyed even the neceſſary arts of agriculture and manufactures; and by the irruption of the barbarous nations, which was occaſioned and facilitated by this ſtate of things. About the eleventh century the people of Chriſtendom were ſunk in the loweſt ignorance and brutality, till the accidental finding Juſtinian's Pandects, at Amalfi, in Italy, about the year 1130, began to awaken and enlarge the minds of men, by laying before them an art that would give ſtability and ſecurity to all the other arts that ſupport and embelliſh life. It is a miſtake to think that the arts were deſtroyed by the irruptions of the northern nations; they had degenerated and decayed before that event.

VER. 692. *What the Goths begun*] Leontius Pilatus was the perſon that reſtored Greek learning in Italy; Gregoris Tiphernas in France; William Grocyn of New College, Oxford, in England. The nine Grecians that came firſt from Conſtantinople into the Weſt, were Beſſarion, Chryſoloras, Demet. Calchondylas, Gaza, J. Argyropulus, G. Trapezuntius, Mar. Muſurus, M. Marullus, J. Laſcaris.

At length Erafmus, that great injur'd name,
(The glory of the Priefthood, and the fhame!)
Stem'd

NOTES.

Ver. 693. *At length Erafmus, &c.*] Nothing can be more artful than the application of this example: or more happy than the turn of the compliment. To throw glory quite round the character of this admirable Perfon, he makes it to be (as in fact it really was) by his affiftance chiefly, that Leo was enabled to reftore letters and the fine arts in his Pontificate. W.

This is not exactly true; others had a fhare in this great and important work.

" I have been afked, whether I would decide the queftion, What was the religion of Erafmus? In one refpect, I account myfelf qualified for the undertaking; for I am unprejudiced, and have nothing to bias me. But I think it beft to leave the reader to judge for himfelf, and to make his inferences from the premifes. Therefore I fhall only obferve, that Erafmus, if he had had an abfolute power to eftablifh a form of religion in any country, would have been a moderate man, and a Latitudinarian, as to the credenda. He would have propofed few articles of faith, and thofe with a primitive fimplicity. This fyftem, indeed, would have been highly difagreeable to the men, who enjoy no comfort in believing, or in pretending to believe, what they think fit, unlefs they can vex, harrafs, and torment, all thofe who will not fubmit to their decifions." This is the candid opinion of Dr. Jortin, in his Life of Erafmus, p. 609.

" I am afraid (faid Erafmus) in one of his epiftles, that not having the firmnefs and fpirit of Luther, I fhould have behaved like St. Peter in the fame circumftances."

Ver. 694. *The glory of the Priefthood, and the fhame!*] Our author elfewhere lets us know what he efteems to be the glory of the priefthood as well as of a chriftian in general, where, comparing himfelf to Erafmus, he fays,

" In Moderation placing all my glory,"

and confequently what he regards as the fhame of it. The whole of this character belonged eminently and almoft folely to Erafmus: For the other Reformers, fuch as Luther, Calvin, and their followers, underftood fo little in what true chriftian liberty confifted, that they carried with them, into the reformed churches, that very fpirit of perfecution, which had driven them from the church of Rome. W.

Stem'd the wild torrent of a barb'rous age,
And drove thoſe holy Vandals off the ſtage.
But ſee! each Muſe, in LEO's golden days,
Starts from her trance, and trims her wither'd bays,
Rome's

NOTES.

VER. 696. *And drove thoſe holy Vandals off the ſtage.*] In this attack on the eſtabliſhed ignorance of the times, Eraſmus ſucceeded ſo well, as to bring good letters into faſhion: to which he gave new ſplendor, by preparing for the preſs correct editions of many of the beſt ancient writers, both eccleſiaſtical and prophane. But having laughed and ſhamed his age out of one folly, he had the mortification of ſeeing it run headlong into another. The Virtuoſi of Italy, in a ſuperſtitious dread of that monkiſh barbarity which he had ſo ſeverely handled, would uſe no term, (for now almoſt every man was become a Latin writer), not even when they treated of the higheſt myſteries of religion, which had not been conſecrated in the Capitol, and diſpenſed unto them from the ſacred hand of Cicero. Eraſmus obſerved the growth of this claſſical folly with the greater concern, as he diſcovered under all their attention to the language of old Rome, a certain fondneſs for its religion, in a growing impiety which diſpoſed them to think irreverently of the Chriſtian Faith. And he no ſooner diſcovered it than he ſet upon reforming it; which he did ſo effectually in the Dialogue, entitled Ciceronianus, that he brought the age back to that juſt temper, which he had been, all his life, endeavouring to mark out to it: Purity, but not pedantry, in Letters; and zeal, but not bigotry, in Religion. In a word, by employing his great talents of genius and literature on ſubjects of general importance; and by oppoſing the extremes of all parties in their turns; he completed the real character of a true Critic and an honeſt Man. W.

VER. 697. *But ſee! each Muſe, in Leo's golden days,*] Hiſtory has recorded five ages of the world, in which the human mind has exerted itſelf in an extraordinary manner; and in which its productions in literature and the fine arts have arrived at a perfection, not equalled in other periods.

The Firſt, is the age of Philip and Alexander; about which time flouriſhed Socrates, Plato, Demoſthenes, Ariſtotle, Lyſippus, Apelles, Phidias, Praxiteles, Thucydides, Xenophon, Æſchylus, Euripides, Sophocles, Ariſtophanes, Menander, Philemon. The Second

Rome's ancient Genius, o'er its ruins spread, 699
Shakes off the dust, and rears his rev'rend head.

Then

NOTES.

Second age, which seems not to have been taken sufficient notice of, was that of Ptolomy Philadelphus, king of Egypt, in which appeared Lycophron, Aratus, Nicander, Apollonius Rhodius, Theocritus, Callimachus, Eratosthenes, Philichus, Erasistratus the physician, Timæus the historian, Cleanthes, Diogenes the painter, and Sostrates the architect. This prince, from his love of learning, commanded the Old Testament to be translated into Greek. The Third age, is that of Julius Cæsar, and Augustus; marked with the illustrious names of Laberius, Catullus, Lucretius, Cicero, Livy, Varro, Virgil, Horace, Propertius, Tibullus, Ovid, Phædrus, Vitruvius, Dioscorides. The Fourth age was that of Julius II, and Leo X, which produced Ariosto, Tasso, Fracastorius, Sannazarius, Vida, Bembo, Sadolet, Machiavel, Guiccardin, Michael Angelo, Raphael, Titian. The Fifth age is that of Louis XIV, in France, and of King William and Queen Anne, in England; in which, or thereabouts, are to be found, Corneille, Moliere, Racine, Boileau, La Fontaine, Bossuet, La Rochefoucault, Paschal, Bourdaloue, Patru, Malbranche, De Retz, La Bruyere, St. Real, Fenelon, Lully, Le Sæur, Poussin, La Brun, Puget, Theodon, Gerradon, Edelinck, Nanteuill, Perrault the architect, Dryden, Tillotson, Temple, Pope, Addison, Garth, Congreve, Rowe, Prior, Lee, Swift, Bolingbroke, Atterbury, Boyle, Locke, Newton, Clarke, Kneller, Thornhill, Jervas, Purcell, Mead, Friend.

Leo the Tenth little imagined, that by promoting the revival of ancient literature, and by the discovery and diffusion of that manly and liberal knowledge which it contained, and which opened and enlarged the bigoted minds of men, into boldness of thought, and freedom of enquiry on all important subjects, he was gradually undermining the absurdity and the tyranny of the Romish church, and emancipating its wretched devotees from ignorance and superstition. In vain, under such circumstances, was the Complutensian edition of the bible given. Cardinal Pole, it is said, with great shrewdness, warned Leo of the consequences of thus enlightening Europe.

In Bayle may be seen, the pains he took, and the expences he incurred, by purchasing curious manuscripts from every country

where

Then Sculpture, and her ſiſter-arts revive;
Stones leap'd to form, and rocks began to live;
With ſweeter notes each riſing Temple rung;
A Raphael painted, and a Vida ſung.
Immortal Vida: on whoſe honour'd brow
The Poet's bays and Critic's ivy grow:

Cremona

NOTES.

where they could be found; and his liberalities to men of genius need not be enlarged upon. One cannot but lament that the charming Arioſto, who was once ſo favoured and careſſed by him, was afterwards neglected and forgotten by this Pope, and denied a preferment which he had promiſed him, which occaſioned the ſeverity with which he treated Leo in his Fifth Satire. It is remarkable, that in the bull which this Pope gave to Arioſto, on the printing his Orlando, he ſpeaks of it as a kind of burleſque poem; as deſcribing, Equitum errantium Itinera, ludicro more, longo tamen ſtudio, &c.

VER. 699. *O'er its ruins ſpread,*] In the ninth century, it was ſaid, there were more ſtatues than inhabitants, at Rome.

VER. 703. *With ſweeter notes*] I have the beſt authority, that of the learned, accurate, and ingenious Dr. Burney, for obſerving, that, in the age of Leo the Tenth, muſic did not keep pace with poetry in advancing towards perfection. Coſtantio Feſta was the beſt Italian compoſer during the time of Leo, and Pietro Aron the beſt Theoriſt. Paleſtrina was not born till eight years after the death of Leo. See Hiſtory of Muſic, Vol. II. p. 336. In the year 1521, Luther wrote a ſerious and preſſing letter to Leo, exhorting him to retire from the ſplendor and vanity of the court, to ſome religious ſolitude, after the example of St. Bernard. We may eaſily imagine how much our polite ſucceſſor of St. Peter was diverted with this remonſtrance of Luther. Leo did not receive the ſacrament before he died; on which, Sannazarius wrote this diſtich;

" Sacra ſub extremâ ſi forte requiritis horâ,
Cur Leo non potuit ſumere? vendiderat.

VER. 705. *Immortal Vida:*] But Vida was by no means the moſt celebrated poet that adorned the age of Leo the Tenth; and muſic received not ſo many improvements, as the other fine arts, at that period. When Vida was advanced to a biſhopric,

he

Cremona now ſhall ever boaſt thy name,
As next in place to Mantua, next in fame!

But

NOTES.

he went to pay a viſit to his aged parents, who were in very low circumſtances; but, unhappily found they were juſt deceaſed. An action more meritorious than writing his Poetics.

The merits of Vida ſeem not to have been particularly attended to in England, till Pope had beſtowed this commendation upon him; although the Poetics had been correctly publiſhed at Oxford, by Baſil Kennet, ſome time before. The Silk-worms of Vida are written with claſſical purity, and with a juſt mixture of the ſtyles of Lucretius and Virgil. It was a happy choice to write a poem on Cheſs; nor is the execution leſs happy. The various ſtratagems, and manifold intricacies of this ingenious game, ſo difficult to be deſcribed in Latin, are here expreſſed with the greateſt perſpicuity and elegance; ſo that, perhaps, the game might be learned from this deſcription. Amidſt many proſaic flatneſſes there are many fine ſtrokes in the Chriſtiad; particularly his angels, with reſpect to their perſons and inſignia, are drawn with that dignity which we ſo much admire in Milton; who ſeems to have had his eye on thoſe paſſages.

Gravina (Della Ragion. Poet. p. 127.) applauds Vida, for having found out a method to introduce the whole hiſtory of our Saviour's life, by putting it into the mouth of St. Joſeph and St. John, who relate it to Pilate. But ſurely this ſpeech, conſiſting of as many lines as that of Dido to Æneas, was too long to be made on ſuch an occaſion, when Chriſt was brought before the tribunal of Pilate, to be judged and condemned to death. The Poetics are, perhaps, the moſt perfect of his compoſitions; they are excellently tranſlated by Pitt. Vida had formed himſelf upon Virgil, who is therefore his hero; he has too much depreciated Homer, and alſo Dante. Although his precepts principally regard epic poetry, yet many of them are applicable to every ſpecies of compoſition. This poem has the praiſe

IMITATIONS.

VER. 708. *As next in place to Mantua,*] Alluding to

"Mantua vae miſerae nimium vicina Cremonae." VIRG.

This application is made in Kennet's edition of Vida.

But ſoon by impious arms from Latium chas'd,
Their antient bounds the baniſh'd Muſes paſs'd.

Thence

NOTES.

praiſe of being one of the * firſt, if not the very firſt, pieces of criticiſm, that appeared in Italy, ſince the revival of learning; for it was finiſhed, as is evident from a ſhort advertiſement prefixed to it, in the year 1520. It is remarkable, that moſt of the great poets, about this time, wrote an Art of Poetry. Triſſino, a name reſpected for giving to Europe the firſt regular epic poem, and for firſt daring to throw off the bondage of rhyme, publiſhed at Vicenza, in the year 1529, Della Poetica, diviſioni quattro, ſeveral years before his Italia Liberata. We have of Fracaſtorius, Naugerius, five de poetica dialogus, Venetiis, 1555. Minturnus, De Poeta, libri ſex, appeared at Venice 1559. Bernardo Taſſo, the father of Torquato, and author of an epic poem, entitled, L'Amadigi, wrote Raggionamento della Poeſia, printed at Venice, 1562. And to pay the higheſt honour to criticiſm, the great Torquato Taſſo himſelf wrote Diſcorſi del poema Eroico, printed at Venice, 1587. Theſe diſcourſes are full of learning and taſte. But I muſt not omit a curious anecdote, which Menage has given us in his Anti-Baillet; namely, that Sperone claimed theſe diſcourſes as his own; for he thus ſpeaks of them, in one of his Letters to Felice Paciotto; "Laudo voi infinitamente di voler ſcrivere della poetica; della quale interrogato molto fiate dal Taſſo, e riſpondendogli io libramente, ſi come ſoglio, egli n'a fatto un volume, e mandato al Signior Scipio Gonzago per coſa ſua, e non mea: ma io ne chiarirò il mondo."

Hence it appears, that our author was miſtaken in ſaying, line 712, that "Critic-learning flouriſhed moſt in France." For theſe critical works here mentioned, by ſo many capital writers in Italy, far exceed any which the French, at that period of time, had produced. "'Tis hard (ſaid Akenſide) to conceive by what means the French acquired this character of ſuperior correctneſs. We have claſſic authors in Engliſh, older than in any modern language, except the Italian; and Spenſer and Sidney wrote with the trueſt taſte, when the French had not one great poet

they

* Victorius's Latin tranſlation of Ariſtotle's Poetics, was publiſhed at Florence, 1560. Caſtelvetro's Italian one at Vienna, 1570.

Thence Arts o'er all the northern world advance,
But Critic-learning flourish'd most in France;
The rules a nation, born to serve, obeys;
And Boileau still in right of Horace sways.
But we, brave Britons, foreign laws despis'd,
And kept unconquer'd, and unciviliz'd;

Fierce

NOTES.

they can bear to read. Milton and Chapelain were contemporaries; the Pucelle and Paradise Lost were in hand, perhaps frequently, at the self-same hour. One of them was executed in such a manner, that an Athenian of Menander's age would have turned his eyes from the Minerva of Phidias, or the Venus of Apelles, to obtain more perfect conceptions of beauty from the English Poet; the other, though fostered by the French court for twenty years with the utmost indulgence, does honour to the Leonine, and the Runic poetry. It was too great an attention to French criticism, that hindered our poets, in Charles the Second's time, from comprehending the genius, and acknowledging the Authority of Milton; else, without looking abroad, they might have acquired a manner more correct and perfect, than French authors could or can teach them. In short, unless correctness signify a freedom from little faults, without enquiring after the most essential beauties, it scarce appears on what foundation the French claim to that character is established."

VER. 714. *And Boileau still in right of Horace sways.*] May I be pardoned for declaring it as my opinion, that Boileau's is the best Art of Poetry * extant. The brevity of his precepts, enlivened by proper imagery, the justness of his metaphors, the harmony of his numbers, as far as Alexandrine lines will admit, the exactness of his method, the perspicacity of his remarks, and the energy of his style, all duly considered, may render this opinion not unreasonable. It is scarcely to be conceived, how much is comprehended in four short cantos. He that has well digested these, cannot be said to be ignorant of any important rule of poetry. The tale of the Physician turning Architect, in the fourth canto, is told with

true

* It was translated into Portuguese verse by Count d'Ericeyra.

Fierce for the liberties of wit, and bold,
We ſtill defy'd the Romans, as of old.
Yet ſome there were, among the ſounder few
Of thoſe who leſs preſum'd, and better knew,
Who durſt aſſert the juſter ancient cauſe,
And here reſtor'd Wit's fundamental laws.
Such was the Muſe, whoſe rules and practice tell,
" Nature's chief Maſter-piece is writing well."

Such

NOTES.

true pleaſantry. It is to this work Boileau owes his immortality; which was of the higheſt utility to this nation, in diffuſing a juſt way of thinking and writing; baniſhing every ſpecies of falſe wit, and introducing a general taſte for the manly ſimplicity of the ancients, on whoſe writings this poet had formed his taſte. Boileau's chief talent was the didactic. His fancy was not the predominant faculty of his mind. Fontenelle has thus characteriſed him; " Il ètoit grand & excellent verſificateur, pourvû cependant que cette louange ſe renferme dans ſes beaux jours, dont la différence avec les autres eſt bien marquée, & faiſoit ſouvent dire Helas! & Hola! mais il n'etoit pas grand poëte, ſi l'on entend par ce mot, comme on le doit, celui qui Fait, qui Invente, qui Cree." It has become faſhionable among the late French writers, to decry Boileau; Marmontel, Diderot, D'Alembert, have done it. The chief fault of Boileau ſeems to be his decrying the great poets of Italy, and particularly Taſſo; but M. Maffei informs us, that the elder ſon of Racine aſſured him, that his friend Boileau did not underſtand Italian, and had not read Taſſo. The high encomium Taſſo gave to Arioſto does him great honour, and ſhews him to be ſuperior to envy.

VER. 723. *Such was the Muſe, whoſe rules and practice tell,*
" Nature's chief Maſter-piece is writing well."

This high panegyric, which was not in the firſt edition, procured to Pope the acquaintance, and afterwards the conſtant friendſhip of the Duke of Buckingham; who, in his eſſay here alluded to, has followed the method of Boileau, in diſcourſing on the various ſpecies of poetry in their different gradations, to no other purpoſe than to manifeſt his own inferiority. The piece is,

indeed,

Such was Roſcommon, not more learn'd than good,
With manners gen'rous as his noble blood; 726
To

NOTES.

indeed, of the ſatyric, rather than of the preceptive, kind. The coldneſs and neglect with which this writer, formed only on the French critics, ſpeaks of Milton, muſt be conſidered as proofs of his want of critical diſcernment, or of critical courage. I can recollect no performance of Buckingham, that ſtamps him a true genius. His reputation was owing to his rank. In reading his poems, one is apt to exclaim with our author,

"What woeful ſtuff this madrigal would be,
In ſome ſtarv'd hackney ſonneteer, or me?
But let a Lord once own the happy lines,
How the wit brightens! and the ſenſe refines.
Before his ſacred name flies every fault,
And each exalted ſtanza teems with thought."

The beſt part of Buckingham's eſſay is that, in which he gives a ludicrous account of the plan of modern tragedy. I ſhould add, that his compliment to Pope, prefixed to his poems, contains a pleaſing picture of the ſedateneſs and retirement proper to age, after the tumults of public life; and by its moral turn, breathes the ſpirit, if not of a poet, yet of an amiable old man.

VER. 725. *Such was Roſcommon,*] An Eſſay on Tranſlated Verſe ſeems, at firſt ſight, to be a barren ſubject; yet Roſcommon has decorated it with many precepts of utility and taſte, and enlivened it with a tale in imitation of Boileau. It is indiſputably better written, in a cloſer and more vigorous ſtyle, than the laſt-mentioned eſſay. Roſcommon was more learned than Buckingham. He was bred under Bochart, at Caen in Normandy. He had laid a deſign of forming a ſociety for the refining, and fixing the ſtandard of, our language; in which project, his intimate friend Dryden was a principal aſſiſtant. This was the firſt attempt of that ſort; and, I fear, we ſhall never ſee another ſet on foot in our days; even though Mr. Johnſon has lately given us ſo excellent a Dictionary.

It may be remarked, to the praiſe of Roſcommon, that he was the firſt critic who had taſte and ſpirit publickly to praiſe the Paradiſe Loſt; with a noble encomium of which, and a rational recommendation of blank verſe, he concludes his performance, though this paſſage was not in the firſt edition. Fenton, in his Obſervations

To him the Wit of Greece and Rome was known,
And ev'ry author's merit, but his own.
Such late was Walſh—the Muſe's judge and friend,
Who juſtly knew to blame or to commend;
To

NOTES.

Obſervations on Waller, has accurately delineated his character. "His imagination might have, probably, been more fruitful, and ſprightly, if his judgement had been leſs ſevere; but that ſeverity, delivered in a maſculine, clear, ſuccinct ſtyle, contributed to make him ſo eminent in the didactical manner, that no man, with juſtice, can affirm, he was ever equalled by any of our own nation, without confeſſing, at the ſame time, that he is inferior to none. In ſome other kinds of writing, his genius ſeems to have wanted fire to attain the point of perfection; but who can attain it?" Edit. 12mo. p. 136.

VER. 729.] Several lines were here added to the firſt edition, concerning Walſh.

VER. 729. *Such late was Walſh—the Muſe's judge and friend,*] If Pope has here given too magnificent an eulogy to Walſh, it muſt be attributed to friendſhip, rather than to judgement. Walſh was, in general, a flimſy and frigid writer. The Rambler calls his works, pages of inanity. His three letters to Pope, however, are well written. His remarks on the nature of paſtoral poetry, on borrowing from the ancients, and againſt florid conceits, are worthy peruſal. Pope owed much to Walſh; it was he who gave him a very important piece of advice, in his early youth; for he uſed to tell our author, that there was one way ſtill left open for him, by which he might excel any of his predeceſſors, which was, by correctneſs; that though, indeed, we had ſeveral great poets, we as yet could boaſt of none that were perfectly correct; and that therefore, he adviſed him to make this quality his particular ſtudy.

Correctneſs is a vague term, frequently uſed without meaning and preciſion. It is perpetually the nauſeous cant of the French critics, and of their advocates and pupils, that the Engliſh writers are generally incorrect. If correctneſs implies an abſence of petty faults, this perhaps may be granted. If it means, that, becauſe their tragedians have avoided the irregularities of Shakeſpeare, and have obſerved a juſter œconomy in their fables, therefore
the

To failings mild, but zealous for deſert;
The cleareſt head, and the ſincereſt heart.
This humble praiſe, lamented ſhade! receive,
This praiſe at leaſt a grateful Muſe may give:
The Muſe, whoſe early voice you taught to ſing,
Preſcrib'd her heights, and prun'd her tender wing,
(Her guide now loſt) no more attempts to riſe,
But in low numbers ſhort excurſions tries:
Content, if hence th' unlearn'd their wants may view,
The learn'd reflect on what before they knew:
Careleſs of cenſure, nor too fond of fame;
Still pleas'd to praiſe, yet not afraid to blame;

Averſe

NOTES.

the Athalia, for inſtance, is preferable to Lear, the notion is groundleſs and abſurd. Though the Henriade ſhould be allowed to be free from any very groſs abſurdities, yet who will dare to rank it with the Paradiſe Loſt? Some of their moſt perfect tragedies abound in faults as contrary to the nature of that ſpecies of poetry, and as deſtructive to its end, as the fools or grave-diggers of Shakeſpeare. That the French may boaſt ſome excellent critics, particularly Boſſu, Boileau, Fenelon, and Brumoy, cannot be denied; but that theſe are ſufficient to form a taſte upon, without having recourſe to the genuine fountains of all polite literature, I mean the Grecian writers, no one but a ſuperficial reader can allow.

VER. 741. *Careleſs of cenſure,*] Theſe concluding lines bear a great reſemblance to Boileau's concluſion of his Art of Poetry, but are perhaps ſuperior.

" Cenſeur un peu facheux, mais ſouvent neceſſaire;
Plus enclin à blâmer, que ſçavant à bien faire."

Our author has not, in this piece, followed the examples of the ancients, in addreſſing their didactic poems to ſome particular perſon; as Heſiod to Perſes; Lucretius to Memmius; Virgil to Mecænas; Horace to the Piſos; Ovid, his Faſti, to Germanicus; Oppian to Caracalla. In later times, Fracaſtorius addreſt P. Bembo; Vida the Dauphin of France. But

neither

Averse alike to flatter, or offend;
Not free from faults, nor yet too vain to mend.

NOTES.

neither Boileau in his Art, nor Roscommon nor Buckingham in their Essays, nor Akenside nor Armstrong, have followed this practice.

I conclude these remarks with a remarkable fact. In no polished nation, after criticism has been much studied, and the rules of writing established, has any very extraordinary work appeared. This has visibly been the case in Greece, in Rome, and in France; after Aristotle, Horace, and Boileau, had written their Arts of Poetry. In our own country the rules of the drama, for instance, were never more completely understood than at present; yet what uninteresting, though faultless, tragedies, have we lately seen? So much better is our judgement than our execution. How to account for the fact here mentioned, adequately and justly, would be attended with all those difficulties that await discussions relative to the productions of the human mind; and to the delicate and secret causes that influence them. Whether or no, the natural powers be not confined and debilitated by that timidity and caution which is occasioned by a rigid regard to the dictates of art; or whether that philosophical, that geometrical, and systematical spirit so much in vogue, which has spread itself from the sciences even into polite literature, by consulting only reason, has not diminished and destroyed sentiment; and made our poets write from and to the head, rather than the heart; or whether, lastly, when just models, from which the rules have necessarily been drawn, have once appeared, succeeding writers, by vainly and ambitiously striving to surpass those just models, and to shine and surprise, do not become stiff, and forced and affected, in their thoughts and diction.

I am happy to find these opinions confirmed by the learned and judicious Heyne, in his Opuscula, p. 116.

"Et initio quidem ipsa ingenii humani doctrinæque humanæ natura haud facile alium rerum cursum admittit, quam ut doctrinæ auctus ingenii damna sequantur; infringitur ipsa rerum copia ingenii vis ac vigor; subtilitas grammatica, historica ac philosophica, in rebus exquirendis ac diluendis, magnos et audaces animi sensus incidit; luxuriantius ingenium a simplicitate ad cultum et ornatum

ornatum, hinc ad fucum et lafciviam prolabitur. Eft idem animorum et ingeniorum, qui vitæ et reipublicæ, ab aufteritate ad elegantiam, ab hac ad luxum et delicias, progreffus; quo gradu uti femel rerum vices conftitere, ad interitum eas vergere neceffe eft."

It is not improper to obferve what great improvements the Art of Criticifm has received fince this Effay was written. For without recurring to pieces of earlier date, and nearer the time in which it was written; the effays in the Spectator and Guardian; Shaftefbury's Advice to an Author; Spence on the Odyffey; Fenton on Waller; Blackwell's Enquiry into the Life and Writings of Homer: even of late years, we have had the Treatifes of Harris; Hurd's Remarks on Horace; Obfervations on the Fairy Queen; Webb on Poetry and Mufic; Brown's Differtation on the fame; the Differtations of Beattie; the Elements of Criticifm, of Kaims; the Lectures of Blair; the Editions of Milton, by Newton and Warton; and of Shakefpeare and Spenfer, by Malone, Steevens, and Upton; the Hiftory of Englifh Poetry; the critical papers of the Rambler, Adventurer, World, and Connoiffeur; and The Lives of the Poets, by Johnfon; the Biographia Britannica; and the Poetics of Ariftotle, tranflated, and accompanied with judicious notes, by Twining and Pye; and the tranflation, with notes, of Horace's Art of Poetry, by Hurd and Colman; and the Epiftles of Hayley.

THE RAPE OF THE LOCK.

AN HEROI-COMICAL POEM.

WRITTEN IN THE YEAR MDCCXII.

TO MRS. ARABELLA FERMOR.

MADAM,

IT will be in vain to deny that I have ſome regard for this piece, ſince I dedicate it to You. Yet you may bear me witneſs, it was intended only to divert a few young Ladies, who have good ſenſe and good humour enough to laugh not only at their ſex's little unguarded follies, but at their own. But as it was communicated with the air of a Secret, it ſoon found its way into the world. An imperfect copy having been offered to a Bookſeller, you had the good-nature for my ſake to conſent to the publication of one more correct: This I was forced to, before I had executed half my deſign, for the Machinery was entirely wanting to complete it.

The Machinery, Madam, is a term invented by the Critics, to ſignify that part which the Deities, Angels, or Demons, are made to act in a Poem: For the ancient Poets are in one reſpect like many modern Ladies; let an action be never ſo trivial in itſelf, they always make it appear of the utmoſt importance. Theſe Machines I determined to raiſe on a very new and odd foundation, the Roſicrucian doctrine of Spirits.

I know how diſagreeable it is to make uſe of hard words before a Lady; but 'tis ſo much the concern of a Poet to have his works underſtood, and particularly by your Sex, that you muſt give me leave to explain two or three difficult terms.

The Roſicrucians are a people I muſt bring you acquainted with. The beſt account I know of them is in a French book called Le Comte de Gabalis, which both in its title and ſize is ſo like a Novel, that many of the Fair Sex have read it for one by miſtake. According to theſe Gentlemen the four Elements are inhabited by Spirits, which they call Sylphs, Gnomes, Nymphs, and Salamanders. The Gnomes or Demons of Earth delight in miſchief; but the Sylphs, whoſe habitation is in the Air, are the beſt conditioned Creatures imaginable. For they ſay, any mortals may enjoy the moſt intimate familiarities with theſe gentle Spirits, upon a condition very eaſy to all true Adepts, an inviolate preſervation of Chaſtity.

As to the following Cantos, all the paſſages of them are as fabulous, as the Viſion at the beginning, or the Transformation at the end; (except the loſs of your Hair, which I always mention with reverence.) The Human perſons are as fictitious as the Airy ones; and the Character of Belinda, as it is now managed, reſembles you in nothing but in Beauty.

If

If this Poem had as many Graces as there are in your Perſon, or in your Mind, yet I could never hope it ſhould paſs through the world half ſo Uncenſured as You have done. But let its fortune be what it will, mine is happy enough, to have given me this occaſion of aſſuring you that I am, with the trueſt eſteem,

MADAM,

Your moſt obedient, humble ſervant,

A. POPE.

THIS Lady was alſo celebrated by Parnell in a poem not publiſhed by Pope, as follows, on her leaving London.

" From town fair Arabella flies:
  The beaux unpowder'd grieve;
The rivers play before her eyes;
The breezes, ſoftly-breathing, riſe;
  The ſpring begins to live.

Her lovers ſwore, they muſt expire:
  Yet quickly find their eaſe;
For, as ſhe goes, their flames retire,
Love thrives before a nearer fire,
  Eſteem by diſtant rays.

Yet ſoon the fair-one will return,
  When ſummer quits the plain;
Ye rivers pour the weeping urn;
Ye breezes, ſadly-ſighing, mourn;
  Ye lovers, burn again.

'Tis conſtancy enough in love
  That nature's fairly ſhewn:
To ſearch for more, will fruitleſs prove,
Romances and the turtle-dove,
  That virtue boaſt alone."

[illegible] had as many Graces as [illegible] your [illegible] of your Mind, yet I could [illegible] [illegible] though the world had [illegible] [illegible] Beauties. [illegible] will [illegible] is [illegible] of [illegible] that I am with the [illegible] respect,

MADAM,

Your most obedient, humble Servant,

A. POPE.

THIS Lady was afterwards [illegible] published [illegible]

[illegible]

Her [illegible], they must [illegible]
[illegible] find their ease;
[illegible] their [illegible]
[illegible]
[illegible]

Yet [illegible]
When [illegible] the plain;
[illegible]
[illegible]
[illegible]

The [illegible]
Then [illegible]
To teach [illegible] with [illegible]
[illegible]
[illegible] virtue shall alone.

IF the moderns have excelled the ancients in any ſpecies of writing, it ſeems to be in ſatire; and, particularly in that kind of ſatire which is conveyed in the form of the epopee, a pleaſing vehicle of ſatire, ſeldom, if ever, uſed by the ancients; for we know ſo little of the Margites of Homer, that it cannot well be produced as an example. As the poet diſappears in this way of writing, and does not deliver the intended cenſure in his own proper perſon, the ſatire becomes more delicate, becauſe more oblique. Add to this, that a tale or ſtory more ſtrongly engages and intereſts the reader, than a ſeries of precepts or reproofs, or even of characters themſelves, however lively or natural. An heroi-comic poem may therefore be juſtly eſteemed the moſt excellent kind of ſatire. The invention of it is uſually aſcribed to Aleſſandro Taſſoni; who, in the year 1622, publiſhed at Paris a poem compoſed by him, in a few months of the year 1611, entitled, La Secchia Rapita, or The Rape of the Bucket. To avoid giving offence, it was firſt printed under the name of Androvini Meliſoni. It was afterwards reprinted at Venice, corrected with the name of the author, and with ſome illuſtrations of Gaſparo Salviani. But the learned and curious Creſcembini, in his Iſtoria della Volgar Poeſia *, informs us, that it is doubtful whether the invention of the † heroi-comic poem ought to be aſcribed to Taſſoni, or to Franceſco Bracciolini, who wrote Lo Scherno degli Dei, which performance, though it was printed four years after La Secchia, is nevertheleſs declared, in an epiſtle prefixed, to have been written many years ſooner. The real ſubject of Taſſoni's poem was the war which the inhabitants of Modena declared againſt thoſe of Bologna, on the refuſal of the latter to reſtore to them ſome towns, which had been detained ever

* Lib. i. p. 78. In Roma, per il Chracas, 1698.

† E tal poeſia puo diffinirſi, e chiamarſi, immitazione d'azione ſeria fatto con riſo. Creſcembini, ibid. See Quadrio alſo.

ſince the time of the Emperor Frederic II. The author artfully made uſe of a popular tradition, according to which it was believed, that a certain wooden bucket, which is kept at Modena, in the treaſury of the cathedral, came from Bologna, and that it had been forcibly taken away by the Modeneſe. Creſcembini adds, that becauſe Taſſoni had ſeverely ridiculed the Bologneſe, Bartolomeo Bocchini, to revenge his countrymen, printed, at Venice, 1641, a tragico-heroi-comic poem, entitled, Le Pazzie dei Savi, ovvero, Il Lambertaccio, in which the Modeneſe are ſpoken of with much contempt. The Italians have a fine turn for works of humour, in which they abound. They have another poem of this ſpecies, called Malmantile Racquiſtato, written by Lorenzo Lippi, in the year 1676, which Creſcembini highly commends, calling it, "Spiritoſiſſimo e leggiadriſſimo poema gioco ſo." It was afterwards reprinted at Florence, 1688, with the uſeful annotations of Puccio Lamoni, a Florentine painter, who was himſelf no contemptible poet. To theſe muſt be added, the lively and amuſing poem called Ricciardetto. In the Adventurer, No. 133, (I formerly endeavoured to ſhew the ſuperiority of the moderns over the ancients, in all the ſpecies of ridicule, and to point out ſome of the reaſons for this ſuppoſed ſuperiority. It is a ſubject that deſerves a much longer diſcuſſion. Among other reaſons given, it is there ſaid, that though democracies may be the nurſes of true ſublimity, yet monarchy and courts are more productive of politeneſs. Hence the arts of civility, and the decencies of converſation, as they unite men more cloſely, and bring them together more frequently, multiply opportunities of obſerving thoſe incongruities and abſurdities of behaviour, on which ridicule is founded. The ancients had more liberty and ſerioufneſs; the moderns more luxury and laughter. In a word, our forms of government, the various conſequent ranks in ſociety, our commerce, manners, habits, riches, courts, religious controverſies, intercourſe with women, late age of the world in which we live, and new arts, have opened ſources of ridicule unavoidably unknown to the ancients.

The Rape of the Lock is the fourth, and moſt excellent of the heroi-comic poems. The ſubject was a quarrel, occaſioned by a little piece of gallantry of Lord Petre, who, in a party of pleaſure, found means to cut off a favourite lock of Mrs. Arabella Fermor's hair. On ſo ſlight a foundation has he raiſed this beautiful ſuperſtructure; like a Fairy palace in a deſart. Pope was accuſtomed to ſay, "what I wrote faſteſt always pleaſed moſt."

The

The first sketch of this exquisite piece, which Addison called Merum Sal, was written in less than a fortnight, in two Cantos only; but it was so universally applauded, that, in the next year, our poet enriched it with the machinery of the Sylphs, and extended it to five Cantos; when it was printed, with a Letter to Mrs. Fermor, far superior to any of Voiture. The insertion of the machinery of the Sylphs in proper places, without the least appearance of its being aukwardly stitched in, is one of the happiest efforts of judgement and art. He took the idea of these invisible beings, so proper to be employed in a poem of this nature, from a little French book entitled, Le Comte de Gabalis,) of which is given the following account, in an entertaining writer. "The Abbé Villars, who came from Thoulouse to Paris, to make his fortune by preaching, is the author of this diverting work. The five dialogues of which it consists, are the result of those gay conversations, in which the Abbé was engaged, with a small circle of men, of fine wit and humour, like himself. When this book first appeared, it was universally read, as innocent and amusing. But at length its consequences were perceived, and reckoned dangerous, at a time when this sort of curiosities began to gain credit. Our devout preacher was denied the chair, and his book forbidden to be read. It was not clear whether the author intended to be ironical, or spoke all seriously. The second volume, which he promised, would have decided the question; but the unfortunate Abbé was soon afterwards assassinated by ruffians, on the road to Lyons. The laughers gave out, that the Gnomes and Sylphs, disguised like ruffians, had shot him, as a punishment for revealing the secrets of the Cabala; a crime not to be pardoned by these jealous spirits, as Villars himself has declared in his book."

The motto to the second edition, when it was enlarged into five cantos, printed in octavo for Lintot, 1714, was from Ovid; as was that to the first:

——— "a tonso est hoc nomen adepta capillo."

Both mottos seem to be happily chosen. No writer has equalled Addison in the happy and dextrous application of passages from the classics for his mottos. Such as that prefixed to the fine paper on the Hoop-petticoat, No. 116 of the Tatler;

"Pars minima est ipsa puella sibi."

To the account of the Spectator's Club, No. 2.

——— "ast alii sex
Et plures uno conclamant ore" ———

To

To No. 8, On Masquerades;

"At Venus obscuro gradientes äëre sepsit,
Et multo nebulæ circum Dea fudit amictu:
Cernere nequis eos" —— VIRG.

To No. 23, On Anonymous Satires;

"Sævit atrox Volscens, nec teli conspicit usquam
Auctorem, nec quo se ardens immittere possit." VIRG.

and many others. The mottos prefixed to the papers in the Rambler and Adventurer, were not so happy. The attempt to translate them was absurd. The one prefixed to Philips's Cyder was elegant.

—— "Honos erit huic quoque pomo?"

Atterbury suggested the interrogation point. Warburton was commended for despising common antagonists, and saying,

"Optat aprum, aut fulvum descendere monte leonem."

But Harrington had said this, in his Oceana, of an adversary. Mr. Walpole, to intimate his high and just opinion of Gray's Ode on Eton College as a first production, wrote on it this line of Lucan;

"Nec licuit populis parvum te Nile videre."

I dare believe the learned and amiable author did not know that Fontenelle had applied the very same line to Newton. A motto to Mr. Gray's few, but exquisite, poems might be, from Lucretius, lib. 4.

"Suavidicis potius quàm multis versibus edam,
Parvus ut est cycni melior canor."——

THE RAPE OF THE LOCK.

[a] Nolueram, Belinda, tuos violare capillos;
Sed juvat, hoc precibus me tribuisse tuis. MART.

CANTO I.

WHAT dire offence from am'rous causes springs,
What mighty contests rise from trivial things,
I sing—This verse to CARYL, Muse! is due:
This, ev'n Belinda may vouchsafe to view:

Slight

NOTES.

[a] It appears by this Motto, that the following Poem was written or published at the Lady's request. But there are some further circumstances not unworthy relating. Mr. Caryl (a Gentleman who was Secretary to Queen Mary, wife of James II. whose fortunes he followed into France, Author of the comedy of Sir Solomon Single, and of several translations in Dryden's Miscellanies) originally proposed the subject to him, in a view of putting an end, by this piece of ridicule, to a quarrel that was risen between two noble Families, those of Lord Petre and of Mrs. Fermor, on the trifling occasion of his having cut off a lock of her hair. The Author sent it to the Lady, with whom he was acquainted; and she took it so well as to give about copies of it. That first sketch (we learn from one of his letters) was written in less than a fortnight, in 1711, in two Cantos only, and it was so printed; first, in a Miscellany of Bern. Lintot's, without the name of the Author. But it was received so well, that he made it more considerable the next year by the addition of the machinery of the Sylphs, and extended it to five Canto's. We shall give the reader the pleasure of seeing in what manner these additions were inserted, so as to seem not to be added, but to grow out of the Poem. See Notes, Cant. I. ver. 19, &c. P.

Slight is the ſubject, but not ſo the praiſe,
If She inſpire, and He approve my lays.

Say what ſtrange motive, Goddeſs! could compel
A well-bred Lord t' aſſault a gentle Belle?
O ſay what ſtranger cauſe, yet unexplor'd,
Could make a gentle Belle reject a Lord?
In taſks ſo bold, can little men engage,
And in ſoft boſoms, dwell ſuch mighty Rage?

Sol through white curtains ſhot a tim'rous ray,
And ope'd thoſe eyes that muſt eclipſe the day:
Now lap-dogs give themſelves the rouſing ſhake,
And ſleepleſs lovers, juſt at twelve, awake:

Thrice

VARIATIONS.

VER. 11, 12. It was in the firſt editions,

And dwells ſuch rage in ſofteſt boſoms then,
And lodge ſuch daring Souls in little Men? P.

VER. 13, &c. ſtood thus in the firſt edition,

Sol through white curtains did his beams diſplay,
And ope'd thoſe eyes which brighter ſhone than they:
Shock juſt had given himſelf the rouſing ſhake,
And Nymphs prepar'd their Chocolate to take;
Thrice the wrought ſlipper knock'd againſt the ground,
And ſtriking watches the tenth hour reſound. P.

NOTES.

VER. 10. *Could make a gentle Belle*] "The characters introduced in this poem were Mr. Caryl, juſt before mentioned; Belinda was Mrs. Arabella Fermor; the Baron was Lord Petre, of ſmall ſtature, who ſoon after married a great heireſs, Mrs. Warmſley, and died leaving a poſthumous ſon; Thaleſtris was Mrs. Morly; Sir Plume was her brother, Sir George Brown, of Berkſhire." Copied from a MS. in a book preſented by R. Lord Burlington, to Mr. William Sherwin.

Thrice rung the bell, the slipper knock'd the ground,
And the press'd watch return'd the silver sound.
Belinda still her downy pillow prest, 19
Her guardian SYLPH prolong'd the balmy rest:
'Twas He had summon'd to her silent bed
The morning-dream that hover'd o'er her head,
A Youth more glitt'ring than a Birth-night Beau,
(That e'en in slumber caus'd her cheek to glow)
Seem'd to her ear his winning lips to lay,
And thus in whispers said, or seem'd to say.

Fairest

NOTES.

VER. 18. *Silver sound.*] Boileau, at an entertainment given by Segrais, was engaged to read his Lutrin; when he came to this passage in the first canto,

"Les cloches dans les airs de leur voix argentines,"

Chapelle, who was one of the company, and who, as usual, had drank freely, stopt him, and objected strongly to the expression, *silver sounds*. Boileau disregarded his objections and continued to read; but Chapelle again interrupting him; "You are drunk," said Boileau; "I am not so much intoxicated with wine (returned Chapelle) as you are with your own verses." It is a singular circumstance, that Boileau was buried in the very spot on which the Lutrin stood.

VER. 19. *Belinda still, &c.*] All the verses from hence to the end of this Canto were added afterwards. P.

VER. 20. *Her guardian Sylph*] When Mr. Pope had projected to give The Rape of the Lock its present form of a mock-heroic poem, he was obliged to find it with its machinery. For as the subject of the epic consists of two parts, the metaphysical and the civil; so this mock epic, which is of the satiric kind, and receives its grace from a ludicrous mimickry of the other's pomp and solemnity, was to have the like compounded nature. W.

It was reserved to Dr. Warburton to say, that the epic consists of two parts, the metaphysical and the civil. It is hard to say what is the metaphysical part of Homer and Virgil.

Faireſt of mortals, thou diſtinguiſh'd care
Of thouſand bright Inhabitants of Air!
If e'er one Viſion touch'd thy infant thought,
Of all the Nurſe and all the Prieſt have taught;
Of airy Elves by moonlight ſhadows ſeen,
The ſilver token, and the circled green,
Or virgins viſited by Angel pow'rs
With golden crowns and wreaths of heav'nly flow'rs;
Hear and believe! thy own importance know,
Nor bound thy narrow views to things below.
Some ſecret truths, from learned pride conceal'd,
To Maids alone and Children are reveal'd:

What

NOTES.

VER. 27. *Faireſt of mortals,*] Theſe machines are vaſtly ſuperior to the allegorical perſonages of Boileau and Garth; not only on account of their novelty, but for the exquiſite poetry, and oblique ſatire, which they have given the poet an opportunity to diſplay. (The buſineſs and petty concerns of a fine lady, receive an air of importance from the notion of their being perpetually overlooked and conducted, by the interpoſition of celeſtial agents.) The firſt time theſe beings were mentioned by any writer in our language was by Sir W. Temple, Eſſays, 4. p. 255. "I ſhould (ſays he) as ſoon fall into the ſtudy of the Roſycruſian philoſophy, and expect to meet a Nymph or a Sylph for a wife or a miſtreſs." They are alſo mentioned in a letter of Dryden to Mrs. Thomas, 1699; "Whether Sylph or Nymph I know not; thoſe fine creatures, as your author Count Gabalis aſſures us, have a mind to be chriſtened, and ſince you deſire a name from me, take that of Corinna, if you pleaſe." Sylphs are mentioned, as inviſible attendants, and as intereſted in the affairs of the ladies, in the 101ſt, 104th, and 195th, of Madame de Sevigné's celebrated Letters; as they are alſo in the ſecond chapter of Le Sage's Diable Boiteaux. M. De Sevigné ſays, remarkably enough, letter 90, "If we had a few Sylphs at our command now, one might furniſh out a ſtory to divert you with."

What tho' no credit doubting Wits may give?
The Fair and Innocent ſhall ſtill believe.
Know then, unnumber'd Spirits round thee fly,
The light Militia of the lower ſky:
Theſe, tho' unſeen, are ever on the wing,
Hang o'er the Box, and hover round the Ring.
Think what an equipage thou haſt in Air,
And view with ſcorn two Pages and a Chair.
As now your own, our beings were of old,
And once inclos'd in Woman's beauteous mould;
Thence, by a ſoft tranſition, we repair
From earthly Vehicles to theſe of air.
Think not, when Woman's tranſient breath is fled,
That all her vanities at once are dead;
Succeeding vanities ſhe ſtill regards,
And tho' ſhe plays no more o'erlooks the cards.
Her joy in gilded Chariots, when alive,
And love of Ombre, after death ſurvive.

For

NOTES.

VER. 47. *As now your own, &c.*] The Poet here forſakes the Roſicrucian ſyſtem; which, in this part, is too extravagant even for ludicrous Poetry; and gives a beautiful fiction of his own, on the Platonic Theology, of the continuance of the paſſions in another ſtate, when the mind, before its leaving this, has not been well purged and purified by philoſophy; which furniſhes an occaſion for much uſeful ſatire. W.

IMITATIONS.

VER. 54, 55. "Quae gratia currûm
Armorumque fuit vivis, quae cura nitentes
Paſcere equos, eadem ſequitur tellure repoſtos."
VIRG. Aeneid. vi. P.

For when the Fair in all their pride expire,
To their firſt elements their ſouls retire:
The Sprites of fiery Termagants in Flame
Mount up, and take a Salamander's name.
Soft yielding minds to Water glide away,
And ſip, with Nymphs, their elemental Tea.
The graver Prude ſinks downward to a Gnome,
In ſearch of miſchief ſtill on Earth to roam.
The light Coquettes in Sylphs aloft repair,
And ſport and flutter in the fields of Air.

Know further yet; whoever fair and chaſte
Rejects mankind, is by ſome Sylph embrac'd:
For Spirits, freed from mortal laws, with eaſe
Aſſume what ſexes and what ſhapes they pleaſe.
What guards the purity of melting Maids,
In courtly balls, and midnight maſquerades,
Safe from the treach'rous friend, the daring ſpark,
The glance by day, the whiſper in the dark,

When

NOTES.

Ver. 67. *Know further yet*;] (Marmontel has, on this idea, framed one of his moſt popular Tales. I muſt again and again repeat, that it is on account of the exquiſite ſkill, and humour and pleaſantry of the uſe made of the machinery of the Sylphs, that this poem has excelled all the heroi-comic poems in all languages. The Ver-vert of Greſſet, in point of delicate ſatire, is perhaps next to it, but far inferior for the want of ſuch machinery.

Ver. 68. *Is by ſome Sylph embrac'd:*] Here again the Author reſumes the Roſicruſian ſyſtem. But this tenet, peculiar to that wild philoſophy, was founded on a principle very unfit to be employed in ſuch a ſort of poem, and therefore ſuppreſſed, though a leſs judicious writer would have been tempted to expatiate upon it. W.

When kind occaſion prompts their warm deſires,
When muſic ſoftens, and when dancing fires?
'Tis but their Sylph, the wiſe Celeſtials know,
Though Honour is the word with Men below.

Some nymphs there are, too conſcious of their face,
For life predeſtin'd to the Gnomes embrace.
Theſe ſwell their proſpects and exalt their pride,
When offers are diſdain'd, and love deny'd:
Then gay Ideas croud the vacant brain,
While Peers, and Dukes, and all their ſweeping train,
And Garters, Stars, and Coronets appear,
And in ſoft ſounds, YOUR GRACE ſalutes their ear.
'Tis theſe that early taint the female ſoul,
Inſtruct the eyes of young Coquettes to roll,
Teach Infant-cheeks a bidden bluſh to know,
And little hearts to flutter at a Beau.

Oft, when the world imagine women ſtray,
The Sylphs through miſtic mazes guide their way,
Through all the giddy circle they purſue,
And old impertinence expell by new.
What tender maid but muſt a victim fall
To one man's treat, but for another's ball?
When Florio ſpeaks, what virgin could withſtand,
If gentle Damon did not ſqueeze her hand?

With

NOTES.

VER. 78. *Though Honour is the word with Men below.*] Parody of Homer. W.

With varying vanities, from ev'ry part,
They ſhift the moving Toyſhop of their heart;
Where wigs with wigs, with ſword-knots ſword-knots ſtrive,
Beaux baniſh beaux, and coaches coaches drive.
This erring mortals Levity may call,
Oh blind to truth! the Sylphs contrive it all.
Of theſe am I, who thy protection claim,
A watchful ſprite, and Ariel is my name.
Late, as I rang'd the cryſtal wilds of air,
In the clear mirror of thy ruling Star
I ſaw, alas! ſome dread event impend,
Ere to the main this morning ſun deſcend,

But

NOTES.

VER. 99. *With varying vanities,*] "The freaks and humours, and ſpleen and vanity of women, (ſays Dr. Johnſon), as they embroil families in diſcord, and fill houſes with diſquiet, do more to obſtruct the happineſs of life in a year, than the pride, ambition, and diſcord of the clergy, (as deſcribed in the Lutrin), in many centuries." I cannot poſſibly aſſent to this obſervation of Dr. Johnſon; who muſt ſurely have forgotten, what he muſt often have read and lamented, the cruelties, the confuſions, the murders, the maſſacres, the rage, and fury, in which Eccleſiaſtical Hiſtory, to the diſgrace of genuine Chriſtianity, ſo much abounds. His zeal therefore, and deſire to place the Rape of the Lock above the Lutrin, on this account, is ill founded. He might have recollected, that Grotius, in his Annals, relates that more than one hundred thouſand Proteſtants periſhed in the Netherlands, by the executioner of Charles V.

VER. 108. *In the clear mirror*] The language of the Platoniſts, the writers of the intelligible world of Spirits, &c. P.

IMITATIONS.

VER. 101.
"Jam clypeus clypeis, umbone repellitur umbo,
Enſe minax enſis, pede pes, et cuſpide cuſpis," &c. STAT. W.

But heav'n reveals not what, or how, or where:
Warn'd by the Sylph, oh pious maid, beware!
This to difclofe is all thy guardian can:
Beware of all, but moft beware of Man!
He faid; when Shock, who thought fhe flept too long,
Leap'd up, and wak'd his miftrefs with his tongue.
'Twas then, Belinda, if report fay true,
Thy eyes firft open'd on a Billet-doux;
Wounds, Charms, and Ardours, were no fooner read,
But all the vifion vanifh'd from thy head.
And now, unveil'd, the Toilet ftands difplay'd,
Each filver Vafe in myftic order laid.

First,

NOTES.

VER. 113. *This to difclofe, &c.*] There is much pleafantry in the conduct of this fcene. The Roficrucian Doctrine was delivered only to adepts, with the utmoft caution, and under the moft folemn injunctions of fecrecy. It is here communicated to a Woman, and in that way of conveyance, which a Woman moft delights to make the fubject of her converfation; that is to fay, her Dreams. W.

VER. 121. *And now, unveil'd, &c.*] The tranflation of thefe verfes, containing the defcription of the toilette, by our Author's friend Dr. Parnell, deferve, for their humour, to be here inferted. P.

" Et nunc dilectum fpeculum, pro more retectum,
Emicat in menfa, quae fplendet pyxide denfa:
Tum primum lympha fe purgat candida Nympha,
Jamque fine menda, coeleftis imago videnda,
Nuda caput, bellos retinet, regit, implet ocellos.
Haec ftupet implorans, ceu cultûs numen adorans.
Inferior claram Pythoniffa apparet ad aram,
Fertque tibi caute, dicatque Superbia! laute,
Dona venufta; oris, quae cunctis, pleno laboris,

 Excerpta

First, rob'd in white, the Nymph intent adores,
With head uncover'd, the Cosmetic pow'rs.
A heav'nly Image in the glass appears,
To that she bends, to that her eyes she rears;
Th' inferior Priestess, at her altar's side,
Trembling begins the sacred rites of Pride.
Unnumber'd treasures ope at once, and here
The various off'rings of the world appear;
From each she nicely culls with curious toil,
And decks the Goddess with the glitt'ring spoil.

This

NOTES.

Excerpta explorat, dominamque deamque decorat.
Pyxide devota, se pandit hic India tota,
Et tota ex ista transpirat Arabia cista;
Testudo hic flectit dum se mea Lesbia pectit;
Atque elephas lente, te pectit Lesbia dente;
Hunc maculis noris, nivei jacet ille coloris.
Hic jacet et munde, mundus muliebris abunde;
Spinula resplendens aeris longo ordine pendens,
Pulvis suavis odore, et epistola suavis amore,
Induit arma ergo Veneris pulcherrima virgo;
Pulchrior in praesens tempus de tempore crescens,
Jam reparat risus, jam surgit gratia visus,
Jam promit cultu, mirac'la latentia vultu;
Pigmina jam miscet, quo plus sua Purpura gliscet,
Et geminans bellis splendet mage fulgor ocellis.
Stant Lemures muti, Nymphae intentique saluti,
Hic figit Zonam, capiti locat ille Coronam,
Haec manicis formam, plicis dat et altera normam,
Et tibi, vel *Betty* tibi vel nitidissima *Letty*!
Gloria factorum temere conceditur horum."

Some of these Latin lines are exceptionable, and not classical.

VER. 122. *Each silver Vase*] Parnell accidentally hearing Pope repeat this description of the Toilette, privately turned them into these Monkish Latin verses, and Pope, to whom he immediately communicated them, was astonished at the resemblance, till Parnell undeceived

This caſket India's glowing gems unlocks,
And all Arabia breathes from yonder box.
The tortoiſe here and elephant unite,
Transform'd to combs, the ſpeckled and the white.
Here files of pins extend their ſhining rows,
Puffs, Powders, Patches, Bibles, Billet-doux.
Now awful beauty puts on all its arms;
The fair each moment riſes in her charms,
Repairs her ſmiles, awakens ev'ry grace,
And calls forth all the wonders of her face;
Sees by degrees a purer bluſh ariſe,
And keener lightnings quicken in her eyes.
The buſy Sylphs ſurround their darling care,
Theſe ſet the head, and thoſe divide the hair,
Some fold the ſleeve, whilſt others plait the gown;
And Betty's prais'd for labours not her own.

NOTES.

undeceived him. Mr. Harte told me, that Dryden had been impoſed on by a ſimilar little ſtratagem. One of his friends tranſlated into Latin verſe, printed, and paſted on the bottom of an old hat-box, a tranſlation of that celebrated paſſage,

"To die is landing on ſome ſilent ſhore," &c.

and that Dryden, on opening the box, was alarmed and amazed.

VER. 131. *From each ſhe*] Evidently from Addiſon's Spectator, No. 69; "The ſingle dreſs of a woman of quality is often the product of an hundred climates. The muff and the fan come together from the different ends of the earth. The ſcarf is ſent from the Torrid Zone, and the tippet from beneath the Pole. The brocade petticoat ariſes out of the mines of Peru, and the diamond necklace out of the bowels of Indoſtan."

VER. 145. *The buſy Sylphs, &c.*] Ancient Traditions of the Rabbi's relate, that ſeveral of the fallen Angels became amorous of Women, and particularize ſome; among the reſt Aſael, who lay with Naamah, the wife of Noah, or of Ham; and who continuing impenitent, ſtill preſides over the women's Toilets. Bereſhi Rabbi in Geneſ. vi. 2. P.

THE RAPE OF THE LOCK.

CANTO II.

NOT with more glories, in th' ethereal plain,
The Sun firſt riſes o'er the purpled main,
Than, iſſuing forth, the rival of his beams
Launch'd on the boſom of the ſilver Thames.
Fair Nymphs, and well-dreſt Youths around her ſhone,
But ev'ry eye was fix'd on her alone.
On her white breaſt a ſparkling Croſs ſhe wore,
Which Jews might kiſs, and Infidels adore.
Her lively looks a ſprightly mind diſcloſe,
Quick as her eyes, and as unfix'd as thoſe:
Favours to none, to all ſhe ſmiles extends;
Oft ſhe rejects, but never once offends.
Bright as the ſun, her eyes the gazers ſtrike,
And, like the ſun, they ſhine on all alike.
Yet graceful eaſe, and ſweetneſs void of pride,
Might hide her faults, if Belles had faults to hide:
If to her ſhare ſome female errors fall,
Look on her face, and you'll forget 'em all.

This

VARIATIONS.

VER. 4. *Launch'd on the boſom, &c.*] From hence the poem continues, in the firſt Edition, to ver. 46.

"The reſt the winds diſpers'd in empty air;"

all after, to the end of this Canto, being additional. P.

This Nymph, to the deſtruction of mankind,
Nouriſh'd two Locks, which graceful hung behind
In equal curls, and well conſpired to deck
With ſhining ringlets the ſmooth iv'ry neck.
Love in theſe labyrinths his ſlaves detains,
And mighty hearts are held in ſlender chains.
With hairy ſpringes we the birds betray,
Slight lines of hair ſurprize the finny prey,
Fair treſſes man's imperial race inſnare,
And beauty draws us with a ſingle hair.
  Th' advent'rous Baron the bright locks admir'd;
He ſaw, he wiſh'd, and to the prize aſpir'd.
Reſolv'd to win, he meditates the way,
By force to raviſh, or by fraud betray;
For when ſucceſs a Lover's toil attends,
Few aſk, if fraud or force attain'd his ends.
  For this, ere Phoebus roſe, he had implor'd
Propitious heav'n, and ev'ry pow'r ador'd,
But chiefly Love—to Love an Altar built,
Of twelve vaſt French Romances, neatly gilt.
There lay three garters, half a pair of gloves,
And all the trophies of his former loves;

With

NOTES.

VER. 25. *With hairy ſpringes*] In alluſion to Anacreon's manner. W.

In what ode of Anacreon?

VER. 28. *with a ſingle hair.*] In alluſion to thoſe lines of Hudibras, applied to the ſame purpoſe,

" And tho' it be a two foot Trout,
'Tis with a ſingle hair pull'd out." W.

With tender billet-doux he lights the pyre,
And breathes three am'rous ſighs to raiſe the fire.
Then proſtrate falls, and begs with ardent eyes
Soon to obtain, and long poſſeſs the prize:
The Pow'rs gave ear, and granted half his pray'r,
The reſt, the winds diſpers'd in empty air.

But now ſecure the painted Veſſel glides,
The ſun-beams trembling on the floating tides:
While melting muſic ſteals upon the ſky,
And ſoften'd ſounds along the waters die;
Smooth flow the waves, the Zephyrs gently play,
Belinda ſmil'd, and all the world was gay.
All but the Sylph—with careful thoughts oppreſt,
Th' impending woe ſat heavy on his breaſt.
He ſummons ſtraight his Denizens of air;
The lucid ſquadrons round the ſails repair:
Soft o'er the ſhrouds aërial whiſpers breathe,
That ſeem'd but Zephyrs to the train beneath.
Some to the ſun their inſect-wings unfold,
Waft on the breeze, or ſink in clouds of gold;
Tranſparent forms, too fine for mortal ſight,
Their fluid bodies half diſſolv'd in light,
Looſe to the wind their airy garments flew,
Thin glitt'ring textures of the filmy dew,
Dipt in the richeſt tincture of the ſkies,
Where light diſports in ever-mingling dyes;

While

IMITATIONS.

VER. 45. *The Pow'rs gave ear,*] VIRG. Aeneid. xi. P.

While ev'ry beam new tranſient colours flings,
Colours that change whene'er they wave their wings.
Amid the circle, on the gilded maſt,
Superior by the nead, was Ariel plac'd;
His purple pinions op'ning to the ſun,
He rais'd his azure wand, and thus begun.

Ye Sylphs and Sylphids, to your chief give ear,
Fays, Fairies, Genii, Elves, and Demons hear!
Ye know the ſpheres, and various taſks aſſign'd
By laws eternal to th' aërial kind.

Some

NOTES.

VER. 75. *Ye know*] Thoſe who are fond of tracing images and ſentiments to their ſource, may, perhaps, be inclined to think, that the hint of aſcribing taſks and offices to ſuch imaginary beings, is taken from the Fairies, and the Ariel of Shakeſpeare; let the impartial critic determine, which has the ſuperiority of fancy. The employment of Ariel in the Tempeſt, is ſaid to be

—— "To tread the ooze
Of the ſalt deep;
To run upon the ſharp wind of the north;
To do—buſineſs in the veins of th' earth,
When it is bak'd with froſt;
—— To dive into the fire; to ride
On the curl'd clouds."

And again,

—— "In the deep nook, where once
Thou call'dſt me up at midnight to fetch dew
From the ſtill-vext Bermoothes."

Nor muſt I omit that exquiſite ſong, in which his favourite and peculiar paſtime is expreſſed.

"Where the bee ſucks, their ſuck I,
In a cowſlip's bell I lie;
There I couch where owls do cry,
On the bat's back I do fly,
After ſun-ſet, merrily;
Merrily, merrily, ſhall I live now,
Under the bloſſom that hangs on the bough."

With

Some in the fields of pureſt Ether play,
And baſk and whiten in the blaze of day.
Some guide the courſe of wand'ring orbs on high,
Or roll the planets through the boundleſs ſky.
Some leſs refin'd, beneath the moon's pale light
Purſue the ſtars that ſhoot athwart the night,
Or ſuck the miſts in groſſer air below,
Or dip their pinions in the painted bow,

Or

NOTES.

With what wildneſs of imagination, but yet, with what propriety, are the amuſements of the fairies pointed out in the Midſummer Night's Dream; amuſements proper for none but fairies!

——— " For the third part of a minute, hence:
Some to kill cankers in the muſk-roſe buds:
Some war with rear-mice for their leathern wings
To make my ſmall elves coats; and ſome keep back
The clamourous owl, that nightly hoots, and wonders
At our quaint ſpirits."———

Shakeſpeare only could have thought of the following gratifications for Titania's lover; and they are fit only to be offered to her lover by a fairy-queen.

" Be kind and courteons to this gentleman,
Hop in his walks, and gambol in his eyes;
Feed him with apricots and dewberries,
With purple grapes, green figs, and mulberries,
The honey-bags ſteal from the humble bees,
And for night-tapers crop their waxen thighs,
And light them at the fiery glow-worm's eyes,
To have my love to bed, and to ariſe;
And pluck the wings from painted butter-flies,
To fan the moon-beams from his ſleeping eyes."

If it ſhould be thought, that Shakeſpeare has the merit of being the firſt who aſſigned proper employments to imaginary perſons, in the foregoing lines, yet it muſt be granted, that by the addition of the moſt delicate ſatire to the moſt lively fancy, Pope, in a following paſſage, (ver. 91.), has equalled any thing in Shakeſpeare, or perhaps in any other author.

Or brew fierce tempests on the wintry main,
Or o'er the glebe distil the kindly rain.
Others on earth o'er human race preside,
Watch all their ways, and all their actions guide:
Of these the chief the care of Nations own,
And guard with arms divine the British Throne.
  Our humbler province is to tend the Fair,
Not a less pleasing, tho' less glorious care;
To save the powder from too rude a gale,
Nor let th' imprison'd essences exhale;
To draw fresh colours from the vernal flow'rs;
To steal from Rainbows ere they drop in show'rs
A brighter wash; to curl their waving hairs,
Assist their blushes, and inspire their airs;
Nay oft, in dreams, invention we bestow,
To change a Flounce, or add a Furbelow.
  This day, black Omens threat the brightest Fair
That e'er deserv'd a watchful spirit's care;
Some dire disaster, or by force, or slight;
But what, or where, the fates have wrapt in night.
Whether the nymph shall break Diana's law,
Or some frail China jar receive a flaw;

Or

NOTES.

VER. 90. *And guard with Arms*] The Poet was too judicious to desire this should be understood as a compliment. He intended it for a meer piece of raillery; such as he more openly pursues on another occasion; when he says,

> "Where's now the Star which lighted Charles to rise?
> With that which followed Julius to the skies.
> Angels, that watch'd the Royal Oak so well,
> How chanc'd you slept when luckless Sorrel fell?" W.

VER. 105. *Whether the nymph, &c.*] The disaster, which makes the subject of this poem, being a trifle, taken seriously; it naturally

Or ſtain her honour, or her new brocade;
Forget her pray'rs, or miſs a maſquerade;
Or loſe her heart, or necklace, at a ball;
Or whether Heav'n has doom'd that Shock muſt fall.
Haſte then, ye ſpirits! to your charge repair:
The flutt'ring fan be Zephyretta's care;
The drops to thee, Brillante, we conſign;
And, Momentilla, let the watch be thine;
Do thou, Criſpiſſa, tend her fav'rite Lock;
Ariel himſelf ſhall be the guard of Shock.

To fifty choſen Sylphs, of ſpecial note,
We truſt th' important charge, the Petticoat:
Oft have we known that ſeven-fold fence to fail,
Tho' ſtiff with hoops and arm'd with ribs of whale;
Form a ſtrong line about the ſilver bound,
And guard the wide circumference around.

Whatever

NOTES.

naturally led the Poet into this fine ſatire on the female eſtimate of human miſchances. W.

VER. 112. *Zephyretta*] The names of his Sylphs are happily choſen. Caſtlevetro mentions an odd circumſtance, that the names which Boiardo gave to his heroes in his Orlando Inamorato, were only the names of ſome of the principal tenants and peaſants on his eſtate of Scandiano.

VER. 118. *The Petticoat:*] It is impoſſible here not to recollect that matchleſs piece of raillery and exquiſite humour, of Addiſon, in the 127th Spectator, on this important part of female dreſs.

IMITATIONS.

VER. 119.—clypei dominus ſeptemplicis Ajax. OVID. W.

VER. 121. *about the ſilver bound,*] In alluſion to the ſhield of Achilles,

" Thus the broad ſhield complete the Artiſt crown'd,
With his laſt hand, and pour'd the Ocean round:
In living Silver ſeem'd the waves to roll,
And beat the Buckler's verge, and bound the whole. W.

Whatever ſpirit, careleſs of his charge,
His poſt neglects, or leave the fair at large,
Shall feel ſharp Vengeance ſoon o'ertake his ſins,
Be ſtop'd in vials, or transfix'd with pins;
Or plung'd in lakes of bitter waſhes lie,
Or wedg'd whole ages in a bodkin's eye:
Gums and Pomatums ſhall his flight reſtrain,
While clog'd he beats his ſilken wings in vain;
Or Allum ſtyptics with contracting pow'r
Shrink his thin eſſence like a rivel'd flow'r:
Or, as Ixion fix'd, the wretch ſhall feel
The giddy motion of the whirling Mill,
In fumes of burning Chocolate ſhall glow,
And tremble at the ſea that froths below!
He ſpoke; the ſpirits from the ſails deſcend;
Some, orb in orb, around the nymph extend;
Some thrid the mazy ringlets of her hair;
Some hang upon the pendants of her ear;
With beating hearts the dire event they wait,
Anxious, and trembling for the birth of Fate.

NOTES.

VER. 125. *Shall feel ſharp*] Our poet ſtill riſes in the delicacy of his ſatire, where he employs, with the utmoſt judgement and elegance, all the implements and furniture of the toilette, as inſtruments of puniſhment to thoſe ſpirits, who ſhall be careleſs of their charge; of puniſhment, ſuch as Sylphs alone could undergo.

If Virgil has merited ſuch perpetual commendation for exalting his bees, by the majeſty and magnificence of his diction, does not Pope deſerve equal praiſes, for the pomp and luſtre of his language, on ſo trivial a ſubject?

THE RAPE OF THE LOCK.

CANTO III.

CLOSE by thoſe meads, for ever crown'd with flow'rs,
Where Thames with pride ſurveys his riſing tow'rs,
There ſtands a ſtructure of majeſtic frame,
Which from the neighb'ring Hampton takes its name.
Here Britain's ſtateſmen oft the fall foredoom
Of foreign Tyrants, and of Nymphs at home;
Here thou, great ANNA! whom three realms obey,
Doſt ſometimes counſel take—and ſometimes Tea.

Hither the Heroes and the Nymphs reſort,
To taſte awhile the pleaſures of a Court;
In various talk th' inſtructive hours they paſt,
Who gave the ball, or paid the viſit laſt;
One ſpeaks the glory of the Britiſh Queen,
And one deſcribes a charming Indian ſcreen;
A third interprets motions, looks, and eyes;
At every word a reputation dies.

Snuff,

VARIATIONS.

VER. 1. *Cloſe by thoſe meads,*] The firſt Edition continues from this line to ver. 24. of this Canto. P.

VER. 11, 12. Originally in the firſt Edition,

In various talk the chearful hours they paſt,
Of, who was bit, or who capotted laſt. P.

Snuff, or the fan, ſupply each pauſe of chat,
With ſinging, laughing, ogling, *and all that.*

Mean while, declining from the noon of day,
The ſun obliquely ſhoots his burning ray;
The hungry Judges ſoon the ſentence ſign,
And wretches hang that Jury-men may dine;
The merchant from th' Exchange returns in peace,
And the long labours of the Toilet ceaſe.
Belinda now, whom thirſt of fame invites,
Burns to encounter two advent'rous Knights,
At Ombre ſingly to decide their doom;
And ſwells her breaſt with conqueſts yet to come.
Straight the three bands prepare in arms to join,
Each band the number of the ſacred Nine.
Soon as ſhe ſpreads her hand, th' aërial guard
Deſcend, and ſit on each important card:
Firſt Ariel perch'd upon a Matadore,
Then each according to the rank they bore;
For Sylphs, yet mindful of their ancient race,
Are, as when women, wond'rous fond of place.

Behold, four Kings, in majeſty rever'd,
With hoary whiſkers and a forky beard;

And

VARIATIONS.

VER. 24. *And the long labours of the Toilet ceaſe.*] All that follows of the game at Ombre, was added ſince the firſt Edition, till ver. 105. which connected thus,

Sudden the board with cups and ſpoons is crown'd. P.

NOTES.

VER. 22. *And wretches hang*] From Congreve.

And four fair Queens whose hands sustain a flow'r,
Th' expressive emblem of their softer pow'r;
Four Knaves in garbs succinct, a trusty band;
Caps on their heads, and halberts in their hand;
And party-colour'd troops a shining train,
Draw forth to combat on the velvet plain.
The skilful Nymph reviews her force with care:
Let Spades be trumps! she said, and trumps they were.
Now move to war her sable Matadores,
In show like leaders of the swarthy Moors.
Spadillio first, unconquerable Lord!
Let off two captive trumps, and swept the board.
As many more Manillio forc'd to yield,
And march'd a victor from the verdant field.
Him Basto follow'd, but his fate more hard
Gain'd but one trump and one Plebeian card.
With his broad sabre next, a chief in years,
The hoary Majesty of Spades appears,
Puts forth one manly leg, to sight reveal'd,
The rest, his many-colour'd robe conceal'd.
The rebel Knave, who dares his prince engage,
Proves the just victim of his royal rage.
Ev'n mighty Pam, that Kings and Queens o'erthrew,
And mow'd down armies in the fights of Lu,
Sad chance of war! now destitute of aid,
Falls undistinguish'd by the victor Spade!

Thus

NOTES.

VER. 53. *Him Basto follow'd,*] The magnificent and majestic style in which this game of cards is described, artfully and finely heightens the ridicule.

Thus far both armies to Belinda yield;
Now to the Baron fate inclines the field.
His warlike Amazon her hoſt invades,
Th' imperial conſort of the crown of Spades.
The Club's black Tyrant firſt her victim dy'd,
Spite of his haughty mien, and barb'rous pride:
What boots the regal circle on his head,
His giant limbs, in ſtate unwieldy ſpread;
That long behind he trails his pompous robe,
And, of all monarchs, only graſps the globe?

The Baron now his Diamonds pours apace;
Th' embroider'd King who ſhews but half his face,
And his refulgent Queen, with pow'rs combin'd
Of broken Troops an eaſy conqueſt find.
Clubs, Diamonds, Hearts, in wild diſorder ſeen,
With throngs promiſcuous ſtrow the level green.

Thus

NOTES.

VER. 65. *Belinda yield;*] It is finely contrived that ſhe ſhould be victorious; as it occaſions a change of fortune in the dreadful loſs ſhe was ſpeedily to undergo, and gives occaſion to the poet to introduce a moral reflection from Virgil, which adds to the pleaſantry of the ſtory. In one of the paſſages where Pope has copied Vida, he has loſt the propriety of the original, which ariſes from the different colours of the men, at Cheſs.

Thus, when diſpers'd, a routed army runs, &c.

"Non aliter, campis legio ſe buxea utrinque
Compoſuit, duplici digeſtis ordine turmis,
Adverſiſque ambæ fulſere coloribus alæ;
Quam Gallorum acies, Alpino frigore lactea
Corpora, ſi tendant albis in prælia ſignis,
Auroræ populos contra, et Phaethonte peruſtos
Inſano Æthiopas, et nigri Memnonis alas."

Thus when diſpers'd a routed army runs,
Of Aſia's troops, and Afric's ſable ſons,
With like confuſion different nations fly,
Of various habit, and of various dye;
The pierc'd battalions diſunited fall,
In heaps on heaps; one fate o'erwhelms them all.

The Knave of Diamonds tries his wily arts,
And wins (oh ſhameful chance!) the Queen of Hearts.
At this, the blood the Virgin's cheek forſook,
A livid paleneſs ſpreads o'er all her look;
She ſees, and trembles at th' approaching ill,
Juſt in the jaws of ruin, and Codille.
And now (as oft in ſome diſtemper'd State)
On one nice Trick depends the gen'ral fate:
An Ace of Hearts ſteps forth: The King unſeen
Lurk'd in her hand, and mourn'd his captive Queen:
He ſprings to vengeance with an eager pace,
And falls like thunder on the proſtrate Ace.
The nymph exulting fills with ſhouts the ſky;
The walls, the woods, and long canals reply.

Oh thoughtleſs mortals! ever blind to fate,
Too ſoon dejected, and too ſoon elate.
Sudden theſe honours ſhall be ſnatch'd away,
And curs'd for ever this victorious day.

For

IMITATIONS.

VER. 101.

"Neſcia mens hominum fati ſortiſque futurae;
Et ſervare modum, rebus ſublata ſecundis!
Turno tempus erit magno cum optaverit emptum
Intactum Pallanta; et cum ſpolia iſta diemque
Oderit." VIRG.

For lo! the board with cups and ſpoons is crown'd,
The berries crackle, and the mill turns round;
On ſhining altars of Japan they raiſe
The ſilver lamp; the fiery ſpirits blaze:
From ſilver ſpouts the grateful liquors glide,
While China's earth receives the ſmoaking tide:
At once they gratify their ſenſe and taſte,
And frequent cups prolong the rich repaſt.
Straight hover round the Fair her airy band;
Some, as ſhe ſipp'd, the fuming liquor fann'd,
Some o'er her lap their careful plumes diſplay'd,
Trembling, and conſcious of the rich brocade.
Coffee (which makes the politician wiſe,
And ſee through all things with his half-ſhut eyes)
Sent up in vapours to the Baron's brain
New Stratagems, the radiant Lock to gain.
Ah ceaſe, raſh youth! deſiſt ere 'tis too late,
Fear the juſt Gods, and think of Scylla's Fate!
Chang'd to a bird, and ſent to flit in air,
She dearly pays for Niſus' injur'd hair!
But when to Miſchief mortals bend their will,
How ſoon they find fit Inſtruments of ill?

Juſt

VARIATIONS.

Ver. 105. *Sudden the board, &c.*] From hence, the firſt Edition continues to ver. 134. P.

NOTES.

Ver. 105.] It is doubtleſs as hard to make a coffee-pot ſhine in poetry, as a plough; yet our author has ſucceeded in giving elegance to a f. miliar object, as well as Virgil.

Ver. 122. *and think of Scylla's Fate!*] Vide Ovid's Metam. viii. P.

Juſt then, Clariſſa drew with tempting grace
A two-edg'd weapon from her ſhining caſe:
So Ladies in Romance aſſiſt their Knight,
Preſent the ſpear, and arm him for the fight.
He takes the gift with rev'rence, and extends
The little engine on his fingers' ends;
This juſt behind Belinda's neck he ſpread,
As o'er the fragrant ſteams ſhe bends her head.
Swift to the Lock a thouſand Sprites repair,
A thouſand wings, by turns, blow back the hair;
And thrice they twitch'd the diamond in her ear;
Thrice ſhe look'd back, and thrice the foe drew near.
Juſt in that inſtant, anxious Ariel ſought
The cloſe receſſes of the Virgin's thought:
As on the noſegay in her breaſt reclin'd,
He watch'd th' ideas riſing in her mind,
Sudden he view'd, in ſpite of all her art,
An earthly Lover lurking at her heart.
Amaz'd, confus'd, he found his pow'r expir'd,
Reſign'd to fate, and with a ſigh retir'd.
   The Peer now ſpreads the glittering Forfex wide,
T' incloſe the Lock; now joins it, to divide.

Ev'n

VARIATIONS.

Ver. 134.] In the firſt Edition it was thus,

As o'er the fragrant ſtream ſhe bends her head. P.

Ver. 147.

First he expands the glitt'ring Forfax wide
T' incloſe the Lock; then joins it to divide:
The meeting points the ſacred hair diſſever,
From the fair head, for ever, and for ever.

All that is between was added afterwards. P.

Ev'n then, before the fatal engine cloſ'd,
A wretched Sylph too fondly interpoſ'd;
Fate urg'd the ſheers, and cut the Sylph in twain,
(But airy ſubſtance ſoon unites again)

The

NOTES.

VER. 152. *But airy ſubſtance*] See Milton, lib. vi. of Satan cut aſunder by the Angel Michael. P.

This line is an admirable parody on that paſſage of Milton, which, perhaps oddly enough, deſcribes Satan wounded:

" The griding ſword, with diſcontinuous wound,
Paſs'd thro' him; but th' etherial ſubſtance cloſ'd,
Not long diviſible."

The parodies are ſome of the moſt exquiſite parts of this poem. That which follows from the " Dum juga montis aper," of Virgil, contains ſome of the moſt artful ſtrokes of ſatire, and the moſt poignant ridicule imaginable.

The introduction of frequent parodies on ſerious and ſolemn paſſages of Homer and Virgil, give much life and ſpirit to heroi-comic poetry. " Tu dors, Prelat? tu dors?" in Boileau, is the " Ευδεις Ατρεος υιε" of Homer, and is full of humour. The wife of the barber talks in the language of Dido in her expoſtulations to her Æneas, at the beginning of the ſecond Canto of the Lutrin. Pope's parodies of Sarpedon in Homer, and of the deſcription of Achilles's ſceptre, together with the ſcales of Jupiter, from Homer, Virgil, and Milton, are judiciouſly introduced in their ſeveral places; are perhaps ſuperior to thoſe Boileau or Garth have uſed, and are worked up with peculiar pleaſantry. The mind of the reader is engaged by novelty, when it ſo unexpectedly finds a thought or object it had been accuſtomed to ſurvey in another form, ſuddenly arrayed in a ridiculous garb. A mixture alſo of comic and ridiculous images, with ſuch as are ſerious and important, adds no ſmall beauty to this ſpecies of poetry, when real and imaginary diſtreſſes are coupled together.

" Not youthful kings in battle ſeiz'd alive,
Not ſcornful virgins who their charms ſurvive," &c.

Which is much ſuperior to a ſimilar paſſage in the Diſpenſary. Canto v.

The meeting points the ſacred hair diſſever
From the fair head, for ever, and for ever!
 Then flaſh'd the living light'ning from her eyes,
And ſcreams of horror rend th' affrighted ſkies.
Not louder ſhrieks to pitying heav'n are caſt,
When huſbands, or when lap-dogs breathe their laſt;
Or when rich China veſſels fall'n from high,
In glitt'ring duſt, and painted fragments lie!
 Let wreaths of triumph now my temples twine,
(The Victor cry'd) the glorious prize is mine!
While fiſh in ſtreams, or birds delight in air,
Or in a coach and ſix the Britiſh Fair,
As long as Atalantis ſhall be read,
Or the ſmall pillow grace a Lady's bed,

While

NOTES.

VER. 165. *Atalantis*] A famous book written about that time by a woman: full of Court and Party ſcandal; and in a looſe effeminacy of ſtyle and ſentiment, which well-ſuited the debauched taſte of the better vulgar. W.

Mrs. Manley, the author of it, was the daughter of Sir Roger Manley, Governor of Guernſey, and the author of the firſt volume of the famous Turkiſh Spy, publiſhed, from his papers, by Dr. Midgley. She was known and admired by all the wits of the times. She wrote three plays; Lucius, the laſt, 1717, was dedicated to Sir Richard Steele, with whom ſhe had quarrelled ſome time before. He wrote the prologue to it, and Prior the epilogue. She was alſo celebrated by Lord Lanſdown. She died in the houſe of Alderman Barber, Swift's friend; and was ſaid to have been the miſtreſs of the Alderman.

IMITATIONS.

VER. 163, 170.

"Dum juga montis aper, fluvios dum piſcis amabit,
Semper honos, nomenque tuum, laudeſque manebunt."

VIRG. P.

While viſits ſhall be paid on ſolemn days,
When num'rous wax-lights in bright order blaze,
While nymphs take treats, or aſſignations give, 169
So long my honour, name, and praiſe ſhall live!
What Time would ſpare, from Steel receives its date,
And monuments, like men, ſubmit to fate!
Steel could the labour of the Gods deſtroy,
And ſtrike to duſt th' imperial tow'rs of Troy;
Steel could the works of mortal pride confound,
And hew triumphal arches to the ground. 176
What wonder then, fair nymph! thy hairs ſhould feel
The conqu'ring force of unreſiſted Steel?

IMITATIONS.

VER. 177.

"Ille quoque everſus mons eſt, &c.
Quid faciant crines, cum ferro talia cedant?"
CATULL. de com. Berenices. P.

THE RAPE OF THE LOCK.

CANTO IV.

But anxious cares the penſive nymph oppreſs'd,
And ſecret paſſions labour'd in her breaſt.
Not youthful kings in battle ſeiz'd alive,
Not ſcornful virgins who their charms ſurvive,
Not ardent lovers robb'd of all their bliſs,
Not ancient ladies when refus'd a kiſs,
Not tyrants fierce that unrepenting die,
Not Cynthia when her manteau's pinn'd awry,
E'er felt ſuch rage, reſentment, and deſpair,
As thou, ſad Virgin! for thy raviſh'd Hair.
For, that ſad moment, when the Sylphs withdrew,
And Ariel weeping from Belinda flew,
Umbriel, a duſky, melancholy ſprite,
As ever ſully'd the fair face of light,

Down

VARIATIONS.

Ver. 11. *For, that ſad moment, &c.*] All the lines from hence to the 94th verſe, that deſcribe the houſe of Spleen, are not in the firſt Edition; inſtead of them followed only theſe,

While her rack'd Soul repoſe and peace requires,
The fierce Thaleſtris fans the riſing fires.

And continued at the 94th verſe of this Canto. P.

IMITATIONS.

Ver. 1. "At regina gravi," &c. Virg. Aeneid. iv. P.

Down to the central earth, his proper scene,
Repair'd to search the gloomy Cave of Spleen.
  Swift on his sooty pinions flits the Gnome,
And in a vapour reach'd the dismal dome.
No chearful breeze this sullen region knows,
The dreaded East is all the wind that blows.
Here in a grotto, shelter'd close from air,
And screen'd in shades from day's detested glare,
She sighs for ever on her pensive bed,
Pain at her side, and Megrim at her head.
  Two handmaids wait the throne: alike in place,
But diff'ring far in figure and in face.
Here stood Ill-nature like an ancient maid,
Her wrinkled form in black and white array'd!
With store of pray'rs, for mornings, nights, and noons,
Her hand is fill'd; her bosom with lampoons.

There

NOTES.

VER. 16. *Cave of Spleen.*]

"Thro' me ye pass to Spleen's terrific dome,
Thro' me, to Discontent's eternal home!
Thro' me, to those who saddend human life,
By sullen humour or vexatious strife;
And here thro' scenes of endless vapour hurl'd,
Are punish'd in the forms they plagu'd the world;
Justly they feel no joy, who none bestow,
All ye who enter, every hope forego!"

It is thus Mr. Hayley, in allusion to Dante's striking inscription over hell-gate, begins his description of the dwelling of Spleen. She and her attendants are afterwards painted with force and spirit in the next 200 verses, and more. His mild and engaging Serena, her prim and sour aunt Penelope, and the good old Squire, are admirable portraits. Whether Pope's Belinda in losing her lock, or Hayley's Serena, in being prevented going to a masquerade, felt the greater mortification and misfortune, is an arduous point that must be determined by the Ladies.

There Affectation with a ſickly mien,
Shows in her cheek the roſes of eighteen,
Practis'd to liſp, and hang the head aſide,
Faints into airs, and languiſhes with pride,
On the rich quilt ſinks with becoming woe,
Wrapt in a gown, for ſickneſs, and for ſhow.
The fair-ones feel ſuch maladies as theſe,
When each new night-dreſs gives a new diſeaſe.
A conſtant Vapour o'er the palace flies;
Strange phantoms riſing as the miſts ariſe;
Dreadful as hermits dreams in haunted ſhades,
Or bright, as viſions of expiring maids.
Now glaring fiends, and ſnakes on rolling ſpires,
Pale ſpectres, gaping tombs, and purple fires:
Now lakes of liquid gold, Elyſian ſcenes,
And cryſtal domes, and Angels in machines.
Unnumber'd throngs, on ev'ry ſide are ſeen,
Of bodies chang'd to various forms by Spleen.
Here living Tea-pots ſtand, one arm held out,
One bent; the handle this, and that the ſpout:
A Pipkin there, like Homer's Tripod walks;
Here ſighs a Jar, and there a Gooſe-pye talks;

Men

NOTES.

VER. 41. *Dreadful, as hermits dreams in haunted ſhades,*
Or bright, as viſions of expiring maids.]

The Poet by this compariſon would inſinuate, that the temptations of the mortified Recluſes in the Church of Rome, and the extatic viſions of their female Saints, were as much the

IMITATIONS.

VER. 51. *Homer's Tripod walks;*] See Hom. Iliad xviii. of Vulcan's walking Tripods. P.

VER. 52. *and there a Gooſe-pye talks;*] Alludes to a real fact, a Lady of diſtinction imagined herſelf in this condition. P.

Men prove with child, as pow'rful fancy works,
And maids turn'd bottles, call aloud for corks.

Safe paſt the Gnome through this fantaſtic band,
A branch of healing Spleenwort in his hand.
Then thus addreſs'd the pow'r—Hail wayward Queen!
Who rule the ſex to fifty from fifteen:
Parent of vapours and of female wit,
Who give th' hyſteric, or poetic fit,
On various tempers act by various ways,
Make ſome take phyſic, others ſcribble plays;
Who cauſe the proud their viſits to delay,
And ſend the godly in a pet to pray.
A nymph there is, that all thy pow'r diſdains,
And thouſands more in equal mirth maintains.
But oh! if e'er thy Gnome could ſpoil a grace,
Or raiſe a pimple on a beauteous face,
Like Citron-waters matrons cheeks inflame,
Or change complexions at a loſing Game.
If e'er with airy horns I planted heads,
Or rumpled petticoats, or tumbled beds,

Or

NOTES.

the effects of hypochondriac diſorders, the Spleen, or, what was then the faſhionable word, the *Vapours*, as any of the imaginary transformations he ſpeaks of afterwards. W.

VER. 53. *Men prove with child,*] Van Swirten, in his Commentaries on Boerhaave, relates, that he knew a man who had ſtudied till he fancied his legs to be of glaſs; his maid bringing wood to his fire, threw it careleſsly down; our ſage was angry and terrified for his legs of glaſs; the girl, out of patience with his megrims, gave him a blow with a log on the parts affected; he inſtantly ſtarted up in a rage, and from that moment recovered the uſe of his glaſs legs.

Or caus'd ſuſpicion when no ſoul was rude,
Or diſcompos'd the head-dreſs of a Prude,
Or e'er to coſtive lap-dog gave diſeaſe,
Which not the tears of brighteſt eyes could eaſe:
Hear me, and touch Belinda with chagrin,
That ſingle act gives half the world the ſpleen.

The Goddeſs with a diſcontented air
Seems to reject him, tho' ſhe grants his pray'r.
A wond'rous Bag with both her hands ſhe binds,
Like that where once Ulyſſes held the winds;
There ſhe collects the force of female lungs,
Sighs, ſobs, and paſſions, and the war of tongues.
A Vial next ſhe fills with fainting fears,
Soft ſorrows, melting griefs, and flowing tears.
The Gnome rejoicing bears her gifts away,
Spreads his black wings, and ſlowly mounts to day.

Sunk in Thaleſtris' arms the nymph he found,
Her eyes dejected, and her hair unbound.
Full o'er their heads the ſwelling bag he rent,
And all the Furies iſſu'd at the vent.
Belinda burns with more than mortal ire,
And fierce Thaleſtris fans the riſing fire.
O wretched maid! ſhe ſpread her hands, and cry'd,
(While Hampton's echoes, Wretched maid! reply'd)
Was it for this you took ſuch conſtant care
The bodkin, comb, and eſſence to prepare?
For this your Locks in paper durance bound?
For this with tort'ring irons wreath'd around?

For this with fillets ſtrain'd your tender head?
And bravely bore the double loads of lead?
Gods! ſhall the raviſher diſplay your hair,
While the Fops envy, and the Ladies ſtare!
Honour forbid! at whoſe unrival'd ſhrine
Eaſe, pleaſure, virtue, all our ſex reſign.
Methinks already I your tears ſurvey,
Already hear the horrid things they ſay,
Already ſee you a degraded toaſt,
And all your honour in a whiſper loſt!
How ſhall I, then, your hapleſs fame defend?
'Twill then be infamy to ſeem your friend!
And ſhall this prize, th' ineſtimable prize,
Expos'd through cryſtal to the gazing eyes,
And heighten'd by the diamond's circling rays,
On that rapacious hand for ever blaze?
Sooner ſhall graſs in Hyde-park Circus grow,
And wits take lodgings in the ſound of Bow;
Sooner let earth, air, ſea, to Chaos fall,
Men, monkeys, lap-dogs, parrots, periſh all!
She ſaid; then raging to Sir Plume repairs,
And bids her beau demand the precious hairs:

(Sir

NOTES.

VER. 121. *Sir Plume repairs,*] Sir George Brown. He was the only one of the Party who took the thing ſeriouſly. He was angry that the Poet ſhould make him talk nothing but nonſenſe; and in truth one could not well blame him. W.

An engraving of Sir Plume, with ſeven other figures, by Hogarth, was executed on the lid of a gold ſnuff box, and preſented to one of the parties concerned; the original impreſſion of a print of it was ſold, at Mr. Gulſton's ſale, for thirty-three pounds.

(Sir Plume, of amber ſnuff-box juſtly vain,
And the nice conduct of a clouded cane)
With earneſt eyes, and round unthinking face,
He firſt the ſnuff-box open'd, then the caſe,
And thus broke out—“ My Lord, why, what the devil!
“ Z—ds! damn the Lock! 'fore Gad, you muſt be civil!
“ Plague on't! 'tis paſt a Jeſt—nay prithee, pox!
“ Give her the hair”—he ſpoke, and rapp'd his box.

It grieves me much (reply'd the Peer again)
Who ſpeaks ſo well ſhould ever ſpeak in vain.
But by this Lock, this ſacred Lock I ſwear,
(Which never more ſhall join its parted hair;
Which never more its honours ſhall renew,
Clip'd from the lovely head where late it grew),
That while my noſtrils draw the vital air,
This hand, which won it, ſhall for ever wear.
He ſpoke, and ſpeaking, in proud triumph ſpread
The long-contended honours of her head.

But Umbriel, hateful Gnome! forbears not ſo;
He breaks the Vial whence the ſorrows flow.
Then ſee! the nymph in beauteous grief appears,
Her eyes half-languiſhing, half-drown'd in tears;

On

NOTES.

VER. 141. *But Umbriel, hateful Gnome! forbears not ſo;*
He breaks the Vial whence the ſorrows flow.]

Theſe two lines are additional; and aſſign the cauſe of the different operation on the Paſſions of the two Ladies. The poem went on before without that diſtinction, as without any Machinery, to the end of the Canto. P.

IMITATIONS.

VER. 133. *But by this Lock,*] In alluſion to Achilles's oath in Homer, Il. i. P.

On her heav'd bosom hung her drooping head,
Which, with a sigh, she rais'd; and thus she said.

For ever curs'd be this detested day,
Which snatch'd my best, my fav'rite curl away!
Happy! ah ten times happy had I been,
If Hampton-Court these eyes had never seen!
Yet am not I the first mistaken maid,
By love of Courts to num'rous ills betray'd.
Oh had I rather un-admir'd, remain'd
In some lone Isle, or distant Northern land;
Where the gilt Chariot never marks the way,
Where none learn Ombre, none e'er taste Bohea!
There kept my charms conceal'd from mortal eye,
Like roses that in deserts bloom and die.
What mov'd my mind with youthful Lords to roam?
O had I stay'd, and said my pray'rs at home!
'Twas this the morning omens seem'd to tell,
Thrice from my trembling hand the patch-box fell;
The tott'ring China shook without a wind,
Nay Poll sat mute, and Shock was most unkind!
A Sylph too warn'd me of the threats of fate,
In mystic visions, now believ'd too late!
See the poor remnants of these slighted hairs!
My hands shall rend what ev'n thy rapine spares:
These

NOTES.

VER. 155. *Where the gilt Chariot*] What aggravating circumstances of solitude!

VER. 163. *The tott'ring China*] The fatal prognostics that preceded the death of Cæsar, in the first Georgic of Virgil, are not imagined with more propriety, or could be more alarming!

These in two sable ringlets taught to break,
Once gave new beauties to the snowy neck;
The sister-lock now sits uncouth, alone,
And in its fellow's fate foresees its own;
Uncurl'd it hangs, the fatal sheers demands,
And tempts, once more, thy sacrilegious hands.
Oh hadst thou, cruel! been content to seize
Hairs less in sight, or any hairs but these!

THE RAPE OF THE LOCK.

CANTO V.

SHE ſaid: the pitying audience melt in tears,
But Fate and Jove had ſtopp'd the Baron's ears.
In vain Thaleſtris with reproach aſſails,
For who can move when fair Belinda fails?
Not half ſo fix'd the Trojan could remain,
While Anna begg'd and Dido rag'd in vain.
Then grave Clariſſa graceful wav'd her fan;
Silence enſu'd, and thus the Nymph began.
Say, why are Beauties prais'd and honour'd moſt,
The wiſe man's paſſion, and the vain man's toaſt?
Why

VARIATIONS.

VER. 7. *Then grave Clariſſa, &c.*] A new Character introduced in the ſubſequent Editions, to open more clearly the Moral of the Poem, in a parody of the ſpeech of Sarpedon to Glaucus in Homer. P.

IMITATIONS.

VER. 9. *Say, why are Beauties, &c.*] HOMER.
" Why boaſt we, Glaucus! our extended reign,
Where Xanthus' ſtreams enrich the Lycian plain;
Our num'rous herds that range the fruitful field,
And hills where vines their purple harveſt yield;
Our foaming bowls with purer nectar crown'd,
Our feaſts enhanc'd with muſic's ſprightly ſound;
Why on thoſe ſhores are we with joy ſurvey'd,
Admir'd as heroes, and as Gods obey'd;

Why deck'd with all that land and ſea afford,
Why Angels call'd, and Angel-like ador'd?
Why round our coaches croud the white-glov'd Beaus,
Why bows the ſide-box from its inmoſt rows?
How vain are all theſe glories, all our pains,
Unleſs good ſenſe preſerve what beauty gains:
That men may ſay, when we the front-box grace,
Behold the firſt in virtue as in face!
Oh! if to dance all night, and dreſs all day,
Charm'd the ſmall-pox, or chas'd old-age away;
Who would not ſcorn what houſewife's cares produce,
Or who would learn one earthly thing of uſe?
To patch, nay ogle, might become a Saint,
Nor could it ſure be ſuch a ſin to paint.

But

IMITATIONS.

Unleſs great acts ſuperior merit prove,
And vindicate the bounteous pow'rs above?
'Tis ours, the dignity they give, to grace;
The firſt in valour, as the firſt in place:
That when with wond'ring eyes our martial bands
Behold our deeds tranſcending our commands,
Such, they may cry, deſerve the ſov'reign ſtate,
Whom thoſe that envy dare not imitate.
Could all our care elude the gloomy grave,
Which claims no leſs the fearful than the brave,
For luſt of fame I ſhould not vainly dare
In fighting fields, nor urge thy ſoul to war.
But ſince, alas! ignoble age muſt come,
Diſeaſe, and death's inexorable doom;
The life which others pay, let us beſtow,
And give to fame what we to nature owe;
Brave tho' we fall, and honour'd if we live,
Or let us glory gain, or glory give."

This paſſage was the firſt ſpecimen our author gave of his tranſlation of Homer; and it appeared firſt in the ſixth volume of Dryden's Miſcellanies.

But ſince, alas! frail beauty muſt decay,
Curl'd or uncurl'd, ſince Locks will turn to grey;
Since painted, or not painted, all ſhall fade,
And ſhe who ſcorns a man, muſt die a maid;
What then remains but well our Pow'r to uſe,
And keep good-humour ſtill whate'er we loſe?
And truſt me, dear! good-humour can prevail,
When airs, and flights, and ſcreams, and ſcolding fail.
Beauties in vain their pretty eyes may roll;
Charms ſtrike the ſight, but merit wins the ſoul.
So ſpoke the Dame, but no applauſe enſu'd;
Belinda frown'd, Thaleſtris call'd her Prude.
To arms, to arms! the fierce Virago cries,
And ſwift as lightning to the combat flies.
All ſide in parties, and begin th' attack;
Fans clap, ſilks ruſtle, and tough whalebones crack;
Heroes' and Heroines' ſhouts confus'dly riſe,
And baſe and treble voices ſtrike the ſkies.
No common weapons in their hands are found,
Like Gods they fight, nor dread a mortal wound.

So

VARIATIONS.

VER. 37. *To arms, to arms!*] From hence the firſt Edition goes on to the concluſion, except a very few ſhort inſertions added, to keep the Machinery in view to the end of the poem. P.

NOTES.

VER. 26. *Curl'd or uncurl'd,*] Fontenelle writes a gallant and pleaſant letter to a beautiful young lady on diſcovering *one* grey hair on her head.

IMITATIONS.

VER. 35. *So ſpoke the Dame,*] It is a verſe frequently repeated in Homer after any ſpeech,

"So ſpoke—and all the Heroes applauded." P.

So when bold Homer makes the Gods engage,
And heav'nly breaſts with human paſſions rage;
'Gainſt Pallas, Mars; Latona, Hermes arms;
And all Olympus rings with loud alarms:
Jove's thunder roars, heav'n trembles all around,
Blue Neptune ſtorms, the bellowing deeps reſound:
Earth ſhakes her nodding tow'rs, the ground gives way,
And the pale ghoſts ſtart at the flaſh of day!

Triumphant

NOTES.

VER. 45. *So when bold Homer*] Homer, Il. xx. P.

The ridicule is moſt artfully heightened by introducing one of the moſt ſublime paſſages in Homer;

" 'Αμφι δ' εσαλπιγξεν μεγας ϐρανος, ϐλυμπος τε
Εδδεισεν δ' υπενερθεν αναξ ενερων Αιδωνευς,
Δεισας δ' εκ θρονϐ αλτο και ιαχε, μη οι επειτα
Γαιαν αναρρηξειε Ποσειδαων ενοσιχθων
Οικια δε θνητοισι και αθανατοισι φανειη,
Σμερδαλε', ευρωεντα, τα τε ςυγεϐσι θεοι περ."

Well might Longinus exclaim, " Do you ſee, O my friend, how the earth burſts aſunder to its centre, Tartarus itſelf is laid open and naked, all things mortal and immortal combat together, and ſhare the danger of this tremendous conflict?"

In none of his many imitations has Virgil ſhewn his inferiority to Homer ſo much as in this paſſage;

" Non ſecus ac ſi qua penitus vi terra dehiſcens
Infernas reſeret ſedes, & regna recludat
Pallida, Dîs inviſa; ſuperque immane barathrum
Cernatur, trepidentque immiſſo lumine Manes."

Æneid. viii. v. 243.

For not to mention that what is part of the Action in Homer, is only a ſimile in Virgil, how tame is ſuperque immane barathrum (even though a magnificent image) to

Δεισας δ' εκ θρονϐ αλτο και ιαχε ——

How or where has terror ever been ſo ſtrongly painted as by this circumſtance of Pluto himſelf, ſuddenly leaping from his throne and ſhrieking aloud?

Triumphant Umbriel on a ſconce's height
Clap'd his glad wings, and ſate to view the fight:
Prop'd on their bodkin ſpears, the Sprites ſurvey
The growing combat, or aſſiſt the fray.

While through the preſs enrag'd Thaleſtris flies,
And ſcatters death around from both her eyes,
A Beau and Witling periſh'd in the throng,
One dy'd in metaphor, and one in ſong.
" O cruel Nymph! a living death I bear,"
Cry'd Dapperwit, and ſunk beſide his chair.
A mournful glance Sir Fopling upwards caſt,
" Thoſe eyes are made ſo killing"—was his laſt.

Thus

VARIATIONS.

VER. 53. *Triumphant Umbriel*] Theſe four lines added for the reaſon before mentioned. P.

Added with great dexterity, beauty, and propriety!

NOTES.

VER. 55. *Prop'd on their*] Like the heroes in Homer, when they are Spectators of a combat.

VER. 64. *Thoſe eyes*] It was the common cant of all the wits and poets of this time to depreciate and laugh at Italian operas. See what Addiſon has ſaid of them, Spectator 18. They would have been of a different opinion, if they could have read what Dr. Burney has ſaid on this ſubject in his Hiſtory of Muſic.

IMITATIONS.

VER. 53. *Triumphant Umbriel*] Minerva in like manner, during the battle of Ulyſſes with the Suitors in the Odyſſ. perches on a beam of the roof to behold it. P.

VER. 64. *Thoſe eyes are made ſo killing*] The words of a ſong in the Opera of Camilla. P.

Thus on Maeander's flow'ry margin lies
Th' expiring Swan, and as he ſings he dies.
  When bold Sir Plume had drawn Clariſſa down,
Chloe ſtepp'd in, and kill'd him with a frown;
She ſmil'd to ſee the doughty hero ſlain,
But, at her ſmile, the Beau reviv'd again.
  Now Jove ſuſpends his golden ſcales in air,
Weighs the Men's wits againſt the Lady's hair;
The doubtful beam long nods from ſide to ſide;
At length the wits mount up, the hairs ſubſide.
  See fierce Belinda on the Baron flies,
With more than uſual lightning in her eyes:
Nor fear'd the Chief th' unequal fight to try,
Who ſought no more than on his foe to die.
But this bold Lord with manly ſtrength endu'd,
She with one finger and a thumb ſubdu'd:
Juſt where the breath of life his noſtrils drew,
A charge of ſnuff the wily virgin threw;

The

NOTES.

VER. 71. *Now Jove, &c.*] Vid. Homer, Il. viii. and Virg. Aen. xii. P.

VER. 74. *At length the wits*] This parody from Homer and Virgil is admirable. Milton improved on this fine fiction in Paradiſe Loſt, Book iv. v. 997. by ſaying, "that when the Almighty weighed Satan in ſuch ſcales, the mounting of his ſcales denoted ill ſucceſs;" and alſo by alluding artfully to the ſign of Libra in the heavens.

IMITATIONS.

VER. 65. *Thus on Maeander's flow'ry margin lies*]
"Sic ubi fata vocant, udis abjectus in herbis,
Ad vada Maeandri concinit albus olor."
Ov. Ep. P.

The Gnomes direct, to ev'ry atom juſt,
The pungent grains of titillating duſt.
Sudden, with ſtarting tears each eye o'erflows,
And the high dome re-echoes to his noſe.
  Now meet thy fate, incens'd Belinda cry'd,
And drew a deadly bodkin from her ſide.
(The ſame, his ancient perſonage to deck,
Her great great grandſire wore about his neck,
In three ſeal-rings; which after, melted down,
Form'd a vaſt buckle for his widow's gown:
Her infant grandame's whiſtle next it grew,
The bells ſhe jingled, and the whiſtle blew;

Then

VARIATIONS.

VER. 83. *The Gnomes direct,*] Theſe two lines added for the above reaſon. P.

NOTES.

VER. 84. *Titillating duſt.*] Boileau and Garth have alſo each of them enlivened their pieces with a mock-fight. But Boileau has laid the ſcene of his action in a neighbouring bookſeller's ſhop; where the combatants encounter each other by chance. This conduct is a little inartificial; but has given the ſatyriſt an opportunity of indulging his ruling paſſion, the expoſing bad poets, with which France, at that time, abounded. Swift's Battle of the Books, at the end of the Tale of a Tub, is evidently taken from this battle of Boileau (Cant. v.), which is excellent in its kind. The fight of the Phyſicians in the Diſpenſary, is one of its moſt ſhining parts. There is a vaſt deal of propriety in the weapons Garth has given to his warriors. They are armed, much in character, with cauſtics, emetics, and cathartics; with buck-thorn, and ſteel-pills; with ſyringes, bed-pans, and urinals. The execution is exactly proportioned to the deadlineſs of ſuch irreſiſtible weapons; and the wounds inflicted, are ſuitable to the nature of each different inſtrument ſaid to inflict them.

IMITATIONS.

VER. 89. *The ſame, his ancient perſonage to deck,*] In imitation of the progreſs of Agamemnon's ſceptre in Homer, Il. ii. P

Then in a bodkin grac'd her mother's hairs,
Which long ſhe wore, and now Belinda wears.)

Boaſt not my fall (he cry'd) inſulting foe!
Thou by ſome other ſhalt be laid as low.
Nor think, to die dejects my lofty mind;
All that I dread is leaving you behind!
Rather than ſo, ah let me ſtill ſurvive,
And burn in Cupid's flames—but burn alive.

Reſtore the Lock! ſhe cries; and all around
Reſtore the Lock! the vaulted roofs rebound.
Not fierce Othello in ſo loud a ſtrain!
Roar'd for the handkerchief that caus'd his pain.
But ſee how oft ambitious aims are croſs'd,
And chiefs contend till all the prize is loſt!
The Lock, obtain'd with guilt, and kept with pain,
In ev'ry place is ſought, but ſought in vain:

With

NOTES.

VER. 105. *Fierce Othello*] Rhymer, with a taſteleſs inſenſibility, laughed at the incident of loſing the handkerchief, as trifling. Neither he, nor the Spectator, ſeem to have known, that this incident, ſo beautifully natural, is in the Italian novel, which Shakeſpeare copied.

VER. 109. *Obtain'd with guilt,*] We are now arrived at the grand cataſtrophe of the poem; the invaluable Lock which is ſo eagerly ſought, is irrecoverably loſt! And here our poet has made a judicious uſe of that celebrated fiction of Arioſto; that all things loſt on earth, are treaſured in the moon. How ſuch a fiction can properly have place in an epic poem, it becomes the defenders of this agreeably extravagant writer to juſtify; but in a comic poem, it appears with grace and conſiſtency. The whole paſſage in Arioſto is full of wit and ſatire; for wit and ſatire were, perhaps, among the chief and characteriſtical excellencies of this incomparable Italian.

In

With such a prize no mortal must be blest,
So heav'n decrees! with heav'n who can contest?

Some thought it mounted to the Lunar sphere,
Since all things lost on earth are treasur'd there.
There Heros' wits are kept in pond'rous vases,
And Beaux in snuff-boxes and tweezer-cases.
There broken vows, and death-bed alms are found,
And lovers hearts with ends of ribband bound,
The courtier's promises, and sick men's pray'rs,
The smiles of harlots, and the tears of heirs,
Cages for gnats, and chains to yoak a flea,
Dry'd butterflies, and tomes of casuistry.

But trust the Muse—she saw it upward rise,
Tho' mark'd by none but quick, poetic eyes:
(So Rome's great founder to the heav'ns withdrew,
To Proculus alone confess'd in view)

A sudden

NOTES.

In this repository in the lunar sphere, says the sprightly Italian, were to be found,

"Cio che in somma quà giù perdesti mai,
Là su saltendo ritrovar potrai."

It is very remarkable, that the poet had the boldness to place among these imaginary treasures, the famous deed of Constantine to Pope Silvester; "if (says he) I may be allowed to say this,"

"Questo era il dono (se pero dir lece)
Che Constantino al buon Silvestro fece."

It may be observed in general, to the honour of the poets, both ancient and modern, that they have ever been some of the first, who have detected and opposed the false claims and mischievous usurpations of superstition and slavery. Nor can this be wondered at, since these two are the greatest enemies, not only to all true happiness, but to all true genius.

Ver. 114. *Since all things lost*] Vide Ariosto, Canto xxxiv. P.

A ſudden Star, it ſhot through liquid air,
And drew behind a radiant trail of hair.
Not Berenice's Locks firſt roſe ſo bright,
The heav'ns beſpangling with diſhevel'd light.
The Sylphs behold it kindling as it flies,
And pleas'd purſue its progreſs through the ſkies.
This the Beau monde ſhall from the Mall ſurvey,
And hail with muſic its propitious ray;
This the bleſt Lover ſhall for Venus take,
And ſend up vows from Roſamonda's lake;
This Partridge ſoon ſhall view in cloudleſs ſkies,
When next he looks through Galilaeo's eyes;

And

VARIATIONS.

VER. 131. *The Sylphs behold*] Theſe two lines added for the ſame reaſon, to keep in view the machinery of the poem. P.

NOTES.

VER. 132. *Through the ſkies.*] One cannot ſufficiently applaud the art of the poet, in conſtantly keeping in the reader's view, the machinery of the poem, to the very laſt: even when the Lock is transformed, the Sylphs, who had ſo carefully guarded it, are here once again artfully mentioned, as finally rejoicing in its honourable transformation.

In reading the Lutrin, I have always been ſtruck with the impropriety of ſo ſerious a concluſion as Boileau has given to ſo ludicrous a poem. Piety and Juſtice are beings rather too awful to have any concern in the celebrated Deſk. They appear as much out of place and ſeaſon, as would the Archbiſhop of Paris, in his pontifical robes, in an harlequin entertainment.

VER. 137. *This Partridge ſoon*] John Partridge was a ridiculous Star-gazer, who in his Almanacks every year never failed to predict the downfal of the Pope, and the King of France, then at war with the Engliſh. W.

IMITATIONS.

VER. 128. "Flammiferumque trahens ſpatioſo limite crinem
Stella micat." OVID. P.

And hence th' egregious wizard ſhall foredoom
The fate of Louis, and the fall of Rome.
Then ceaſe, bright nymph! to mourn thy raviſh'd hair,
Which adds new glory to the ſhining ſphere!
Not all the treſſes that fair head can boaſt,
Shall draw ſuch envy as the Lock you loſt.
For after all the murders of your eye,
When, after millions ſlain, yourſelf ſhall die;
When thoſe fair ſuns ſhall ſet, as ſet they muſt,
And all thoſe treſſes ſhall be laid in duſt,
This Lock, the Muſe ſhall conſecrate to fame,
And 'midſt the ſtars inſcribe Belinda's name.

UPON the whole, I hope it will not be thought an exaggerated panegyric to ſay, that the Rape of the Lock is the beſt Satire extant; that it contains the trueſt and livelieſt picture of modern life; and that the ſubject is of a more elegant nature, as well as more artfully conducted, than any other heroi-comic poem. Pope here appears in the light of a man of gallantry, and of a thorough knowledge of the world; and indeed he had nothing, in his carriage and deportment, of that affected ſingularity, which has induced ſome men of genius to deſpiſe, and depart from, the eſtabliſhed rules of politeneſs and civil life. For all poets have not practiſed the ſober and rational advice of Boileau;

" Que les vers ne ſoient pas votre eternel emploi;
Cultivez vos amis, ſoyez homme de foi.
C'eſt peu d'etre agréable et charmant dans un livre;
Il fait ſavoir encore et converſer, et vivre."

L'Art Poetique, chant. iv.

Our nation can boaſt alſo, of having produced ſome other poems of the burleſque kind, that are excellent; particularly the Splendid Shilling, that admirable copy of the ſolemn irony of Cervantes,

Cervantes, who is the father and unrivalled model of the true mock-heroic; and the Muſcipula, written with the purity of Virgil, whom the author ſo perfectly underſtood, and with the pleaſantry of Lucian; to which I cannot forbear adding, the Scribleriad of Mr. Cambridge, the Machinæ Geſticulantes of Addiſon, the Hobbinol of Somerville, and the Trivia of Gay; the Battle of the Wigs of Thornton, and the Triumph of Temper of Hayley.

If ſome of the moſt candid among the French critics begin to acknowledge, that they have produced nothing in point of ſublimity and majeſty equal to the Paradiſe Loſt, we may alſo venture to affirm, that in point of delicacy, elegance, and fine-turned raillery, on which they have ſo much valued themſelves, they have produced nothing equal to the Rape of the Lock. What comes neareſt to it, is the pleaſing and elegant Ver-vert of Greſſet, in which the foibles of the Nuns are touched with ſo delicate a hand, and ſuch nice ridicule, that it cannot diſguſt the moſt religious prude. I dare not even mention La Pucelle of Voltaire, except to lament that ſuch a rich vein of ſterling and uncommon wit, ſhould be debaſed by the groſs alloy of ſo much abominable obſcenity.

The learned and ingenious Mr. Cambridge has, in the Preface to his Scribleriad, made a remark ſo new and ſo ſolid, as to deſerve examination and attention.

He ſays, that in firſt reading the four celebrated mock-heroic poems, he perceived they had all ſome radical defect. That at laſt he found, by a diligent peruſal of Don Quixote, that propriety was the fundamental excellence of that work. That all the marvellous was reconcileable to probability, as the author leads his hero into that ſpecies of abſurdity only, which it was natural for an imagination, heated with the continual reading of books of chivalry, to fall into. That the want of attention to this was the fundamental error of thoſe poems. For with what propriety do Churchmen, Phyſicians, Beaux, and Belles, or Bookſellers, in the Lutrin, Diſpenſary, Rape of the Lock, and Dunciad, addreſs themſelves to heathen gods, offer ſacrifices, conſult oracles, or talk the language of Homer, and of the heroes of antiquity?

This acute obſervation bears hard on the conduct of more than one of the heroi-comic poems above-mentioned.

Nothing is here ſaid of Hudibras; becauſe its unrivalled excellence could not be diſcuſſed in a note. It is one of the poems that gives peculiar luſtre to our nation and language. One circumſtance only I will here mention, that the ancients had

no

no notion of ſuch ſort of Poems. The cruel wars between Pompey and Cæſar, and the execrable proſcriptions of Auguſtus, were never treated in a burleſque ſtyle, as the horrors of the league in France, and the bloody civil war in England, were deſcribed in the Satyre Menippée, and in Hudibras. One of the moſt accurate Greek ſcholars, of our time and nation, is of opinion, that the Batracomachia is not by Homer, but a burleſque poem in imitation of his manner, by ſome ancient poet, who, though he adopted the words and expreſſions of the Greek Bard, formed his metre according to the pronunciation of his own country. With equal confidence we may pronounce the Margites to have been a forgery, though there are only four lines of it extant, three of which are quoted by Plato and Ariſtotle; but in theſe we have a compound verb, with the augment upon the prepoſition (ηπιςατο), which Homer's grammar did not admit. Knight's Analytical Eſſay on the Greek Alphabet, page 30.

E L E G Y

TO THE MEMORY OF AN

UNFORTUNATE LADY*.

WHAT beck'ning ghoſt, along the moon-light ſhade
Invites my ſteps, and points to yonder glade?
'Tis ſhe;—but why that bleeding boſom gor'd,
Why dimly gleams the viſionary ſword!
Oh ever beauteous, ever friendly! tell,
Is it, in heav'n, a crime to love too well?
To bear too tender, or too firm a heart,
To act a Lover's or a Roman's part?
Is there no bright reverſion in the ſky,
For thoſe who greatly think, or bravely die?

Why

NOTES.

* See the Duke of Buckingham's verſes to a Lady deſigning to retire into a monaſtery, compared with Mr. Pope's Letters to ſeveral Ladies, p. 206. quarto Edition. She ſeems to be the ſame perſon whoſe unfortunate death is the ſubject of this poem. P.

VER. 1. *What beck'ning ghoſt,*] Who does not, by this ſtriking abruptneſs, imagine, with the poet, that he ſuddenly beholds the phantom of his murdered friend? He might, perhaps, have a paſſage of Ben Jonſon in his head, in an elegy on the Marchioneſs of Wincheſter, which opens thus;

"What gentle ghoſt beſprent with April dew,
Hails me ſo ſolemnly to yonder yew?
And beck'ning wooes me?"——

The

Why bade ye else, ye Pow'rs! her soul aspire
Above the vulgar flight of low desire?
Ambition first sprung from your blest abodes;
The glorious fault of Angels and of Gods:
Thence to their images on earth it flows,
And in the breasts of Kings and Heroes glows.
Most souls, 'tis true, but peep out once an age,
Dull sullen pris'ners in the body's cage:
Dim lights of life, that burn a length of years
Useless, unseen, as lamps in sepulchres;

Like

NOTES.

The cruelties of her relations, the desolation of the family, the being deprived of the rights of sepulture, the circumstance of dying in a country remote from her relations, are all touched with great tenderness and pathos, particularly the four lines from the 51st.

By foreign hands thy dying eyes were clos'd;

Which lines may remind one of that exquisite stroke in the Philoctetes of Sophocles, who, among other afflicting circumstances, had not near him any σύντροφον ὄμμα. ver. 171. The true cause of the excellence of this elegy is, that the occasion of it was real; so true is the maxim, that nature is more powerful than fancy; and that we can always feel more than we can imagine; and that the most artful fiction must give way to truth, for this Lady was beloved by Pope. After many and wide enquiries, I have been informed that her name was Wainsbury; and that (which is a singular circumstance) she was as ill-shaped and deformed as our author. Her death was not by a sword, but, what would less bear to be told poetically, she hanged herself. Johnson has too severely censured this elegy, when he says, "that it has drawn much attention by the illaudable singularity, of treating suicide with respect;" and, "that poetry has not often been worse employed, than in dignifying the amorous fury of a raving girl." She seems to have been driven to this desperate act by the violence and cruelty of her uncle and guardian, who forced her to a convent abroad; and to which circumstance Pope alludes in one of his letters.

Like Eaſtern Kings a lazy ſtate they keep,
And, cloſe confin'd to their own palace, ſleep.

From theſe perhaps (ere nature bade her die)
Fate ſnatch'd her early to the pitying ſky.
As into air the purer ſpirits flow,
And ſep'rate from their kindred dregs below;
So flew the ſoul to its congenial place,
Nor left one virtue to redeem her Race.

But thou, falſe guardian of a charge too good,
Thou, mean deſerter of thy brother's blood!
See on theſe ruby lips the trembling breath,
Theſe cheeks now fading at the blaſt of death;
Cold is that breaſt which warm'd the world before,
And thoſe love-darting eyes muſt roll no more.
Thus, if eternal juſtice rules the ball,
Thus ſhall your wives, and thus your children fall:
On all the line a ſudden vengeance waits,
And frequent herſes ſhall beſiege your gates;
There paſſengers ſhall ſtand, and pointing ſay,
(While the long fun'rals blacken all the way)
Lo! theſe were they, whoſe ſouls the Furies ſteel'd,
And curs'd with hearts unknowing how to yield.
Thus unlamented paſs the proud away,
The gaze of fools, and pageant of a day!
So periſh all, whoſe breaſt ne'er learn'd to glow
For others good, or melt at others woe.

What can atone (oh ever-injur'd ſhade!)
Thy fate unpity'd, and thy rites unpaid?

No friend's complaint, no kind domeſtic tear
Pleas'd thy pale ghoſt, or grac'd thy mournful bier.
By foreign hands thy dying eyes were clos'd,
By foreign hands thy decent limbs compos'd,
By foreign hands thy humble grave adorn'd,
By ſtrangers honour'd, and by ſtrangers mourn'd!
What tho' no friends in ſable weeds appear,
Grieve for an hour, perhaps, then mourn a year,
And bear about the mockery of woe
To midnight dances, and the public ſhow?
What tho' no weeping Loves thy aſhes grace,
Nor poliſh'd marble emulate thy face?
What tho' no ſacred earth allow thee room,
Nor hallow'd dirge be mutter'd o'er thy tomb?

Yet

NOTES.

VER. 59. *What tho' no weeping Loves, &c.*] "This beautiful little Elegy had gained the unanimous admiration of all men of taſte. When a critic comes—But hold; to give his obſervation fair play, let us firſt analize the Poem. The Ghoſt of the injured perſon appears to excite the Poet to revenge her wrongs. He deſcribes her Character—execrates the author of her misfortunes—expatiates on the ſeverity of her fate—the rites of ſepulture denied her in a foreign land: Then follows,

"What tho' no weeping Loves thy aſhes grace," &c.
"Yet ſhall thy grave with riſing flowers be dreſt," &c.

Can any thing be more naturally pathetic? Yet the Critic tells us, he can give no quarter to this part of the poem, which is eminently, he ſays, diſcordant with the ſubject, and not the language of the heart. But when he tells us, that it is to be aſcribed to imitation, copying indiſcreetly what has been ſaid by others, [Elements of Crit. vol. ii. p. 182.] his criticiſm begins to ſmell furiouſly of old John Dennis. Well might our Poet's laſt wiſh be to commit his writings to the candour of a ſenſible and reflecting judge, rather than to the malice of every ſhort-ſighted and malevolent critic." W.

Yet ſhall thy grave with riſing flow'rs be dreſt,
And the green turf lie lightly on thy breaſt:
There ſhall the morn her earlieſt tears beſtow,
There the firſt roſes of the year ſhall blow;
While Angels with their ſilver wings o'erſhade
The Ground, now ſacred by the reliques made.

So peaceful reſts, without a ſtone, a name,
What once had beauty, titles, wealth, and fame.
How lov'd, how honour'd once, avails thee not,
To whom related, or by whom begot;
A heap of duſt alone remains of thee,
'Tis all thou art, and all the proud ſhall be!

Poets themſelves muſt fall like thoſe they ſung,
Deaf the prais'd ear, and mute the tuneful tongue.
Ev'n he, whoſe ſoul now melts in mournful lays,
Shall ſhortly want the gen'rous tear he pays;
Then from his cloſing eyes thy form ſhall part,
And the laſt pang ſhall tear thee from his heart,
Life's idle buſineſs at one gaſp be o'er,
The Muſe forgot, and thou belov'd no more!

PROLOGUE TO MR. ADDISON'S TRAGEDY OF CATO.

THE Tragedy of Cato itſelf, is a glaring inſtance of the force of party; ſo ſententious and declamatory a drama would never have met with ſuch rapid and amazing ſucceſs, if every line and ſentence had not been particularly tortured, and applied to recent events, and the reigning diſputes of the times. The purity and energy of the diction, and the loftineſs of the ſentiments, copied, in a great meaſure, from Lucan, Tacitus, and Seneca the philoſopher, merit approbation. But I have always thought, that thoſe pompous Roman ſentiments are not ſo difficult to be produced, as is vulgarly imagined; and which, indeed, dazzle only the vulgar. A ſtroke of nature is, in my opinion, worth a hundred ſuch thoughts, as

"When vice prevails, and impious men bear ſway,
The poſt of honour is a private ſtation."

Cato is a fine dialogue on liberty, and the love of one's country; but conſidered as a dramatic performance, nay, as a model of a juſt tragedy, as ſome have affectedly repreſented it, it muſt be owned to want action and pathos; the two hinges, I preſume, on which a juſt tragedy ought neceſſarily to turn, and without which it cannot ſubſiſt. It wants alſo character, although that be not ſo eſſentially neceſſary to a tragedy as action. Syphax, indeed, in his interview with Juba, bears ſome marks of a rough African; the ſpeeches of the reſt may be transferred to any of the perſonages concerned. The ſimile drawn from Mount Atlas, and the deſcription of the Numidian travellers ſmothered in the deſart, are indeed in character, but ſufficiently obvious. How Addiſon could fall into the falſe and unnatural cuſtom of ending his three firſt acts with ſimilies, is amazing in ſo chaſte and correct

 a writer.

a writer. The loves of Juba and Marcia, of Portius and Lucia, are vicious and insipid episodes, debase the dignity, and destroy the unity of the fable. Cato was translated into Italian by Salvini; into Latin, and acted by the Jesuits at St. Omers; imitated in French by De Champs, and great part of it translated by the Abbé Du Bos.

The Prologue to Addison's Tragedy of Cato, is superior to any prologue of Dryden; who, notwithstanding, is so justly celebrated for this species of writing. The prologues of Dryden are satyrical and facetious; this of Pope is solemn and sublime, as the subject required. Those of Dryden contain general topics of criticism and wit, and may precede any play whatsoever, even tragedy or comedy. This of Pope is particular, and appropriated to the tragedy alone, which it was designed to introduce.

PROLOGUE TO MR. ADDISON'S TRAGEDY OF CATO*.

To wake the ſoul by tender ſtrokes of art,
  To raiſe the genius, and to mend the heart,
To make mankind, in conſcious virtue bold,
Live o'er each ſcene, and be what they behold:
For this the Tragic Muſe firſt trod the ſtage,
Commanding tears to ſtream through ev'ry age;
Tyrants no more their ſavage nature kept,
And foes to virtue wonder'd how they wept.
Our author ſhuns by vulgar ſprings to move
The hero's glory, or the virgin's love;
In pitying love, we but our weakneſs ſhow,
And wild ambition well deſerves its woe.

Here

NOTES.

* This Prologue, and the Epilogue which follows, are the moſt perfect models of this ſpecies of writing, both in the ſerious and the ludicrous way. W.

The former is much the better of the two; for ſome of Dryden's, of the latter kind, are unequalled.

VER. 7. *Tyrants no more*] Louis XIV. wiſhed to have pardoned the Cardinal de Rohan, after hearing the Cinna of Corneille.

VER. 11. *In pitying love,*] Why then did Addiſon introduce the loves of Juba and Marcia? which Pope ſaid to Mr. Spence, were not in the original plan of the play, but were introduced in compliance with the popular practice of the ſtage.

Here tears ſhall flow from a more gen'rous cauſe,
Such tears as Patriots ſhed for dying Laws:
He bids your breaſt with ancient ardour riſe,
And calls forth Roman drops from Britiſh eyes.
Virtue confeſs'd in human ſhape he draws,
What Plato thought, and godlike Cato was:
No common object to your ſight diſplays,
But what with pleaſure Heav'n itſelf ſurveys,
A brave man ſtruggling in the ſtorms of fate,
And greatly falling with a falling ſtate.
While Cato gives his little Senate laws,
What boſom beats not in his Country's cauſe?
Who ſees him act, but envies ev'ry deed?
Who hears him groan, and does not wiſh to bleed?
Ev'n when proud Caeſar 'midſt triumphal cars,
The ſpoils of nations, and the pomp of wars,
Ignobly vain, and impotently great,
Show'd Rome her Cato's figure drawn in ſtate;
As her dead Father's rev'rend image paſt,
The pomp was darken'd, and the day o'ercaſt;
The Triumph ceas'd, tears guſh'd from ev'ry eye;
The world's great Victor paſs'd unheeded by;
Her laſt good man dejected Rome ador'd,
And honour'd Caeſar's leſs than Cato's ſword.

Britons,

NOTES.

VER. 20. *But what with pleaſure*] This alludes to a famous paſſage of Seneca, which Mr. Addiſon afterwards uſed as a motto to his play, when it was printed. W.

VER. 27. *Ev'n when*] The twenty-ſeventh, thirtieth, thirty-fourth, thirty-ninth, and forty-fifth lines, are artful alluſions to the character and hiſtory of Cato himſelf.

Britons, attend: be worth like this approv'd,
And ſhow you have the virtue to be mov'd.
With honeſt ſcorn the firſt fam'd Cato view'd
Rome learning arts from Greece, whom ſhe ſubdu'd;
Your ſcene precariouſly ſubſiſts too long
On French tranſlation, and Italian ſong.
Dare to have ſenſe yourſelves; aſſert the ſtage,
Be juſtly warm'd with your own native rage:
Such Plays alone ſhould win a Britiſh ear,
As Cato's ſelf had not diſdain'd to hear.

NOTES.

VER. 37. *Britons, attend:*] Spence told me that Pope had written it—"Britons, ariſe"; but that Addiſon, frightened at ſo ſtrong an expreſſion, as promoting inſurrection, lowered and weakened it by the word, attend.

VER. 42. *On French tranſlation,*] He glances obliquely at the Diſtreſt Mother of his old antagoniſt Philips, taken, evidently, from Racine. Cato's laſt ſoliloquy is tranſlated with great purity and elegance by Bland.

It is a little remarkable that the laſt line of Cato is Pope's; and the laſt of Eloiſa is Addiſon's.

VER. 45. *Such Plays alone*] Addiſon, having finiſhed and laid by, for ſeveral years, the firſt four acts of Cato, applied to Hughes for a fifth; and Dr. Johnſon, from entertaining too mean an opinion of Hughes, does not think the application ſerious. When Hughes brought his ſupplement, he found the author himſelf had finiſhed his play. Hughes was very capable of writing this fifth act. The Siege of Damaſcus is a better tragedy than Cato; though Pope affected to ſpeak ſlightingly of its author. An audience was packed by Steele on the firſt night of Cato; and Addiſon ſuffered inexpreſſible uneaſineſs and ſolicitude during the repreſentation. Bolingbroke called Booth to his box, and gave him fifty guineas for defending the cauſe of liberty ſo well, againſt a perpetual dictator.

VER. 46. *As Cato's ſelf, &c.*] This alludes to that famous ſtory of his coming into the Theatre, and going out again, related by Martial. W.

Britons, ... be worth like th

And ... you have the virtue to be

With ... from the first fam'd C

... me charming arts from Greece, w

Your scene precariously subsists too

On French translation, and Italian

Dare to have sense yourselves; assert

Be justly warm'd with your own na

Such Plays alone should win a Briti

As Cato's self had not disdain'd to.

NOTES.

VER. ... Britons, attend,] ...

VER. 42. On French translation,] ...

EPILOGUE TO MR. ROWE'S JANE SHORE.

THE Epilogue to Jane Shore is written with that air of gallantry and raillery which, by a ſtrange perverſion of taſte, the audience expects in all epilogues to the moſt ſerious and pathetic pieces. To recommend cuckoldom, and palliate adultery, is their uſual intent. I wonder Mrs. Oldfield was not ſuffered to ſpeak it; for it is ſuperior to that which was uſed on the occaſion. In this taſte Garrick has written ſome, that abound in ſpirit and drollery. Rowe's genius was rather delicate and ſoft, than ſtrong and pathetic; his compoſitions ſoothe us with a tranquil and tender ſort of complacency, rather than cleave the heart with pangs of commiſeration. His diſtreſſes are entirely founded on the paſſion of love. His diction is extremely elegant and chaſte, and his verſification highly melodious. His plays are declamations, rather than dialogues; and his characters are general, and undiſtinguiſhed from each other. Such a furious character as that of Bajazet, is eaſily drawn; and, let me add, eaſily acted. There is a want of unity in the fable of Tamerlane. The death's head, dead body, and ſtage hung in mourning, in the Fair Penitent, are artificial and mechanical methods of affecting an audience. In a word, his plays are muſical and pleaſing poems; but inactive and unmoving tragedies. This of Jane Shore is, I think, the moſt intereſting and affecting of any he has given us: but probability is ſadly violated in it by the neglect of the unity of time. For a perſon to be ſuppoſed to be ſtarved, during the repreſentation of five acts, is a ſtriking inſtance of the abſurdity of this violation.

It is probable that this is become the moſt popular and pleaſing tragedy of all Rowe's works, becauſe it is founded on our own hiſtory. I cannot forbear wiſhing, that our writers would

would more frequently search for subjects, in the annals of England, which afford many striking and pathetic events, proper for the stage. We have been too long attached to Grecian and Roman stories. In truth, domestica facta are more interesting, as well as more useful; more interesting, because we all think ourselves concerned in the actions and fates of our countrymen; more useful, because the characters and manners bid the fairest to be true and natural, when they are drawn from models with which we are exactly acquainted. The Turks, the Persians, and Americans, of our poets, are, in reality, distinguished from Englishmen, only by their turbans and feathers; and think and act, as if they were born and educated within the Bills of Mortality. The historical plays of Shakespeare are always grateful to the spectator, who loves to see and hear our own Harrys and Edwards, better than all the Achilleses or Cæsars that ever existed. In the choice of a domestic story, however, much judgment and circumspection must be exerted, to select one of a proper æra; neither of too ancient, or of too modern a date. The manners of times very ancient, we shall be apt to falsify, as those of the Greeks and Romans. And recent events, with which we are thoroughly acquainted, are deprived of the power of impressing solemnity and awe, by their notoriety and familiarity. Age softens and wears away all those disgracing and depreciating circumstances, which attend modern transactions, merely because they are modern. Lucan was much embarrassed by the proximity of the times he treated of.

I take this occasion to observe, that Rowe has taken the fable of his Fair Penitent, from the Fatal Dowry of Massinger and Field. His very spirited translation, which does not seem sufficiently regarded, is perhaps his best work; and one of the best translations in our language, of the only classic, said Addison, not explained for the use of the Dauphin.

EPILOGUE TO MR. ROWE'S JANE SHORE.

DESIGNED FOR MRS. OLDFIELD.

PRODIGIOUS this! the Frail-one of our Play
From her own Sex ſhould mercy find to-day!
You might have held the pretty head aſide,
Peep'd in your fans, been ſerious, thus, and cry'd,
The Play may paſs—but that ſtrange creature, Shore,
I can't—indeed now—I ſo hate a whore—
Juſt as a blockhead rubs his thoughtleſs ſkull,
And thanks his ſtars he was not born a fool;
So from a ſiſter ſinner you ſhall hear,
"How ſtrangely you expoſe yourſelf, my dear?"
But let me die, all raillery apart,
Our ſex are ſtill forgiving at their heart;
And, did not wicked cuſtom ſo contrive,
We'd be the beſt, good-natur'd things alive.
There are, 'tis true, who tell another tale,
That virtuous ladies envy while they rail;
Such rage without betrays the fire within;
In ſome cloſe corner of the ſoul, they ſin;
Still hoarding up, moſt ſcandalouſly nice,
Amidſt their virtues a reſerve of vice.
The godly dame, who fleſhly failings damns,
Scolds with her maid, or with her chaplain crams.

Would you enjoy ſoft nights and ſolid dinners?
Faith, gallants, board with ſaints, and bed with ſinners.
Well, if our Author in the Wife offends,
He has a Huſband that will make amends:
He draws him gentle, tender, and forgiving,
And ſure ſuch kind good creatures may be living.
In days of old they pardon'd breach of vows,
Stern Cato's ſelf was no relentleſs ſpouſe:
Plu—Plutarch, what's his name, that writes his life?
Tells us, that Cato dearly lov'd his Wife:
Yet if a friend, a night or ſo, ſhould need her,
He'd recommend her as a ſpecial breeder.
To lend a Wife, few here would ſcruple make,
But, pray, which of you all would take her back?
Tho' with the Stoic Chief our ſtage may ring,
The Stoic Huſband was the glorious thing.
The man had courage, was a ſage, 'tis true,
And lov'd his country,—but what's that to you?
Thoſe ſtrange examples ne'er were made to fit ye,
But the kind cuckold might inſtruct the City:
There, many an honeſt man may copy Cato,
Who ne'er ſaw naked ſword, or look'd in Plato.
If, after all, you think it a diſgrace,
That Edward's Miſs thus perks it in your face;

To

NOTES.

VER. 44. *Who ne'er ſaw*] A ſly and oblique ſtroke on the ſuicide of Cato; which was one of the reaſons, as I have been informed, why this epilogue was not ſpoken.

VER. 46. *Edward's Miſs*] Sir Thomas More ſays, ſhe had one accompliſhment uncommon in a woman of that time; ſhe could read and write.

To ſee a piece of failing fleſh and blood,
In all the reſt ſo impudently good;
Faith, let the modeſt Matrons of the town 49
Come here in crouds, and ſtare the ſtrumpet down.

Thomſon in his Epilogue to Tancred and Sigiſmunda ſeverely cenſures the flippancy and gaiety of modern Epilogues, as contrary to thoſe impreſſions intended to be left on the mind by a well-written tragedy. The laſt new part Mrs. Oldfield took in tragedy was in Thomſon's Sophoniſba; and it is recorded that ſhe ſpoke the following line;

Not one baſe word of Carthage for thy ſoul,

in ſo powerful a manner, that Wilkes, to whom it was addreſſed, was aſtoniſhed and confounded. Mrs. Oldfield was admitted to viſit in the beſt families. George II. and Queen Caroline, when Princeſs of Wales, condeſcended ſometimes to converſe with her at their levees. And one day the Princeſs aſked her if ſhe was married to General Churchill; "So it is ſaid, may it pleaſe your Highneſs, but we have not owned it yet." Her Lady Betty Modiſh, and Lady Townly, have never yet been equalled. She was univerſally allowed to be well-bred, ſenſible, witty, and generous. She gave poor Savage an annual penſion of fifty pounds. And it is ſtrange that Dr. Johnſon ſeems rather to approve of Savage's having never celebrated his benefactreſs in any of his poems.

END OF THE FIRST VOLUME.

www.ingramcontent.com/pod-product-compliance
Lightning Source LLC
Chambersburg PA
CBHW020544300426
44111CB00008B/784
9783744675192